The Wenner-Gren Foundation
For Anthropological Research, Inc.

Ritual Communication

Wenner-Gren International Symposium Series

Series Editor: Leslie C. Aiello, President, Wenner-Gren Foundation for Anthropological Research, New York.

Since its inception in 1941, the Wenner-Gren Foundation has convened more than 125 international symposia on pressing issues in anthropology. These symposia affirm the worth of anthropology and its capacity to address the nature of humankind from a wide variety of perspectives. Each symposium brings together participants from around the world, representing different theoretical disciplines and traditions, for a week-long engagement on a specific issue. The Wenner-Gren International Symposium Series was initiated in 2000 to ensure the publication and distribution of the results of the foundation's International Symposium Program.

Prior to this series, some landmark Wenner-Gren volumes include: *Man's Role in Changing the Face of the Earth* (1956), ed. William L. Thomas; *Man the Hunter* (1968), eds Irv DeVore and Richard B. Lee; *Cloth and Human Experience* (1989), eds Jane Schneider and Annette Weiner; and *Tools, Language and Cognition in Human Evolution* (1993), eds Kathleen Gibson and Tim Ingold. Reports on recent symposia and further information can be found on the foundation's website at www.wennergren.org.

The Wenner-Gren Foundation

For Anthropological Research, Inc.

Ritual Communication

Edited by

Gunter Senft and Ellen B. Basso

Routledge
Taylor & Francis Group
LONDON AND NEW YORK

First published 2009 by Berg Publishers

Published 2020 by Routledge
2 Park Square, Milton Park, Abingdon, Oxon OX14 4RN
605 Third Avenue, New York, NY 10017

Routledge is an imprint of the Taylor & Francis Group, an informa business

Library of Congress Cataloging-in-Publication Data

A catalogue record for this book is available from the Library of Congress.

British Library Cataloguing-in-Publication Data

A catalogue record for this book is available from the British Library.

ISBN13: 978-1-8478-8296-7 (hbk)

ISBN13: 978-1-8478-8295-0 (pbk)

Typeset by JS Typesetting Ltd, Porthcawl, Mid Glamorgan

Contents

Figures

Acknowledgments

This book is the result of a symposium on ritual communication sponsored by the Wenner-Gren Foundation for Anthropological Research. In 1999, meeting for the first time in Mainz, Germany, we began to explore ritual communication as a topic for extensive discussion that might interest an international group of linguistic anthropologists. We thank Richard Fox, former director of the foundation, and Leslie Aiello, its current director, for their interest and encouragement, which led to the acceptance of our proposal. The conference was eventually held in a most beautiful setting, the Hotel Palácio de Seteais in Sintra, Portugal, on March 16–23, 2007. The planning work by the foundation's conference program associate, Laurie Obbink, on behalf of all participants was exceptional, and we thank her again for making the meeting special indeed. Leslie Aiello and Victoria Malkin, the foundation's anthropologist, not only contributed to the discussions during the meeting but also performed important work as liaisons with the publishers.

We are grateful to our three conference discussants, Richard Bauman, John Lucy, and Charles Briggs, whose lively remarks greatly enhanced the discussion during our Sintra stay. Richard Bauman also provided us with extensive written comments, some of which we used in preparing our introduction. We also gratefully acknowledge the participation of our symposium monitor, Antonio Jose B. da Silva, then a graduate student at the University of Arizona. During the production of the book, the efficient and professional contributions of Victoria Malkin at Wenner-Gren and Anna Wright at Berg were invaluable. Thanks also to Jane Kepp for her help with preparation of the manuscript. Above all, we thank our Jaffrey and Senft families for their unstinting patience and loving support during the preparation of this volume.

Ellen B. Basso
Gunter Senft

Contributors

Felix K. Ameka, Leiden University
Ellen B. Basso, University of Arizona (emerita)
John W. Du Bois, University of California, Santa Barbara
N. J. Enfield, Max Planck Institute for Psycholinguistics
Maurizio Gnerre, University of Naples
Cliff Goddard, University of New England (Australia)
John B. Haviland, University of California, San Diego
Ingjerd Hoëm, Kon-Tiki Museum and University of Oslo
Corinne A. Kratz, Emory University
Joel C. Kuipers, George Washington University
Suzanne Oakdale, University of New Mexico
Gunter Senft, Max Planck Institute for Psycholinguistics
Michael Silverstein, University of Chicago

Introduction

Ellen B. Basso and Gunter Senft

Ritual communication is an undertaking or enterprise involving a making of cultural knowledge within locally variant practices of speech-centered human interaction. The position adopted in this book is that ritual communication is artful, performed semiosis, predominantly but not only involving speech, that is formulaic and repetitive and therefore anticipated within particular contexts of social interaction. Ritual communication thus has anticipated (but not always achieved) consequences. As performance, it is subject to evaluation by participants according to standards defined in part by language ideologies, local aesthetics, contexts of use, and, especially, relations of power among participants.

In this poetic-pragmatic view of ritual language or ritual communication, "meaningfulness" is both a retrospective and a prospective process. Participants use local, inherited understandings and experiences, both collective and personal, to create new events and prospective selves and to project these forward into an anticipation of the future. In all places and times, people appear to describe types of talk, which persons use them, how their use is experienced, their effects and relations to each other, and what happens when they are misused. Although some claim that the actual relationships between rules and consequences are often unclear—uncertain even to the speakers themselves—in fact many resources are available to local speakers for use in new contexts of ritualization. Most important among these resources are narratives about actual conversational and other discursive examples of the linguistic forms in past practice and of persons who spoke concretely in particular ways in the past. Because they are narratives, these texts also provide considerable information regarding the precursor and subsequent instances of speech that surround a particular spoken instance and give it a semiotic framing and sociocentric footing. These and other metacommunicative models remind us that people do remember and comment upon ongoing events that are highly marked in both formal and pragmatic ways.

Our consideration of ritual communication as a special mode of semiotic behavior is of course a value-laden sociohistorical artifact, the result of a long history of inquiry, anthropological and otherwise, into the nature of human behavior, beginning with a framework that contrasted European modes of behavior and language use with those discovered among newly colonized people around the world. Though not always known as such, ritual communication has been a long-standing subject in anthropology. Most important, it emerged through a long history of thinking about one of the core themes of Americanist anthropology, the relationship between language and "culture."

The use of "ritual" as a metaphor has much to do with Erving Goffman's "sociology of occasions" (1967: 2), the study of interpersonal gestures, including speech, in which the term served as a trope for the social organization of interaction. Goffman's use of "ritual" emphasized the degree to which ordinary, face-to-face interactions of the everyday are structured and performed. In fact it is not so easy to distinguish this everyday ritual practice (which might be termed "ritualization") from large-scale public ritual events. During our conference, we frequently returned to the examination of similar structural and sociopsychological elements in such events. As various chapters in this book show, ritual involves "formal patterning"—that is, it comprises events that feature heightened, intensified, and "increased code structuring" (Irvine 1979). And as Richard Bauman commented, "formal patterning sets up a dynamic of expectation (or arousal) and fulfillment that elicits participative involvement."

The view of ritualization adopted here also emphasizes its inherent multimodality, in which the human body, temporalization, and formally categorized spatial settings all play crucial roles. Through multimodal events of display, the meanings and values of remembered past events, made manifest through special verbal registers, costuming, and musical activities, offer strategies for constructing links to contemporary social settings, with the aim of constructing new or refigured communicative practices.

Because anthropologists are now far more aware than they once were of the complexity and non-uniformity of social meanings and values, their understandings of ritual events as sites of challenge to traditions and to existing power relations are furthered by a historically contextualized emphasis. Consequently, over time, the power of Goffman's metaphor has become the source of greater focus upon the participatory, experiential side of ritual events. Ritual is not only something done but also something experienced in the doing. The ritualization of culture has thus come to be treated as a highly "self-oriented" enterprise, in which human imagination and the dialogical figuration of sociality produce important reflexive "sites" or "centers" of semiosis, dialectical segments of a complex network of semiotic pathways (Du Bois, this volume; Silverstein 2004).

Early Boasian writers such as Robert Lowie, Ruth Benedict, Margaret Mead, as well as Bronislaw Malinowski and the British social anthropologists in the Durkheimian tradition often used examples of joking relations, avoidance between certain kin, and oratory to emphasize what they understood as significant differences between the societies they studied and modernist Euro-American societies. Although some scholars, such as Edmund Leach, understood early on that ritual could be treated as a message-making activity (Parkin 2001: 13368), rarely were such examples of ritual communication truly contextualized in terms of narratives of individual lives or the changing character of interpersonal relations. They were taken "as is" to be representative of larger social patterns or of social "needs" such as the lessening of conflict. Linguistic matters were acknowledged implicitly (Malinowski was something of an exception), but usually ethnographers presented their examples as if they were translations of "texts" or actual events. It is rare in the older literature to find good examples of utterances in original languages, carefully analyzed.

A. R. Radcliffe-Brown, in his essay on the topic (1940), considered joking relations in southern Africa a sociological "problem" insofar as they appeared to contradict rules for appropriate behavior among young and old, men and women. The many discussions of Radcliffe-Brown's "solution" to the problem called field anthropologists' attention to such activities in many other parts of the world. We have now accumulated substantial evidence of the worldwide prevalence of distinctive verbal locutions that follow local standards of comportment and of speaking, a seeming language universal that cries out for theoretical commentary.[1]

Even for more recent anthropologists, "ritual" has long been a key category for entry into the understanding of non-Western societies. Among some groups, ritual life was so prominent and pervasive an apparatus for ordering society that it gave those societies, in anthropologists' eyes, a special definition. Many are represented in the classic ethnographic literature. As anthropologists have written about ritual, it has been received as a rather narrow concept, associated with formal, public, collective activity oriented toward an allegedly transcendent religious ideology. As Rappaport wrote (1999: 404): "To sing or dance in concert or in unison with others, to move as they move and speak as they speak is, literally, to act as part of a larger entity, to participate in it; and as the radical separation of the everyday self dissolves in the communitas of participation—as it sometimes does—the larger entity becomes palpable." In this view, common in ethnographic analysis, ritual is treated as something that helps practitioners define the sociopolitical order in which they participate, and it must include language. By this definition, ritual is the medium through which social values are expressed.

Views of Ritual from Linguistic Anthropology

More recent means of understanding communication in anthropology involve subtler and more nuanced concerns about formality, creativity, voicing, stance, power manipulations, and intertextuality. Since the 1974 Wenner-Gren conference on secular ritual (Moore and Myerhoff 1977), newer approaches to "ritual" have separated it topically from "religion" and have involved studying its place in both community and individual practice, creative improvisation, and people's participation in newly emergent communities of practice. Even so, scholars have found the link between ritual and religion useful for understanding relations between emotion and language. For example, Roy Rappaport's model of "effective ritual" linked linguistic practice to certain kinds of emotional effects: it entailed "the union in ritual of the numinous, a product of emotion, with the sacred, a product of language" (Rappaport 1999: 396).

In his review of work on religious language, Webb Keane (1997a: 47) wrote that "the sources of words, as well as the identity, agency, authority, and even the very presence of participants in an interaction, can be especially problematic." We agree, and we understand that this is true of all communicative (ritualized) events. Yet the features of religious language reviewed by Keane turn out to be present in "non-religious" language as well, leading to the unavoidable conclusion that this contrast might not be entirely useful after all. For example, Keane observed that religious situations may involve the suspension of assumptions about participants, because some are "invisible"; a question exists about "who is participating and what counts as the relevant context of 'here' and 'now'" (1997a: 50). In this volume, Ellen B. Basso describes something similar in regard to Kalapalo leaders' talk. Michael Silverstein (1981: 54) observed that a ritual speech form "serves as metapragmatic figure for the accomplishment of the successive stages of the action being undertaken." Sometimes metapragmatic statements are recontextualized discourse forms that have taken on this function. As Keane put it: "Their linguistic form remains the same, but their function shifts. Rather than being construed as accounts of actions that were carried out in the past, the words are taken as reports on and directives for the action they themselves carry out in the moment of speaking" (1997a: 51). We see the same thing taking place in the data described by Joel Kuipers and Corinne Kratz in this volume.

Finally, Keane described the use of religious genres that involve esoteric knowledge. The use of esoteric forms is also characteristic of Kalapalo leaders (Basso, this volume). Keane noted that scholars have debated questions of intentionality and responsibility in the context of communication with invisible beings. But in the case of Kalapalo leaders' talk, speakers use languages that many visiting observers cannot understand; hence the use of nonverbal codes.

Paying special attention to ritual or ritualized communication is a useful way to examine, comparatively, the cultivation of self, family, and community. This is particularly the case if such matters are treated not as the old Durkheimian "things" of society but as processes and practices of relationship. The separation of ritual from a magico-religious domain of culture also leads to important insights into ritual communication that were not forthcoming in the past. From a focus on symbolic meaning and the relation of beliefs, cosmologies, and the like to ritual practice, as in the classic works of Raymond Firth (1967), Clifford Geertz (1957, 1973), Max Gluckman (1954, 1963), and Victor Turner (1967, 1969, 1975), we have come to look at the *experiencing* of ritual. Indeed, this emphasis comes directly from Turner's work, in which participants' experience became a central focus.

Although the earlier idea of "secular ritual," developed by anthropologists influenced by Turner's "symbolic" approach to ritual, sought to capture the tension between traditional order and contemporary improvisation, conflict, and meaning creation, work along those lines incorporated little data on language. In this book we do not attempt to contrast secular and religious; rather, we consider that ritual involves the interpretation of social reality, and we use the term "ritual communication" to emphasize the linguistic materials used in such interpretation. We are also concerned with more recent theoretical ideas that go beyond understanding as "interpretation" and that orient the researcher toward practice and experience. We reject the contrast between sacred and profane, as well as between ordinary and ritual communication and between formal and informal communication, which usually sets ritual communication against "strategic interaction" and ritual against "secular" contexts and activities.

To summarize, rather than looking at the objects of what we call ritual communication, as the earlier Boasian patternist and British functionalist anthropologists did, we are concerned with the conditions or contextualizations of such activities as fundamentally historical and even as having important implications for the understanding of human evolution. The features we emphasize integrate questions about the multimodal, the dialogical or interactive, the interpersonal, and the experiential with questions about human history. The pervasive integration of psychological, historical, and linguistic issues in the study of narratives, greetings, protests, and other communicative genres has promoted a new look at ritual communication. Thus we see relatively formalized aspects of speaking such as greetings and departures (see chapters by Ameka and Enfield) and civility registers (Basso, Haviland) linked with narrative discourse (Oakdale), rites of passage (Kratz, Silverstein), forms of theatricality (Hoëm), and political protest marches (Kuipers). Collective social practice is also linked with instances of personal or individual ritual practice (Basso, Oakdale, Silverstein, Du Bois).

Evolutionary Issues with Regard to Rules of Communicative Behavior

In addition to Goffman's metaphoric notion of "micro-sociological rituals," the notion of ritual turns up in the work of a number of writers who have transposed the ethological or the evolutionary with the anthropological (see Rappaport 1999: 24ff.). Julian Huxley's (1966a) notion of "cultural ritualization" crossed the ethological with the cultural, and more recently the evolutionary and the symbolic served Roy Rappaport (1999) for developing his notion of "effective ritual." Other recent important work suggests close connections between strategic communication and ritual communication when they are viewed both from an evolutionary perspective and one of metasignaling and metadiscourse (Urban 2002).

Huxley, in his classic introduction to the symposium "A Discussion on Ritualization of Behavior in Animals and Man" (1966a), discussed the evolution and the forms of human and nonhuman ritual. Influenced by Huxley and by the (human) ethological approach toward ritual and ritual communication (see Eibl-Eibesfeldt and Senft 1987), Gunter Senft, writing about Trobriand Islanders in chapter 3 of this volume, points out that speakers of a natural language must also learn the rules of communicative behavior that are valid for their speech community in order to understand and duplicate the construction of the speech community's common social reality. The social construction of reality must be safeguarded with respect to possible "sites of fracture" such as cooperation, conflict, and competition within the community. This safeguarding, however, does not always work. Senft characterizes ritual communication as a type of strategic action that, in the Trobriands, serves functions such as social bonding and the blocking of aggression. Aggressive conflict is usually suppressed because of the "general societal requirement to 'be nice' even when people do not feel that way." Through ritual communication, tensions can be calmed, and voicing can be repressed. A society as open as that of the Trobriand Islanders depends on its members' having a strong sense of tact: sometimes one has to pretend not to hear or observe things. It is the general requirement of tactful behavior, the necessity to be nice, and the positive and successful effects of ritual communication that contribute to social harmony in such a society. It remains an open question whether forms of ritual communication can be seen as culture-specific manifestations of universal human interaction strategies, as hypothesized within the framework of human ethology—that is, whether ritualized behavior elements evolved phylogenetically or developed culturally under selection pressure for unambiguous signaling to improve social communication.

Ritual Communication and the Microsocial-Macrosocial Polarity

Some readers might find the contributors to this book to be overconcerned with microanalyzing portions of larger ritual events or with levels of ritual communication that seemingly lie on the margins of such "type-case" rituals. In such a view, "micro" references interpersonal interactions, and "macro" references the social, representational, Durkheimian collective consciousness. A variant of this contrast is that made between "public" and "private," which Judith Irvine (1979: 786) wrote "actually references degrees of centralization of situational focus and positional identities." The ethnographic examples Irvine used, although varied, were all public occasions, or "meetings," suggesting that anthropologists' own sociocultural ideas about formality tend to exclude more private situations. But might formal properties of code, situation, or model as described by Irvine occur in such microsociological situations? And what about settings in which no more than one person is included? In this volume, a number of contributors critique the association of "formality" with "public" or "macrosociological."

Forms of ritual communication associated with the everyday—joking relations, avoidance practices, greetings, leave-takings, the languages of the marketplace, and chiefly oratory—have become known to every undergraduate anthropology major through the texts of classical modernist ethnography. The modernists understood this incredible variety of ritual communication as central to the development and maintenance of community, as well as to the processes of self-fashioning characteristic of particularly distinct cultures (see Geertz 1957, 1963). Practitioners of the earlier folkloristic and ethnopoetic approaches, in their emphasis on language in ritual as "verbal art," described the linguistic features of the speech of shamans, mediums, and storytellers and of prayer, confession, and dream narratives. This substantial body of data forces us to challenge the contrast between private and public, micro- and macrosociological events.

For researchers in the tradition of Goffman, the category of everyday ritual permeates well beyond these easily recognized microsociological exchanges; they emphasize the ritual nature of just about every move people make in social interaction. Although our contributors differentiate between everyday forms and other, more complex forms of ritual and ritual communication, many of them raise the question of which kinds of communicative events we want to subsume under the label "ritual communication." Some actually challenge the contrast between the everyday and the ritual, proposing that "ritual" events can be described as a cline. Nicholas Enfield points out in this regard that formal ritual and everyday ritual represent regions on a continuum. Using data from the Kri, a Vietic community of upland central Laos, he further differentiates between "ritualized communicative behavior in an ethological sense…, which captures all linguistic and other human symbolic behavior," formal ritual, or "socially marked events" such as weddings and other rites of passage, and everyday ritual, such as greetings and politeness formulas.

Indexicality provides one important means of linking forms of ritual communication. In addition to Enfield's discussion, John Haviland's example, in chapter 1, of a "little ritual" on the road—a greeting ritual between a respected elder and a passing religious party in Chiapas, Mexico—involves an encounter of experts highly competent in ritual communication. These are the sorts of people whom Richard Bauman, in his commentary during our conference, called "ambulatory centers of ritual semiosis." Haviland illustrates that even in the briefest communicative encounters, the biographies and social histories of the interactants play important roles. He reveals resonances between this brief wayside encounter and the great tradition of highly complex forms of ritual communication, and he elaborates on this indexical linkage between communicative features and the patterns that occur in them.

Another means of linking forms of ritual communication is ideology. In an important paper on Roy Rappaport's evolutionist theory of ritual, Joel Robbins (2001a) discussed the relationship between linguistic ideology and ritual. He referenced linguistic ideologies (ideologies of communication) for understanding variation in ritual performance and the performative indexicality of ritual signs. He was concerned with examining linguistic ideologies in terms of Rappaport's interest in the way a heterogeneous community, including nonbelievers, is united by cumulative ritual activities into a homogeneously committed ritual whole that yields a collective message. In this view, language ideology shapes participants' attitudes toward ritual.

Many of the contributors to this volume suggest that this approach toward linguistic ideologies and ritual performance is somewhat simplified, particularly when considered in light of the ethnographic data concerning cultural "recontextualization." In chapter 12, Maurizio Gnerre discusses two forms of ritual communication that are still performed by the Amazonian Shuar and Achuar, Jivaroan speakers in Ecuador and Peru. He emphasizes the importance of historical processes that modify "specific kinds of ritual communication," sometimes giving them additional strength and efficacy. The genres that Gnerre examines—shamanic chants and privately sung incantations—are deeply intertwined with Jivaroan language ideology. The Shuar highly value individuality, and with it, unique proper names and words. They implement such words in rhetorical performances, in shamans' displays of magical power, and in privately performed songs. The morphology of the language allows for endless innovations through recombination of morphemes, and innovations are taken to enhance the enunciative power of words and to strengthen the efficacy of speech and discourse. This ideology is framed in the Shuar and Achuar attitude of being open to everything new. External influences come from new media, from English, and from contact with speakers of Spanish and Quechua.

The changed sociocultural conditions of Shuar and Achuar life have resulted in new human-to-nature and human-to-human relations. Shifts in demography and in forms of human aggregation have direct consequences on all forms of communication. The changes in the two forms of Shuar and Achuar ritual communication reveal both the anticipatory and the vanguard roles of ritual communication in changing communicative practices.

Continuing the exploration of the microsocial-macrosocial polarity in ritual communication, Felix Ameka, in chapter 5, contrasts complex access rituals with simple, conventional openers and well-being inquiries as a special form of greeting. Gunter Senft, in chapter 3, illustrates simple, special, and extraordinary forms of ritual communication, noting, however, that it is more appropriate to locate specific forms of ritual communication on a cline of structural and social complexity.

Formality and Moral Poetics

The Durkheimian moral essence of society is perhaps best recognized and grasped through its personal implications, by means of formally intensified enactments of the collective conscience and of participants' commitment to it. Such forms of ritual communication are domains of moral poetics: they are display events in which the values of a society are embodied and enacted in an intensified way. They are public behaviors employed to affect others' mental states and statuses. Therefore, the form or manner of ritual communication is constrained by the requirement that it be recognizable to others. In ritual, the manner of an action becomes a sign in its own right. The self-conscious performance of formal behavior then provides an opportunity for moral assessment of the status and identity of participants. Ritual behavior requires cooperation with one's peers in treating something as a natural fact when it is merely a social fact; it requires acquiescence to social conventions and thus constrains interactants' freedom to act. As many of the contributors show in their chapters, this observance of formal constraints is controlled, and not adhering to such conventions is morally sanctioned. Thus, ritual is a site in which the local moral order is displayed, exercised, and contested. If inherent ritual constraints are contravened, the coerciveness of ritual becomes manifest in social sanctions.

As long ago as 1979, Irvine's discussion of "formality" showed that quite different descriptive dimensions were subsumed under that term. As she wrote, some of these analytic dimensions "concern properties of code while others concern properties of a social situation; some focus on observable behavior while others invoke the conceptual categories of social actors" (Irvine 1979: 774–775). These elements do not necessarily correlate with one another. Nonetheless, they are interdependent properties that "social actors can exploit by altering their behavior to bring about a redefinition of the situation and of the identities that are relevant to it" (Irvine 1979: 785). One particularly important manifestation of interdependence is created through the "emergence of a centralized situational focus in a public ritualized situation" (Irvine 1979: 786). It is this that has led many anthropologists to consider the large-scale public event to be the ritual type case.

In contradistinction, John Du Bois, in chapter 13, discusses individual ritual communication outside of a social context. There we see the important role of formality and formalization in distinguishing ritual communication from other kinds of communicative events. Du Bois explores the dialogical dimensions of ritual voicing through the analysis of a rarely documented kind of discourse that forms a regular part of the lives of many religious believers. A man alone in a room performs a daily ritual reading of calendrically prescribed texts that deal with "the sacred." He then responds aloud in his own voice to the biblical and exegetical texts he has just been co-voicing. This alternation of textual reading and reader response creates a kind of dialogical tension.

Formality and Power

Irvine also raised the issue of how the formality of a social occasion (including code formality) might relate to political coercion. She concluded that "formalizing a social occasion reduces its participants' political freedom ... only in limited ways" (Irvine 1979: 784). In chapter 4, Cliff Goddard writes that the use of English and Malay proverbs in everyday interaction indicates reference to traditional authorities and invokes interdiscursive relationships. These formulaic practices of everyday life claim to be based on a specific moral poetics in representing value judgments that control and legitimate social behavior in present-day contexts, offering strategies for dealing with recurrent situations. Proverbs are small forms of authoritative discourse, formulaic expressions in which language ideologies and social in-group politics are condensed and in a way petrified. Malay proverbs (*peribahasa*) index "Malayness" and thus are used to contextualize culture according to group-specific political interests and ideologies.

Felix Ameka, in chapter 5, provides the cultural ethnopragmatic scripts for complex West African "sitting" visits, with their ritualized and stereotypical opening, central, and closing sequences, and for the ritualized verbal and nonverbal acts and forms of behavior that are appropriate and expected during these social visits. A feature of these encounters is that they involve not only a host and a visitor but also a spokesperson who acts as an intermediary through whom messages are sent from one party to the other. This triadic communication does not involve the usual sender-receiver participant structure. Instead it includes the speaker of the source utterance, the intermediary as first receiver and relayer of this utterance, and the targeted receiver of the utterance, who of course has overheard the source utterance when it was addressed to the spokesperson. That a message which has already been spoken is immediately relayed can be seen as an enactment of the authorization and traditionalization of discourse. It is an act of metasemiosis that manifests the interdiscursive, iterative quality of ritual communication. The ritualistic formulas exchanged during these visits do not have just phatic functions but also rich illocutionary meanings. As sites of collective memory, they reinforce ideologies of gratitude, communality, inclusiveness, interdependence, and religious belief in God, but they also enact cultural ideologies of inequality.

Haviland, too, illustrates the coercive interactive effects of ritual forms. Zinacantec shamanic prayer is highly interactive because it implies various sorts of "uptake" from the patient. The curer's words prompt secondary prayer in the patient, partly as echo and partly as response. Shamans can hint that certain actions ought to be performed, but skilled patients can also change the course of the shaman's prayer by their responses.

Voicing and the Experiencing of Ritual Communication

Many of the features described by Goffman and then developed by Du Bois (2007) in his discussion of stance could be used in discussing forms of ritual communication that fall more on the "macro" side of interaction, insofar as large numbers of people are involved and explicit stance-taking may be required of the participants (see also Kockelman 2004). Where the performance and experiencing of ritual take place in a multilingual situation, nonverbal indexes of stance-taking (e.g., music, bodily decoration, gestures) are used (Basso 1985). As we see in the chapters by Basso, Senft, Kratz, and Kuipers, ritual communication should be thought of as an especially elaborated, multimodal form of behavior, a point made earlier by anthropologists who wrote about music in ritual (Basso 1985; Feld 1982; Hill 1993; Roseman 1991; Seeger 1987).

Initiation and other liminal rituals have long been sources of information about the psychological shaping of ritual experience as well as the psychic struggles of participants engaged in ritual communication (see, e.g., much of the work by Victor Turner). Yet the linguistic features of other kinds of ritual events, such as personal narratives, are also important for helping us understand the problems of voicing (Bakhtin 1973 [1929]; Hill 1993; Urban 1989; Voloshinov 1973), including questions about the multiplicity of a single person's voices, the understanding of different kinds of dialogicality in interpersonal contacts, and phenomena associated with the suppression of voicing in the face of perceptions of power and violence in a relationship.

In chapter 6, Suzanne Oakdale explores the autobiographical and biographical aspects of rituals in several lowland South American societies. Biographical narratives merge with autobiographical ones, narrators assume the identities of ancestral figures, and the identity of the ancestral figure becomes subsumed by the identity of the narrator. The effect of these performances is a kind of circulation of experiences and perspectives among subjects from different time periods and distinct communities. Performances of these autobiographical and biographical narratives, which are embedded in ritual events, are key moments both in the construction of personal identities and memories and in the imagining of emergent kinds of social groups and historicities. The nuanced understanding of the play of voices in interpersonal relations (including, as Du Bois shows in chapter 13, interaction between the voice of a text and that of a living commentator) and the topic of voicing and power together afford a special opportunity for critical scrutiny of autobiographical rhetoric.

The contributors to this volume emphasize newer understandings of the play of voices in interpersonal relations, including the multiplicity of voices uttered by the same speaker. They look at the way images of sociality are foregrounded through stance-taking and the recontextualizing of communicative practices that dispute, reinforce, or elaborate such images. The authors of several chapters are concerned with the suppression of voicing (including its self-suppression, or what Senft calls "tact"), with the open violation of learned discursive forms in the face of perceptions of "rules" (Kuipers, Hoëm), and with the coercive power in a relationship that makes talk about certain subjects taboo (Silverstein).

Images of sociality are thus consequences of newly constituted participation frameworks that serve as "ritual centers of semiosis." Du Bois shows how intersubjective processes of dialogicality frame the voicing of the ritual text. We see that multivocal dialogic sequences between the person as a reader of a ritual text and the same person as commentator on the text are triggered by something in the text that its reader finds salient and that motivates a shift from uttering the words to responding to them. This resonance is sometimes divergent, sometimes convergent. Thus the ritual comes in voices that are able to say many things; the question is whether we want them to speak within us.

Du Bois emphasizes that dialogic voices exist in all kinds of discourses, and he links this insight to the theory of distributed cognition. Full acknowledgment of the implications of distributed cognition demands that we not only expand the concept of individual cognition to encompass its social dimension but also recognize social voicing within the cognition of the solitary individual. This implies that the individual social actor is built for intersubjective cognition within the practice of self-understanding as well as externally, and there is potential for socially distributed agency in any utterance.

In chapter 11, Michael Silverstein focuses on two kinds of private, solitary rituals in two societies. For the Chinookans of North America's Columbia River, the ritual comprises a preadolescent's securing of a "spirit power," and for the Australian Aboriginal Worora, it has to do with the way a man becomes "fecund by-and-with a child," determining the child's "great name." In each ritual a person has a conventionally structured yet out-of-observation encounter with alterity—with nonhuman spirits or natural substances or species—and comes away from it culturally endowed for a new phase of life. Silverstein deals with the different kinds of voicing that take place in these encounters and with the micropolitical effects the encounters may have for the individual, effects that might even reverberate in macropolitical realms in the public domain if their seeking for power is successful. That such a ritual encounter has taken place is proprietary information, communicable only in restricted contexts, by, for example, demeanors that index life-transforming experiences. Contrary to many other rituals, such private rituals entail anxiety about whether the person will have such an encounter, whether he or she really has had such a ritual experience, and what consequences the encounter will have for the person's future behavior. Rituals and forms of ritual communication can fail, and so it is risky to engage in them (see also Senft, this volume).

Ellen B. Basso's chapter, too, spans the realms of private and public as well as the domains of the micro- and macropolitical. She highlights the coercive power and interactive effects of different forms of ritual communication that are voiced by different interactants. Even simple forms of ritual communication display resonances to more complex forms, thus increasing their pragmatic force and efficacy. Ritual communication is used to reproduce micro- and macropolitical systems of power; it controls people and situations, indexes authority, and gives participants a sense of being in control of a fraught situation.

The resonance of ritual activities in two different contexts is similarly described by Ingjerd Hoëm, in chapter 8. Hoëm explores the reception of a ritualized performance in two different social environments. Polynesian *faleaitu* ("house of spirits") are skits or comedies constituting a conventional genre that can be an instrument of severe social control but also allows for the breaking of social conventions. Its actors play on turning established social roles upside-down and overturn relationships of respect and authority. As a communicative genre it offers protection to those who enter its ritualized space and gives them license to talk about issues "one does not talk about" otherwise. It is a safeguard to defuse and divert potentially dangerous conflicts related to topics that the society consciously suppresses. Thus it allows for the mirroring of, and provides an opportunity to reflect upon, the sometimes difficult sides of village life. People who perform in *faleaitu* try finally to create an atmosphere that brings everyone together in joy and excitement.

The Recontextualization of Culture through Ritual Communication

A number of chapters highlight some of the ways in which ritual communication enables the "recontextualization" of culture, that is, the reconfiguration of meaning and new contextualization of older practices as well as the creation of new forms of ritual communication from historically older forms. The chapters also illustrate the way old ritual practice contextualizes and recontextualizes culture and the way forms of ritual communication cope with rapid social changes in various cultures. These "practices" vary from indexical grammatical features to whole ritual performances.

Affinal civility, discussed by Basso, and the majority of the proverbs discussed by Goddard illustrate conservative strategies that forms of ritual communication in everyday interaction can activate in recontextualizing culture. We have already discussed the way the songs of the Amazonian Shuar and Achuar (Gnerre) and the narratives and shamanic songs of other South American lowland societies (Oakdale) show how flexible and open for change and innovation even relatively complex forms of ritual communication can be. Historical processes have modified these narratives and songs. Innovations due to cultural changes are reflected and incorporated in the specific semiotic codes of these forms of ritual communication. Even more important, these innovations are understood as providing additional enunciative and performative strength for the narratives and songs. The plasticity of inherited forms of ritual communication helps South American lowland societies negotiate social relations between ethnic groups. The forms of ritual communication remain meaningful because the ancestors' perspectives can be incorporated into the contemporary perspectives of the present-day performers of these rituals.

The Amazonian rituals described by Basso, Oakdale, and Gnerre are not all ritualized to the same degree. The most ritualized events on a continuum of forms of ritual communication show the greatest degree of formal patterning and condensation. As Oakdale shows, lowland rituals encourage a circulation or generalization of a point of view in different ways by drawing on concepts of the "I" in narrative discourse. She differentiates the everyday "I" from the narrative "I" and subcategorizes the narrative "I" into a projective "I," in which speakers speak as if they have become merged with the presented character, and a theatrical "I," in which speakers speak through the character they represent. Moreover, there is an "I" that is almost but not quite projective; in this case, narrators have not completely identified with the character they are presenting, but there is more subjective identification than in theatrical role-playing. Oakdale shows how lowland rituals present images of extreme sorts of sociability by featuring the discourse "I," which allows living persons to partake in the perspectives and stories of others who are unusually distant. They take on the "I" of mythic or deceased ancestors and of enemies, both human and supernatural. This is also true of Kalapalo leaders' talk during large-scale ceremonial gatherings (Basso). In Oakdale's case, the "circulation of experiences" among subjects from different times lends itself to a constructed notion of chronology that has helped preserve the continuity of the indigenous cultures.

Recontextualized rituals have also played a role in the restructuring of communities. In chapter 7, Corinne Kratz discusses parallels and differences between the encouraging addresses (*ceerseet*) given during Okiek female initiation ceremonies in Kenya and addresses offering wedding advice to young couples, and between Okiek marriage arrangement meetings, men's meetings, and new forms of political meetings. She argues that defining and understanding ritual communication requires not only analyses of the ways various modes of communication are used and combined in particular ritual events but also analyses that trace the historical transformations of ritual occasions and ritual communication and that cut across different events and contexts. She sketches the way different kinds of Okiek speeches and meetings relate to one another in terms of event and participation structures, discursive themes, and pragmatic patterns and processes.

Returning to chapter 8, Hoëm discusses the contrast between the performance and efficacy of a play produced by a Tokelauan theater group in two very different settings: Wellington, New Zealand, and the island territory of Tokelau itself. The performance space in New Zealand is closer to that of a Western theater performance. Hoëm looks at the consequences of the ritualized performance in terms of subsequent group formation, power struggles, and discourse about the definition of Tokelauan tradition.

In chapter 9, Joel Kuipers examines a case from the Indonesian island of Sumba in which the definition of what counted as ritual communication was undergoing rapid change. In 1998, a protest demonstration, or "expression of feeling," that was initially only a challenge to the bureaucratic authority of the district regent, a member of the Weyewa ethnolinguistic group, was reinterpreted by his supporters as a challenge to his person. They in turn organized their own demonstration to support him. Another group, however—Lolinese ritual celebrants who, coincidently, had gathered near the town for a festival—recoded this counterdemonstration in more traditional terms and interpreted it as a threatening act of territorial violation. Ultimately the two groups clashed, and at least several dozen people died. Later, traditional leaders from the Weyewa and Loli subdistricts organized a reconciliation event in which they delivered orations in ritual speech. Although Loli and Weyewa are different languages, the ritual speech discourse provided a common idiom for expressing their reconciliation. Kuipers shows that the escalation of the events was due to different interpretations of forms of ritualized protest and to changing ideas about the structure and function of ritual communication on Sumba. He understands these events as a dynamic process of metasemiosis in which conflicting ideologies of expression, humility, and ritual etiquette came together in an atmosphere of general crisis. His analysis of the incidents illustrates the way participants in ritual events mutually monitor one another's uses of local and cosmopolitan models of ritual communication—sometimes with tragic consequences.

Among the Kalapalo, as described by Basso, the affinal civility register, with all its features and strategies, seems to provide the grounding for the ceremonial agency of hereditary leadership expressed in "the leader's talk." This form of ritual communication is distinctive to male Kalapalo hereditary leaders, who engage in these oratory-like speeches during large-scale ceremonial gatherings involving people of more than one community and often more than one language. This is an inherited style that is learned by young leaders, who practice it with older relatives. A speaker's skillful use of the style enables him to connect the present ritual event and its participants with others that took place in the distant past, indexing the continuity of customary behavior initiated by ancestral leaders as well as the specific genealogical underpinning of the speaker's status.

A number of contributors explore difficulties that arise with attempts at recontextualization. In Silverstein's two examples, people are primed and prepared to have private ritual encounters, and the disappointment is great when this kind of encounter "either does not take place or seems to have taken place to no effect." Thus, one can remain powerless (in the Chinookan case) and childless (in the Worora case), unvalidated as "a citizen of a culture one exquisitely understands."

The Communicative Cline

Many of the contributors to this volume discuss models of communication as a matter of degree, organizable as a series of "clines" of features such as the following:

1 Degrees of prospective and retrospective indexicality
2 The performance focus, which emphasizes how degrees of control over and thus responsibility in speech are effected (Du Bois 1986; Rumsey 2000; Urban 1989)
3 Poetic enregisterment: the use of more or less elaborate features of other genres; degrees of difficulty with entextualization; the contrast between things that must be said and what is felt by the speakers (ideological disjunctures, tact, etc.)
4 Degrees of illocutionary force (Austin 1962) in the verbal mode of ritual communication
5 Degrees of metapragmatic content: reference to the participants, location, and temporality of the discursive contents

Is it the case that all language tends toward ritualization (as Haviland claims for Tzotzil speech), and if so, are there degrees of ritualization of speech exhibited by all speakers in all societies? Are large-scale public ("explicit," "religious"?) events only the most obvious kinds of ritual communication (especially to the anthropological outsider)? Are there in fact many kinds of ritual communications, even in private, micropolitical contexts? Are there communities in which all speech is ritualized? And going further, is all speech actually ritualized, so that our current polarity between "ordinary" and "ritual" speech is due for a serious overhaul? If all talk is ritualized, and if ritualization is a "matter of degree," then understanding the ritualization of language must involve foregrounded communicative phenomena (as on a cline, for example). We believe the chapters in this volume provide important theoretical considerations that can serve as bases for further research geared toward finding adequate answers to these important questions.

Note

1. Although this has become an important issue for the newer evolutionists in our field, comparative linguistic materials to substantiate the numerous claims about cognitive origins and functions are strangely absent (e.g., in Liénard and Boyer 2006, there is a curious absence of anything to do with language). For a discussion of this issue in linguistics, see, for example, Cowie 1998 and Földes and Wirrer 2004.

one

Little Rituals

John B. Haviland

Mexican folk discourses partake of several great traditions of ritual language, including the codified responsive dialogues of the Catholic catechism and the massive parallel diphrasism of Mesoamerican emotionally charged or powerful speech. Sometimes, in the Tzotzil of Zinacantán, Chiapas, the two forms are partially merged—for example, in the prayer of shamans and religious officeholders. Resonances of both these great traditions resound in interactions of more mundane sorts in Zinacantán, from domestic conversations to performances in political meetings, markets, and other public spaces. In this chapter I concentrate on these "little rituals," in which echoes of more thoroughly regimented, formulaic, and contextually bound ways of using language can be heard. What do such echoes tell us about the people who produce them, about what they are doing, and about talk and interaction in general? The Zinacantec material underlines the way ritual forms, themselves inherently multimodal, tend to leak beyond the boundaries of full-blown ritual events. Such leakage in turn illustrates again the profound indexicality of talk in interaction and begins to explain some of the coercive effects of ritual talk, on which I focus.

Zinacantec Tzotzil and its closest neighbors have been classic exemplars in the taxonomic study of "ways of speaking" (Gumperz and Hymes 1972), starting with the foundational works of Bricker (1974) and Gossen (1973,1974a, 1974b). My own studies of Zinacantec gossip (Haviland 1977a, 1977b, 1998) amplified but also somewhat undermined the early taxonomies. Irvine's (1979) critique of the notion of formality made it impossible to continue to confound distinct senses of the word—talking without elaboration of "formal language," for example—and a similar critical exercise could be mounted against the term "ritual language." Further, Bauman's development of the notion of performance (1977; Bauman and Briggs 1990) highlighted both interactive and social-structural (or even ethical) aspects of ways of speaking missing in the classic formulations.

My understanding of the social life of talk draws on several foundations: the idea of interaction and face elaborated by Goffman (1981a, 1983); Silverstein's (1976) emphasis on indexical dimensions of language use, linking speech to contexts both assumed and imposed; and the recognition of the social historicity and multiple voicing of speech in work by Bakhtin and his circle (Bakhtin 1981 [1934], 1986). Goffman's insistence on placing talk in a wider interactive frame and his "interaction rituals" are obvious inspirations for the phrase "little rituals." Similarly, one could understand "ritualization" to be a displacement or recalibration of distinct but laminated contexts indexically projected, in Silverstein's parlance, by talk in interaction. Finally, the ritual echoes in quotidian Zinacantec interaction clearly reflect the generic leakage characteristic, for Bakhtin, of "secondary genres," but with somewhat more sociological bite.

A *Merolico*

I start not in highland Chiapas but in a central plaza of downtown Mexico City, the Alameda, where many of the city's poor go on Sundays for "free" entertainments. Among these are the spectacles provided by *merolicos,* celebrated fast-talkers who purvey everything from fortunes, herbs, and joke books to spells and recipes for conquering lovers or vanquishing enemies (Bauman 2004; Haviland 1993, 2005b; Sobrevilla del Valle 2000).

An accomplished *merolico* is Felix, who takes money from people in return for a magical talisman and an offer of spiritual and practical advice. At a crucial point in his performance, when he has arranged his public in a tight circle around him, arms outstretched, fists clasping their talismans, and each person having already "donated" a few small coins to him for his blessing, Felix demonstrates his extraordinary powers by inserting a steel ice pick into his nostril and apparently straight into his brain. As the public gasps and stares, he walks around the circle, ice pick projecting from his face, touching each person in turn. Then he kneels in the center of the circle. After incanting a blessing, he appropriates a piece of the catechism designed to ensnare the audience willy-nilly in a responsive commitment to his purposes. In the following portion of a transcription of such an exchange, M is the *merolico,* and A is the audience:

13 m; *Todos decimos…*
Let us all say…
14 *¡Así sea!*
So be it!
15 a; *Así sea*
16 m; *Ave María purísima* [placing his right palm over his heart]
Hail Mary most pure,
17 a; *Sin pecado concebida*
Conceived without sin.
18 m; *Ave María purísima* [louder]
19 a; *Sin pecado concebida*
20 m; *Ave María purísima*
21 a; *Sin pecado concebida*

Having secured the participation of the public—following his direct command (13), the assembled crowd repeats his "So be it" (15)—he goes on (16) to elicit, first somewhat uncertainly (17), then with perfect coordination in the repetitions (19–21), the appropriate response from the audience to his "Hail Mary most pure": "conceived without sin." He then induces the members of the audience to cross themselves, seemingly involuntarily, at the appropriate moment (24–27):

22 m; *En el nombre sea de dios bendito todopoderoso*
In the name of blessed, all powerful God,
23 *Danos tu bendición*
Give us your blessing.
24 *En el nombre del padre*
In the name of the Father,
25 *Del hijo*
Of the Son,
26 *Del espíritu*
And of the
27 *Santo*
Holy Spirit.
28 *Amen*

Felix now sits back on his heels and engages an entirely different though equally powerful set of folk religious traditions, oriented less toward the reflexive responses of Catholic ritual than toward the awe and fear associated with Mesoamerican magic. He assumes in sequence, via the hypothetical ascriptions of others, the roles of witch, sorcerer, animal spirit companion (the *nagual* of Aztec tradition), snake charmer, diviner, spiritist (*santero,* i.e., devotee of a cult of saints), and shaman, pronouncing himself, finally, "teacher of teachers":

30 m; *Me dicen brujo*
They call me a witch.
31 *Me dicen hechicero*
They call me a sorceror.
32 *Me dicen nagual*
They call me a spirit companion.
33 *Perdónenme*
Excuse me,
34 *Otros me dicen pitonista*
Others call me a snake charmer.
35 *Hay quien me dice adivino*
There are some who call me a psychic.
36 *Señor*
Sir,
37 *Soy santero*
I am a worshipper of saints.
38 *Soy curandero*
I am a curer.
39 *Soy*
I am
40 *Maestro de maestros*
Teacher of teachers.

The *merolico* endows himself (and by extension his talisman) with a variety of powers: those of priest and intermediary to God, of the saints and the Virgin, of sorcery and witchcraft, of divination, and of healing. He borrows language from Catholic and popular traditions to accomplish both crowd and mind control. He has earlier demonstrated his control over snakes, and most recently over a six-inch steel shank inserted apparently straight into his brain. As he speaks he now exercises his power over the members of the crowd, causing them to move their bodies and respond on his command. These same powers, or fear of them, will ultimately cause many in the audience to part with up to a week's earnings before they can be freed from Felix's circle.

Zinacantec Ritual Language

Let me turn now to Chiapas and to a seemingly inconsequential snippet of interaction. In August 2004, as I accompanied the entourage of a prestigious ritual officer ("cargoholder") en route to an important fiesta, we stopped at a village on the road to pick up several helpers. My ninety-year-old *compadre,* P, blind and nearly deaf, made his way out to the road to meet the passing group, and there ensued a brief encounter while the truck was being loaded with people and provisions. A senior helper and the cargoholder's wife greeted the old man and exchanged a few words, and the cargoholder's official *tot-meʔ* (lit., 'father-mother', or ritual adviser) offered him a few sips of cane liquor. There could scarcely be a more prosaic interaction than this—a chance meeting between acquaintances, a mere parenthesis to a much larger ritual event. Before looking at its details, let me proceed to an extremely abbreviated mini-ethnography of Tzotzil ritual speech.

The language of prayer in Zinacantec Tzotzil is organized into parallel structures. Song (Haviland 1967), formal denunciation (Laughlin 1975), and some ordinary talk (Haviland, 1996) share with prayer the use of stylized images and sentiments, lexicalized as more or less fixed pairs (and sometimes triplets or quadruplets) of expressions structured tightly together (see Gossen 1974, 1974b, 1985, for Chamula prayer; see Laughlin 1980, Haviland 1967, 2000 for Zinacantán).

In its canonical form, a Zinacantec curer's prayer proceeds as a series of strictly parallel lines that differ from one another in only a single element—sometimes a lexeme, sometimes just a root. Although every Zinacantec can muster at least some couplets, and other Zinacantec specialists may be extraordinarily proficient at the elaborate parallel speech of religious ritual, curing prayer is considered a gift from the gods. In Zinacantec theory, the ability to cure one's fellow human beings—and crucially, the ability to pray fluently—is bestowed by ancestral gods in a dream. It is not something one can *learn* to do.

In the following prayer fragment, a curer (C in the transcript) addresses the spirits of the mountain cave where the ceremony is taking place, to try to reverse witchcraft that has caused her patient's (P's) symptoms:

Example 1. A shaman prays to reverse witchcraft

1 c; *k'elavil la jtot // k'elavil la kajval*
Look here, father // look here, my lord.
2 *muʔnuk o chal t avalabe /*
Your child didn't say anything //

3 *muʔnuk o chal ta anich'nab une*
Your offspring didn't say anything.
4 p; *an ch'ay xkaʔi*
Why, I forgot.
5 c; *pero yuʔun me chamelzanbon //*
But still I want you to fix for me,
6 *yuʔun me chachapabon ech'el*
I want you to prepare for me
7 *ti jchamel une // ti jlajel une*
The sick one // the hurt one,
8 *li joyijel une // ti tz'epp'ujel une*
The spinning one // the tripping one.
9 *liʔ la chkom ta yo laveʔeb une //*
May it remain here in your eating place,
10 *liʔ la chkom ta yo lavuch'eb une*
May it remain here in your drinking place,
11 *ti ip une // ti k'ux une*
The sickness // the pain.

There are two highly productive aspects to the parallel structure of prayer. First are the paired doublets (or triplets), which alternate in the frame of a single sequence of lines. For example, the paired verbal roots *cham* 'be sick' // *laj* 'finish' refer in prayer to disease and death. Zinacantecs employ these paired roots with appropriate morphological elaboration as full words. Thus, (7) involves the pair *j-cham-el* 'sick person' // *j-laj-el* 'dying person' (with an agentive prefix *j-* and a nominalizing suffix *-el*), but one could equally well form a doublet around fully inflected verb forms: *ch-i-cham* 'I am sick' // *ch-i-laj* 'I am dying'. The morphological creativity of the language thus augments the already large inventory of paired roots, creating many possible doublets tailored to particular contexts of speech. More important, at the level of cultural meaning, these doublets have a dual character. On the one hand, they are the cells from which the tissue of prayer grows, the irreducible units of ritual expression. On the other, they are highly evocative images compressed into minimal elements of speech. Thus *cham // laj* makes available a means for referring to sickness, and it also incorporates a "stereoscopic" image (Fox 19741977) involving both the painful process of sickening and dying (the meaning of *cham*) and its ultimate finality (*laj*, lit., 'finish, come to an end'). An alternative image for a related concept is found in the doublet *ʔip* 'sickness' // *k'ux* 'pain' (11), which focuses on suffering.

The second productive aspect of prayer involves the frames within which doublets appear. Sometimes a pair of lines consists of nothing more than the couplets themselves, appropriately dressed syntactically and morphologically. Usually, however, there is a wider frame: parts of a line that are repeated without change in a parallel construction. These frames themselves comprise a restricted set of possibilities reflecting the conventionalized content of prayer, just as the inventory of doublets represents its conventional imagery. In the preceding transcript, line (1) uses the conventional summons *k'elavil* (lit., 'look and see'). Sometimes a particular phrase in prayer always co-occurs with a particular doublet, but sometimes a single frame admits a number of different paired doublets, resulting in slightly different meanings. The summons (1) is here directed at the lord of the cave, represented by the doublet *j-tot* 'my father' // *k-ajval* 'my lord', though elsewhere it might have other addressees.

Prayer as a code thus employs a limited constructional syntax and a large but heavily conventionalized imagistic lexicon. In fluent prayer, curers enter an almost trancelike state. They deliver the words rapidly, without hesitation, and with remarkably little repetition. Each line exhibits one of a characteristic range of repetitive melodic and rhythmic cadences, with several lines grouped into phrases whose prosodic structure exhibits the same kind of repetition as its wording. Zinacantecs cite the difficulty of the genre as evidence that the ability to pray is a gift from the ancestral gods. Skilled shamans can pray for hours at a sitting, improvising appropriate, nonrepetitive prayers throughout ceremonies that can last for more than twenty-four hours. Despite the Zinacantec metatheory of divine inspiration, the constrained structure of ritual language clearly facilitates the remarkable fluency a skilled shaman brings to curing prayer.

Dialogicity, Interactivity, and Uptake

Although shamanistic prayer often appears monologic—typically performed by a lone curer, who nominally addresses one or more supernatural authorities—and textual sediments of prayer have mostly been presented that way (e.g., Laughlin 1980), prayer, like virtually all other Zinacantec talk, is highly interactive, implying various sorts of "uptake" and response between interlocutors.[1] Previously (Haviland 2000) I argued that the participant structure (and consequently the set of interactive stances and implicated voices) of prayer is fluid, rapidly shifting, and constantly renegotiated in the moment. That is, specific addressees, both real and virtual, are invoked and constantly shuffled in the course of even single lines of prayer.

What is more, the shaman is frequently accompanied in prayer by the patient or the patient's proxy. Much like a professional leading a novice in song or dance, the curer's words prompt appropriately refashioned prayer from the companion. The secondary prayer is thus partly an echo and partly a response. (There are moments when the priority is reversed, and a particularly fluent patient can apparently change the course of the shaman's prayer.) This tendency for one participant to repeat and transform the words of another is characteristic of Tzotzil interaction, conversational as well as ritual, and it is widely reported in Mayan languages (e.g., Brody 1991; Brown 1997) and elsewhere in Mesoamerica.

It is also typical of prayer and other highly parallel ritual genres such as song that they allow indirect interaction, operating like hints or cues to ancillary participants who are not directly addressed. Just as Zinacantec musicians signal to attentive helpers that liquor is to be served by singing a verse mentioning *xiʔobil // sk'exobil,* lit., 'the cause for fear, the cause for shame'—that is, cane liquor—so shamans, by incorporating appropriate elements into their prayers, can indicate that certain actions important to a curing ceremony ought to be performed. Indeed, in the curing prayer fragment shown in example 1, lines 2 and 3, which are addressed directly to the lord of the cave (the "you" of "your offspring"), explicitly prod the "child // offspring" in question—namely, the patient—to begin to pray herself. Her remark "Oh, I forgot," at line 4, registers her chagrin at being reminded, and shortly thereafter she begs forgiveness in her own prayer. Here is a hint that, like the allusions to the Catholic catechism in the *merolico*'s routine, ritual forms in Zinacantán can also have a coercive interactive effect—here a gentle but effective chiding reminder.

Multimodality

Moreover, in prayer as in other kinds of talk, participants' whole bodies are typically involved. Rather than "ritual language," it is perhaps more appropriate simply to speak of "ritual action," which includes not only talk but also postures (including features of mutual gaze or its absence), demeanor, aspects of dress and grooming, spatial disposition, ancillary activities, and even props. The prayer session in the cave illustrates the point in several obvious ways. The prayer is the spoken accompaniment to quite specific sorts of action.

First, the interaction between shaman and patient is characterized by the stylized greetings or acknowledgments that take place between any two Zinacantecs in situations of sufficient gravity. At points of transition—when starting or stopping a prayer sequence, for example—the patient bows to her curer, with accompanying responsive spoken couplets. Such greetings are, indeed, expected concomitants to opening and closing *all* interactions, at least as I was taught them as a novice ethnographer in the 1960s. When two interactants are of unequal age, the younger bows to the older (in Tzotzil, *-nupbe sk'ob* 'meets her hand'), presenting her forehead, which the older person gently touches with the back of her hand (in Tzotzil, *-ak'be sk'ob* 'gives her hand'). When two people are of equal age, they may shake hands (if they are male) or, in certain ceremonial contexts, mutually bow to one another. Alternatively, especially if they are female or physically distant, they may simply acknowledge each other's presence by uttering the appropriate words without touching. Strikingly, in certain highly charged contexts, people will rise from their chairs (or from their mats on the floor if they are female) to walk across a crowded room to exchange a full-body greeting with a senior person.

Second, integral to these greetings is an elaborate calculus of address terms, based mostly on kin formulas, that specifies uniquely for almost any dyad what the correct term of address should be. Thus, if I greet an unknown senior woman, I will "meet her hand," saying, *meʔtik* 'ma'am'. If she knows my name, she will intone it back to me as she "gives me her hand"; if not, she will merely touch my forehead without a word, call me *kere* 'boy', or perhaps utter the formula *laʔ chabot* 'come and be cared for'. Age differences can be neutralized terminologically by certain special relationships: *compadres* call each other "compadre" (but bow to each other according to age); cargoholders and other officeholders substitute cargo titles for names or kin terms, and so on. Thus the greeting is a mini-ritual rich with social structural, social historical, and contextual meaning, of which the words are but one, albeit especially pregnant, component.

In the anti-witchcraft cave, further actions are integrated with the prayer. The shaman lights the candles and otherwise arranges offerings to the Lord of the Earth, in whose dominion the cave lies. She gently strikes the patient's back, shoulders, arms, and legs with pine boughs to cleanse her soul of maladies. Liquor is exchanged and consumed, and helpers arrange offerings and other paraphernalia. Parts of the prayer explicitly refer to these accompanying actions. For example, lines 9–10 ask that the patient's sickness remain there in the cave, characterized in couplets as "your eating place, your drinking place," an indirect reference to offerings that the shaman simultaneously prepares for the Earth Lord to "eat and drink."

Knowledge, Competence, and Power

Shamanistic prayer and its malevolent witchcraft cousins are the most specialized, formulaic, and contextually constrained kinds of speech in the Zinacantec repertoire. At the same time, prayer is fluid, creative, and—in the Zinacantec scheme of things—the most highly efficacious sort of talk imaginable. It can effect a cure and thus transform the world. On Silverstein's (1976) cline, prayer is thus at once highly presupposing, because to pray at all requires that appropriate circumstances obtain, and highly creative, because it is explicitly designed to transform the circumstances in which it is embedded.

Other related speech genres in Zinacantec Tzotzil are similarly formulaic, partake of the same shared repertoire of code elements (the same stereoscopic doublet imagery, for example), and relate in different ways to specialized knowledge and power to which Zinacantecs can aspire. These, too, are kinds of "formal" language, in Irvine's "positional identities" sense—language appropriate to and indeed expected of persons who occupy roles of specific kinds.

The most obvious and widespread examples of such ritual talk are the prayers, greetings, salutations, and elaborate thanks exchanged between cargoholders in the ceremonies and meals that are the main business of the civil-religious hierarchy (see Cancian 1965, 1992. Unlike shamanistic curing prayer, this sort of talk is never performed alone. Instead, it typically occurs in responsive dyads, where the content of the talk is linked to the immediate context of the ritual and where what one person says is matched to what the other says, with appropriate adjustments for the asymmetries in roles between them. These exchanged words are also accompanied by bowing and touching of the head or, in the case of the specially clad cargoholders depicted in figure 1.1, the touching of one's partner's rosary to one's forehead.

When one ritual officeholder offers bottles of liquor to another in order to invite him to put on special ritual garments during Holy Week, he says something like the following:

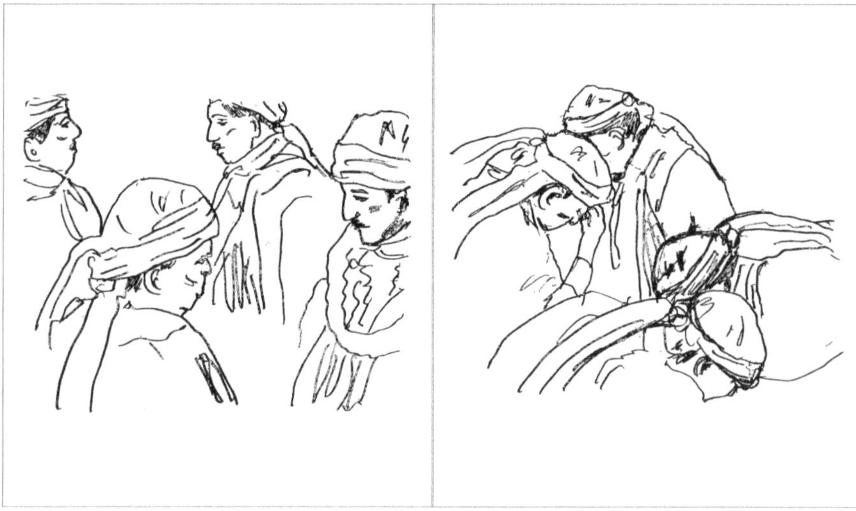

Figure 1.1. Cargoholders greet each other at the doorway of a house.

Example 2. Offerer's part of fragment of cargo prayer (t920413)

1 *ak'o pertonal*
Give pardon.
2 *o to jset'uk // o to jutebuk*
There is still a pinch // there is still a bit,
3 *xiʔobil // sk'exobil*
Of the cause for fear // the cause for shame,
4 *li jch'ul man vinajele // jch'ul man lorya*
Of the holy buyer of heaven // the holy buyer of glory.
5 *ta jlap o jk'uʔtik //*
With it shall we put on our clothes //
6 *ta jlap o jpok'tik*
With it shall we put on our scarves.
7 *ba jkuxbetik yoʔon //*
We will go to rest the heart //
8 *ba jvik'betik ti sat*
We will go to open the eyes.
9 *jlikeluk // chaʔ-likeluk*
For a moment // for two moments.
10 *nichimal jmanvanej // nichimal jtojvanej*
The flowery buyer of souls // the flowery payer of souls.

His partner responds, simultaneously or with a fractional delay, with exactly the same words, except that for the first two lines he substitutes the following:

1 *bweno kolaval*
Well, thank you.
2 *mi o to jset'uk // o to jutebuk*
Is there still a pinch? // Is there still a bit?

All adults are thought in principle to be able to learn to muster such talk, unlike curing prayer, although novice cargoholders need explicit instruction in exactly which formulas to use for which circumstances. One primary task of a *tot-me?,* or ritual advisor—a senior man contracted to give advice to a cargoholder during his year in office—is to instruct the cargoholder in appropriate ritual speech. An enormous store of specialized knowledge is associated with such ritual talk, and just as it is (in principle at least) a source of pride and a mark of adult maturity and success to perform in the cargo hierarchy, knowing how to talk in these ritual contexts is also a valued skill.

Nor is it only religious ritual that gives occasion for such formulaic exchanges. Other events involve such greetings: baptismal meals, weddings, funerals, and associated events such as resolving elopements or divorce; the beginnings and endings of formal dispute settlements; housewarming fiestas; ceremonial visits to ask for loans or wives or ritual help; and so on. Because some people are simply better at such performance than others, more tongue-tied Zinacantecs make sure that to accomplish important business they take along a *j-k'opojel* 'spokesperson'. Expert talkers take a leading role in guiding less accomplished partners through the motions, sometimes truncating or simplifying a sequence when no appropriate response is forthcoming, and otherwise supplying single-handedly the whole content in the face of mumbled and halting replies.

Sometimes a specific social role demands speaking abilities that surpass those a given incumbent may possess. For example, the *jpetom,* lit. 'embracer', or godparent at a wedding—a person usually chosen more for economic might than for verbal prowess (see Haviland 1996)—is expected to deliver wedding instructions to the bride and groom in fluent parallel speech. But a career selling flowers or driving a truck, although it might have produced wealth, might not have prepared the godfather for fluent and elegant speech, so wedding exhortations sometimes fall short of the Zinacantec formal ideal. Often couplets begin but fail halfway. Sometimes, instead of a parallel line, a godfather produces just a repetition or nonparallel "ordinary" talk.

In one wedding I attended, the exhortation began with an elaborate greeting between the godfather and the father of the groom, the latter a man with considerable cargo experience, a fluent master of the genre, who used ritual doublets to invite the other man to give advice to the newlyweds. As a measure of fluency, in 35 seconds of responsive parallel greeting, the father produced 5.5 syllables per second, whereas the less accomplished godfather managed a respectable but considerably lower average of 3.7. The godfather went on to give a halting, partly extemporized although substantively expert set of instructions to bride and groom, with encouraging additions from the father and another senior relative, and in counterpoint with his wife, the couple's godmother, who largely addressed nonparallel speech to the bride (fig. 1.2).

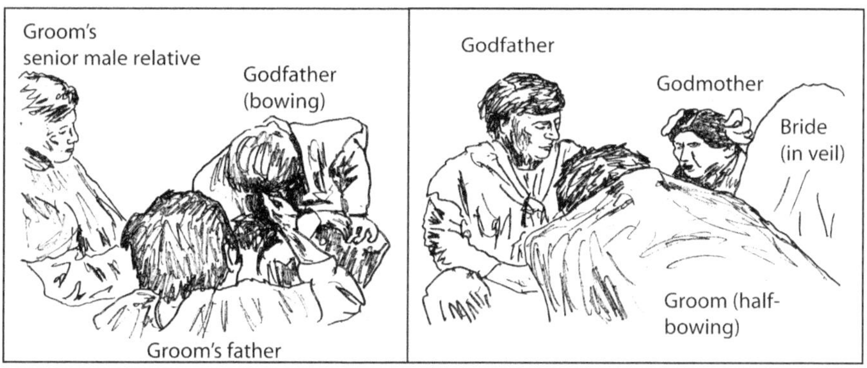

Figure 1.2. The godfather at a wedding, with elders and newlyweds.

The reciprocal relationship between the bride and groom and their linguistically semicompetent godfather illustrates a kind of ramshackle ritualization. Just as the godfather was only sporadically able to summon the sort of linguistic structure appropriate to the wedding exhortation, so the newlyweds seemed occasionally reluctant to respond with appropriate gestures of respect. In this same wedding, the father of the groom found it necessary from time to time to admonish his son, directing him explicitly at awkward transitional moments to "meet his godfather's hand"—that is, to bow and give thanks for the instruction he was receiving. The multimodal concomitants of ritual speech, that is, were as halting as the speech meant to elicit them. But once again, the ritual form itself provides a mechanism for bringing potential insubordination—in this case, on the part of a groom uncomfortable at being lectured about how to behave, especially in the presence of his domineering father—back under control. Let me explore a bit further the gentle coercion associated with ritual language. A shaman shows power in part by marshaling the parallel structure of prayer. In the mouths of cargoholders and wedding godparents, parallel constructions index authority. In the transitional moments of other quotidian rituals, lapsing into ritual speech indicates solemnity and respect, or sometimes high emotion. Even the burlesque transformation of ritual language that drunks sometimes emit can have a kind of authority almost despite itself.

In the final days of the fiesta of San Lorenzo in August 2005, one of the helpers of a senior cargoholder—his brother-in-law—took it upon himself to lecture his teenage niece, the cargoholder's daughter, about appropriate behavior (fig. 1.3). The girl, who was trapped making bean tamales for an important ritual meal, resisted her tipsy uncle's harangue, which became ever more insistent and couplet-filled as it progressed. She made fun of his choice of images, turned his words back on him, and generally tried to brush him off, especially when his admonition—

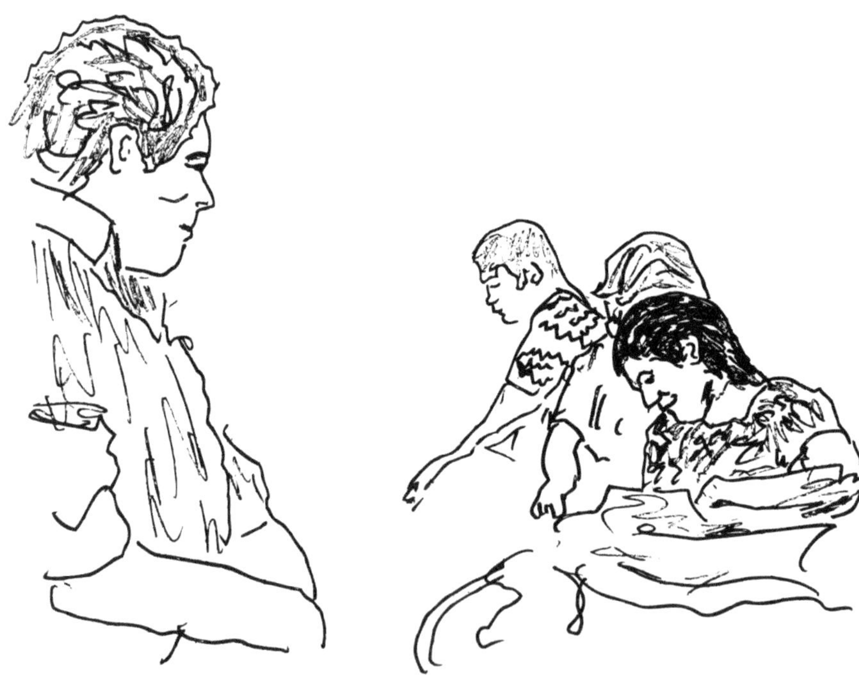

Figure 1.3. A tipsy uncle harangues his niece.

itself a kind of burlesque of a wedding godfather's instructions to a bride—turned to the acutely embarrassing subject of her own eventual courtship and marriage. Nonetheless, despite insurrectionist giggles and ridiculing asides, the girl was willy-nilly drawn into the interactive form, until eventually she capitulated to the "positional identity" it cast upon her, bowing and offering formulaic polite thanks to ("meeting the hand" of) her uncle (fig. 1.4).

Figure 1.4. Harangued niece reluctantly bows to admonishing uncle.

Genres of Interpersonal Relations

Working in the nearby Tzotzil community of Chamula, Gossen (1985) linked the structure of prayer to a metaphor of "heat." Prayer "is exalted, ritually significant, hot, and fixed; it can be said only in a formal context" (1985: 86). Furthermore, according to Gossen, "emotional speech ... is a key to understanding what happens to language when the 'heart is heated.' In a word, it multiplies; the same information is repeated"(1985: 86). Hence, the elaborate parallelism and repetition are direct icons of the character of the heated heart. "Emotional speech occurs in countless contexts of everyday and ritual life. It invariably leans toward the redundant and formal, for such are the qualities of the heated heart of a Tzotzil speaker" (Gossen (1985: 92).

Whatever the native Tzotzil theory of parallelism, Zinacantecs tend to break into couplets in many circumstances when emotions run high. In angry denunciation, in lamentation and weeping, and in scolding, allusions to the parallel constructions of prayer (as well as doublets more scatological and scathing, characteristic of scolding) tend to emerge (see Haviland 2005a). Gossen's remarks suggest that the apparent leakage of ritual linguistic forms into nonritual contexts (Haviland 1994) derives not simply from a Bakhtinian revoicing or borrowing of primary genres by secondary ones but from a deeper interpersonal psychodynamic through which parallel form erupts almost spontaneously. The link between strong emotion and ritual language characteristic of power, authority, and coercion reemerges in the tiny encounter between the old man and the cargo party, to which I return shortly.

The vast literature on honorifics and respectful language (Agha 1994) and on politeness (Brown and Levinson 1978), and the classic work on competing dimensions in pronominal systems (Brown and Gilman 1960), repeatedly makes two observations relevant to the current argument. First is that simple dichotomies implied by terms such as "respectful" and "polite" fail to capture the multidimensional subtlety of multifold social relationships. Failing to be polite is not (necessarily) to be impolite, and appropriate "respect" may require extraordinarily polite words (or none at all) with some people but explicit vulgar joking with others. Second, we are reminded that respect or politeness is virtually never a matter of mere words, but rather that words are simply one part in a multimodal symphony of "respectful" behaviors.

Wracking my ethnographic brain for exemplary counterpoles to the highly parallel ritual language of Zinacantán, I am hard-pressed to identify any completely "*non*ritual" language to counterpose. I find no unmarked sort of "natural conversation" unconstrained by its own contextual conditions, no "informal" talk on any of Irvine's dimensions. I consider in turn a few apparently promising types.

There is what might be called "idle chat" in Zinacantán, a kind of maximally empty "polite" dialogue, massively repetitive, highly formulaic (Zinacantecs also turn, in awkward social moments, to the weather), and, in precisely Malinowski's sense (1923), phatic, because the point is seemingly never to convey propositional information. Learning how to ape such a form was one of my own first achievements as a novice Tzotzil speaker, a testimony to its emptiness and thus its ritualization in an ethological sense.

Another kind of nonritual talk, often juxtaposed with prayer and other ritual forms, is common to male helpers in Zinacantán, who often stand around killing time in the lulls between intense ceremonial activity. It, too, has a typical generic form and a characteristic content: boasting, tall tales, sexual innuendo, and hyperbole. Formally, such boasting talk is also highly marked, not by parallel constructions (although it is almost aggressively repetitive), but lexically by the heavy use of affective verbs (Laughlin 1975) and exaggerated positional images, and prosodically by elongated vowels and occasional falsetto voice. It is interactively competitive, filled with overlap, struggles for the floor and for the right to deliver punchlines—reminiscent of Zinacantec gossip (Haviland 1977b). Like the most intimate of conversational forms in Zinacantán, it is also punctuated by routinized joking, mostly in the form of punning and wordplay (Gossen 1974a), like the standard Mexican *albur* though usually not as sexually tinged. Such punning also takes a distinctive parallel interactive form.

I mention these generic forms and contrast them with a nonexistent hypothetical neutral conversational form because (for this ethnographer at least) they have a highly salient shared feature: they have to be learned. "Knowing how to speak Tzotzil" in a grammatical sense is simply not enough to be able to joke or boast with the guys, just as it is not enough to allow one to respond to a cargoholder's greeting or to pray in a cave. Instead, there is a veritable hegemony of genres, in which every utterance, like every interaction, has a character that is linked to and informed by its position on multiple dimensions of interpersonal relations. Like walking the right way, wielding a machete, holding a weaving stick, or tying a belt (Devereaux 1995), talking in Zinacantán is *always* a tiny formulaic ritual. Waking up, washing one's face, sitting down by the fire to start the day—these moments are pervaded by routines and have their *smelol,* their 'right way', indexed *always* to the co-presence of specific social alters. And so it is with talk.

The Old Man and the Passing Ritual Entourage

With this schematic preamble, let me return, finally, to the little interaction between my *compadre* and the passing cargo party. Working through the talk, I try to point to the "ritual" resonances I hear. The scene begins with the old man (P) checking with the senior helper (C) and the ritual adviser (M) about the exact calendar of events. When would the ritual activity finish in the distant town to which the group was heading?

1 p; *lunex to*
(You will stay) until Monday.
2 c; *yech to:*
Until then.
[
3 m; *a yech to leʔe=*
Yes, until then.
4 p; *=yech to*
Until then.
[
5 c; *yech to:*
Until then.
[
6 m; *e:y*
Okay.
[
7 p; *lunex to chmuy ta xmal k'ak'al*
They come back up on Monday at sundown.
[
8 c; *ji:*
Yes.
[
9 m; *jaʔ to*
Not until then.
10 p; *yech to*
Until then.
[
11 c; *yech un*
Then.
12 m; *ji:*
Yes.
13 c; *yech to un*
Until then, indeed.

In fact P is well aware of these details; in the isolation of his blindness and deafness, he spends his hours calculating and recalculating the crucial dates of the ritual calendar, anchoring himself in a world of ritual to which he has dedicated his life and which he carries around in his head. It is P who supplies (7) the fact that Monday is the day when the cargoholder himself will "climb" up the mountain from the other village back to Zinacantán to mark the end of the fiesta. Notice that both of P's interlocutors assume the role of "answerer," showing their agreement by multiply repeating his pronouncements.

P knows that the cargo party is in a hurry, only passing through his village. Having confirmed the dates, he immediately initiates a polite end to the interaction with a standard, formulaic preclosing:

14 p; *ji: te . k'el abaik aʔa*
Yes. So take care of yourselves.
15 *pas avokolik*
Do your job.
[
16 m; *teyuk aʔa kumpa:*
Agreed, compadre,
17 p; *ch'omiloxuke*
You who are helpers.
[
18 c; *teyu:k*
All right.
[
19 m; *teyu:k*
All right.
20 c; *teyu:k*
All right.

Both interlocutors repeat the equally formulaic *teyuk,* lit., 'let it be then/there', that is, "agreed." (As M's reply to P [16] shows, the two men are *compadres.*)

A more intimate sequence ensues. C is P's relative, and the old man has served as ritual adviser for C's own cargo career. C now expresses more personal concerns before taking leave of the older man. (P is, in the meantime [23–24, 26], checking details with M about where they will await the arrival of the cargoholder, who is walking down to the other village in the saint's entourage.) C tells P to "watch after himself," addressing him as *tot* 'father', a term reserved for close older male relatives. P recognizes C's turn as a preclosing, a preamble to C's leaving the interaction, and he addresses him directly (by name [27]) with a series of polite leave-taking formulas, repetitively acknowledged in turn by the other.

22 c; *k'el aba un tot*
Look after yourself, father.
[

<table>
<tr><td>23</td><td>p;</td><td>- ta ba sten-
At the mea-</td></tr>
<tr><td>24</td><td></td><td>ba stenteje
At the meadow.
[</td></tr>
<tr><td>25</td><td>c;</td><td>te k'el aba
Look after yourself.</td></tr>
<tr><td>26</td><td>m;</td><td>jaʔ bi aʔa
Yes, indeed.</td></tr>
<tr><td>27</td><td>p;</td><td>pas avokolik c.
Do your work, c.</td></tr>
<tr><td>28</td><td></td><td>pas avokolik un
Do your work.
[</td></tr>
<tr><td>29</td><td>c;</td><td>teyuk
Okay.
        [</td></tr>
<tr><td>30</td><td>m;</td><td>   teyuk xa o:
        All right, then.</td></tr>
<tr><td>31</td><td>c;</td><td>teyuk
All right.</td></tr>
<tr><td>32</td><td></td><td>te k'el aba
Look after yourself.
                [</td></tr>
<tr><td>33</td><td>p;</td><td>   te k'el abaik
                Look-</td></tr>
<tr><td>34</td><td>c;</td><td>teyuk
All right.</td></tr>
<tr><td>35</td><td>p;</td><td>jiʔ
Yes.
[</td></tr>
<tr><td>36</td><td>c;</td><td>teyuk cheʔe tot
All right then, father.
             [</td></tr>
<tr><td>37</td><td>m;</td><td>   jiʔ
             Yes.</td></tr>
<tr><td>38</td><td>p;</td><td>bweno
Okay.</td></tr>
</table>

C knows that the older man cannot see. Because the circumstances resonate with ritual, however, he cannot simply truncate his leave-taking and slip away. P is a man who has passed through an extraordinarily distinguished cargo career, having served in the same cargo that these helpers now serve and having maintained strong links to the ritual hierarchy throughout his life, as cargoholder, ritual adviser, and "holy elder"—a kind of ritual super-rank. C therefore goes to great lengths to "meet the hand" of the older man. "Can you see, father?" he asks (39), and utters a formulaic farewell (40, 43–44), bowing his head so low that he actually brings his forehead into contact with the older man's lowered right hand (fig. 1.5).

39 c; *mi chavil tot*
Can you see, father...
40 *chibat che?e tot*
Good-bye, then, father.
[
41 p; *teyuk un*
All right.
42 *te xak'el aba ech'el*
Take care as you go.
[

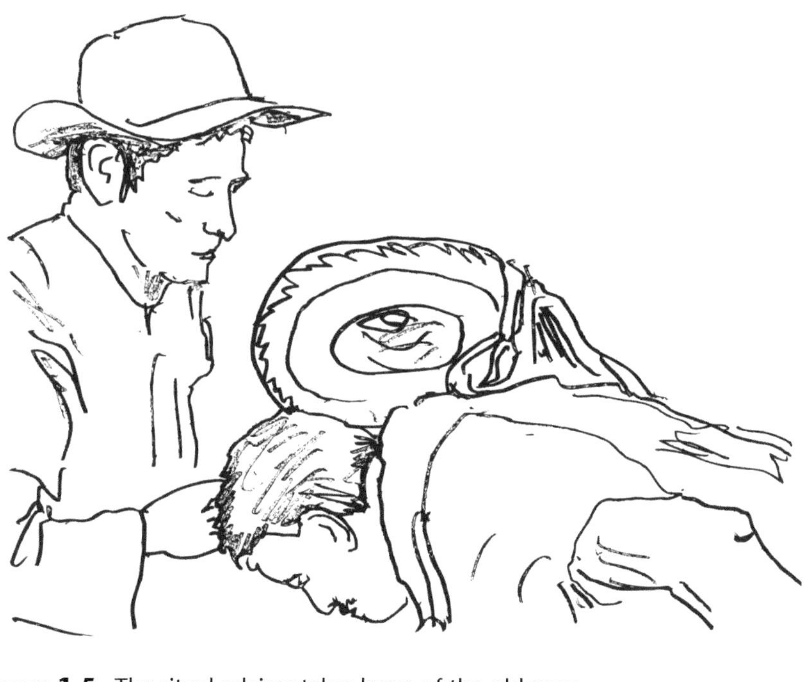

Figure 1.5. The ritual adviser takes leave of the old man.

43 c; *chibat tot*
Good-bye, father.
44 *chibat che?e:*
Good-bye, then.
[
45 p; *an teyuk un*
Why, all right.

The ritual adviser, M, himself a very senior man, follows suit, taking his leave with an elaborate bow. (P is, in fact, one of the very few men to whom M has had to bow during several weeks of intense ceremonial activity.) P cannot see him and is prompted by another man, J (48), to touch the other's forehead.

46 m; *chibat kumpare:*
Good-bye, compadre.
[
47 p; *mi chabat kumpare*
Are you leaving, compadre?
48 j; *ak'o lak'ob kumpa*
Give your hand, compadre!
49 m; *chibat*
Good-bye.
50 p; *te xabat kumpare*
Go, then, compadre.
51 m; *mm, teyuk un*
Hmm, all right.

There follows an especially poignant sequence. P assumes that C's wife, Mal, is present, as well as M's wife—his *comadres*—and he addresses them with preclosings (52, 54) on the basis of that polite and ritually completive assumption:

52 p; *te me xabatik ma:l*
Good-bye, then, Mal.
[
53 x; *teyan nox tot=*
Just stay there, father.
54 p; *=te xabatik kumale:*
Good-bye, comadre.

Instead, the woman present is X, the cargoholder's wife, a principal in the entourage. X gives P a preclosing of her own, tailored to the circumstances. "Just stay here, father," she says (53, 56), reflecting the fact that she is leaving and he is staying. He finally recognizes who she is, greeting her formulaically (57). She acknowledges the greeting (58, 61) and tells P that she will take along his daughter as helper. P chokes back tears of emotion (59–60, 63)—remorse, I surmise, for his blindness, chagrin that he has not recognized or acknowledged X's presence, and despair at his incapacity to participate more fully in ritual events on which he has centered his life.

56 x; *teyan nox . tot*
Just stay there, father.
57 p; *liʔote?*
You're here?
58 x; *jiʔ liʔone*
Yes, I'm here.
[
59 p; *mi-*
Are-
60 *a:y=*
Ay.
61 x; *=liʔone*
I'm here.
62 *jiʔ yuʔun xkik' ech'el aYe*
I am taking your (daughter) Y with me.
[
63 p; *mi nox-*
Have—

P recovers his composure, partly by again asking about procedures: Has the entire entourage set out for the other village? There is a reply and the expected "polite" repetition (66–68):

64 *mi tal xa skotol avajch'omtak*
Have all your helpers come
65 *mi o to komem*
Or did some still stay behind?
[
66 x; *ali te to komem jkot karro*
Uh, one carload of them has stayed behind.

67 j; *a karajo .*
Ah, damn!

68 p; *oy te komem jkot karo ..*
One carload has stayed behind?

69 *a bweno*
Ah, okay.

The two men C and M have already officially exited the interaction. But there is one more bit of ritual etiquette to accomplish. M, as the cargoholder's ritual adviser, has for days never ventured out in public without a small bottle of strong cane liquor that he presents to all men of sufficient religious status, a kind of roaming prestation from the cargoholder. Although P no longer drinks and rarely leaves his house compound, he is a man with a vast store of such status. M thus returns to proffer the bottle, using an elaborate self-humbling ritual formula to refer to it (72, 74) (fig. 1.6).

71 m; *mi cha—*
Will you—

72 *mi- mi muk' chanup jtz'uj kunen ch'amem voʔ kumpa*
Won't you sip a bit of my little bit of poured-off water, *compadre*?

Figure 1.6. The ritual adviser offers a ceremonial drink to the old man.

73 p; *jej?*
Huh?
74 m; *mi muk' chanup jtz'uj kunen ch'amem voʔ?*
Won't you sip a bit of my little poured-off water?
75 p; *oy ach'amem voʔ?*
You have some poured-off water?

P, as custom dictates, demurs by referring to his incapacities (78, 82):

76 *yo:s*
Lord!
[
77 m; *oy jch'amem voʔ*
I have poured off water.
78 p; *yuʔun me mu xkil un kumpa*
But I can't see, compadre.
[
79 m; *vaʔi*
Here.
80 *muʔyuk aʔa*
No, you can't.
81 *vaʔi*
Here.
82 p; *jaʔ xʔelan lisoke:*
Since I am disabled.
[
83 m; *paso preva jtz'uj*
Just try a little.

M, as custom also dictates, insists, using a phrase lifted from cargo prayer (84). P (85, 89) and M (87, 88) then exchange formulaic drinking salutations:

84 *chʔech' o me sk'in ti jtotik santorensoe*
To celebrate the fiesta of Our Father San Lorenzo.
[
85 p; *kich'ban kumpa:*
I take it, compadre.
86 *kolaval ta (jnup) to*
Thank you, I will sip it.
[

87 m; *ich'o kumpare*
Take it, compadre.
88 *ich'o kumpare*
Take it, compadre.
[
89 p; *kich'ban kumpare*
I take it, compadre.

In normal circumstances, when a cargoholder or his proxy offers a drink, the recipient takes three long swigs from the bottle, each one bracketed by verbal insistence and exchanged toasts, before the interaction can close. Here, there can be no insistence (although there is an echo of it in M's pre-offer in 93), but P himself shortcuts the ritual by touching M's bottle to his lips three times before returning it with multiple thanks (91, 92, 94) (fig. 1.7). M acknowledges P's thanks with his own standard self-deprecatory formula (95–96):

91 p; *kolaval kumpa:*
Thank you, compadre.
92 *(kolaval lach'amem voʔ kumpa)*
Thank you for your liquor, compadre.
[

Figure 1.7. The old man drinks three times.

93 m; *mi xuʔ o chavaʔi kumpa*
Is that enough for you, compadre?
94 p; *kolaval xchiʔuk kajvaltik*
Thank you and Our Lord.
[
95 m; *jset'-*
a little
96 *jset' tajme:k*
Just a little.

Conclusion

I began with a straightforward example of permeable generic boundaries, in which the Mexico City *merolico* imported simulacra of religious and magical language into his performance, apparently to draw on their coercive power. I then considered different sorts of Zinacantec ritual communications, trying to arrange them along scales of formulaicity, contextual presupposition, and embeddedness in wider ceremonial activities, recalling that language is just one component in a whole-body performance. Finally, I presented a short Zinacantec interaction to illustrate how resonances of an entire ritual life permeate even a brief, chance encounter on the road.

Ritual communication in Zinacantán begins with form: from the highly structured parallelism of prayer to the plain repetition of secular genres; from the echoing responsiveness of cargo greetings to the minimal formulaic responses of common courtesy; from morphological elaboration of paired lexical doublets to creative lexical distortion in punning or proliferated affective verbs and positional roots in male boasting. In Zinacantán there hardly seems to exist any completely nonformulaic, unmarked conversation, any talk that is generically uncontaminated (i.e., allusive) or—correlatively—socially nonprojective. For form is linked to force. Every communicative act, even at its most truncated, carries both its formulaic load and its socially indexical resonances. Ritual language is linked to ritual not simply by being part of it but from a prospective and retrospective reliance on it. Even a mocking allusion to matrimonial exhortation recalls past marriages and anticipates future unions. The old man's life as a ritual officeholder and his truncated phrases of ceremonial courtesy energize an entire ritual apparatus in miniature.

Different time lines exist in ritual communication as well. One is the familiar Bakhtinian chain of utterances, a kind of discursive time in which every utterance looks both forward and backward. Another is the course of a life. We know little about how ritualized forms of talk are learned in Zinacantán. Some children seem to know the cadence of prayer even before they know words (Lourdes de León, personal communication). Contrarily, some old people manage to pass through life, even through ritual office, without apparently learning more than how to mumble a few parallel couplets. Who are the master speakers, the apprentices, the bumblers? My aged *compadre*'s "little ritual" on the road demonstrates the weight of biography and of social history more generally on even the briefest communicative encounters.

A final theme has been the coercion of ritual forms, a variant of Bloch's argument that what he calls "formalized language" in political oratory "is a way whereby one speaker can coerce the response of another [and thus] ... can be seen as a form of social control" (Bloch 1975a: 20), and further, that formulaic language, being the special province of experts, "is thus a form of power for the powerful rather than simply a tool of coercion available to anybody" (1975: 23). The *merolico* almost magically manipulates his crowd, inducing members of the public to move arms and tongues. The curer controls patient and spirits alike. The tipsy haranguer brings even the insubordinate child into line. The blind old man's courtesy extracts due respect almost despite his own self-deprecation, as though his very person—invoked by his words—embodies the entire ritual hierarchy to which he has dedicated himself.

The coercive force of ritual forms of talk (and ritual action more generally) and their ability to smooth out potential conflict by suppressing insubordination are evident not only in the vignettes presented here but also in Zinacantec metatheory. To the person who, from incapacity or inattention, fails to respond to a greeting, a toast, or a ritual formula, one says *Tak'avan la* 'Answer the person!' The bowed head needs to be touched; the first half of the couplet cries out for its second half. Ritual form, that is, implies both an interactive and a moral order, implicit in the Tzotzil couplet for "wisdom": *jp'el // chaʔ p'el, rason // mantal* 'one word // two words, of reason // of order'.

Notes

Some material in this chapter was presented during an invited talk at SALSA at the University of Texas, Austin, in April 2005. I am indebted to the organizers of that session and to other participants for their comments, as well as to the other participants at the Wenner-Gren symposium in Sintra that gave rise to the current volume.

1. In fact prayer is virtually the only form of Zinacantec speech that does not *require* specific interactive uptake in the form of highly repetitive and almost institutionalized "back channel." The role of *jtak'vanej*, or "answerer" (Haviland 1988, 1996) is a near requisite for most Zinacantec speech. When someone addresses a group, one person usually assumes the role of the official answerer, supplying appropriate assessments and continuers (Goodwin 1986; Goodwin and Goodwin 1987), usually in the form of partial repetitions. Without such a ratified addressee, speech quickly falters and grinds to a halt. Gossen (1985: 88) claims that the phase-final enclitic *-e* in Tzotzil provides "a cue to listeners for appropriate moments in which to offer supportive or participatory statements," that is, "back-channel" (Yngve 1970).

two

Everyday Ritual in the Residential World

N. J. Enfield

> Instead, then, of merely an arbitrary period during which the exchange of messages occurs, we have a social encounter, a coming together that ritually regularizes the risks and opportunities face-to-face talk provides, enforcing the standards of modesty regarding self and considerateness for others generally enjoined in the community.
>
> —Erving Goffman, "Replies and Responses"

This chapter is about everyday ritual in the residential world of the Kri, speakers of a Vietic (Austroasiatic) language of upland central Laos. I examine the relationship between the spatial layout of the Kri house and the everyday ritual behavior of the people in it. When inside a house, no matter whose house it is, a Kri person is not free to be just anywhere he or she likes. When carrying out everyday activities such as eating, working, sleeping, sitting, smoking, or talking, a Kri speaker may occupy space in a given house that is a function of that person's kin relation to the household and his or her status in terms of age and rank.

To give a simple preview of the phenomenon, figure 2.1 shows two Kri families relaxing, seated at the fire pit in the center of their houses' interiors. Their seating placement is not random but proper according to Kri norms. The man of the house sits toward the outer-upper corner of the fire pit (see fig. 2.2). His wife sits toward the inner-upper corner. The photographer, as guest, is properly seated farther toward the outer wall of the house. In this chapter I lay out the cultural logic of the Kri house floor plan in terms of inner, outer, upper, and lower dimensions and some ways in which Kri people ritually regiment their behavior (and that of others) in accordance with this logic.

(a)

(b)

Figure 2.1. Members of two Kri families relaxing at home. The man of the house sits to the outer-upper corner of the fire pit, his wife sits to the inner-upper corner. In both photographs, the man sits slightly farther in the "upper" direction.

The ethnographic facts suggest some general properties of human ritual communication, whether it be in formal rituals such as weddings and initiations (Bloch 1974; Fortes 1966; Tambiah 1985) or in everyday rituals such as handshakes and observances of table manners (Goffman 1967; Leach 1966). Formal rituals and everyday rituals are not different species but, as is widely acknowledged, represent relative regions on a continuum.[1] They share many of their important defining features. First, both formal rituals and everyday rituals are public behaviors concerned primarily with wielding influence in the social world. Their desired effects are brought about by affecting others' mental states and statuses. Because of this, the form or manner of those behaviors is constrained by the requirement that their meaning be recognizable to others. This recognizability is a general requirement of any social behavior (ritualized behavior most broadly construed; Huxley 1966a), but in ritual the manner of action becomes another sign in itself. Kinds of ritual can differ in the degree to which this formal component of the ritual behavior is thematized—that is, the degree to which it is a focus of attention or a consciously foregrounded feature of the current action.

Second, and relatedly, the formal behavior of ritual provides a public opportunity for moral assessment of the status and identity of participants. How well I am regarded as an Australian middle-class boy may depend in part on whether I keep my elbows off the table at dinnertime. My status as a Lao man may be judged in part on whether I have been ordained as a monk at some point in my youth, and if so, for how long. Others can use such behavior as a basis of (moral) assessment of me in terms of how well I inhabit my status and identity. Correspondingly, I can strategically display such behavior to exploit these normative patterns of assessment and thereby manage others' impressions of me (Goffman 1967; cf. Krebs and Dawkins 1984; Owings and Morton 1998).

How Manner Meets Manners in Everyday Ritual

Manner: Formal Constraint for Recognizability and Evaluation

Through formalization, ritual behavior is a way of acting in the world (Huxley 1966b: 258; Leach 1966: 403). As Leach pointed out, "rational technical" behaviors have brute means-to-ends relations (e.g., chopping down a tree), whereas both communicative behaviors (e.g., Englishmen shaking hands) and magical behaviors (e.g., swearing an oath) depend on social agreement to be effective. Although many researchers have wanted to distinguish firmly between the communicative and the magical in ritual (cf. everyday versus formal), Leach argued that any such distinction was "either illusory or trivial," and so the term "ritual" should embrace both categories. They are alike in that they operate not by natural law but by virtue of social agreement that they should so operate (Watts 1999). An example is money: "It is only given the institution of money that I now have a five dollar bill in my hand. Take away the institution and all I have is a piece of paper with various gray and green markings" (Searle 1995: 27; see also Searle 1969: 51).

In order that these effects are possible, the actions by which we communicate must be sufficiently formalized to guarantee that the meaning of our behavior is recognizable to others. It is this recognizability alone that causes our communicative actions to work at all. This is true of nonhuman ritual behavior in the ethological sense. An example is the behavior of *Labroides dimidiatus,* a tropical fish that removes parasites from the bodies of other fish (Wickler 1966). Other fish make invitation displays before allowing the Labroides to feed on their bodies, and the Labroides also often does "a sort of dance" to elicit such invitation (Wickler 1966: 473). Nibbling on the bodies of other fish brings about the effects it does (the Labroides obtains food) by means of physically causal processes. By contrast, the efficacy of the Labroides' dance and of other fishes' gestural invitations depends on those actions being recognizable to the creatures involved (hence, as Wickler documents, the possibility of mimicking by other fish who attack the bodies of the submissive species instead of feeding on them). All of language, along with the rest of our symbolic resources, is predicated upon this notion of norm-governed recognizability of meaning (or action or intention).

The mechanistic requirement that ritual behavior be formally recognizable is a key conservative force in cultural practice generally. Accordingly, Sacks (1992) defined culture as "an apparatus for generating recognizable action."[2] To effectively transform the world in a brute sense, one merely requires instrumental efficacy. If you want to break something, it doesn't much matter how you swing the hammer. But the communicative efficacy of a ritual action depends on its being socially recognizable by others as an instrument for its intended function. This constraint on form is thematized and exaggerated in formal rituals such as initiation rites, weddings, and political parades, where the defining actions need to be performed in just the right way if they are going to properly effect a social transformation (Austin 1962: 14ff.). As a result, social-cultural norms prescribe manner of action far more narrowly than would otherwise be required for purely instrumental purposes. A social task—be it requesting, complaining, telling, or grooming—is, and should be, done in a quite particular manner, even when doing it in that manner is not causally necessary to achieving its function. Hence the local cultural tweaking of even the most everyday actions. For example, we can often recognize locals just by the way they walk, sit, or smoke a cigarette. We are usually oblivious to it, but the locally conservative nature of our conforming social behavior imports a strong sense of ritual to everyday social action (Goffman 1959, 1967).

Manners: Ritual and the Cooperative Moral Order

Ritual behavior requires two things that are both puzzling in human evolution and definitive of our species: cooperation and moral order (see, among others, Axelrod 1984; Boyd and Richerson 2006a, 2006b; Danielson 1998; Joyce 2006; Key and Aiello 1999; Knight, Power, and Watts 1995). Human groups cooperate in maintaining the collective illusions necessary for sustaining the meaning of ritual:[3]

> Humans who participate collectively in magico-religious ritual performances do so precisely in order to instill belief in fictional "other worlds." Representations of such fictions are more than epiphenomenal; they are central in securing cognitive acknowledgement of an allegiance to the contractual intangibles underpinning cooperation in human social groups. Given the characteristically collaborative, cooperative nature of the rituals designed to generate such illusions, the "deceptions" which emerge may be dubbed "collective deceptions," corresponding to Durkheim's classic notion of "collective representations." (Knight, Dunbar, and Power 1999: 6; see also Knight, Power, and Watts 1995)

Knight and colleagues were referring to the kinds of illusions entailed by religious beliefs and associated rituals (e.g., entertaining the reality of souls without bodies and of objects with souls, "a counterfactual and counterintuitive world of supernatural agents" [Atran 2002: 4; see also Bloom 2004; Boyer 1994, 2002]). But nonmagical, nonreligious, everyday institutional facts, like all forms of symbolic meaning, are equally dependent upon collective illusion. The idea that a piece of paper with gray and green markings can be equal in value to vital food or medicine is one such illusion. So is the idea that the noise corresponding to the phonetic transcription [kʰæt] is inherently connected with the essence of a feline. And so is the Kri idea that a son-in-law cannot approach the upper-outer corner of his father-in-law's house. Although the objects of these beliefs are not intrinsic, natural truths (no physical force literally prevents the son-in-law's movement), they nevertheless become true by virtue of being collectively, publicly treated as true.[4]

In this way, to engage in ritual behavior is to cooperate with one's group-mates in treating something as a natural fact when it is merely a social fact. This acquiescence to local convention is embodied in the observance of formal constraints on behavior and in the collective illusion (and attendant regimenting moral order) required to sustain them. We become constrained in our freedom to act, even in the most casual, everyday settings. Durkheim (1982 [1895]: 52) recognized this in defining social facts as "manners of acting, thinking and feeling external to the individual, which are invested with a coercive power by virtue of which they exercise control over him." As Knight wrote (1999: 234), ritual is inherently unfair. If I am a Nuer boy having my brow cut to the bone as I ritually transition to manhood (Evans-Pritchard 1940: 249), I might wonder why I wasn't born a girl. This is why ritual can be a political and a moral matter: political, because it invokes acquiescence to institutional facts, diminishing our individual agency (Kockelman 2007), and moral, because although ritual may not be fair, a person who does not acquiesce when he or she should is liable to sanction. And this moral sanction costs: "Moralistic punishment can stabilize any arbitrary behavior—wearing a tie, being kind to animals, or eating the brains of dead relatives … when moralistic punishers are common, being punished is more costly than performing the sanctioned behavior" (Boyd and Richerson 2006b: 461).

All these arbitrary behaviors are ritualized in the more general sense of Leach (1966) and Huxley (1966b). Whether it's fair or not that as a Nuer boy I must let my brow be cut to the bone or that as a Kri son-in-law I must cower in the inner corners of my father-in-law's house, it's the right thing to do. If I am going to do the right thing, I have to "suspend doubt and simply follow the prescribed practices" (Tambiah 1985: 131).[5] This is not unique to formal ritual. It comes with any collective illusion, including such innocuities as "It's good to say *Please* and *Thank you*" and "It's bad to approach the *rồông* of your father-in-law's house." And the very ideas of good and bad, at the conceptual core of moral value (Wierzbicka 1996), are themselves inherently institutional; that is, that such-and-such is considered good or bad in a culture is necessarily an arbitrary, institutional, collective illusion, because it could be otherwise.

Formal ritual is more easily seen as coercive than is everyday ritual (Bloch 1974). But everyday ritual is equally constraining. When Durkheim (1982 [1895]: 53) wrote of social "currents"—social facts not given by any explicit form of social organization—he said, "If perhaps I abandon myself to them, I may not be conscious of the pressure they are exerting upon me, but that pressure makes its presence felt immediately I attempt to struggle against them" (see also Wittgenstein 1953: §1.129). We are seldom aware of being subject to coercion by tacit norms, just as we remain unaware of the air we breathe: "Thus air does not cease to have weight, although we no longer feel that weight" (Durkheim 1982 [1895]: 53). If we were to feel that weight, it might be enlightening (Whorf 1956: 209), but it might also be unbearable. Goffman vividly described the price paid by those who depart from normal or expected patterns of social conduct (Goffman 1963; see also Garfinkel 1967). Like formal ritual, everyday ritual "is not a 'free expression of emotions' but a disciplined rehearsal of 'right attitudes'" (Tambiah 1985: 134; see also Geertz 1966; Langer 1951). To sit in the right place in the Kri house is to display one's discipline. Yet unlike formal rituals, such everyday ritual practices do not thematize the formal discipline on display. The message is given off rather than given (Goffman 1959: 2). Practicing the ritual indexes commitment to the collective norms and willingness to exercise the required self-discipline in a way that is publicly evaluable.[6] As I show later, the discipline is regimented by cooperative adherence to normative practices.

Summary: Everyday Ritual Is Where Manner and Manners Meet

The key idea I want to draw from the foregoing discussion is the following: In all social communication, the manner in which an action is carried out is formally constrained by the requirement that it be recognizable to others as having the meaning it has. In *ritual* communication, of both the formal and everyday varieties, the manner of action is not merely instrumental in achieving public recognizability of the action's meaning. It is also itself made available for evaluation as a token of the actor's acquiescence to a constraint of social convention. Ritual is then a site in which the local moral order is displayed, exercised, and no doubt contested. In formal ritual, this evaluable manner of action tends to be a focus of attention, whereas in everyday ritual it tends not to be. But the coercive and regimenting nature of everyday ritual comes readily to the surface when the constraints are contravened.

Kri Residence

The Kri are a group of about 250 people living in the upper reaches of the Ñrong Valley, in a protected rainforest in the easternmost area of

Nakai District of Khammouane Province, Laos. They live within a day's walk of the Vietnamese border at Ha Tinh Province. The Kri language belongs to the Vietic sub-branch of the Austroasiatic language family (Enfield and Diffloth 2009).

In this section I describe the Kri house and its meaning in Kri daily life, looking particularly at the way people engage in practical interpretation of its meaning, regimented by the moral constraints of everyday ritual.

Plan of the Kri House

As is the case in any other culture, the spatial layout of the Kri house is charged with social meaning. The house "serves as much to reveal and display as it does to hide and protect..., the physical structure, furnishing, social conventions and mental images of the house at once enabling, molding, informing and constraining the activities and ideas which unfold within its bounds" (Carsten and Hugh-Jones 1995: 2; see also, among others, Bourdieu 1990: 271ff.; Duranti 1981: ch. 4; Frake 1975; Lévi-Strauss 1963: ch. 8, 1987; Waterson 1990). The Kri word for house is *krnooq* (derived from *kooq* 'to live, remain, be somewhere', with infixation of the nominalizer *-rn-*). The design of all Kri houses follows a standard, modular plan. The house is built entirely by hand, using machetes and no other tools. Materials are available exclusively from the forests surrounding the village: timber of various gauges for the main structure, varieties of bamboo for flooring, walls, and light structure, varieties of rattan for tying the structure together (no nails are used), and umbrella-size leaves of the *culoo* palm (*Licuala grandis*) for thatching. Houses differ in size as a function of individual necessity and motivation. A man may be more or less interested in having a large house. He might or might not want certain optional features such as a covered verandah in addition to an open-air verandah, or indeed, any kind of verandah. Numbers and sizes of internal partitioned rooms also differ, but the general layout is always the same.

The floor plan of the Kri house interior is basically a square, onto whose two dimensions are mapped kinship (inner-outer) and social rank (upper-lower). Another way to think of it is that the house has four sides: upper, lower, inner, and outer. Figure 2.2 shows the plan of the house in which I stayed during field trips in 2005 and 2006. The house is fairly complete by Kri standards, featuring both a covered verandah and an open verandah.

Social meaning is mapped onto the floor space by a simple organizing principle that crosses an inner-outer with an upper-lower axis. These

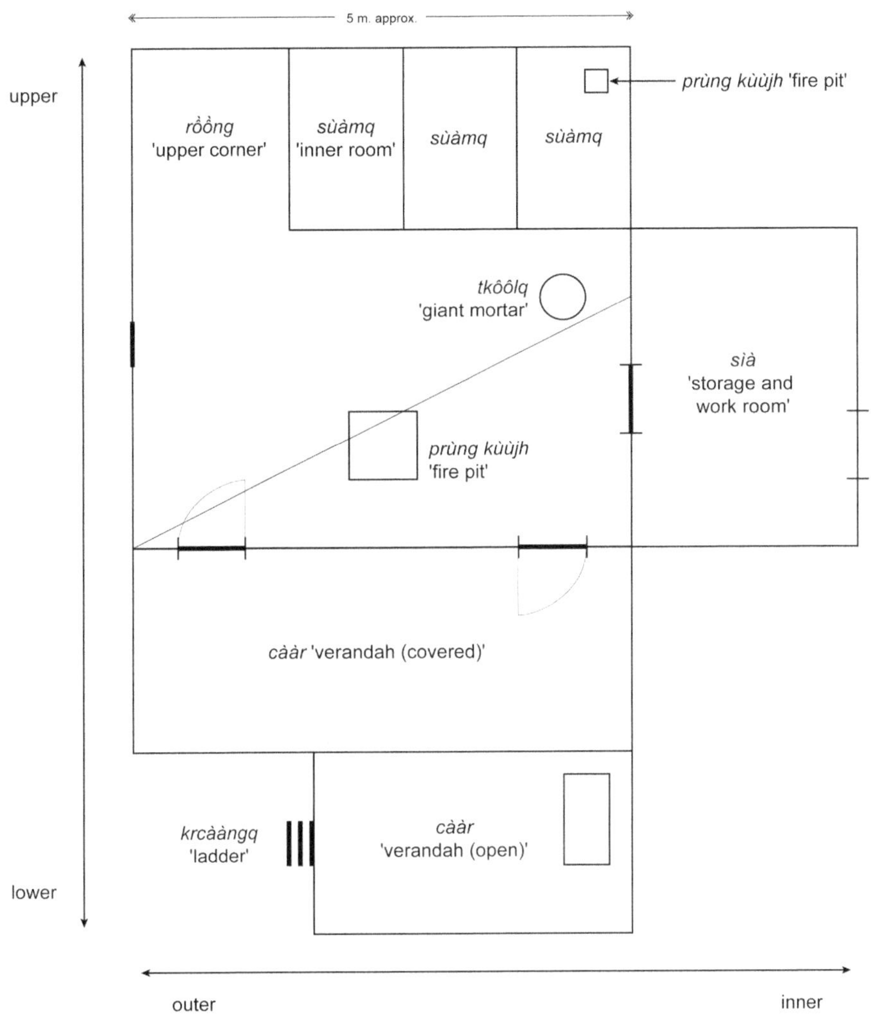

Figure 2.2. Plan of a typical Kri house.

two axes more or less map onto a distinction of "in" versus "out" of a kin circle and "high" versus "low" on a scale of rank, defined by age and other indices of status. The lower side of the house is the side where people enter and exit. (There is no other passage in or out.) The lower side might be termed in English the front of the house. The upper side is the side farthest from the entrance. It corresponds to what would be called in English the back of the house. The upper-lower axis of the house is typically aligned with an up-down axis in local physical space, either the upstream-downstream orientation of the nearest river or stream or the uphill-downhill orientation of the land on which the house is built (or both, since these are usually aligned with each other).

Along the left-right axis as one enters the house, the inner side is the side of the house where family activities such as pounding rice (at a giant mortar, labeled *tkôôlq* in figure 2.2), husking corn, and preparing and storing food take place.[7] A storage and work room called the *sìà* is attached to the main structure of the house on this side.

The outer side is where non-kinfolk should be. Certain signs make it publicly clear which is the outer side. The ladder up onto the house leads up on that side, and inside the house are other clues, such as the clear space called the *rồồng* in the upper-outer corner and the large diagonal beam running down along the roof, which joins the lower (front) wall of the house at the outer-lower side entrance.

The house has a third spatial dimension as well: the vertical dimension, or above versus below. The Kri house is literally raised above ground level, as shown in figure 2.3. For talking about the various spatial relations within the house, Kri speakers use the following spatial terms:

Above, upstream	*tồồl* 'above, upper, upstream place'
	lêêh 'there (above, upstream)'
	saaw 'ascend'
Below, downstream	*từrk* 'below, lower, downstream place'
	cồồh 'there (below, downstream)'
	cììh 'descend'
Across (in-out)	*seeh* 'there (across ways)'

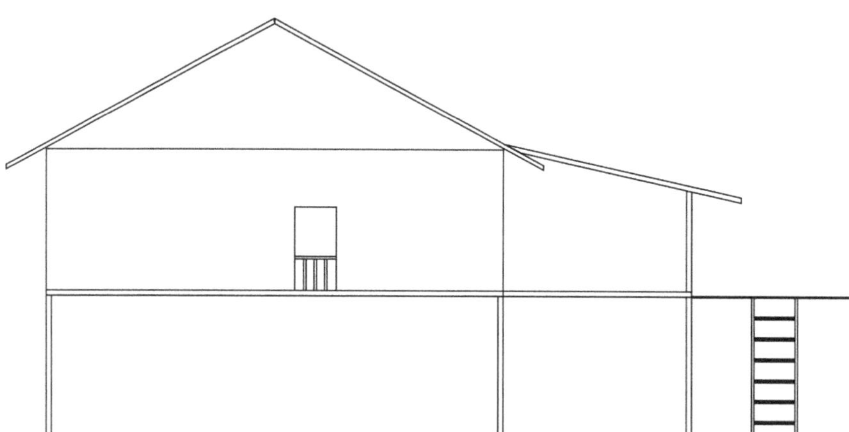

Figure 2.3. Elevation of a Kri house, looking from the outer side—that is, from the left of figure 2.2.

Social Aspects of the Kri House

The house plays a central role in Kri social organization. For one thing, it is where a great deal of social interaction takes place—where meals are shared, where gossip is exchanged, where stances are contested, where bonds are built, maintained, and eroded. In addition, the house has a special status in terms of kinship organization. Kri kinship is anchored in *kmuuc krnooq* 'spirits of the house', which belong to the man of the house. Each person belongs to the spirits of a single house, as determined by who owns the spirits of the house into which one is born (this may be one's father or grandfather). When formal rituals are performed for these spirits, as happens a few times a year, the rituals take place around a tiny, ceremonial fire pit located in the inner-uppermost corner of the house interior (fig. 2.2).

A man's house spirits are not necessarily located physically in his own dwelling. For example, as a young man's nuclear family grows, he may build his own house and move to live there with his family while his father is still alive—as usually happens, given the physical constraints of houses. Because the son does not have his own spirits in his house, it is considered not a real *krnooq* 'house' but merely a *tuup* 'hut', despite its being structurally identical to a house.

The structure shown in figure 2.4 (top) is regarded as a real *krnooq* 'house'. It has its own spirits. Accordingly, there is a tiny fire pit in the innermost room (*sùàmq;* see fig. 2.2). The structure in figure 2.4 (bottom) belongs to a son of the man who built the first house. The Kri insist that the son's dwelling is not a real *krnooq* but a *tuup,* using the word for a simple little raised hut in the rice fields (fig. 2.5). Accordingly, although the house is fully functional, it has no such tiny fire pit in the inner sanctum. When the son, along with his family, performs formal rituals to his kin spirits, he does so in the father's house.

The use of the word *tuup* for the house in figure 2.4 (bottom) is an example of the everyday collective illusion that defines ritual and other symbolic behavior for Knight, Dunbar, and Power (1999). To insist that the son's house in figure 2.4 is a "hut" is to ritually suspend the normal way of talking. It may be compared to any kind of avoidance behavior, such as using the word "mask" for "face" in fox-hunting, or avoiding words that sound like the names of recently deceased persons (see Dixon 1971).

(a)

(b)

Figure 2.4. Father's house (top) and son's house.

Figure 2.5. The usual referent of *tuup* 'field hut'.

Practical Interpretation of the Kri Residence: Behaving in Accordance with Norms

Kri people's daily behavior surrounding the house constitutes a domain of everyday ritual in which members of the community constantly display their cooperation with morally sanctionable social norms. Adhering to these constraints is, on the one hand, a *product of* these norms (i.e., the norms are what cause the behavior) and, on the other, a way of *bringing about* or reinforcing the norms, by instantiating the normative behavior and thereby producing public signs that those norms apply. The norms are further reinforced when their contravention results in public sanctioning behavior, which involves thematization and explicit articulation of the normative practices and their meaning.

I use the term "practical interpretation" to refer to people's behavior insofar as it constitutes evidence of their understanding of meaning in the physical world (Kockelman 2006). If I take a key and open a locked door with it, these actions constitute a display of evidence to any onlooker that I know what these instruments are for (i.e., what their designers had in mind by designing them) and what may be achieved by their use. Similarly if I pick my teeth with a sliver of bamboo, I display a practical interpretation of that object. I display that I recognize one of its affordances (or perhaps its function, if the sliver had been fashioned for that purpose). The same logic applies to actions of a more cultural nature. In general, the way we orient to things and events constitutes (evidence of) our understanding of those things. This may be evident, for example, in the physical world of affordances, instruments, and actions or in the cultural world of language, culture (roles, identities), and social interaction (Kockelman 2006; Sacks 1992). The spatial layout of the Kri house has meaning in this sense. Behavior that is oriented to the house in particular ways constitutes a range of interpretants of the house, and thereby a practical interpretation.[8]

Physical behavior not only supplies an interpretation of what the house means but, more important, expresses an individual's commitment to and identification with social categories (roles and identities) that are implicated in those meanings. As a son-in-law, when I cower in the inner corner of my father-in-law's house, I am not just being a son-in-law, I am "doing" being a son-in-law (see Sacks 1992: 215ff.). I do what sons-in-law do, and in doing so I display that I am a (good) son-in-law. I categorize myself as a son-in-law by recognizably behaving like one. And the cause-and-effect relationship goes both ways: I act like this because I am a son-in-law; I am (categorized as) a son-in-law because I act like this.

Goffman (1963: 2) observed that "society establishes the means of categorizing persons and the complement of attributes felt to be ordinary and natural for members of each of these categories." We have, then, roles such as *matààm* 'son-in-law' and identities such as *Kri* 'of Kri ethnicity' (Kockelman 2006). "We lean on these anticipations that we have, transforming them into normative expectations, into righteously presented demands" (Goffman 1963: 2).[9] It is the business of ethnographers (for types of roles or identities and for types of relationships implied by these) and biographers (for individuals and relationships between individuals) to define what constitutes such normative expectations in a community.

I now turn to some of the everyday ritual constraints that Kri people are subject to. A first phenomenon is the forbidding (*kềềl* 'taboo') of certain people, at certain times, from going up into certain houses at all. For instance, when a women is menstruating, she is not to ascend any house but must 'stay down below' (*kooq qùù tìrk cồồh*) or 'stay down on the ground' (*kooq qùù qatak cồồh*). At these times she sleeps in a separate menstruation hut (fig. 2.6).

(a)

(b)

Figure 2.6. Top: The woman holding the baby is menstruating and is not allowed to ascend the house. Her grandmother is on the verandah, helping with water, food for the baby, and so forth. The family's menstruation hut is visible in the left background. Bottom: The woman is inside the menstruation hut, talking with her husband, who stands outside.

Other forms of contamination can keep people down on the ground. For instance, the man pictured in figure 2.7 is contaminated from assisting with a childbirth some days earlier. He is not allowed (i.e., it is *kə̀ə̀l* 'taboo' for him) to ascend any house in the village other than his own house until such time as his contamination is resolved (*qapùrh*) by formal ritual.

Figure 2.7. This man is contaminated because of having assisted during a childbirth some days prior. He cannot ascend another's house until his contamination is ritually resolved (*qapùrh*).

These are examples of the kinds of inconvenience to which people acquiesce on the basis of collective illusions about what can or cannot happen and what might happen as a result. The substance of the rule is illusory; there is nothing physically keeping them on the ground. Its effect is an inconvenience, and an unfair one at that: it's your tough luck if you happen to be affected. But cooperatively enforced social, moral norms turn the illusion into effective reality. As Boyd and Richerson (2006b: 461) point out, with moral enforcement, the alternative to the arbitrary behavior quickly becomes costlier than the inconvenience itself. More positively framed, the payoff of carrying out the arbitrary behavior is the opportunity to be judged a good person in terms of roles such as son-in-law or identities such as Kri.

I now turn to normative Kri practical interpretation of the house's floor plan. The inner side is where family members tend to reside, where housework (winnowing, pounding rice, etc.) takes place, where family members eat, and where they enter and exit the house. The outer side is more for non-kin, that is, guests. Women tend to sit toward the inner side of the house, and men, toward the outer side. On the upper-lower axis, people of higher status tend to sit toward the upper side, and those of lower status toward the lower side. By these criteria, it is often crystal clear where certain individuals ought to be. For example, a high-ranking guest who is not a family member sits toward the upper-outer corner. A son-in-law sits toward the inner-lower corner. The high rank of the man of the house tends to position him farther toward the outer side than his female housemates. An illustration of these principles concerns the problem of where in the house to place *kamàang* 'tray tables' for eating (fig. 2.8).

Figure 2.8. Kri speakers eating around a *kamàang* 'tray table' (here, placed toward the house's inner side).

On a normal day during my fieldwork, the tray table at which I ate, always separately from my hosts, was placed on the floor on the outer side of the house, while the household's tray tables were placed toward the inner side. My tray table was typically placed slightly higher—that is, slightly more toward the upper side—than the family's tables. This placement accorded with my status as non-kin (outer) and honored guest (upper).

A case illustrating the principle of respecting the mapping of outer-inner in terms of guests versus insiders arose when I visited a house while other visitors were also present. Food was served, and four tray tables were laid out across the house along the outer-inner axis. From outer side to inner, the groups seated at these tables were (1) the ethnographer and his official Lao government associate, (2) the man of the house, his son, and a Vietnamese hiker-trader guest, (3) the woman of the house, her daughter, and her niece, and (4) the son-in-law and his wife (fig. 2.9). The last two sat out in the *sìà* itself.

The occasion depicted in figure 2.9 was purely informal. Other kinds of functional contexts result in other kinds of configurations. Figure 2.10 shows a different occasion on which I observed four tray tables laid out in a line, this time during a formal ritual called *qjàk sii* 'tying of (string on) the arms' (related to the Lao ritual called *basii*). The key event in this ritual is the tying of cotton strings around the wrists of an individual or members of a small group. The ritual is carried out ad hoc under a range of circumstances, such as a farewell, a return to good health after illness, or the death of a relative. A small number of people are targets of the ritual and have the strings tied around their wrists, one by one, by the many other participants present. Those who ritually tie the strings on the guests of honor do so as a kind of well-wishing, and these people may be anyone from children to seniors, kin to outsiders. Associated with the string-tying component of the ritual event is eating and drinking. Because this is a formal ritual, the eating is ceremonial—that is, everyone has already eaten dinner at home earlier, and (unlike in the scene illustrated in fig. 2.9) the central goal of the event is not that everyone be full until the next meal. Those who are given food are the honored, respected guests, and naturally they are seated in the outer half of the house. In contrast to the layout of four tray tables for an everyday meal, in this case the tray tables were laid out not across the house but along the upper-to-lower axis, lined up on the outer side of the house (fig. 2.10).

This arrangement accorded with the food-giving of the event's being oriented exclusively to guests; hence all tray tables were on the house's

(a)

(b)

Figure 2.9. Layout of four tray tables, across the house, from outer side (foreground in photo) looking toward inner side. The people are (A) ethnographer (not shown in photo); (B) government chaperone of ethnographer (arm and knee visible to right of frame); (C) man of the house (leftmost in frame), (D) Vietnamese hiker-trader, passing through (next to his radio set), (E) C's son, (F) C's daughter, (G) C's wife, (H) C's niece, (I) C's eldest daughter, and (J) I's husband and C's son-in-law (visible in far background of photo).

(a)

(b)

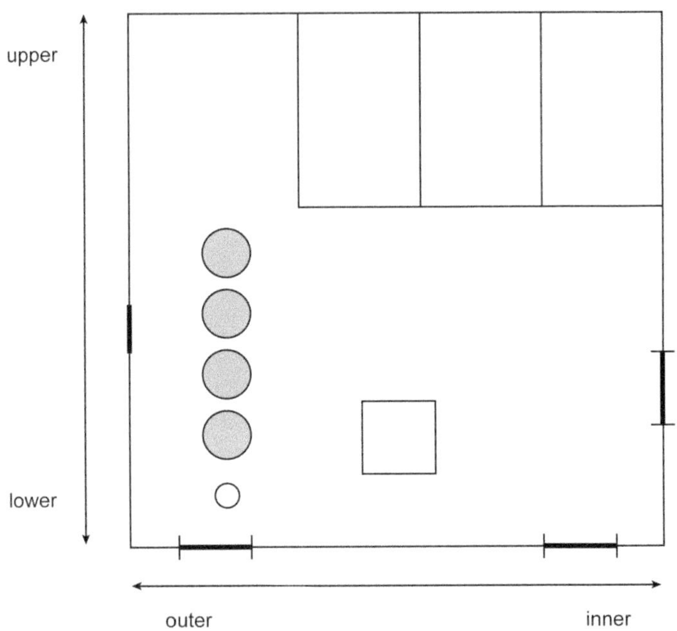

Figure 2.10. Tray tables laid out vertically on the outer side of the house for ritual eating during a *qjàk sii* 'string-tying' event.

outer side. Within that placement, the seating of guests at each tray table was arranged from lowest to highest rank along the lower-upper axis. Naturally, the guests of honor—in this case, the ethnographer and his government sidekick—were seated at the uppermost of the four tray tables.

An earthen jar called *boomq* in Kri—visible in the photograph in figure 2.10 at the far end of the row of tray tables, with long bamboo straws sticking out of it—was full of brewed liquor, to be drunk after the eating. It was placed at the lower side of the house, a best compromise given that the practice of drinking must incorporate everyone, including sons-in-law, who would be forbidden from entering the upper-outer corner. Such festivities invariably evolve into long drinking sessions involving men of all ranks.[10] The upper-outer quadrant (*rồồng*) remains clear for guests to relax in.

Spatial Distributions and Diagrammatic Iconicity

The patterns by which people in the Kri world regularize their spatial distribution in the house provide an external, physical representation of the conceptual structure underlying norms of Kri social organization. The Kri house functions as a diagram, a type of cognitive artifact (Norman 1991) by which people's inhabiting of different roles and identities can be read from their spatial behavior. Looking at where people place themselves in a given house is like looking at pieces on a chessboard. In the scenes I have considered so far, one sees people physically mapping their own token roles and identities onto type-sanctioned spatial positions, the meaning of which has been inscribed through traditions of practical interpretation of the floor plan. When participants position themselves appropriately, the entire structure becomes literally embodied, visible in space. The bodies occupying the house become nodes on a life-size diagram of their own roles and (inter)relationships. (On diagrams, see Enfield 2009: ch. 6 and references therein; on diagrammatic iconicity, see Peirce 1965 [1932].)

Sanction of Norms: Making the Tacit Explicit

Just as people's actions constitute evidence of the way they interpret the world around them (Kockelman 2006), so do their words . Most of the time, when life runs as it should, patterns of everyday ritual behavior go unquestioned. The norms themselves, or the formal aspects of behavior that embody them, remain out of any focus of attention. But when transgressions occur, norms are thematized, made explicit, articulated, characterized, and reasoned about. It is when things depart from the plan that the norms behind everyday ritual come to the surface. By contrast, in formal ritual, participants are aware of the event's special status and to some degree of its social meaning.

Early in my first extended field trip working with Kri speakers, I was blissfully unaware of the meaning of the Kri house. At a certain point I sat down, randomly, against the front wall of the house in the lower-inner quadrant, and my host joked, "*Vòòk nik tôô matààm* [Grandfather Nick is a son-in-law!]." It drew much laughter, as any in-law joke should do. This is when I first became explicitly aware of the social significance of the Kri house's floor plan. The normally implicit had to be articulated. Since then, I have invited many Kri speakers to explain to me the social meaning of the house's spatial layout. Their accounts are more or less identical: family to the inner side, guests to the outer side, high status to the upper side, low status to the lower side. It is also agreed that these are not unbreakable rules but general tendencies.

The Kri speaker who joked about my sitting in the wrong part of the house treated my error as innocuous, if nevertheless worthy of remark. Perhaps as omni-ignorant ethnographer, I could not have known better. By contrast, I have heard sanction of outsiders who it seems *should* know better because they are regular overnight lodgers in these villages. These are the Vietnamese hiker-traders who engage in small-time trade throughout the area. A group of women once described to me, with disapproval, some of these men's lack of observance of the meaning of the Kri house's floor plan. Some of these guests simply walk unhindered around the house—for example, crossing to the inner side and entering the *sìà* 'work and storage room' to look for a knife, a bowl, or the like. It is not that an outsider is forbidden from doing this. But when one does need to contravene the norm, whether as a guest crossing to the inner side or a household member crossing to the outer side, one ought to display an explicit orientation to the problematic nature of this little transgression.

The proper thing is to draw to the attention of those present that one needs to approach an inappropriate part of the house (requiring acknowledgment, thus as if asking permission) and to bow forward, lowering one's head and upper body while entering the problematic area. This marked *manner* of acting—creeping rather than walking—is an everyday ritual for displaying one's *manners,* one's willingness to cooperate with the local moral order. Failing to do so attracts moral condemnation. In passing moral judgments on their unmannered hiker-trader guests for failing to correctly "ritually regularize the risks" of these social encounters (Goffman 1976), the Kri women added that this behavior caused them to feel afraid of their guests. This supports the view that ritual is a means of social control (Bloch 1974). When people fail to observe required behavioral constraints, they become unpredictable and therefore menacing (see Burgess 1962). In the context of a moral order that needs upholding, they are, simply, "bad." Such expressions of disapproval are where cultural values are made explicit.[11]

Another case of sanctioning concerns the behavior of children. When guests are present, children are told by their elders not to cross to the outer side of the house, and especially not to cross to the upper-outer corner (*rồồng*). This admonishment is especially likely to occur during formal ritual occasions, when manner of action is generally in the foreground. On one occasion, I was the guest of honor at a hand-tying ceremony. As was proper, I was situated in the upper-outer corner of the house (fig. 2.11). At a certain point during the string-tying part of the event, three young girls who were seated across the other side of the fire pit (*prùng kùùjh*) from me wanted to come to where I was in order to tie strings on my wrists. They had two paths available, the more direct one being to pass above the fire pit, and the other, to pass below it (fig. 2.12). As they set out to pass above, they were halted and sternly admonished by the man of the house, Non, who insisted they pass below the fire pit.

This redirection would have been unlikely in a context other than formal ritual—for example, if one of the girls was simply going to pass me a spoon while I ate my evening meal in my usual spot in the upper-outer corner. But in a context in which "doing a cultural practice" was thematized (as is seen to be definitive of formal ritual), it was more important that things be (seen to be) done *in the right way*.[12] As I argued earlier, in ritual, the *manner* of action becomes a sign in itself that may be inspected and evaluated for how well it conforms to local constraints. In a formal ritual setting such as this, when manner of action is a focus of attention, there is no doubt that Non's sanctioning behavior itself was a chance for him to display that he was a good Kri man by insisting that things be done right. His admonition to the girls served as a sign on multiple levels. Among other things, it was (1) an instruction for the girls to go the other way, (2) a sign that it would be "not good" to take the upper route in this situation, reiterating the moral norms at hand, and (3) a sign that he was a good Kri man for caring.

A subtler form of explication of the norms of spatial meaning in the house is people's daily insistence, in the most informal situations, that I

(a)

(b)

Figure 2.11. Two views from the *rồông* (upper-outer corner) during the ritual ceremony *qjàk sii*, or "tying of the hands." Note the position of the women to the outer side (left background) in both pictures. In the top image, a son-in-law of the household can be seen in the far background, wearing a black-and-white jacket. In the bottom photo, the strings being draped on this ritually decorated tray table will be tied one by one around the wrists of the guests of honor.

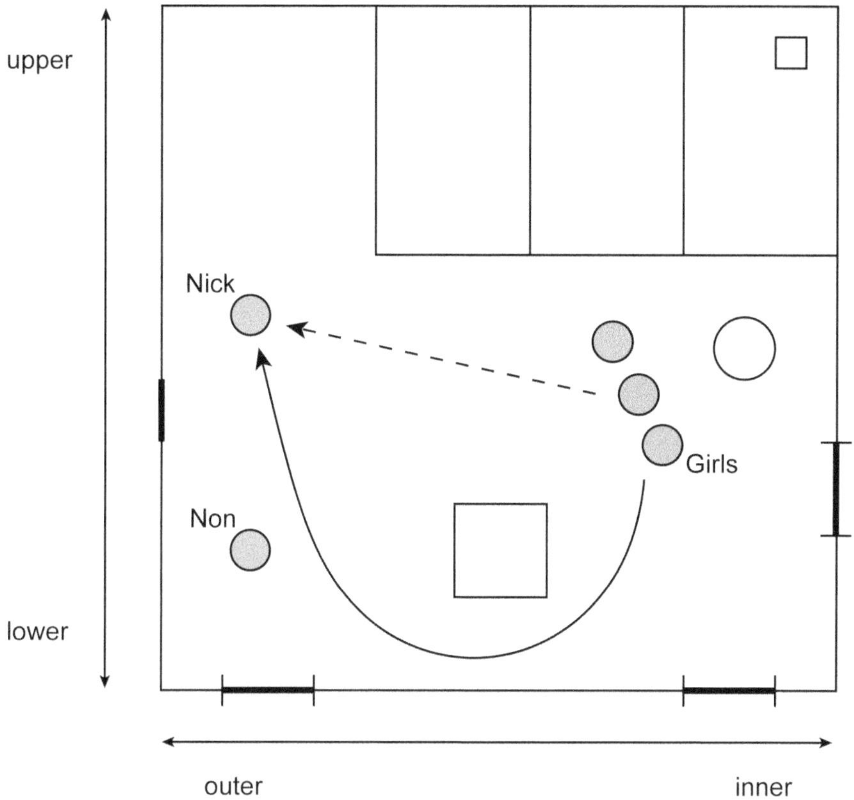

Figure 2.12. Example of sanction during ritual ceremony. Three girls need to cross the house to tie strings on Nick's wrists. As they set out to take the most direct route (dotted-line arrow), they are admonished by the man of the house (Non), who tells them to take the correct lower route (solid-line arrow).

sit in the upper-outer corner. If I sit close to the doorway, too far to the lower side, they usher me back (using the verb *saaw* 'ascend'). Again, this displays both the content of the norm itself and the degree to which people (want to be seen to) care about such norms' being followed.[13]

In each of these cases of sanction, my hosts and I participate in the regimentation of norms. People are morally obliged to orient themselves properly (i.e., to produce normative interpretants) toward the physical behavior that the house invites. The required discipline constrains the actual possibilities to a tiny fraction of the conceivable next moves. So the restraint (an institutionally founded constraint) that morality imposes is ritual(ized) in this way (Hauser 2006). All these examples constitute the substance of norms in the sense that (1) the practices are observed (evidence that people are disposed to follow the norms); (2) when they are not observed, this occasions surprise, sanction, or both; and (3) when they are observed, no such surprise or sanction is evinced (or, to be precise, if anyone oriented himself or herself toward observance of these norms with surprise or sanction, that itself would occasion surprise or sanction).

Conclusion

Why does a Kri son-in-law confine himself to the lower-inner edges of his father-in-law's house? Why is an honored guest ushered to the upper-outer corner? Why, when a Kri man and wife sit down at home for a smoke after a long day in the fields, does the man sit on the outer corner of the fire pit while his wife sits toward the inner side? These everyday ritual behaviors provide ways of making public one's role or identity (whether given or given off; Goffman 1959) and to knowingly display *how well* one inhabits one's role or identity. This practical interpretation is at once a product of the individual's understanding of local norms, an index of those norms (constituting onlookers' evidence for them, whether as learners or users of the system), and a regimenting force for the cooperative, morally invested regularization of those norms. Practical interpretation of the semiotics of Kri residence allows community members to signal, relatively cheaply, their commitment to current norms, with motivators such as a moral order and an emotional intelligence to enforce it, driving people both to conform and to enforce conformity. To paraphrase the passage from Goffman quoted at the opening of this chapter, by interpreting the spatial meaning of the house in these normative ways, Kri speakers ritually regularize the risks and opportunities that co-presence provides, enforcing the standards generally enjoined in the community.

These everyday ritual practices substantiate and perpetuate social facts under the guise of brute facts (Searle 1995). No natural, causal law prevents a son-in-law from being in the upper-outer corner of his father-in-law's house, but for him it is truly as if he is physically subject to an external constraint (Durkheim 1982 [1895]: 59; Lévi-Strauss 1966: 221). Logically, Searle is right to say that money is just paper, worth only what we socially agree it is worth. But our firsthand experience is the same as the experience Kri speakers have with the social diagram inscribed in their house floor plan. No amount of logic will divorce our sense of investment in the worth of money—or the pressure upon the son-in-law to stay in his place. This gives ritual its power.

As Goffman (1967, 1976) stressed, even the most mundane social encounter entails joint interpersonal commitment. Regardless of the nature of the exchange, one is obliged to pay attention to and engage with others, and one obliges others to pay attention and engage in return. Huxley's definition of ritual communication (1966b: 258) featured the twin objectives of "reducing damage" and "promoting bonding" in social relations. These are not so much about harmony as about politics (Bloch 1974),[14] and everyday politics is delicate. Human inhibition and the morality associated with it mean that none but the most desperate Machiavellian intentions can be effected, baboonlike, with a random blow to the head in passing (Silk 2002). Human social interaction seldom if ever goes without some attention to everyday ritual, buckling to its constraints as in formal ritual. The difference is whether the manner or formal execution of action is a focus of participants' attention. In both cases, the manner of action is available for moral evaluation. In this way, ritual behavior is both weapon and shield for handling the political and moral delicacy of social co-presence that characterizes human interaction.

Notes

I received useful suggestions on written versions of this paper from Grant Evans, Steve Levinson, Gunter Senft, Ellen Basso, and three anonymous reviewers. I also received careful commentary from Paul Kockelman, who helped me clarify a number of points. Subsequent input from my fellow participants in Sintra helped me further improve this work. Many thanks to these colleagues. Deficiencies are due to me alone. I gratefully acknowledge Ludy Cilissen's expert assistance with the illustrations and the Max Planck Society's support of the research, as well as the Wenner-Gren Foundation's role in funding and hosting the Sintra symposium. Photographs are by the author. I thank the Kri-speaking community for welcoming me into their world and allowing me to publicize it. This chapter is dedicated to Grant Evans, with thanks for a decade of generosity, intellectual and otherwise.

1. The term "ritual" is used in the literature for at least three kinds of phenomena: *ritualized communicative behavior* in an ethological sense (Huxley 1966b), which captures all linguistic and other human symbolic behavior

(Leach 1966: 404; Watts 1999); *formal ritual,* or "symbolic actions relating to the sacred" (Firth 1972: 3)—that is, more socially marked events such as weddings, initiations, swearings-in, and other rites of passage; and *everyday ritual,* the far more casual yet still formal procedures "of a communicative but arbitrary kind, having the effect of controlling or regularizing a social situation" (Firth 1972: 3)—for example, greetings ("Good morning") and politeness formulas ("Thank you"). For some, the category of everyday ritual permeates well beyond these easily recognized little exchanges. Goffman (1959, 1967), for example, pointed to the ritual nature of just about every move we make in social interaction. Whether or not scholars of ritual collectively wish to include under ritual communication both a wedding ceremony and a chat between cousins at the reception later on, we should be able to characterize the similarities and differences between those things that have been described as ritual to date and keep them terminologically distinct.

2. Thanks to Federico Rossano for pointing out Sacks's phrase to me.

3. I use the term "illusion" to avoid the agency implied by the word "deception" in the quoted passage.

4. Learned disgust (e.g., at certain foods) is a good case of transposing the institutional to the brute (or social to causal, or cognitive to behavioral).

5. This kind of unquestioning acceptance is arguably an innate form of docility (Simon 1990). Recent researchers evoke this as a key mechanism in cultural evolution and cultural learning: "The psychology of social learning should plausibly be arranged so that people have a strong tendency to adopt the views of the majority of those around them" (Richerson and Boyd 2005: 122; see also Boyd and Richerson 2005; Gergely and Csibra 2006). It appears to be adaptive and economical to adopt the practices of one's consociates (i.e., those with whom we identify) without asking why those things are (1) *to be done* and (2) to be done *in that way.* Although a cultural practice might be maladaptive (as some cultural practices are), chances are that if it has survived to be passed on, it is not maladaptive, and it may even be positively adaptive. At least, no (immediate) harm will likely be done in taking it on. Inconveniences ranging from keeping one's elbows off the dinner table to lying still while one's brow is cut to the bone are all, it seems, readily accepted by those who are inconvenienced by them.

6. The inconvenience of ritual is far more apparent in formal rituals such as subincision, scarification, and circumcision, but in everyday ritual it is still there. This is especially clear when we compare ourselves with other beasts and note that only we humans are capable of inhibiting our compulsions to a degree sufficient to, for instance, remain in the dentist's chair for the duration of an appointment or refrain from reaching over in the subway and grabbing someone else's food when we are hungry (see Hauser 2006).

7. There is no fixed or absolute left-right mapping of the inner-outer axis. Some houses have the inner side on the left (e.g., fig. 2.1), and others, on the right (e.g., fig. 2.9). Compare the images in figure 2.4 , where the ladders leading up at the houses' outer sides are opposite to each other.

8. Also following Kockelman (2006), I am interested in affordances and instruments as among those aspects of our world that are semiotic (see also Gibson 1979) and through which we may observe people interpreting their residential world. There is much to say regarding the affordances incorporated into the Kri house. To pick just one, there is the set of possibilities afforded by split-bamboo flooring: One may spit and drop rubbish through the floor at will. Description of the incorporation of affordances into the complex instrument called the *krnooq* 'house' is reserved for a more complete ethnography of Kri residence.

9. Returning to the normally tacit, unthematized nature of everyday norms and rituals, Goffman (1963: 2–3) went on: "Typically, we do not become aware that we have made these demands or aware of what they are until an active question arises as to whether or not they will be fulfilled." Stigma arises when "usualness" is noticeably absent.

10. Drinking has to be done in a certain order, because there is only one vessel to drink from. As for the serving of after-meal tea, its order is strictly by rank and is determined with great seriousness.

11. This kind of explicit talk is part of the broader set of mechanisms for enculturation beyond mere practical-behavioral habituation. Although Bourdieu's theory of practice (1977, 1990) is often taken to deliver culture "without articulation," it is clear from Bourdieu's work that it matters a great deal how people *talk* about their cultural world (Goddard 2002: 69; Hanks 2005).

12. Accordingly, during formal rituals among the Kri, I have observed those in charge bicker about "the right way to do it," or to self-sanction, saying that they themselves don't know how to do it. This is especially common among younger people during phases of the *qjàk sii* ritual in which one is required to chant short conventional phrases, which few people seem to have memorized correctly. This is not to say that the norms are absent in less formal contexts but merely that they are relatively relaxed and unthematized. But this is only relative. Some aspects of behavior and meaning of the house are strictly observed. For example, the constraint against a son-in-law or daughter-in-law being on the outer side of the house, especially in the outer-upper corner, is strong and laden with emotional response. People report that they simply could not bring themselves to step into that part of their parents-in-law's house.

13. There are practical issues, too. Wherever I am sitting, others will not want to sit "above" me, so if I sit too far toward the lower end of the house, an open area of house space becomes unusable for others.

14. This is in line with Owings and Morton's (1998) model of animal vocal communication (following Krebs and Dawkins 1984). Their model is constructed on an assessment-management mechanism. The individual's powers of assessment (not necessarily dedicated to social interaction) are presupposed and exploited in the formulation of communicative behaviors in order to change the world in ways desired by the formulator of a message. In other words, what senders do is driven by what they anticipate receivers will do in response.

three

Trobriand Islanders' Forms of Ritual Communication

Gunter Senft

Many discussions of ritual and ritualization, such as Goffman's (1967) essays on face-to-face behavior, emphasize functional criteria and point out that one of the most important functions of rituals is to create and stabilize social relations. Social rites that serve the functions of bonding and aggression-blocking are central to the interaction of living beings. Humans, however, do not have to rely on nonverbal signals to develop rituals; they can also use verbal means to reach this aim.

Thus, with humans we observe not only ritualized patterns and forms of nonverbal behavior that are used as signals in acts of communication but also, and especially, ritualized patterns and forms of verbal communication. In what follows, the term "ritual communication" (RC) subsumes verbal as well as nonverbal patterns and forms of behavior that function as signals that originate and have been generated in processes of ritualization (see Senft 1991: 43).

It is a trivial insight that anyone who wants successfully to research the role of language, culture, and cognition in social interaction must know how the researched society constructs its reality. It is a prerequisite that researchers must be on "common ground" with the researched community. However, as Goffman pointed out, this essential precondition is a rather general one: Every speaker of a natural language must learn the rules of nonverbal and verbal communicative behavior that are valid for her or his speech community. In the course of this learning, one of the most important objectives is to understand and duplicate the construction of the speech community's common social reality. Verbal and nonverbal patterns and modes of behavior must be coordinated and harmonized, too.

The duplicated social construction of reality must be safeguarded and secured, especially with respect to possible "sites of fracture" such as cooperation, conflict, and competition within the community. The safeguarding of the duplicated social construction of reality is achieved partly through the ritualization of verbal and nonverbal communication. The ritualization of communication can contribute to relieving tension in critical social situations and to regulating social differences and dissension by increasing the harmonizing functions of speech, by creating and stabilizing social relations, and by distancing emotions, impulses, and intentions. Ritualization of communication can increase the predictability of human behavior; moreover, it can open up space where behavior can be tried out without fear of social sanctions.

Therefore, one can characterize RC broadly as a type of strategic action that, among many other things, helps promote social bonding, block aggression, and dispel elements of danger that might affect a community's social harmony. It acts within the verbal domain by enabling people to voice these elements of danger and bring them up for discussion (see Eibl-Eibesfeldt and Senft 1987: 75ff.).[1]

It goes almost without saying, however, that this does not always work. As Ellen Basso (personal communication) has pointed out, the duplication of the social construction of reality or the social truth of a locution does not always accord with either the speaker's or the listener's experiencing of that situation or one alluded to in the locution. Aggression that might result from this failure is usually suppressed because of the strong general societal requirement to "be nice" even when people do not feel that way. Thus emotions can be calmed, and voicing can be repressed. A society as open as the one in the Trobriand Islands in which I have been studying forms of RC (and any other that offers few closed personal spaces to ensure privacy for its members) depends on its members' having a strong sense of tact. Sometimes one has to pretend not to (over)hear and not to note things, and one must learn at an early age that one does not talk about these things—so the atmosphere is indeed often tense.[2] The general requirement of tactful behavior, the necessity to be nice, and the positive and successful effects of ritual communication contribute to and create the necessary social harmony in a society such as the one I have been researching.

Forms of Ritual Communication in the Trobriand Islands

Since 1982 I have been studying the language and culture of the Trobriand Islanders. Their language, Kilivila, is one of forty Austronesian languages spoken in the Milne Bay Province of Papua New Guinea. It is an agglutinative language, and its unmarked word order pattern is Verb-Object-Subject (VOS). The Austronesian languages spoken in Milne Bay Province are grouped into twelve language families, one of which is labeled Kilivila. The Kilivila family encompasses the languages Budibud (or Nada, with about 200 speakers), Muyuw (or Murua, with about 4,000 speakers), and Kilivila (or Kiriwina, Boyowa, with about 28,000 speakers). Kilivila is spoken on the islands Kiriwina, Vakuta, Kitava, Kaile'una, Kuiawa, Munuwata, and Simsim. The languages Muyuw and Kilivila are each split into mutually understandable local dialects. Typologically, Kilivila is classified as a Western Melanesian Oceanic language belonging to the Papuan-Tip-Cluster group (Senft 1986: 6).

The Trobriand Islanders have become famous, even outside of anthropology, because of the ethnographic masterpieces on their culture published by Bronislaw Malinowski, who did field research there between 1916 and 1920 (Young 2004; see also Senft 1999, 2006). The Trobrianders belong to the ethnic group called Northern Massim. They are gardeners, doing slash-and-burn cultivation of the bush; their most important crop is yams. They are also famous for being excellent canoe builders, carvers, and navigators, especially in connection with the ritualized *kula* trade, an exchange of shell valuables that covers a wide area of the Melanesian part of the Pacific (see Malinowski 1978 [1922]; Persson 1999). The society is matrilineal but virilocal.

With respect to its communicative forms and sociocultural contexts, ritual communication in the Trobriand Islands, as elsewhere, can be relatively simple and everyday-like—Haviland (this volume) refers to these forms of RC as "little rituals"—or highly complex and situation-specific. These forms can be located on a continuum or cline of structural, (con)textual, and sociocultural complexity. In what follows I illustrate a selection of typical forms of RC that can be observed in the Trobriand Islands. I start with greetings as simple, everyday forms of RC. Then I present and analyze more complex forms of RC that are manifested in insinuating "ditties" and magical formulas. Finally I discuss and illustrate *wosi milamala,* songs that are sung only during the Trobriand Islanders' harvest festival, after the death of a Trobriander, and during the first mourning ceremonies for the deceased. *Wosi milamala* represent a situation-specific, complex, sophisticated, and extraordinary form of RC in the Trobriand Islands.

Greetings

Greetings are probably the best known and described forms of everyday RC (see, e.g., Caton 1986; Duranti 1997). Besides nonverbal greetings such as a friendly smile, a nod, showing the open palm of one's hand, and quickly raising one's eyebrows (Eibl-Eibesfeldt 1989: 118, 453), Trobriand Islanders use the verbal greeting formulas *bwena kaukwa* 'good morning', *bwena lalai* 'good day', *bwena kwaiyai* 'good afternoon', and *bwena bogi* 'good evening' or 'good night'.[3]

These formulas, however, are used primarily at relatively formal occasions such as official welcomings of invited guests. The informal way of greeting consists of the question "*Ambeya?* [Where are you going to?]" (see also Malinowski 1923: 314). The question is asked first by the greeter and then by the greeted, and both parties answer it truthfully. This greeting ritual continuously assures Trobrianders not only of their integration into a community that cares for its members but also of their protection by the community's social net, which guarantees safety wherever they are. If anything should happen to persons who are greeted like this, whether by accident or because of bad ghosts or black magic, they can be sure that other people know of their whereabouts and will come search for them and help them if necessary. Therefore, this formulaic greeting not only is a ritual of friendly encounter but also creates a social bond and implies safety.

For the sake of completeness, I should add that the official greeting formula used for opening public speeches is "*Agutoki guyau, agutoki misinari, agutoki tommota*... [Dear chief, dear missionaries, dear people of (name of village)]." Greeting formulas constitute a special register of Kilivila that is metalinguistically labeled *biga taloi* 'the language of greeting'. Other everyday forms of RC in the Trobriands are, for example, forms of requesting, giving, and taking and what Malinowski defined as "phatic communion," but I do not discuss these forms in detail here (see Senft 1987, 1996a).

Insinuating Ditties

Among the more complex forms of RC in the Trobriands are insinuating verses, songs, and lullabies that Malinowski (1978 [1922]: 299) called "ditties." Many of these ditties accompany games that children (and sometimes also adults) play, and most of them are not just insinuating but explicitly sexual. Every society has things, topics, and themes that are tabooed; one simply does not speak of them. Many such taboos concern sexuality and talk about sexual matters. Sexuality has always been closely connected with taboos in the Trobriand Islands, although it is still true that "sex as such is not tabooed" (Malinowski 1929: 381).

That taboos are ignored and violated—and all the more, the more strictly a society demands observance of them—is well known but often more or less consciously suppressed. A society can secure its members' observance of certain taboos, especially those that are important for its social construction of reality, by allowing the taboos, especially the sociologically less important ones, to become topics of discourse and conversation. A society may even allow its members to imagine the ignorance of taboos—in a fictitious way, of course. This is exactly how and why so-called safety-valve customs develop (see Eibl-Eibesfeldt 1989: 380ff.). The probably prototypical verbal safety-valve custom is the joke. I have described elsewhere how subtle jokes in the Trobriand Islands fulfill this function (Senft 1985a, 1985b), and I illustrate this phenomenon here with insinuating ditties that accompany string figures (see Senft and Senft 1986).

String figures are called *ninikula* in the Kilivila language, and the ditties accompanying them are *vinavina ninikula*. Some of them topicalize mythical incidents, animals and plants, the environment in general, events in the lives of the islanders, and individuals and their actions, which are either praised or ridiculed. The vast majority, however, play with sexual allusions or simply are bawdy or obscene jokes. I illustrate two of these *vinavina*. The first (Senft and Senft 1986: 211ff.) thematizes sexual intercourse, which is tabooed while people are working in the gardens (see Malinowski 1929: 68, 455):

Tokwelasi bila va bagula	Tokwelasi will go to the garden.
bibani natala vivila	He will find a girl (there).
ebikelasisi	They will whore.

The second *vinavina* (Senft and Senft 1986: 154ff) thematizes the verbal breaking of the "supreme taboo of the Trobrianders: the prohibition of any tender dealings between brother and sister" (Malinowski 1929: 437). This *vinavina* clearly constitutes a safety-valve custom:

Tobabane Tobabane	Tobabane, Tobabane,
kwakeye lumta	You screw your sister.
kwalimati	You fuck her to death.
kusivilaga	You turn around,
kuyomama	You feel weak and tired.

Whenever I discussed this taboo-breaking behavior with Trobrianders, even those who were fully aware of due social decorum justified their tolerance of such verses and the fun people have reciting them by labeling them *biga sopa,* "joking or lying speech, indirect speech, speech that is not vouched for." Besides the *vinavina,* the ditties, Trobrianders differentiate and linguistically label a number of other genres, such as *sopa* 'joke, lie, trick', *kasilam* 'gossip', and *wosi* 'songs'. These genres constitute the *biga sopa*. All of them have specific formal and functional characteristics and are easily recognized by members of the speech community.

This variety is absolutely characteristic of Trobriand forms of talk. It is based on the fact that Kilivila, like any other natural language, is marked by features that include vagueness and ambiguity. Its speakers use these features as stylistic means to avoid possible distress, confrontation, or too much and—for Trobriand Islanders, at least—too aggressive directness in certain speech situations.

If hearers signal that they may be insulted by a certain speech act, speakers can always retreat from what they have said by labeling it *sopa,* something they did not really mean to say. The simple but pragmatically clearly marked formula *asasopa wala* 'I am just joking', or its shortened version *sopa wala* '(It's) just (a) joke', then regulates and controls the reactive behavior of the addressees. It signals speakers' "unmarked non-commitment to truth" (Bill Hanks, personal communication). Trobriand etiquette prescribes that hearers must not be offended by utterances explicitly labeled by this formula as *sopa*—that is, as utterances detached from truth.

Trobriand Islanders have told me—and I have observed this day after day over the last twenty-five years—that they employ this variety of rhetoric in everyday conversation, in small talk, in flirtation, in public debates, in admonitory speeches, and in games, songs, and stories as a means to avoid conflicts and to relax the atmosphere of the speech situation. The *biga sopa* variety also contributes to putting forward arguments, because it allows speakers to disguise their thoughts verbally and to disagree in a playful way without risking too much personal exposure. Moreover, the *biga sopa* variety is used for mocking people.

As a means of irony and parody, it can be used to criticize certain forms of sociologically deviant behavior, asking, relatively mildly, for immediate correction. Finally, the *biga sopa* variety offers Trobrianders their only license for the verbal breaking of taboos and even for the use of many (but not all) insults and swear words (which are labeled *matua*). Genres of the *biga sopa* variety in which taboos are violated are first and foremost classified as *sopa*—as play, as something fictitious in Trobriand society.[4] This register thus generates a forum in which the breaking of taboos—and the use of "bad language" (*biga gaga*), that is, situationally and stylistically inadequate language—is allowed, if it is done verbally. This forum permits a specially marked way of communication about something "one does not talk about" otherwise.

In sum, the *biga sopa* variety and its constituting genres, such as the *vinavina ninikula,* help channel emotions and keep possible aggression under control. The register and its constituting genres secure harmony in Trobriand society and contribute to maintaining islanders' "social construction of reality" (Berger and Luckmann 1966).

Magical Formulas

Another, more complex form of ritual communication is constituted by magical formulas. The Kilivila label *megwa* refers to these formulas (and all formulas accompanying rites). The formulas constitute the register of Kilivila called *biga megwa* 'magic speech'. Until recently, Trobriand Islanders believed strongly in the power of the magical word; they used magic as a means to reach certain aims and to control nature. They distinguish between "black magic," which causes illness or even death, beauty and love magic, magic that is used in building canoes, safety magic against witches and sharks, garden magic, and weather magic. Many of the magical formulas have special labels, such as that for a specific kind of love magic, *kasina*. There are specialists for certain kinds of magic, and all magic is regarded as personal property.

While reciting—or rather, whispering and murmuring—magical formulas, the magician's accentuation of the words and phrases creates a special, characteristic rhythm. Malinowski (1935: 213) and Weiner (1983: 703) rightly praised the phonetic, rhythmic, alliterative, onomatopoetic, and metaphorical effects, the repetitions, and the prosodically specific characteristics of the language of magic. It is especially these phonetic, suprasegmental, and poetic characteristics that mark the special status of magical formulas as a genre of their own. Moreover, in the majority of these formulas one finds so-called magical words, names (of the formula or its former owners), things (such as feathers and spears), and references (to the moon, animals, rivers, and taboos) the meanings of which are unknown even to the magicians themselves (see Senft 1997). Expert magicians perform their rites upon request and are compensated for their services. Their fame depends on their success.

In what follows I present one of Tobwabwana's magical formulas against wild pigs, which may destroy Trobrianders' yam and other gardens. Tobwabwana lives in Tauwema, the village on Kaile'una Island that has been my place of residence since 1982. The formula is used to attract a wild pig to the magician, who waits in the vicinity of the garden with a group of hunters who will help him kill the pig (see Senft 1997: 384):[5]

bulivaleva bulivaleva	Wild pig, wild pig
bulivaleva bulimalema	Wild pig, wild pig come
bulimalema bulimalema	Wild pig come, wild pig come
badududem	I will charm and kill you
basobalem kwapusiga	I will call you over and kill you at your flank
pusigam asamla	Your flank I kill
asamla asamla	I kill, I kill
amwala asamla	Your head I kill
asamla kudum	I kill your tooth
asamla asamla ampola	I kill I kill your brow
asamla asamla togitem	I kill I kill your loin
asamla asamla tobulumalem	I kill I kill your belly (streaky bacon)
asamla asamla lopem	I kill I kill your stomach
asamla asamla katem	I kill I kill your innards
asamla asamla kopuvem	I kill I kill your lung
asamla asamla sile'um	I kill I kill your belly
asamla asamla sileveaka	I kill I kill your large intestine
asamla asamla silekekita	I kill I kill your small intestine
asamla asamla kaikem	I kill I kill your hind leg
asamla asamla yamam	I kill I kill your foreleg
asamla asamla	I kill I kill
bulivaleva	Wild pig
bulivaleva bulivaleva	Wild pig, wild pig
bulimalema bulimalema	Wild pig come, wild pig come

bulimalema badudulem	Wild pig come, I will put a spell on you and kill you
basibalem	I will call you over and kill you
pwapu pusigam	(At your) shoulder, your flank
asamla	I kill
ema kudokeva	It comes, you are bleeding from your mouth
kuditilava	You are bleeding your heart's blood
ikapitoki	It closes the mouth
atakubila	I raise the spear to strike
akoluma	I stick you
yegula Tobwabwana psss	I myself Tobwabwana *psss*

The formula begins with the magician's ordering the wild pig to come to him (lines 1–3) and the announcement that he will put a spell on the animal and kill it (line 4). The noun the formula uses to refer to the wild pig is a magical word; in everyday contexts the noun *bwarodina* refers to this animal. The verbal expressions *badududem/badudulem, basobalem/basibalem,* and *asamla* are magical expressions as well.

The second part of the formula (lines 5–21) lists fourteen body parts of the wild pig and with every part reiterates that the magician will kill it. The list starts with the pig's flank, the place where pigs are usually killed with a spear that is driven through the flank into the heart. This important part of the body is mentioned twice (lines 5–6), and then the formula names the body parts of the pig, beginning with its head and continuing down to its legs. The verbal expression *asamla,* which refers to the act of the magician's killing the pig, is repeated twenty-eight times in this part of the formula.

The third part of the formula (lines 22–25) is a repetition of the first lines of the formula, and the fourth part (lines 26–28) almost identically repeats the first two lines of the second part of the formula (lines 5–6), again mentioning the flank that is so important for killing the animal.

The last part of the formula starts with the statement that the pig comes (line 29), continues with the magician's direct address to the pig, in which he describes what will happen to the animal after he has struck it with the spear in the process of its dying (lines 29–30), and a neutral description of the pig's last action in its death (line 31). It ends with a reference to the magician's actions in killing the pig and an explicit mention of the magician's name. The final onomatopoetic sound *psss* is uttered to distribute the spell into the air so that it will reach the pig, wherever it is.

This formula is typical for the Trobriand *megwa*. Magicians direct all magical formulas toward specific addressees, among whom are animals, as in this case, things, natural powers, substances, and spirits (see Senft 1997). All these addressees are personalized in the formulas. Some of the addressees are mediating substances (Tambiah 1985: 41) that, like go-betweens, take up the verbal assertions of the formulas, pass them on, and convey them to the final recipient of the magic.

All formulas pursue certain aims, which they will achieve by commanding their addressees to do or change something, by foretelling changes, processes, and developments that are necessary for reaching these aims, or simply by describing the conditions and effects at which the formula aims. Malinowski (1974: 74) characterized this aspect of magic by writing that "it is the use of words which invoke, state, or command the desired aim." About sixty years later, Tambiah (1985: 60, 78) connected this observation with Austin's speech act theory (Austin 1962) and rightly called these verbal acts "illocutionary" or "performative" acts.

The speech situation in which magicians in the Trobriand Islands find themselves engaged is special indeed. According to my consultants and to all the magicians who presented me with or sold me their formulas, the act of whispering, carrying, or saying the magic is not monological. On the contrary, the magicians emphasize that they engage in a kind of conversation with their addressees. For Trobriand magicians, the addressees of their formulas have to behave like partners in a conversation—at least they have to take the function of listeners—because the power of the magical words forces them to do so. According to my Trobriand consultants, the interactants in the communicative situation of magic are the magician, on one side, and the intermediate or immediate addressee or addressees of the magical formula, on the other. Magicians address their "vis-à-vis" verbally, and the addressees may then be compelled to react nonverbally. That is, they may have to fulfill the commands they hear in the formula and see that its described aims are reached. If they do not react to the magician's formula, it is either because they have to obey another magician's more powerful formula or because the magician has broken a taboo or made a mistake in reciting the formula and therefore cannot successfully force the power of his or her magic onto the addressees. Thus, whether communication between magicians and their addressees is successful or not—from the point of view of the magicians, of course—is completely dependent on the nonverbal reaction of the verbally addressed. From the Trobrianders' point of view, the emic perspective, the performance of magic is always a communicative event characterized by a verbal-nonverbal conversation between magician and personalized addressee, regardless of whether the addressee is animate or inanimate. The magician talks to an addressee, which listens and reacts, and therefore both are engaged in a special type of conversation.

This elucidates the dialectics of RC. Rituals and forms of RC can fail, and so it is a risky business to engage in them (see also Howe 2000). If the communication between magicians and their addressees is unsuccessful, magicians can plead the aforementioned explanations for the failure of their magic. If they do this too often, however, they quickly lose their reputation. And not only do they lose face, but the reputations of generations of their relatives who handed down their formulas to their young apprentices are at stake.

For the Trobriand Islander, magic is certainly "a dialectical and dialogical pattern of activity," as Tambiah (1985: 22) pointed out. Tambiah also emphasized that "magical acts are ritual acts" (Tambiah 1985: 60). Werlen's (1984: 81) general characterization of ritual as "institutionalized, expressive action" certainly encompasses Trobriand magic, with its emphasis on speech-action. Like many other rituals, Trobriand magic "ritualize[s] man's optimism … [and] enhance[s] his faith in the victory of hope over fear" (Malinowski 1974: 90)—especially with respect to his fear of nature and its forces. Trobriand magic is a specific form of ritual, and the verbal manifestations of this ritual—the magical formulas—are relatively complex forms of ritual communication.

As I mentioned earlier, it is characteristic for Trobriand discourse and communication to use linguistic vagueness and ambiguity as a stylistic means to avoid possible distress, confrontation, or too much and too aggressive directness in everyday speech situations. The magical formulas clearly contradict this observation. With their formulas, Trobriand magicians attempt to force their will on their addressees, and even far-reaching requests are expressed without moderation. Such directness, which strips away the ambiguity and vagueness with which one normally can disguise one's thoughts, is characteristic of the *biga pe'ula* or *biga mokita* register—"heavy" or "true, direct" speech. The use of this variety in Trobriand verbal interaction inevitably demands action that for either party involved in the speech event may be dangerous or even fatal.

Yet Trobriand Islanders regard magical formulas as constituting the *biga megwa* register, a language variety in its own right. Magicians pointed out to me that the explicit stylistic marking of the magical formulas as something special and extraordinary was a means to signal addressees that these speech acts were different from the speech acts of general, everyday speech situations—that they will and must put a great strain on the communicative interaction between magicians and their addressees (see also Wheelock 1982: 62). Thus, the formal characteristics of the formulas constitute pronounced signals (Senft 1997: 389). By means of the formal verbal domain, license is sought to strain the communicative interaction. The *biga megwa* concept uses this license to relieve the tension in this critical situation of social interaction and to ward off any undesirable consequences of its strains. If one characterizes RC as a type of strategic action that, by verbalizing elements of danger more or less explicitly and bringing them up for discussion, contributes to promoting social bonding, blocking aggression, and banning elements of danger that may affect the community's social harmony, then magical formulas are a complex and important form of RC.

Wosi Milamala

Wosi milamala, the songs of the harvest festival that are also sung after the death of a Trobriander and during the first mourning ceremonies, constitute *biga baloma* or *biga tommwaya,* 'speech of the spirits of the dead' or 'old peoples' speech', an archaic variety of Kilivila. Only a few of the elderly living in the Trobriands still know the meaning of these songs, although they are passed on from members of the older generation to a few interested members of the younger one. The genre is in danger of being lost to Trobriand culture.[6]

For Trobrianders, the most important event in the course of the year is still the period of harvest festivals that were first described by Malinowski (1935; see also Senft 1996b: 385ff.). This period is called *milamala,* and it used to last for almost three months. Since the mid-1990s, the Milne Bay government and the Council of Chiefs in the Trobriands have been trying to cut the *milamala* down to just one day and one night. During my last visits to the Trobriands in 2006 and 2008, I got the impression that these bodies had finally realized their plan. This development illustrates that, especially in the present time of globalization, the ritualization of culture can be manipulated. It seems that this manipulation preferentially affects highly complex and extraordinary forms of RC that, as in the case of the harvest festival, preserve in a specific way important aspects of culture, in this case the Trobriand Islanders' indigenous eschatology.

In the traditional harvest festival, after getting in the yam harvest, Trobrianders open the *milamala* with a cycle of festive dances accompanied by drums and songs—the *wosi milamala.* Upon the decision of the village chief, the important garden magicians, and the expert dancing instructor, the villagers formally present yams, taro, sweet potatoes, fish, sugarcane, and betel nuts to the *baloma,* the spirits of the dead (Malinowski 1974), just before sunrise. This food distribution is called *katukaula.* Trobrianders believe that at this time the *baloma* leave their "underworld paradise" on Tuma Island and visit their former villages.

Then most men and some girls dress up carefully in their traditional clothes. All the dancers decorate their faces with asymmetrical ornaments in red, white, and black. They anoint their bodies with coconut oil and an essence made of fragrant herbs, sprinkle their torsos with small yellow leaves, and put white cockatoo feathers in their hair. They wear armlets made of natural fibers on their upper arms; these emphasize the men's muscles and frame the girls' breasts, thus increasing the wearers' physical beauty. Some of the dancers also wear necklaces, tortoise-shell earrings, and boars' tusks. Moreover, some dancers wear belts made of small white cowrie shells around their waists, knees, or ankles. Most of these adornments mark their wearers' wealth and status within the highly stratified Trobriand society, with its clans and subclans (see Weiner 1976: 237ff.).

After some final magical rites in which the dancers' relatives or the village dance master whispers magical spells on their bodies to make them dance more gracefully, the dancers gather at the center of the village, where in the meantime a group of mostly elderly men, some with drums and some with long sticks, has gathered. As soon as this group begins to sing and drum, the dancers start dancing in circles around them. The *wosi milamala* are intoned and ended in a specific way. They consist of verses of two to nine lines each, are repeated ad libitum, and have a characteristic melody. The singing and dancing may last for more than three hours. The *milamala* songs are sung in the language of the *baloma,* which represents the speech of the ancestors, the "old people," as a salute to the spirits of the dead and to honor and celebrate them (see Senft 2003). The songs are verbal manifestations of the Trobrianders' belief in an immortal spirit, the *baloma,* that lives in a kind of paradise in the underworld of Tuma Island (see Malinowski 1974). The songs poetically and erotically describe the "life" of the spirits of the dead in their Tuma Island paradise. Trobriand Islanders believe these spirits can be reborn; they can also visit their former villages, and they do so regularly during the *milamala*. During these visits the *baloma* control whether the villagers living there now still know how to garden, how to celebrate a good harvest, and how to behave even while celebrating exuberantly. "Depending on whether or not they are pleased with what they see, the spirits enhance or hinder the next year's production" of yams (Damon 1982: 231).

Together with the *katukaula,* the food distribution for the spirits of the dead, the *wosi milamala* and the song-accompanying dances mark the official beginning of the *milamala,* the period of harvest festivals. Until the mid-1990s, *wosi milamala* were also sung in the late evenings during the *milamala,* and sometimes they formed the transition from one day to the next at this time. This period was characterized by conviviality, flirtation, and amorous adventures. During such festive periods, social norms, rules, and regulations were interpreted more liberally and generously than at other times. This might have led to jealousies and rivalries that, in escalation, would have threatened the community. As my consultants told me, the mere fact that *wosi milamala* were sung prevented such a development. The songs reminded Trobrianders of the presence of the *baloma* and of social norms that were valid even for the spirits of the dead, "living" in their paradise. Thus the guardians of the norms of the past were present, checking whether that past was still present in their former villages. The *baloma* must not be offended by unseemly and indecent behavior, which includes jealousy among bachelors. Keeping this in mind, Trobrianders must control their behavior, especially their emotions, because no one would dare offend the spirits of the dead.

Thus, the past is present during the *milamala,* and the present during this period is deeply anchored in, and must be similar to, the past. The singing of *wosi milamala* assures the community that there is a virtually transcendental regulator controlling its members' behavior and thus warding off developments that might prove dangerous for the community. These features of *wosi milamala* are central for the characterization of RC that I propose.

The importance of the *wosi milamala* as a complex form of RC in Trobriand society becomes even more evident when one considers that they are also sung, without accompanying drumming, after the death of a Trobriander and during the first mourning ceremonies (see Senft 1985c; Weiner 1976). Trobriand Islanders believe that the *baloma* of dead persons, before they go to Tuma Island, stay with their relatives until the corpse is buried. This eschatological "fact" is the link between mourning ritual and the harvest festival. On the basis of this belief, the *wosi milamala* that are sung during the mourning ritual, especially those that describe the carefree life of the spirits in their Tuma paradise, can be interpreted as easing the *baloma's* grief upon parting. The songs should also console the bereaved, reminding them that dying is just a rite of passage (van Gennep 1909), a transition from one form of existence to another. The songs remind islanders that the present and the future are anchored in the past, and for the *baloma* the future is not at all different from the past. Life in the Tuma underworld is always the same. There is only a "present." After a few days in the underworld, *baloma* forget their past, and it is only when they grow tired of their carefree lives there and think of being reborn that a future opens up for them.

Referring to this common knowledge coded in the community's religious superstructure, the songs sung in the *biga baloma* variety of Kilivila contribute to channeling and controlling emotions during the mourning ceremonies and to maintaining bonds between members of a community that has been struck by death. *Wosi milamala,* then, not only are sung on specific and more or less "extraordinary" occasions but also can be regarded as a complex and extraordinary form of RC that secures the construction of the society's social reality (Berger and Luckmann 1966) through their norm-controlling and bonding functions. This form of RC also preserves in a specific way important aspects of Trobriand indigenous culture in oral tradition.

Before I present an example of such songs, I want to complete my description of the *milamala* festival by noting how the end of this period is still officially and publicly marked. In the complete *milamala* period that I observed in Tauwema village, on Kaile'una Island, the festival ended as the villagers, especially the youngsters, chased the spirits of the dead back to their Tuma underworld by throwing stones, sand, and rotten coconuts and yams toward the invisible *baloma*. The "past," which was present until then in the villagers' consciousness, was thus chased away. This rite clearly signified that ordinary time, with its clear separation between past, present, and future, would take over again.

In my corpus of Kilivila data I have documented 21 *wosi milamala* song cycles, with 204 stanzas altogether (including cycles with as few as 2 and cycles with as many as 17 stanzas). Until the mid-1960s the Trobriand Islanders also used this genre to communicate news to their deceased. Most of these songs, however, describe the "lives" of the spirits of the dead in their underworld paradise. In the example that follows, I have ordered the stanzas in such a way that the story told in the cycle emerges.[7] With only one exception, I never heard *wosi milamala* cycles sung with ordered stanzas—especially not during the actual *milamala* festival. That the informed Trobriander immediately assigns a story to a stanza belonging to a specific *wosi milamala* cycle further highlights the "insider knowledge" that is intertwined with this genre.

The following *wosi milamala* cycle illustrates the genre. The cycle is called "Wosi Oruvekoya"; Oruvekoya is the name of a place near the freshwater grotto Tuyabwau, in the bush close to the village Tauwema:

"Wosi Oruvekoya"	"Oruvekoya Song"
Kwatuyavesa waga	Turn 'round the canoe's sail,
rakeda milaveta	its road is to the open sea.
Igineda—igibwau	Our wind—it is very strong,
kwatura'ema tevau	it blows us off the land, men.
Kwatuyavesa waga	Turn 'round the canoe's sail,
rakeda milaveta	its road is to the open sea.
Isirara—Namgereva—budibudi	A girl with two men—Namgereva—island far away.
Kaugepwasa waga—	The wrecking of the canoe—
nagega milaveta	we wonder about it at the open sea.
Kusiunisa ina	You sit together, girls,
bukagonusa buita	you make wreaths of flowers.
Bisuya	She will string the flowers,
Namirumeru	Namirumeru,
biruveyem kunugu	she will put it in her hair.
Kumnabegu ina	You stay with me, girls,
kusiunisa tau	you stay with the men.
Bukwasana guwosi	You will like my song.
Bigoegu	He'll cry for me with joy
vaponu	between waves and sand.
Mbutumgwa venu	The noise of the village,
miliobu—vaogu	*Miliobu*—yam house—my body,
bokone'isa tau	they will look for the man,
kusiunegu siporu	you sit and sing songs.
Sikevai nubegu	Their flirting, my friend,
mkwebwau urata	the singing of the young men,

rokumavai va'ogu—	her liking of my body—
bidam Valuekoya	it will get quiet at Valuekoya.
[*Kaila*]	[*Kaila* (joining part of the song, refrain)]
Sikevai nubegu—	Their flirting, my friend—
kwatudelisa napunuponu	you walk in line, young girls,
kulimatusa biga	you use the (right) language.
Basikemrura	I will sit between the two points,
bivanisegu Tadou	she will refute me (Bwe-)Tadou.
Okunevotu bukwiyayema	In front of the beach you will love
tevau	the men.
Mkwebwau urata,	Your singing, young men,
rokumevai vavogu—	her liking of my body—
bidam Varuvekoya	it will be quiet at Varuvekoya.
[End of *Kaila*]	
Kwatupelemgwa venu	You change the place of your village,
be'ura'emgwa nogu	it will open my mind,
okega'ila nogu	it will change my mind,
bimyegu unata	she whispers to me, young man.
Kapisim gwadi	I am sorry, child,
bakina koya	I will see the mountain.
Yoyuvanogu varam	My mind remembers the crying,
gunuvenu	my village.

This song cycle describes the grief of a young man's *baloma* that has just arrived in a village in the Tuma underworld. The man's name is Bwetadou, and he is still between the worlds of the living and the dead. He has died in a shipwreck and bewails the loss of his girlfriend, whom he knows cannot but refute him now and have love affairs with other men. When she changes her village, he will know that she has married another man. Then he will change his mind and turn toward the *baloma* girls in the underworld. He feels sorry about what has happened and what will happen—and he still remembers how he was bewailed only a few days ago at his village.

Summary

The forms of Trobriand ritual communication that I have described all contribute to safeguarding and securing the islanders' construction of social reality. Greetings are socially integrative devices that continuously help strengthen bonds and stabilize social relations among members of the society. Trobriand ditties, especially the insinuating ones, provide a forum for topicalizing themes that one does not otherwise talk about. Thus they contribute to channeling emotions and keeping frustrations and aggression, caused by the society's strict requirements to adhere to certain taboos, under control. The power of magical words bequeathed by the ancestors to following generations helps strengthen the belief that Trobrianders can master their environment no matter how dangerous and hostile it might be at times. And *wosi milamala* are verbal manifestations of the Trobrianders' belief in immortal spirits. During the harvest festival these spirits are believed to control people's possibly aggressive behavior patterns, which could turn out to be dangerous for the community. After the death of a Trobriander and during the first mourning ceremonies, the eschatological knowledge encoded in these songs contributes to channeling and controlling emotions and to maintaining bonds among members of a grieving community.

With the exception of the relatively simple forms of greeting, all the forms of Trobriand Islanders' ritual communication that I have described are results of what Ellen Basso and I, in our introduction to this volume, called "artful, performed semiosis." They are "formulaic and repetitive and therefore anticipated within particular contexts of social interaction," and they usually (but not always, as I pointed out in connection with magical formulas) have anticipated consequences. Moreover, they are performed and therefore "subject to evaluation by participants according to standards that are defined in part by language ideologies, ... contexts of use, and ... relations of power among participants" (Basso and Senft, this volume). In a very specific way, they preserve important aspects of Trobriand Islanders' cultural identity.

There is no metalinguistic expression in Kilivila that can be compared to the "etic" concept of RC. All the Kilivila examples of RC presented in this chapter, however, are metalinguistically labeled, not only with respect to the speech genre to which they belong but also with respect to the variety (or register) of Kilivila they co-constitute. Thus, basic considerations constitutive for the etic concept of RC may have emic equivalents in Kilivila.

Concluding Remarks on Two Daring Hypotheses

Human ethologists such as Irenäus Eibl-Eibesfeldt have argued that rituals and forms of RC can be referred back to so-called basic interaction strategies (Eibl-Eibesfeldt 1984: 642–645, 1989: 425–547). They claim that all humans have a finite set of these conventionalized strategies at their disposal and assume that these strategies are universal. Eibl-Eibesfeldt differentiated between strategies of group maintenance and bonding, of social learning and teaching, of rank striving, and of fighting. He assumed that the ways people in different cultures try to acquire status, get a gift from someone, invite someone, or block aggression follow in principle the same basic patterns. On the basis of his human ethological field research he concluded: "The superficial appearance of human interactive behaviors varies enormously from culture to culture, but with closer examination we can recognize that the various strategies of social interactions share a universal pattern, based upon a universal rule system (Eibl-Eibesfeldt 1989: 522). Thus—according to Eibl-Eibesfeldt—many rituals and forms of RC can be traced back to, or at least be understood as, the differentiation of these elemental interaction strategies. Despite their richness of variation, they are just culture-specific expressions of these strategies.

Recently, Stephen Levinson (2006b: 61), on the basis of his anthropological-linguistic field research, also postulated a "universal systematics of interaction." He pointed out that "as we learn more about conversational organization ... we see that there are relatively few crucial organizing principles" (2006: 61). This observation, explicitly linked with Conversation Analysis, seems to be in agreement with Eibl-Eibesfeldt's claims with respect to probably universal human elementary interaction strategies. These strategies seem to be part of Levinson's "building blocks for cultural diversity in social interaction," provided by what he called the "interaction engine" (2006b: 62). This interaction engine is understood as "a set of principles that can interdigitate with local principles, to generate different local flavors" (Levinson 2006b: 56). Thus, this set of basic organizing principles "provides the parameters for variation with default values that account for the surprising commonalities in the pattern of ... interchange across cultures" (Levinson 2006b: 62). To put it differently, the enormous variety of human interaction to be observed in different cultures can be attributed to and explained by a few such organizing principles or interaction strategies.

These are daring, though certainly interesting, hypotheses, and they open up another promising approach for researching RC. However, I file a strong caveat here—that to verify or falsify such hypotheses requires a vast amount of empirical and comparative research into the phenomenon.

Notes

I thank the national and provincial governments in Papua New Guinea, the Institute for PNG Studies, and the National Research Institute for their assistance with and permission for my research projects. I express my great gratitude to the people of the Trobriand Islands, above all the inhabitants of Tauwema and my consultants, for their hospitality, friendship, and patient cooperation over all these years. Without their help, none of my work on the Kilivila language and Trobriand culture would have been possible. Thanks are also owed to the participants in the Wenner-Gren symposium on ritual communication, in which a first draft of this chapter was discussed.

1. This list of some of the many (cross-cultural and possibly also culture-specific) features that are characteristic and constitutive of forms of RC is the result of joint research and many discussions with Ingrid Bell-Krannhals, Irenäus Eibl-Eibesfeldt, Karl Grammer, Volker Heeschen, Reinhard Schropp, Barbara Senft, and Wulf Schiefenhövel. See also Eibl-Eibesfeldt and Senft 1987; Heeschen 1987; Senft 1987.

2. The concept of tact is an important part of the Trobriand Islanders' moral order. Among other things, it highlights the importance of silence in and for ritual communication. Parents and older members of children's "own little communit[ies]" (Malinowski 1929: 53) explicitly instruct small children in what to do and what not to do. For example, one of the many things one should not do is peep through the mats woven of coconut palm leaves that enclose the wooden frames of the houses. One man of Tauwema lost his eye while doing this as a child—another boy sitting inside the house gouged out his eye with a wooden stick as he peeped through the mats. When children try to do this in Tauwema, one often hears the admonition, "Don't do that, or would you like to look like [the man who lost his eye]?" For further information, see Malinowski 1929: esp. chs. 3 and 8.

3. For Kilivila orthography, see Senft 1986: 14–16.

4. I do not insinuate here that this "play" is ritualized. What is ritualized is the culturally expected reaction of participants in verbal interactions. A Trobriand Islander must not feel offended by utterances that are explicitly labeled *sopa* by use of the formulaic expression *asasopa wala* 'I'm just joking' or *sopa wala* '(It's) just (a) joke'. The *biga sopa* variety thus allows the breaking of almost all taboos in a kind of "inversed world," without fear of facing severe consequences. Only the five most severe curses in the Trobriands can never be labeled *sopa*.

5. All my remarks about this formula, and my comments about the characteristic communicative features of *biga megwa* in general, are based on

long and intensive discussions I have had with owners of magical formulas, especially with Weyei, the renowned weather magician of Tauwema.

6. My description of *wosi milamala* and its importance for Trobriand Island society is based on intensive discussions with consultants who still know the meaning of these songs. What I present here is thus an emic account of the role of *wosi milamala* that I present in my etic analysis of forms of RC in the Trobriands.

7. This ordering of the stanzas was approved by my consultants.

four

"Like a Crab Teaching Its Young to Walk Straight"

Proverbiality, Semantics, and Indexicality in English and Malay

Cliff Goddard

How are proverbs connected to notions of ritual, ritual communication, and ritualized communication? Along with greetings and partings, apology formulas, and the like, proverbs fall squarely under the rubric of "small *r*" ritual, in the sense of formulaic communicative practices of everyday life: utterance forms with a quality of ready-madeness, fixity, and iteration, drawn from (and understood to be drawn from) a limited corpus. To be sure, they are not situation-specific in the same way greetings and partings are. Rather, proverbs are typically used to impose particular construals upon situations. Like scriptural allusions and quotations, proverbs epitomize "double-voicing," in Bakhtin's terms, standing aside from the ongoing flow of discourse even while being integrated into it. They necessarily bring a complex interdiscursivity into the speech situation. As Hasan-Rokem (1992: 129) put it: "The application of a proverb imbues the specific situation with cultural meaning by linking it to a chain of situations all of which may be interpreted by the same proverb."

Proverbs can also be seen as falling under the rubric of ritual communication—or better, "ritualized" communication—in that they recapitulate and reproduce established cultural values. They are communicative vehicles that both enact traditional authority and are partially constitutive of it. They are "small forms" of authoritative discourse, as against large forms such as ritual liturgies and magical spells. As I show later, in some contexts proverbs may become the objects or instruments of a "ritualization of culture," as when Malay *peribahasa* (proverbs) are used as emblems in a project of ethno-identity maintenance or construction.

To write as I have been doing assumes that definitional clarity exists about what qualifies as a proverb, at least as a cross-linguistically applicable analytic type (as opposed to a culture-specific genre; see Ben-Amos 1969). Whether this condition is fully satisfied is perhaps debatable, but there is general agreement that the properties of a proverb include relative fixity of form, brevity, appealing stylistic features, traditionality, and the status of presenting "folk wisdom" (Norrick 1985: ch. 3). Traditional paremiology (see Mieder 2001, 2004) has catalogued proverbs, often in their thousands, from many cultures and classified them by form and subject matter. A number of insightful studies in linguistic anthropology and ethnopoetics have inquired into the culture-specific formal and functional properties of proverbs and into their performance dimension—how they are deployed and integrated into ongoing social interaction (see, among others, Arewa and Dundes 1964; Briggs 1988; Obeng 1996). It is clear that culture-specific genres approximating the analytic type "proverb" differ somewhat from culture to culture and language to language (see Goddard n.d.), as do their functional and performance aspects. For example, Briggs, in his study of the performance of Mexicano "proverbs" (*dichos*), identified the citation of a certain person with whom the proverb is associated as a crucial element, which "emanates from the belief that proverbs are, in a sense, 'owned' by individuals" (Briggs 1988: 106). Mexicano proverb performances are, furthermore, almost invariably closed by a series of validation statements about the truth of the proverb. Neither of these features is associated with contemporary uses of English and Malay proverbs, with which I deal in this chapter.

From a formal point of view, the brevity of proverbs—perhaps better termed "semantic compression" (Gándara 2004: 348)—is one of their most conspicuous features. As unitary, free-standing, fixed utterances, they minimize processing demands, and their typical stylistic characteristics, such as vivid imagery, rhyme, alliteration, parallelism, and contrast, make for easy memorization. Even so, inculcating hundreds or even thousands of proverbial items during language socialization is such a costly investment that it must serve important communicative and—presumably—cognitive functions. As Sweeney (1987: 97) remarked in a brilliant study of orality in premodern Malay society: "The discourse of an oral culture is heavily dependent upon the use of relatively fixed utterances in stylised form, such as proverbs and other 'sayings.' … Such utterances are not merely used to underline a point: they *are* the point. The individual *thinks* in these formulas" (emphasis in original).

From the vantage point of linguistic semantics, it is striking how little progress has been made on the question of how the meanings of proverbs (in the sense of proverb texts) can be stated, if at all. The simplistic and impressionistic "literal paraphrases" typically offered by proverb dictionaries and researchers—such as *Make hay while the sun shines:* "Act while propitious conditions prevail" (Norrick 1985: 113)—are inadequate in many ways. It is unsurprising that some researchers have preferred to say that proverb texts are "semantically incomplete" (Mukařovský 1971 [1942–1943]: 285, cited in Briggs 1988: 132) until or unless they are contextualized by being inserted into real social interaction. One of my purposes in this chapter is to challenge this view. Like White (1987: 152), I believe that "certain key understandings make up a kind of kernel of proverb meaning, even though such meanings may be shifted or elaborated in particular contexts of use." Using a well-established methodology of semantic description, I demonstrate that it is possible to "unpack" the meanings of proverb texts rigorously and precisely.

The semantic approach I follow is the Natural Semantic Metalanguage (NSM) approach, which employs reductive paraphrase as its method of meaning representation (see Ameka, this volume; Goddard 2006, 2008; Goddard and Wierzbicka 2002; Peeters 2006; Wierzbicka 1996, 2003). The paraphrases, known as explications, are composed within a small metalanguage of simple meanings (putative semantic primes), such as 'someone', 'something', 'people', 'this', 'say', 'do', 'happen', 'want', 'know', 'good', 'bad', 'because', 'can', and 'if'. The inventory of semantic primes is tabulated in the appendix to the chapter. The NSM approach has been employed in numerous semantic and ethnopragmatic studies across many languages (see bibliography at the NSM website, www.une.edu.au/bcss/linguistics/nsm). Paraphrase in terms of semantic primes allows for fine-grained resolution of semantic detail, wards off any danger of definitional circularity, and enables a higher level of intuitive accessibility than is possible with more technical modes of representation.

Although the semantic (symbolic) meanings of proverb texts may be amenable to precise description, such a description does not exhaust the full significance of a proverb utterance in context. As is widely recognized in the literature on proverb usage and other formulaic verbal arts, the full significance of a proverb utterance (or any generically shaped utterance) depends also on indexical meanings that arise in specific spatiotemporal and culture-historical contexts. Indexical meaning is not susceptible to paraphrase and is often below the limits of awareness of ordinary speakers. Considerations of ethnopragmatics (cultural pragmatics) and interdiscursivity (intertextuality) are fundamental to understanding context-bound indexical meaning (see Bauman 2005; Briggs and Bauman 1992; Goddard 2002, 2006; Hill 2005; Silverstein 2005).

Consistent with the themes of this volume, my objective is to give a balanced, contrastive treatment of the textual semantics, cultural-historical positioning, and interdiscursivity of proverbs in two widely different speech cultures. In what follows, I look first at contemporary English, addressing the way proverbs, as instances of a language-specific category, can be identified on linguistic evidence. I propose a template in the NSM metalanguage to articulate the semantic framing inherent in the proverb genre (essentially, the semantic content of "proverbiality") and demonstrate the utility of the approach with a full analysis of several English metaphorical proverbs ("A stitch in time saves nine") and maxims ("Practice makes perfect"). I discuss aspects of the interdiscursivity of proverbs in English, with particular reference to the ethos of modernity. In the remainder of the chapter, I apply a parallel analysis and discussion to proverbs (*peribahasa*) in contemporary Malay, including the metaphorical Malay proverb *Seperti ketam mengajar anak berjalan betul* 'like a crab teaching its young to walk straight'.

Proverbs in Contemporary English

The ultimate criterion for whether something qualifies as a proverb (in the genre sense) is that ordinary people can refer to it as such in ordinary discourse—for example, by means of a "metalexical tag" (Goddard 2004) such as "as the proverb goes" (or "says"). Unlike its counterparts in other languages (Čermák 2004), this tag is not particularly common in contemporary English. A related and more frequent tag is "as the old saying goes." Compatibility with this tag is an intuitively straightforward test that helps delimit the class of items of interest. For example:

(1) a. "A stitch in time saves nine," as the old saying goes.
b. As the old saying goes, "Don't count your chickens before they hatch."

The word "old" is important, because the simpler tag "as the saying goes" can apply to a much broader range of "sayings," including not just proverbs but also well-known quotations and modern sayings, such as "Let's cut to the chase, as the (*old) saying goes." However, even with the inclusion of the modifier "old," the tag does not delimit proverbs as such, because it can also be used with well-known "old" quotations and other sayings: "Revenge is sweet, as the old saying goes." In short, whereas all proverbs are old sayings, not all old sayings are proverbs.[1]

A contrast is often drawn between metaphorical proverbs, such as "A stitch in time saves nine," and "plain" proverbs, or maxims, such as "Practice makes perfect."[2] To separate these classes using linguistic tests is not difficult. Metalexical tags such as "so to speak" and "as it were," which are diagnostic of "active metaphor" generally (Goddard 2004), will identify metaphorical proverbs. The metalexical modifier "the proverbial" also works ("the proverbial stitch in time"), though ironically, it is not restricted to proverbs but can be applied to any metaphorical but clichéd expression ("We were up the proverbial creek").

How, then, can the meaning of a classic metaphorical proverb such as "A stitch in time saves nine" be stated using the techniques of reductive paraphrase? Can its meaning (qua proverb text) be captured in an extended paraphrase composed from simple, everyday words?

A Semantic Template for Proverb Text Meanings

After an extensive process of semantic-conceptual experimentation, I propose and illustrate here a five-part semantic template for English proverbs. For reasons of space, only a few samples can be presented from a larger body of work (Goddard n.d.). The structure of the template can be depicted as in figure 4.1.

The framing sections recur with exactly the same wording in all the examples to be considered here. Section [a], labeled TRADITIONALITY in the explications to follow, establishes that the words used are fixed and have long been used by people to express the subsequent message content. Section [e], labeled STATUS AS FOLK WISDOM, "caps" the content of

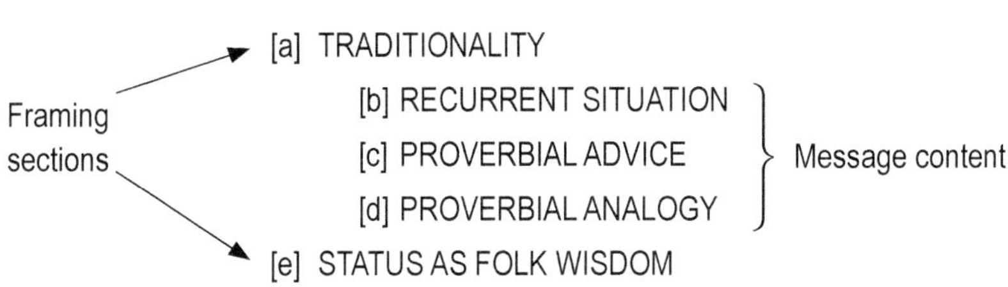

Figure 4.1. Structure of semantic template for proverb text meanings.

each explication with an endorsement of its status as an item of traditional wisdom. This section presupposes, and in a sense projects, the assumption that there *is* some body of collective traditional knowledge and that aspects of this knowledge can be relevant and helpful in certain situations. The semantic content of these framing sections is spelled out in the metalanguage of semantic primes, as shown below:[3]

[a]	for a long time people have said these words when they want to say something like this: —	TRADITIONALITY
[e]	many people have lived for a long time because of this, these people know many things this is one of these things it can be good for someone if this someone thinks about this at some times	STATUS AS FOLK WISDOM

The message content of the individual proverb is given in the three middle sections, [b], [c], and [d]. To anticipate, I will say that the tripartite structure—RECURRENT SITUATION, PROVERBIAL ADVICE, PROVERBIAL ANALOGY—is maximal. Most metaphorical proverbs require all three sections, but maxim-style proverbs lack the PROVERBIAL ANALOGY, and some metaphorical sayings (such as "Out of the frying pan, into the fire") lack the PROVERBIAL ADVICE section. Before considering these variations, however, let me work carefully through a couple of examples of the full structure.

Explications of Some English Proverb Texts

Explication [A] is for "A stitch in time saves nine." The explication exhibits a great deal of semantic compression: twenty lines of semantic text are packed into six words. It also shows how the tripartite structure of the message content works. The RECURRENT SITUATION in section [b] is introduced as 'something like this often happens: —' (see Burke 1967: 296). The word 'often' can be regarded as equivalent to the expression 'at many times.' The PROVERBIAL ADVICE in section [c] spells out the didactic message, typically a way of avoiding the recurrent situation just presented. Then comes the PROVERBIAL ANALOGY in section [d], introduced by 'it is like this: —.' What follows is usually based on everyday experience. As Taylor (1962 [1931]: 10) put it: "A novel application of a familiar scene arrests our attention, imprints itself on our minds, and drives home the lesson."

[A] Semantic explication for *A stitch in time saves nine:*

[a] for a long time people have said these words — TRADITIONALITY
when they want to say something like this:

[b] something like this often happens: — RECURRENT SITUATION
someone has to do many things at some time,
because this someone did not do one small thing at some time before
this is bad for this someone

[c] because of this, when someone knows that they have to do — PROVERBIAL ADVICE
something small,
it is not good if this someone thinks like this: "I will do it after some time"
it is good if this someone thinks like this: "I will do it now"

[d] it is like this: — PROVERBIAL ANALOGY
when there is a *tear in someone's *clothes,
after some time someone has to do something to these *clothes
if they do it when the *tear is small, they can do one small thing
if they don't do this one small thing, after some time the *tear will not be small anymore
because of this, this someone will have to do many things
this is bad for this someone

[e] many people have lived for a long time — STATUS AS FOLK WISDOM
because of this, these people know many things
this is one of these things
it can be good for someone if this someone thinks about this at some times

Notice that the wording of the proverb is related to section [d], PROVERBIAL ANALOGY, but not necessarily in a simple one-to-one fashion. For example, in the case of "A stitch in time saves nine," it is unnecessary to mention in the explication any "stitching" as such, let alone to refer to the number nine. "A stitch" (i.e., one stitch) stands for doing one small thing, as opposed to "nine (stitches)," which stands for doing many things. To spell out the content of the analogy, it *is* necessary, however, to refer to the situation of having a tear in one's clothing, and consequently some semantically complex words ('clothes' and 'tear,' marked with asterisks) are used in this section. In this and subsequent explications, I have tried to keep the number of such words to a minimum and to use only words that seem essential to spelling out the analogical content in a plain and intuitively appealing fashion. I hypothesize that these concrete lexical items are cognitively "real" in the sense that they are involved in the speaker's actual representation of the analogy.

Explication [B] is for "Too many cooks spoil the broth." Only the message content sections of the explication are given. The RECURRENT SITUATION section again depicts an undesirable situation, which the PROVERBIAL ADVICE section provides counsel on how to avoid. The PROVERBIAL ANALOGY essentially describes a dysfunctional kitchen scene, though the only semantically complex words that seem to be needed are 'make' and 'eat.'[4]

[B] Partial semantic explication for *Too many cooks spoil the broth*

[b] something like this often happens: RECURRENT SITUATION
many people in one place want something to happen in this place
because of this, they all want to do some things
for some time they all do the same things in the same place at the same time
because of this, none of these people can do these things well
because of this, it doesn't happen as they want
this is bad

[c] because of this, when many people in a place all want the same thing to happen, PROVERBIAL ADVICE
it is not good for these people if they all do the same things in the same place at the same time

[d] it is like this: PROVERBIAL ANALOGY
sometimes some people in one place do some things at one time because they want to *make some good things for people to *eat
if these people all do the same things at the same time, none of them can do these things well
because of this, they can't *make something good
this is bad

Let me now look briefly at some simpler proverbs—simpler in the sense that they lack one or another set of semantic components found in the classic metaphorical proverb. As noted earlier, many common English proverbs are of the maxim variety. "Practice makes perfect," for example, consists of plain words used in their plain meanings. If we unpack the intended meaning, we will find that a recurrent situation is implied, along with some schematic advice, but obviously there is no proverbial analogy. Conversely, there are some metaphorical proverbs—such as "Out of the frying pan, into the fire" and "Birds of a feather flock together"—that characterize recurrent situations, pairing them with a proverbial analogy but without offering any particular advice. Explication [C] illustrates with "Out of the frying pan, into the fire." The analogy is about what speakers describe as a "little critter (or creature)" of some kind. This is rendered in section [c] as a 'small living thing'. Early versions of the saying actually referred to a flounder. For example, Heywood's (1546) compendium has "As the flounder dothe, Leape out of the frying pan into the fyre."

[C] Partial semantic explication for *Out of the frying pan, into the fire*

[b] something like this often happens: RECURRENT SITUATION
something bad is happening to someone at some time
this someone does something at this time because this someone wants it not to be like this anymore
after this, something very bad happens to this someone because of it

[d] it is like this: PROVERBIAL ANALOGY
if a small living thing is in a *frying pan above a *fire, it can't not feel something bad because of this
if this small living thing moves in one moment because it wants it not to be like this anymore, after this it can be in the *fire because of this
if this small living thing is in the *fire, it can't not feel something very bad because of this

This handful of English examples raises many questions, but I believe they are sufficient to establish the viability of the general project of explicating proverb text meanings in extended reductive paraphrases via the proposed semantic template. (For more extensive argumentation and exemplification, see Goddard n.d.). Now let me turn to the interdiscursive positioning of proverbs and proverbiality in contemporary English.

Modern English Proverbs: Contextualization and Interdiscursivity

In any language and culture, interdiscursivity of the proverb genre is (naturally) type-interdiscursivity (Silverstein 2005). The chronotopes of all items in the genre, as members of the set of "old sayings," project backward to some hypothetical past, some vague "long time ago."[5] In this backward-looking stance, as well as in its trope of quasi-quotation and its reverence for traditional collective authority, the proverb genre in contemporary English is at odds with the prevailing Anglo ethos of modernity. Modernity defines itself through its sense of rupture with the past. It is forward-looking, it valorizes originality, it rejects the very notion of traditional wisdom. In this climate, proverbs are open to being seen as mere clichés, and their messages, as platitudes.

It was not always so, as is detailed in Obelkevich's (1994 [1987]) study of the social history of proverbs and associated speech genres in Europe. The sixteenth and early seventeenth centuries were the golden age for proverbs in England, when they were studied, treasured, and used in abundance by educated people, as well as by the illiterate. Obelkevich charted the way the educated classes' enthusiasm for proverbs then began to wane and, in the early eighteenth century, gave way to outright rejection: "The expulsion of the proverb from learned culture is a landmark in social and linguistic history" (Obelkevich 1994 [1987]: 230). This development coincided with the onset of the Enlightenment, a loss of reverence for the past, and the abandonment of the notion of traditional collective wisdom. The same period, however, saw the rise of a new and rival genre, the aphorism—more literary, more abstract, more individual. Later, in the Victorian years, proverbs enjoyed a short-lived revival, and a new and even more "personalized" alternative genre emerged: the great quotation. This genre in turn has gradually lost its gloss, and originality and individuality have triumphed as the leading values of the times.

Among educated people, Obelkevich observed, apart from the occasional allusion, proverbs are now taboo: "Only when old sayings can be made to say something new, whether by irony or by more drastic means, are they accepted, but in the process they cease to express the wisdom of the community and become raw material for the wit and originality of the individual speaker" (Obelkevich 1994 [1987]: 239). There is no doubt an element of hyperbole in this dictum. It has been established that full proverb usage persists, for example, in the speech of political leaders (Charteris-Black 2005; Gándara 2004; Mieder 2005), for rhetorical reasons that are not difficult to appreciate, such as to invoke the sanction of tradition or notions of common sense or to pursue a "folksy" quality. Nonetheless, the general validity of Obelkevich's observations is evident.

These observations, furthermore, help make sense of some more mundane proverb phenomena that have been documented by linguists. As Norrick (1985: 102) pointed out, "many scholars have accepted or asserted that the completely metaphorical proverb describing a concrete scene, call it the scenic proverb, represents the archetypal proverb." Certainly this proverb type is the most frequent in published compendiums of English proverbs. On the other hand, corpus studies and familiarity ratings indicate that the most common "full" proverbs in contemporary English are not metaphorical but are of the maxim variety (Charteris-Black 1999; Higbee and Millard 1983). The paradox is easily resolved given that from a conceptual point of view, the category "proverb" implies an old saying. Metaphorical proverbs tend to employ archaic imagery, archaic vocabulary, or both (e.g., from the farm or the household in preindustrial days), which makes them more prototypical in this respect. On the other hand, the "modern" attitude militates against actual usage of old-fashioned sounding proverbs.

It also helps us to understand why, on the contemporary scene, proverb "fragments" and other proverb variations and manipulations are a good deal more common than full proverbs in their traditional forms. Charteris-Black (1999) showed, for example, that in a 330-million-word corpus, the phrase "Birds of a feather" occurred 190 times, in comparison with 6 occurrences of the full proverb, "Birds of a feather flock together." Advertising, branding, and the like are particularly fertile domains for the creative manipulation of proverbs. Winick (1998) emphasized "proverbial innovation" in contemporary English-language popular culture. Sherzer (2002: 56–61) emphasized the role of proverb usage in the strategic operation of conversation and for humorous purposes, in both of which contexts they are frequently subject to forms of manipulation such as abbreviation, inversion, and playful literal interpretation.

Proverbs (*Peribahasa*) in Contemporary Malay

Traditional Malay culture was richly verbal. Linguistic etiquette was elaborate and highly valued, relying on artful indirectness and allusion as well as on a variety of prescribed formal devices (honorific address forms, lexical variants, etc.). People knew and used innumerable *peribahasa* (roughly, folk sayings and phrases), *pantun* (rhyming four-line verses), and *teka-teki* (riddles), and in the case of the last two folk genres, they innovated and improvised freely. In the older Malay oral culture (Sweeney 1987), formulaic speech was ubiquitous. The colonial commentator Swettenham stressed "the Malay's fondness for proverbs, for epigrams and wise saws," adding that "in his conversation he never fails to introduce one or the other, when he sees an opportunity for their fitting application" (1906: 169, cited in Lim 2003: 23). Despite modernization and the multiethnic, multilingual character of modern Malaysia, many of these practices persist in contemporary Bahasa Melayu, especially as spoken by the Malay population. The usage examples in this chapter have been garnered from blogs and other Internet sources.[6]

Before moving to some cultural and semiotic background on Malaysia and on *peribahasa* and then to explications of a selection of Malay proverb texts, it is helpful to review Malay ethnoclassification and related metalexical indicators. *Peribahasa* is a rather general term, subsuming idioms (*simpulan bahasa*) as well as proverbs in the English sense. For the latter, three terms are in current use. *Pepatah* are concise traditional sayings that can serve as "clinching" or decisive contributions to discussion. This is the closest Malay term to the English "proverb." *Bidalan* are explicitly moralistic, similar to maxims or adages except that they can be metaphorical in wording. And *perumpamaan* (a nominalization on *umpama* 'like') are sayings introduced by one of several words meaning 'like,' such as *seperti, macam, bagai, bak,* and *ibarat* (the last two, like *umpama* itself, are archaic).

Although some Malay writers treat these terms as if they were mutually exclusive in their referential ranges, this is not really so. For example, *pepatah* that strongly imply advice can also be considered *bidalan,* and some *pepatah* can be prefaced with *seperti* 'like' (or equivalents), in which case they can be termed *perumpamaan.*

As in English, Malay sayings can be introduced in various ways. The most generic is *kata orang* 'people say', followed by *kata orang-orang tua* 'old people say'. Also common are the metalexical tags shown in (2), which employ the categories just mentioned. Notice that it is possible to include the ethnolinguistic descriptor *Melayu* 'Malay' in some of these metalexical tags. This is a linguistic index of the strong ethnic affiliation of the genre as a whole.

(2)	*bak pepatah (Melayu)...*	'as the (Malay) *pepatah* [goes],...'
	bak peribahasa (Melayu)...	'as the (Malay) *peribahasa* [goes],...'
	bidalan lama (or: *orang tua)...*	'the old (or: old people's) *bidalan* [goes]...'
	ibarat kata...	'the *ibarat* says...'

Because Malaysia is unlikely to be familiar to most readers, I review the larger context before addressing the semantic content of some Malay proverbs.

Malay Proverbs: Contextualization and Interdiscursivity

Formed in 1957, previously a British colony, Malaysia is a multiethnic, multilingual nation. Politics is constituted on strongly communalist lines, and the major political parties are aligned with the three main *bangsa* 'ethnic-racial groups' (in Malaysian English, "races"), which are usually identified as Malay, Chinese, and Indian. The primary distinction is between "the Malays," on the one hand, at more than 50 percent of the population, and the next largest ethnic-racial segment, "the Chinese," at about 25 percent. The substantial Chinese population consists mostly of native-born descendants of Chinese laborers who were encouraged to come to the region by the British. Generally speaking, Chinese Malaysians (a term rarely used in Malaysia) are today more strongly represented than Malays in business and commerce and in urban areas, although complex positive discrimination measures favoring Malays (and other so-called *bumiputra* (lit. 'sons of the soil') have been in place to offset this situation for many years. Political leadership, on the other hand, has been dominated by a Malay political elite. The ruling party, the United Malays National Organization (UMNO), has held power continuously since independence, in coalition with a conservative Chinese-based party (on Malaysian politics, see Case 2002). Religion also divides along *bangsa* lines, with almost all Malays being Muslims (indeed, under the Malaysian constitution they are required to be Muslims).

There is a substantial historical and political literature on the construction of the contemporary "Malay" identity, which arguably began in British times (Barnard 2004; Kahn 2006; Kessler, Kahn, and Wah 1992). A key element of this process has been the construction of an imagined Malay tradition, in the sense of Anderson (1991), and, as integral to this, the "ritualization of culture" by way of school textbooks, museums, public displays, national festivals, and the like (see Hobsbawm and Ranger 1992).

How do *peribahasa* fit into this situation? First and most obviously, as a self-styled genre of traditional collective wisdom—indeed, as one of the vehicles for the interdiscursive construction of tradition—they are highly salient semiotic materials for the construction and maintenance of the Malay cultural "brand." At a subtler level, the lexicon of the *peribahasa* (the imagery of rice farming, fishing, and forest) evokes echoes of the *kampung* (roughly, 'village community'), which is held to be the locus of the essential Malay culture.

Certainly in the last fifty years *peribahasa* have become one of the leading emblems of Malay identity. Numerous *peribahasa* dictionaries and guides have been published, both for the general public and for schools. Ding and Arba'eyah (2002) mentioned that no fewer than thirty *peribahasa* books were published between the 1950s and 2001, and several websites now exist as well. Children are required to learn *peribahasa* at school and are examined on them. The codification and institutionalization of *peribahasa* in Malaysia, and their introduction into formal education, can be seen as part of a state project of capturing, valorizing, and reproducing the cultural-political identity of "Malayness" at the level of national ideology. (Ironically, but not unexpectedly, institutionalization has coincided with a decline in everyday usage; see Sweeney 1987.)

In semiotic terms, the chronotopes of Malay *peribahasa* differ radically from those of English proverbs, insofar as they encompass attachments to a particular ethnic-racial social collectivity situated in an idealized *kampung* world. Drawing on conceptual vocabulary from a different source, one can say that in the contemporary Malaysian context, *peribahasa* involve complex "indirect indexicality" (Bauman 2005; Hill 2005; Ochs 1990: 295), in that they carry with them and project a set of naturalized assumptions about "Malayness"—for example, that Malays come from villages (*kampungs*), that they are modest, well-mannered, kind, and ethically correct. All this is in implicit contradistinction to other ethnic groups (*bangsa*) in Malaysia, particularly "the Chinese," and also in contradistinction to an imagined "West."

Consequently, choosing to use a "Malay saying" in Malaysia provides speakers with a rhetorical opportunity to position themselves, their interlocutors, or both within a complex identity politics, for multiple purposes and with multiple effects.[7] This applies as much (or perhaps more) to the new public spaces of the media and Internet as to face-to-face social interaction, as I show in some of the examples to follow.

On the other hand, I would not want to give the impression that the role of *peribahasa* in contemporary Malay is solely a matter of the interdiscursive construction of identity and tradition. Though modernizing in many ways, Malaysia is by no means fully converted to Anglo-European modernity. In an earlier work (Goddard 2000), I argued that Malaysia is still characterized by the widespread acceptance of an absolutist approach to ethics and morality, a belief that in all or most situations there is a correct or appropriate (*patut*) way to act that can potentially be known. Hence, Malays place a high premium on obtaining advice (*nasihat*) and guidance (*panduan*) from people such as religious leaders (*iman*), Islamic scholars (*ulama*), government leaders (*pemimpin*), and old people (*orang tua*) generally. In this environment, the proverb genre has a much greater functionality and much higher status than in the contemporary Anglo world.

With this background, let me now examine some Malay proverb texts and comment on some of their uses in context.

Semantic Explications for Some Malay Peribahasa *Texts*

A canonical Malay cultural value is *rendah diri* 'to lower oneself' (Goddard 2000). A common *peribahasa* referring to and reinforcing this value tells people to "follow the way of the rice plant (*padi*)." The analogy, which is sometimes spelled out explicitly, as in (3a), is that the more the rice plant grows full (with grain), the more it bows over. Sometimes the rice plant is contrasted with the useless *lalang* 'long grass'. An online *peribahasa* dictionary gives the explanation in (3b). The English translations are mine.

(3a) *Ikut resmi padi, makin berisi makin tunduk, jangan ikut resmi lalang, semakin tegak tiada berisi.*
Follow the way of the rice plant, the more it grows full the more it bows, don't follow the way of the long grass, as it stands up higher with never anything inside.

(3b) *Hendaklah merendah diri walaupun kita berilmu dan berpangkat dan jangan sombong.*
We have to want to lower ourselves, even though we have knowledge and status, and not be arrogant.

As suggested by the gloss in (3b), the proverb implies that the "fuller content" of a person can involve greater knowledge, as well as higher status or greater capabilities (see Lim 2003: 44). In usage, it is certainly applied to situations where what is at issue is popularity or recognition. For example, on a Malaysian blog, a music fan, commenting on the success of the singer Ning, quoted the "way of the rice plant" saying and then continued in English: "I hope Ning will stay modest if she goes international." By citing the proverb, the blogger seemingly reinforced his discursive identification with canonical Malay values, even though most of the blog was composed in Malaysian English (the unofficial "youth" lingua franca of Malaysia).

In an online interview, a young self-made Malay millionaire was quizzed about his success and about how he wanted to act as a "motivator" for other young Malays.[8] Despite his success, he said he hoped to emulate the low-key style of Bill Gates. Again, invoking this canonical saying enabled the speaker to position himself as a Malay insider still:

(4) *Tetapi di Amerika Syarikat seperti Bill Gates sendiri, dia beri ceramah pakai baju T biasa sahaja. Yang penting kejayaan dia. Saya kalau boleh hendak menjadi seperti resmi padi—semakin berisi semakin tunduk.*
But in the United States, Bill Gates himself, he gives presentations wearing just an ordinary T-shirt. What counts is the person's success. So if I can, I want to adopt the way of the rice-plant—the more it grows full, the more it bows over.

In explication [D], the meaning of the "way of the rice plant" saying is articulated in the same five-part template developed for English metaphorical proverbs. The one difference is the addition of the specification 'in this place' to the TRADITIONALITY framing component (in view of the more highly localized affiliation noted earlier).

The RECURRENT SITUATION starts with someone having certain knowledge and capabilities and an appropriate self-lowering attitude. Subsequent to this, this person comes to know more and to be able to do more. When this happens in life, no doubt many people change their way of thinking, but the PROVERBIAL ADVICE delivered here is that to do so is not good. On the contrary, it is good if the person thinks his or her humble thoughts more often. The PROVERBIAL ANALOGY section sets out the well-known facts about the rice plant.

Another well-known Malay saying alludes to the transparent hypocrisy of people who instruct others in how to behave well while behaving in the opposite way themselves. This saying is *Seperti ketam mengajar (menyuruh) anak berjalan betul* 'like a crab teaching (or: telling) its young to walk straight', sometimes continued as *tetapi diri sendiri berjalan senget* 'but she herself walks crooked'. A *peribahasa* compendium glosses it as *Memberi nasihat pada orang lain padahal diri sendiri tidak betul* 'Giving advice to other people despite being not correct oneself'. Notice that the image in this proverb is not a realistic one, in that no one believes crabs teach their young anything, let alone to walk straight. Compare the English "Like the pot calling the kettle black." An even more dramatic "impossible image" is the English "People who live in glass houses shouldn't throw stones."

[D] Semantic explication for *Ikut resmi padi, (semakin berisi, semakin tunduk)*
'Follow the way of the rice plant (the more it grows full, the more it bows over')

[a] for a long time people in this place have said these words when they want to say something like this: TRADITIONALITY

[b] something like this often happens: RECURRENT SITUATION
at one time, someone knows some things, this someone can do some things
at this time, this someone thinks like this:
"I know some things, not many things, I can do some things, not many things
I am not someone above other people, I am someone below other people"
some time after this, this someone knows more, this someone can do more

[c] when it is like this, it is not good if this someone doesn't think like this anymore PROVERBIAL ADVICE
it is good if this someone thinks like this more often

[d] it is like this: PROVERBIAL ANALOGY
after a *rice-plant has some *rice-seeds, it *bows over
[i.e. the top of it is below the place where it was before]
after the *rice-seeds are big, it *bows over more

[e] many people have lived for a long time STATUS AS FOLK WISDOM
because of this, these people know many things
this is one of these things
it can be good for someone if this someone thinks about this at some times

As one might imagine, the "crab teaching its young" proverb finds plenty of application in the political sphere. For example:

(5) *Di manakah letaknya maruah orang Melayu? Ke manakah perginya budi bahasa? Barangkali Datuk Seri Rais Yatim ada jawapannya . . . janganlah kita menjadi ketam yang mengajar anaknya berjalan betul; mengajar rakyat berbudi bahasa sedangkan pemimpin2 biadap dan kurang ajar!* Where has the dignity and self-respect of the Malays been put? Where has proper behavior gone? Maybe Datuk Seri Rais Yatim has the answers... Let's not be the crab that teaches its young to walk straight; instructing the public to be well-mannered while the leaders are discourteous and ill-bred!

In this example we see a *peribahasa* being employed seemingly for twofold effect. The topos is itself the (legendary) "dignity and respect" of Malays, which according to the writer is under threat by uncivil behavior by some in high places. By employing the canonical Malay saying, the writer manages to advocate his position from the platform of collective agreement and at the same time avoid direct criticism of his implied target. For reasons I have discussed elsewhere (Goddard 2000), direct public criticism is difficult in Malaysia. The proverb genre, as long observed, enables a "depersonalization" of discourse. Such depersonalization, however, is not relevant to all uses of this proverb. In example (6), the target of the criticism is the impersonal "West":

(6) *Itulah sikap Barat terhadap Islam—mereka menilai bahawa ideologi merekalah yang terbaik, tetapi pada hakikatnya mereka ini tidak ubah seperti ketam yang menyuruh anaknya berjalan dengan betul.*
So this is the attitude of the West towards Islam—they believe that their ideology is superior, but as a result they won't change, like the crab that tells its young to walk straight.

Coming now to the precise message content, I believe that this Malay proverb text lacks any direct PROVERBIAL ADVICE. It gets its "sting" simply by depicting a certain undesirable recurrent situation. A couple of points of detail in the RECURRENT SITUATION section of explication [E] are, first, that the person being criticized is someone "higher" than other people (as suggested by the image of a mother or father crab and its young, and by the verbs *mengajar* 'teach, instruct' and *menyuruh* 'tell to do, instruct') and, second, that the hypocritical attitude is presented as being obvious to everyone ('other people can know ... they can't not know'). The latter element is implied by the PROVERBIAL ANALOGY with the crab. Everybody knows that a crab doesn't walk straight; in fact, 'people can't not know this'.

For a Malay saying that lacks a proverbial analogy, consider example (7). The need for verbal caution is a canonical theme of traditional Malay culture (Goddard 2000). Variant forms include *Tersilap cakaplah binasa badan* 'from a slip of speech, the body suffers', and *Binasa badan telajak lidah* (or: *bahasa*) 'the body suffers when the tongue (or: speech) overshoots the mark'.

(7) *Ingatlah sebelum berkata-kata ... ibarat kata ... binasa badan kerana mulut.*
Think before you say anything ... as the saying goes ... the body suffers on account of the mouth.

[E] Partial semantic explication for *Seperti ketam mengajar anak berjalan betul* 'like a crab teaching its young to walk straight'

[b] something like this often happens: RECURRENT SITUATION
someone is above someone else
this someone says something like this to this someone else about some things:
"when you do things like this, I want you to do it in one way,
it is not good if you do it in another way"
other people can know that when this someone does the same things,
this someone does these things in this other way
other people can't not know this
it is not good if someone is like this

[d] it is like this: PROVERBIAL ANALOGY
everyone knows that a *crab doesn't ever *walk *straight
people can't not know this

This saying might seem to employ metaphorical wording, but although the body (*badan*) stands for a person and the mouth (*mulut*) stands for this person's words, this is as far as it goes. There is no implicit analogy about a real body suffering on account of a real mouth (see Box F).

[F] Partial semantic explication for *Binasa badan kerana mulut* 'The body suffers because of the mouth'

[b] something like this often happens: RECURRENT SITUATION
someone says something to someone else
it can be something very small
this someone does not think about it well before
afterwards something very bad happens to this someone because of this

[c] because of this, it is not good for someone if this someone PROVERBIAL ADVICE
says something when this someone has not thought
about it well before

From this exegesis of a few Malay proverbs, the value of the reductive paraphrase technique should be clearer. With familiar English proverbs, it is all too easy to believe that the message content is simple and obvious. When we encounter proverbs from a different culture, sometimes making reference to unfamiliar analogies (with rice plants, crabs, etc.) and often embodying value orientations different from our own, the cognitive complexity and semantic compression of proverbs becomes more evident. Although the small number of examples considered in this chapter prohibits any far-reaching generalizations, it seems likely that, as White (1987: 152) expressed it, "the fact that proverbs represent generalized knowledge, applied in the interpretation of particular events, suggests that they may tell us something about enduring models of cultural experience."

Concluding Remarks: Proverbiality, Semantics and Indexical Meaning

Proverbs are ritualized communication in miniature. In this chapter I have endeavored to combine what are sometimes called "textual" and "contextual" approaches and to show that the two are not incompatible, let alone antithetical. On the textual side, I have tried to show that proverbs in English and Malay have determinable semantic content. This semantic content is substantial in its "volume" and complex in its internal structure. It cannot be accurately represented in a conventional gloss, but it can be pinned down and articulated by way of extended reductive paraphrases (explications). In general terms, this result parallels Ameka's finding (1987, 2006, this volume) that linguistic routines in different languages have rich and culture-specific semantic content that goes far beyond their social and phatic functions. More specifically, by establishing the viability of a particular semantic template for proverb explications, I have sought to disclose the internal meaning structure of the proverb genre: how the individual message content is embedded in a semantic frame that presupposes and projects a claim to traditionality and wisdom, and how the message content itself has a substructure involving (in the maximum case) identification of a recurrent situation, advice about what it is good to do in such situations, and a supporting analogy based on a scene from everyday life.

On the contextual side, I have attempted to shed light on the ways in which the semantic content of proverb texts and the semantic framing of proverbiality (as capturable in paraphrases) tell only part of the story about the significance of proverb usages in social interaction. Semantic (symbolic) meanings are irrevocably intertwined in discourse with indexical meanings. I hope that my culture-historical comparisons of contemporary English and contemporary Malay have made it abundantly clear that proverbiality can be interdiscursively positioned in radically different ways in varying culture-historical contexts and social formations. Ritualized communication is positioned differently under different ideologies of interdiscursivity. It follows that proverbs in different communicative contexts offer their users not only a remarkable expressive resource but also varying creative possibilities for positioning themselves, their utterances, and their interlocutors.

Appendix

*Semantic Primes, English Exponents**

Substantives: I, YOU, SOMEONE, SOMETHING/THING, PEOPLE, BODY
Relational substantives: KIND, PART
Determiners: THIS, THE SAME, OTHER/ELSE
Quantifiers: ONE, TWO, SOME, ALL, MUCH/MANY
Evaluators: GOOD, BAD
Descriptors: BIG, SMALL
Mental predicates: KNOW, THINK, WANT, FEEL, SEE, HEAR
Speech: SAY, WORDS, TRUE
Actions, events, movement, contact: DO, HAPPEN, MOVE, TOUCH
Location, existence, possession, specification: BE (SOMEWHERE), THERE IS, HAVE, BE (SOMEONE/SOMETHING)
Life and death: LIVE, DIE
Time: WHEN/TIME, NOW, BEFORE, AFTER, A LONG TIME, A SHORT TIME, FOR SOME TIME, MOMENT
Space: WHERE/PLACE, HERE, ABOVE, BELOW, FAR, NEAR, SIDE, INSIDE
Logical concepts: NOT, MAYBE, CAN, BECAUSE, IF
Intensifier, augmentor: VERY, MORE
Similarity: LIKE/WAY

*Primes exist as the meanings of lexical units (not at the level of lexemes). Exponents of primes may be words, bound morphemes, or phrasemes. They can be formally complex. They can have combinatorial variants (allolexes). Each prime has well-specified syntactic (combinatorial) properties.

Notes

My thanks to Anna Wierzbicka for many helpful discussions and suggestions. Anna Gladkova and Zhengdao Ye also made valuable suggestions about the explications. My fellow participants at the Wenner-Gren symposium "Ritual Communication" made numerous valuable suggestions on an earlier version of this chapter, which led to substantial additions. I am particularly indebted to Richard Bauman for a number of ideas presented in the introductory section, and to Felix Ameka. Three anonymous reviewers and the editors of this volume provided further helpful input. This research was supported by the Australian Research Council.

1. According to various authorities, the following are "modern proverbs": "What comes around goes around"; "If anything can go wrong, it will"; "Shit happens"; "Garbage in, garbage out"; and "Those who can, do; those who can't, teach." On linguistic evidence, however, these do not qualify as proverbs because they are not referred to as such in ordinary speech. Nor do they qualify as old sayings.

2. Many maxim-style proverbs, and presumably the genre itself, were popularized (if not originated; see Taylor 1962 [1931]: 75) by Benjamin Franklin in his *Poor Richard's Almanac* (1733–1758). For example: "Where there's a will, there's a way," and "Nothing ventured, nothing gained." Franklin also popularized some important figurative proverbs, including "The early bird catches the worm," "A rolling stone gathers no moss," and "All that glitters is not gold."

3. Explications composed in a limited vocabulary of simple words do not, of course, sound like everyday speech. They may be clear and comprehensible, but for many readers they will be unfamiliar in style. Indeed, there is a strong intertextual dissonance between the simple wording of NSM explications and the complex, high-register vocabulary of most academic writing, particularly writing with the linguistic virtuosity and conspicuous intellectualism of much current linguistic anthropology. As with any new genre and register, a period of familiarization and stylistic habituation is usually necessary before these dissonance effects subside.

4. "Too many cooks spoil the broth" is sometimes said to have an antonym in "Many hands make light work." Notice therefore, that the RECURRENT SITUATION and PROVERBIAL ADVICE in explication [B] would not apply to the prototypical situations for "Many hands make light work," that is, sharing a "distributed" physical task such as moving a heavy load.

5. Of course individual proverbs can have distinctive chronotopes and invoke idiosyncratic indexicality effects. Some people are aware, for example, of Benjamin Franklin's advocacy of certain proverbial sayings associated with the ethos of hard work, self-reliance, enterprise, and so forth (see note 2). A different kind of indexical association—namely, a kind of local affiliation—

was mentioned by Sherzer (2002: 59), who observed that in the Texas legislature, legislators sometimes used folksy proverbs about Texas wildlife, flora, and agriculture in their speeches, "in order to be seen as more rural and traditional—and also to be purposely funny—even if they are actually urban attorneys."

6. The contexts for these Internet examples are rather attenuated, insofar as the response from the readers or listeners is unclear. The same applies to proverb usage in mass media statements by politicians and political commentators and in popular culture products such as films and cartoons. All are radically decontextualized from face-to-face encounters. As Winick (1998: 8) pointed out, it is hardly possible to analyze such uses if the face-to-face encounter continues to be taken as the "normative speech event."

7. Many older English proverbs use (or used) biblical language: "Who sows the wind will reap the whirlwind"; "No man can serve two masters"; "The love of money is the root of all evil." When the sources of such words are recognizable to speakers, they carry resonances of faith, religion, and shared identity. Not surprisingly, in view of the role of Islam as a marker of Malay identity and the resurgence of conspicuous public piety, Koranic sayings are currently enjoying an upsurge in Malaysia.

8. The sources of the Malay examples (4)–(6) are as follows, all accessed December 29, 2006: www.rahsiainternet.com/media/mingguan.htm; http://kadirjasin.blogspot.com/2006/09/peluang-dan-cabaran-kekalahan-dr.html; http://tintapermata.blogspot.com/2005_10_02_tintapermata_archive.html.

five

Access Rituals in West African Communities

An Ethnopragmatic Perspective

Felix K. Ameka

> Semantic analysis must be integrated with ethnographic information if we want to provide an adequate pragmatic analysis of speech activities within and across speech communities.
>
> —Alessandro Duranti, "Universal and Culture-Specific Properties of Greetings"

One can think of access rituals as verbal and nonverbal communicative acts that mark boundaries at the beginning and closing phases of social interaction. Goffman (1967, 1971) classified greetings and farewells as access rituals because "greetings mark the transition to a condition of increased access and farewells to a state of decreased access" (Goffman 1971: 79). Levinson (2006a, 2006b) suggested that access ritual activities were among the ethologically grounded behavioral proclivities driven by cognitive predispositions for human interaction "that are at source independent of variations in language and culture" (Levinson 2006b: 40). Even though access rituals have generally been subsumed under greetings and farewells, and the former have been privileged in many cases over the latter (e.g., Duranti 1997; Firth 1972), I argue that greetings and farewells stricto sensu are components of opening and closing access rituals and are not coextensive with them. These access rituals are forums in which members of various communities of practice "enact through linguistic practices cultural ideologies of . . . [e.g.] inequality in West Africa" (Foley 1997: 359).

Ethnographic and sociolinguistic accounts of "greetings" in some West African societies have pointed to the enactment of an ideology of inequality in which participants with inferior status assume the role of initiator of greetings, with its possible manipulations and attendant responsibilities (see, e.g., Goody 1972 on Gonja and Lodagaa; Irvine 1974 on Wolof; Schottman 1995 on Baatombu; Youssouf, Grimshaw, and Bird 1976 on Touareg). However, in some other West African communities that are also status conscious but not as stratified, the ideology of inequality seems not to be acted out in greetings or, more generally, access rituals. Even in these celebrated cases, interactional asymmetry is just one among many other values. Thus Perrino (2002) found that in Wolof ethnomedical greetings, inequality was enacted but was "tempered" by a projection of intimacy. I demonstrate later in this chapter that in several communities of practice along the West African coast, other cultural values are played out in the performance of access rituals. These include hospitality, interdependence, harmony, and inclusiveness. For reasons of space, I use Ewe-speaking communities as the prototype and draw parallels with practices in other communities, such as Akan and Ga. My discussion is based on participant observation, ethnographic interviews, and recorded texts from different communities of practice. With respect to Ewe, I also draw on my native knowledge of these communicative practices.

The aims of this chapter, then, are manifold. First, I want to show that greetings and farewells are parts of, rather than being, the conventional openings and closings of social interactions. Openings and closings are phases in interaction in which mutual access is negotiated, and they are made up of several act sequences (see Schegloff 1968). Second, I want to demonstrate that even though the boundaries of social encounters are marked through ritual communicative acts, these ritual acts do not have just social (e.g., acknowledgment) and phatic functions. They have rich illocutionary meanings that can be analyzed and represented in a rigorous fashion using, for example, the methods and modes of representation of the Natural Semantic Metalanguage framework (see, e.g., Ameka 1999; Goddard 1998; Wierzbicka 2003). A third aim is to characterize expectations, norms of interaction, cultural ideologies, and values with respect to access rituals and modes of interpreting them in cultural or ethnopragmatic scripts (see, e.g., Goddard 2006; Goddard and Wierzbicka 2004).

A fourth goal is to address a specific issue concerning routinized greeting questions and their answers. Much theorizing about the ritualistic nature of greetings, and especially about greeting questions, has concentrated on an Anglo and Western attitude toward such questions. In English, it has been argued that "How are you?" is not a question but a greeting (Leech 1983). Some writers, including Sacks (1975), have demonstrated that such questions are preferentially answered by lying. Wirerzbicka (2003) argued that "How are you?" is a Pollyanna question that has to be answered positively. I show that in some cultural linguistic groups in West Africa, greeting questions are genuine questions that have to be faithfully and felicitously answered.

The complexity of openings and closings everywhere depends on several factors, including the period of absence, the status and age of participants, and, importantly, the type of encounter and associated sociocultural conventions. Therefore, in the following section I outline different types of encounters that may occur between interlocutors in West Africa. Next, I describe a particular type of encounter—a social visit—drawing out its constitutive factors and elucidating the linguistic routines that may be used in such situations. I then focus on a variety of conventional opening acts for negotiating interaction, arguing that "greetings" are but a subcomponent of openings. I claim that the enactment of well-being inquiries is an avenue for displaying cultural values such as inclusiveness and harmony in West African communities, and I show that expectations about the questions vary cross-culturally. Finally, I consider changes due to cultural contact in the norms associated with greeting behavior in West Africa and conclude by reflecting on the relationship between access routines and ritual communication.

Toward a Typology of Encounters

Interactions between people who do not live in the same place may occur as chance meetings or as planned encounters. Chance meetings occur just because the interlocutors happen to be in the same place at the same time. Their paths cross as they go about their individual activities. This implies that chance meetings take place between interactants, either as individuals or as groups, none of whom could be said to be at their place of abode or work. In West Africa, encounters of this kind occur between people who meet in the street, in the neighborhood, at the riverside, on the way to the market, to the farm, to school, and so forth. Such meetings are usually brief and involve, minimally, the exchange of greeting routines. They can be accompanied by brief general conversations. They could also develop into a sort of "purposeful" encounter in which the interlocutors retire to a spot with some shade and exchange news, ideas, or gossip.

Planned meetings, on the other hand, have a defined social or transactional purpose. In this case one can identify two or more participants or groups of participants: a host, who is construed to be at "home" either in reality or at least functionally (Naden 1980, 1986), and a visitor or visitors, who are not at home or do not function as such. Thus a trader in the market, a teacher at school, and a farmer on the farm are all functionally at home. A customer in the market and a visitor to the school or farm are not at home. Such encounters may vary in their level of formality (Irvine 1979), their length and content, and, above all, their purpose.

In the West African context, one person can visit another for the purpose of paying respect to neighbors and relatives or to exchange greetings and just check on the well-being of others. Thus the Ewe utterance in (1) can be used either as a parting expression or as an answer to the question, "Where are you going?"[1]

(1) *me-yi má-dó gbe ná asímasí má-vá*
1SG-go 1SG: POT-put voice to so-and-so 1SG: SUBJV-come
I am going to greet So-and-So, and I'll be back.

Similarly, one can visit another to express one's best wishes to a new parent or a sick person, offer condolences to a bereaved person, or give thanks to a benefactor. The cultural importance of visits as an interactional habit of members of West African communities is enshrined in traditional sayings such as the following ones in Ewe:

(2a) *nɔví-kpɔ́-kpɔ́-é nyé nɔví-wɔ-wɔ*
Sibling-RED-see-FOC COP sibling-RED-do
Seeing (visiting) friends is making friends.

(2b) *Afɔ mé-gblḛ́-á ame dome o*
foot NEG-spoil-HAB person between NEG
Lit.: foot/leg does not spoil relations between people
Going by foot to visit people does not destroy friendships/relationships.

These social visits can be of varying lengths. They might be "flying" visits, in the sense that the visitor comes around to say hello and soon departs, or they might be "sitting" visits, in which the visitor accepts a seat from the host and spends some time with him or her. Sitting visits may be for the exchange of news or for some economic transaction, such as the visitor's wanting to negotiate a loan from the host.

Each of the interactions is defined by or has cultural-situational frames. To provide a frame for looking at access rituals, I next concentrate on social "sitting" visits, characterizing the act sequences that make up the opening, central, and closing phases. An "exchange of news" event in which a visitor goes to a host with the specific purpose of giving him or her a piece of news is taken as an example.

A Frame for a Social Visit

I adopt the SPEAKING model proposed by Hymes (e.g., 1968, 1972; see also Duranti 1985; Saville-Troike 2003) in the description of a speech event of news exchange. We can assume that the setting of this event is a compound house with seats in the courtyard (and children playing around). The participants are a host and a visitor. Each of them may assume the role of speaker or addressee in the act sequences that constitute the event. In addition, there may be a spokesperson for each of the host and visitor or just one person acting as spokesperson for both parties. The spokesperson serves as an intermediary (or channel) through whom messages are sent from one party to the other. The addressor may whisper the content of his thought to the spokesperson, who frames it in good language and verbalizes it to the addressee (or through the addressee's spokesperson). Alternatively, the addressor-speaker invites the spokesperson to pass on the information while he says the message for the hearing of the addressee (and his spokesperson). During social visits of this kind, the second option is usually adopted (on triadic communication in West Africa, see Ameka 2004; Ameka and Breedveld 2004; Yankah 1995; and references therein). I now turn to the sequences of acts that make up the speech event of news exchange, focusing on the boundary acts that are used to ask for and grant access and to terminate access. The enactment of these involves adjacency pairs and, in most cases, standardized expressions.

Opening Sequences

The opening sequences in the speech event include attention-calling, the welcome, the offer of a seat, the offer of water, the host's identification of the visitor, and an exchange of greetings. Some of these are required, and others are optional.

Attention-Calling The visitor initiates the action by attracting the host's attention outside the house. The visitor uses vocative and hailing routines such as *agoo* 'I want you to know I am about to do something'

(Ameka 1994); *kɔ́kɔ́kɔ́kɔ́* 'ideophone copying the sound of knocking on the door'; and a phrase such as *mi-le é-me-a?* 'Are you (pl) inside?" Nonverbal signs such as physically knocking or clapping at the gate may also be used. The effect of this act is to draw the host's attention to the visitor. It also helps the addressee ascertain whether the host is available or not.

If the host (or someone in the host's home) is available, he or she gives an appropriate response to the hailing routine—for instance, *amee!* 'I want you to do what you say you want to do', the standard response to *agoo;* the answer particle *ehẽ́* 'yes'; or any expression that signals "come in," such as the Ewe *gé ɖé é -me* (lit. 'drop toward its inside'), "come in."

Welcome This is an optional move, and its execution depends on where the visitor is coming from. If the visitor is from the same village or neighborhood, then there is no need for this act. If the visitor has come from another village or is perhaps returning from work or the farm, then the host welcomes him or her. The routines used include the interjectional expressions *a..túúù* 'We embrace each other'; dz*áà* 'I am very happy to see you'; *wò / mìawó-é zɔ* 'YOU (sg/pl) walked!'; *wò / mìawó-é de* 'YOU (sg/pl) have been and back'; and *ɖó afé* 'reach home' (see Ameka 1992, 1994 for their semantics).

Seat Offer Immediately after the visitor enters the compound, he or she is offered a seat. In this respect Ewe practice differs from that of the Ga. In Ga practice, according to Kropp Dakubu (1981, 1987), the visitor is seated and offered water only after the initiation of greetings. The verbal routines used in Ewe to offer the seat are usually variations on the idea that there is a seat for the visitor. These routines are usually accompanied by a pointing gesture: *zi le mia té* [chair be.at 2PL under] 'There is a seat/chair under you'; *zikpui / nɔfé li* [chair/ seat be.at: 3SG] 'There is a chair/seat'. The visitor can decline the seat if this is a passing visit, and then the offer of water will also be omitted. If a host does not offer the visitor a seat, the visitor may interpret it as a sign of being unwelcome. Thus, even though this may be an automatic ritual, its non-occurrence when it is expected is loaded.

Offer of Water This act depends on whether the visitor is a traveler or not—whether she or he has come from some other village or is just visiting from the same village. When the visitor is offered water, she or he pours a little bit on the ground and then drinks the rest. The pouring of water on the ground is done as an offering to ancestors and to ask for peace in the transactions that follow. Traditional prayer in West African communities is always accompanied by the pouring of some liquid, whether alcoholic or simply water, on the ground as an offering to God and the ancestors. Hence one could argue that when the visitor pours some water on the ground, it is a kind of prayer. Even if the visitor is not thirsty, she or he must take a sip of the water before giving it back. It is considered bad manners to reject the offer of water without performing these rituals.

Identification There is a phase in the opening in which the host identifies the visitor by the use of special address terms that place the visitor in the lineage, generation, or social category to which she or he belongs. For instance, in several Ewe communities of practice, this identification makes reference to the day of the week on which the person was born. These identification terms in the context of access rituals are a recognized category in Ewe called *dzedzeŋkɔ́* 'salutation name'. This is similar to a category of names used in greetings in some Central and East African communities, such as among the Luo, who label it *empaako* (Byakutaaga 1991; Ndoleriire 2000: 278–280). Typically, in Akan communities the address term for identification relates to the origin or lineage of the interlocutors, especially clan affiliation. In the context of a social visit this move may also include a real question about the visitor's identity. The position of this move in the sequence is relative. It may occur immediately before the exchange of greetings, or it may occur earlier.

Exchange of Greetings After the preliminary acts of attention-calling, welcome, and offers of a seat and water, the interlocutors are ready to exchange greetings. The Ewe folk label for this is *gbe-lɔ̃-lɔ̃* 'voice-intertwining'. This label is instructive, for it suggests that the turn-taking among greeting participants is viewed as the interweaving of their voices, as is evident in the sample greeting exchange that follows. Perrino (2002: 239) reported a similar image for Wolof greetings, which were said to be "like a braid."

The greeting itself may be preceded by a pre-greeting sequence. If it is performed, it may be initiated by either the host or the visitor. When the visitor initiates it, its purpose is to alert the host and seek permission, as it were, to greet him. An adjacency pair for a pre-greeting initiated by a visitor is the following:

(3) Visitor:	*má-dó*	*gbe*	*ná*	*mi*	*ló!*
	1SG: SBJV put	voice	to	2PL	UFP
	May I greet you!				
Host:	*yoo,*	*gbe-a*		*né-vá*	
	Okay,	voice-DEF		JUSS-come	
	Okay, let the greeting come!				

In essence, the host's response acknowledges his or her preparedness to receive the greeting. When the host initiates the move, the same utterance without the assent-giving signal *yoo* is used. Another routine expression used to invite greeting exchange is *mí-lɔ̃ gbe* [1PL-weave voice] 'let's greet'. Either the host or the visitor can proffer this when the two are ready for this phase of the interaction. The other participant simply acknowledges it.

After the pre-greeting sequence, the visitor initiates a series of greeting acts. In this case, Ewe practice is similar to that of the Ga, among whom greetings are initiated by the visitor (Kropp Dakubu 1987: 508). However, Ewe practice may be different from what obtains in other West African societies, such as the Gonja (Goody 1972: 40), the Bisa (Naden 1980), and the Baatombu (Schottman 1995), among whom it appears that hierarchical status in terms of age or office determines who initiates the greeting exchange.

Greeting exchanges in Ewe are made up of a series of speech act sequences. These may be broadly divided into greeting, "how-are-you," and thanking sequences. The greeting sequence is made up of routines referring to the time of day, such as *ŋdí* 'morning' or the adapted word *mɔ́ni* 'morning' and *ŋdɔ* 'afternoon'. The how-are-you sequence consists of several question-and-answer pairs during which the interlocutors in turn ask about the well-being of each other, their relatives, parents, children and the people in the household they belong to, or the people at the place they have been associated with just before the interaction, such as fellow travelers (see Agblemagnon 1969: 57ff.). The thanking or "gratitude" segment of the greetings exchange is present in other West African communities as well. The expressions used in enacting it are based on "thanks for yesterday" and "thanks for the other day" formulas that have become routinized as parts of daily greeting rituals (Ameka 2006). They are used to acknowledge the services that people render to each other daily by virtue of being part of the same community. The Ewe expressions are:

(4) *Etsɔ/nyitsɔ/gbaɖégbe* *fé* *dɔ́*
Yesterday/day.before.yesterday/the.other.day POSS work
Thanks for yesterday/the other day.

As part of the routinization, the expressions may be reduced in syntactic complexity or in lexical or phonological form. In Ewe, for instance, in the greeting context, the full forms of the expressions in (4) may be reduced to just the temporal nouns. Furthermore, the nominals in the expression *etsɔ fé dɔ́* 'yesterday's work' may be compounded to form *dɔ̌–tsɔ* 'work-yesterday' and used in the greeting context.

A further indication of the ritualization of these expressions in the greeting context is that they do not elicit any of the standard responses to gratitude expressions (Ameka 2006). Rather, they are responded to by echoing the expression. The echo response shows that the speaker wants to say the same kind of thing back to the addressee as a return greeting.

Another set of expressions used in the gratitude segment of greetings emphasizes the continued support that members of the community give to each other. These expressions incidentally use the second person plural pronoun as the subject, namely, *mia-wó-é le dɔ dzí / wɔ-ḿ* lit. 'YOU (PL) are working' and *mia-wó-é le ame ta/dzí kpɔ́-ḿ* lit. ' YOU (PL) are looking after people'. Such expressions are responded to with *yoo, mia-wó hã* [Okay 2PL-PL also] 'Okay, you too' or simply with *Máwú-é* 'it is God'. The former response acknowledges the participants' mutual involvement in the good things that are supposed to have been done. The latter shifts the responsibility for the things to an external divine being, reinforcing a communal cultural belief that things that happen to people are brought about by supernatural beings such as God (Ameka 1987, 1994). Thus, even though it is ritualistic, this enactment and its choice of expressions reinforce not only ideologies of gratitude, communality or inclusiveness, and interdependence but also religious belief in God and a view of the causality of things that happen in the world.

There are two modes of interweaving the greeting exchange in Ewe. In one, the initiator posits a proposal, and the interlocutor responds in one move and then follows it with a second move in the same turn by positing a question or proposition. The next turn consists of similar moves by the other interlocutor. Thus, the pattern in terms of moves is A BB AA BB AA BB, and so forth. This is the mode employed in the inland Ewe dialects. An example of this pattern in greeting during a chance meeting on the street is the following:

(5a) Inland Ewe greeting exchange pattern:

A: *ŋdí* *loo!*
Morning UFP
Good morning.

B: *ŋdí*
Morning.
afé-á *me* *ɖê?*
house-DEF containing.region Q
Morning, how is the house/how are the people at home?

A: *Wó-dɔ̌*
3PL-spend.time
Mì-le *agbe-a?*
1PL-be.at: PRES life-Q
They are fine. Are you well? (lit: They have spent the night. Are you alive?)

B: *Ee!* *Na-vá* *kábá*
Yes 23G: SUBJV-come quickly
Yes, come back early.

A: *Yoo*
Okay.

Apart from the first and final turns in the preceding excerpt, all turns consist of two moves, one in response to the immediately adjacent pair and the other a proposition or a question.

By contrast, in the southern dialects, the pattern is that the initiator remains the initiator through many turns, but at the end of the how-are-you enquiries, the roles are reversed, and the interlocutor becomes the questioner. The pattern is A B A B A B. Consider the following exchange, which follows this pattern (Ameka and Essegbey n.d.):

(5b) Southern Ewe greeting exchange pattern:

Titsa Kɔdzó: *Yoo,* *xɔ* *ŋdɔ* [GREETING SEQUENCE]
Okay get afternoon
Okay, good afternoon to you.

Aƒétɔ́ Gemegá: *ŋdɔ* *goo,*
Afternoon UFP
mɔ́-dzí-tɔ́-wó? [HEALTH INQUIRIES]
way-top-PERS-PL
Good afternoon! How are the people on the road?

Titsa Kɔdzó: *Wó-dɔ́*
3PL-spend.time
They are fine.

[INTERRUPTION]

Afétɔ́ Gemegá:	*Aléké-é,*	*afí*	*ka*	*ne-tsó*	*fífíá?*
	How-FOC	place	CQ	2SG-come.from	now
	How is it? Where are you coming from now?				

Titsa Kɔdzó:	*Me-tsó*	*Ho*
	1SG-come.from	Ho
	I come from Ho.	

[HEALTH INQUIRIES RESUMED]

Afétɔ́ Gemegá:	*ã,*	*Ho-tɔ́-wó?*
	INTERJ	Ho-PERS-PL
	Okay How are the people at Ho?	

Titsa Kɔdzó: *Wó-dɔ́*
3PL-spend.time
They are fine.

Afétɔ́ Gemegá:	*Wó*	*ame-wó?*
	3PL	person-PL
	How are the people?	

Titsa Kɔdzó: *Wó-li*
3PL-exist
They are fine.

Afétɔ́ Gemegá: *Dziwòláwó?*
bear-2SG-ER-PL
Your parents?

Titsa Kɔdzó: *Wó-dɔ́*
3PL-spend.time
They are fine.

Afétɔ́ Gemegá: *Nɔví-wò-wó?*
sibling-2SG-PL
Your brothers and sisters?

Titsa Kɔdzó: *Wó-li*
3PL-exist
They are fine.

Afétɔ́ Gemegá:	*Mie-dɔ́*	*nyúíé-a?*
	2PL-spend.time	well-Q
	Are you well?	[SIGNALING ROLE SWITCH]

Titsa Kɔdzó: *Ee*
Yes.

	Aféme-tɔ́-wó?		[CHANGE TO QUESTIONER]
	home-PERS-PL		
	The people at home?		
Afétɔ́ Gemegá:	*Wó-dɔ*		
	3PL-spend.time		
	They are fine.		
Titsa Kɔdzó:	*Ɖeví-wó?*		
	child-PL		
	The children?		
Afétɔ́ Gemegá:	*Wó-li*		
	3PL-exist		
	They are fine.		
Titsa Kɔdzó:	*Mie-dɔ́*	*nyúíé-a?*	
	2PL-spend.time	well-Q	
	Are you well?		
Afétɔ́ Gemegá:	*Ee*		
	Yes.		
	Wo-é *zɔ* *kékéké*		
	2SG-FOC walk very.much		
	Yes, (we are fine). Welcome, welcome.		
[SIGNAL TO END GREETING PHASE]			
Titsa Kɔdzó:	*Yoo*		
	Okay.		

Propositional questions, as opposed to topic-only questions, are used to signal that a speaker is giving up the role of questioner. Once both have had their turn in the role of questioner, the whole greeting phase is rounded off by the host's welcoming of the visitor once more. The greeting exchange could be accompanied by a handshake, especially if the interlocutors are both male.

The Central Sequence

The middle part of a speech event involving news exchange consists of an inquiry about the purpose of the visit. The folk Ewe label for it is *amanié bɔ́bɔ́* lit. 'recounting of news' (*bɔ́ amanié* 'recount news' is a phrase that has diffused from Akan into Ewe as well as Ga). This segment of the interaction is initiated by the host.

Various combinations of formulas are used. These are illustrated in the following excerpt from Nyaku (1985: 3) involving the use of the spokespersons *Ametefé* and *Tsiami*. The host is named Bokɔ́, using the title for his role as a diviner.

(6a) Bokɔ́:	*Ametefé*	*se-e*	*né*	*wò-a-tu*	
	NAME	hear-3SG	COMP	3SG-SBJV-reach	
	va-vá-lá wó				
	RED-NZER-ER-PL				
(6b)	***wó-nyá-ná***	***hã̰***	***wó-biá-ná***	***amaniɛ́-***	***a?***
	3PL-know-HAB	too	3PL-ask-HAB	news	Q

Ametefe, hear it and pass it on to the visitors. (It is said that) even though one may be aware of it one can still ask. What's the news/mission?

(6c) Ametefé:	*tɔ--nye-tɔ́-wó*		*mie-se*		
	POSSPRO-1SG-PERS-PL		2PL-hear		
	gbe-a	*ɖá-a?*			
	voice-DEF	VS-Q			
(6d)	***bokɔ́***	***bé***	***ye***	***gbɔ́***	***fá***
	diviner	QUOT	LOG	place	become.cool

My friends, have you heard the message? The diviner says everything is peaceful here.

(6e) Tsiami:	*mié-se-e*	...	***miá-wó***		***hã̰***		
	1PL hear 3SG		1PL	PL	too		
(6f)	***mié-le***		***afɔ***	***vɔ̰́***	***áɖéké***	***dzí***	***o***
	1PL: NEG-be.at: PRES		foot	bad	any	top	NEG

We have heard it ... we have also not come with any bad mission.

A number of routines in this excerpt shed further light on aspects of the "inquiry of purpose" component in Ewe social encounters. These expressions are shown in boldface in the excerpt (lines b, d, and f).

One stereotyped phrase used as a pre-question or disclaimer in the inquiry turn is *wó-nyá-ná hã̰ wó-biá-ná* 'even if one knows one (still) asks' (line 6b). This phrase is used as a preface to other inquiring expressions in situations in which the visitor's mission seems predictable because of its context. For instance, in the preceding example, the host is a diviner, so when people come to his place, it can be assumed that they are coming to ask for his services in that role, as is the case with these visitors. Hence it is appropriate that the diviner prefaces his inquiry with this phrase. The phrase is also appropriate in contexts in which meetings are prearranged. In such cases, the host may have had some prior notice of the purpose of the encounter. The force of the expression seems to be, "I am asking the obvious question." Thus this pre-question gives an indication of the scheduled nature of such interactions and is used to establish a common ground for the interaction. In the foregoing example, the pre-question routine is followed by a question:

amaniɛ́-a? 'the news?' The significance of the routine *amaniɛ́-a?* could be paraphrased as follows:

I think you are in this place because you want us to do something together.
I don't know what you want us to do.
I want to know it.
I say: I want you to say what you want us to do (here).
I say it because I want you to say something that would cause me to know it.

The next turn after the host's inquiry is the response, in which the visitor spells out the broad outline of his mission or topic. A final part of the inquiry about the purpose of the visit is that in which the visitor may enquire about any news or business that the host may have at his place. This can be done only after the visitor's mission and purpose have been established. This turn is usually included when the visitor comes from another village. In such situations, the host may recount some of the things that have happened or are in the planning at his village, such as recent deaths and festivities.

The Closing

It appears that in cultures in which the terminal boundaries of encounters are recognized, closings tend to have a tripartite structure: a preclosing phase in which one of the participants signals his or her intention to bring the encounter to a close; a leave-taking phase enacted through various social rituals such as thanking; and the final departure (see, e.g., Aijmer 1996: 59ff; Schegloff and Sacks 1973: 317). In West Africa, too, closings take place in three stages: a permission-to-leave phase; a leave-taking phase that might comprise a formal gesture of leave-taking; and a final departure phase.

The Preclosing When an interlocutor wants to terminate an encounter, she or he cannot do so without first asking permission to leave (Ameka 1999). The request for permission to leave is a genuine one and can be answered positively or negatively. A positive response may be accompanied by other supportive acts such as thanking the visitor for coming and expressing displeasure at having to let him go. If the response is negative, the host signals that he or she would like the visitor to participate in other activities. The visitor can accede to the request and delay departure or may decline and repeat the request, adding a justification for being unable to stay longer. If the visitor agrees to stay, he or she will have to act out the permission-seeking again at the end of the activities that have been introduced into the agenda. This phase is omitted if the meeting is a chance one, and it is minimally realized if the encounter is purposeful but informal. It is obligatory and fairly elaborate if the situation is a formal one, such as a traditional ceremony of name-giving or one of certain types of funerals, marriages, arbitrations at the chief's court, and other events. The following cultural script, presented according to Natural Semantic Metalanguage principles, is proposed to represent the communicative practice of requesting permission before leaving a host (for justification, see Ameka and Breedveld 2004: 172):

[A] Cultural script for permission to leave
[people think like this:]
when I am with someone in this person's place because I wanted to do some things with this person
if I think like this: "I don't want to be here in this person's place anymore"
I have to say something like this to this person:
"I think that there is nothing more you want us to do now
I think that there is nothing more you want to say to me now
if it is like this, I want to be somewhere else a short time after this
I want to do something because of this
I know that I can't do it if you don't say to me 'You can do it'
I want you to say it"

The salience of this preclosing phase of leave-taking in West Africa is reflected in the folk linguistic action labels used to talk about it in different languages—for instance, *srɛ kwan* 'beg way' (Akan), *bí gbɛ* 'ask way' (Ga), *tɔkusú* 'ask road' (Sɛkpɛlé), and *biá mɔ̌* 'ask way, ask permission' (Ewe). It is also reflected in the transfer of this communicative practice to the varieties of English and French used in that part of the world. The phrase *on va demander la route* has become a routine expression in West African French. In Anglophone West African countries such as Ghana, similar standardized phrases are emerging, such as the adjacency pair "Permission to fall out" and the response, "Permission granted." The following fragment is the permission-to-leave phase of the encounter between the visitors and the diviner cited in (6):

(7) Tsiami: ...*fífiá,* *míá-biá* *mɔ̌*
...now 1PL-ask way
...Now, we will ask permission to leave.

Bokɔ́:	*mɔ̌*	*li*	*faa;*	*mià-de*	*afé.me*	*nyúíe*
	way	exist	freely	2PL-reach	home	well
	You may go. Have a safe journey home.					
Tsiami:	*yoo*					
	Okay.			(Nyaku 1985: 9)		

The Leave-taking In some encounters, especially those involving elders and more formal occasions, all present perform a physical gesture to show that the encounter has been completed. The spokesperson is asked to lead them in this. This act occurs after permission has been granted to the visitor to leave. The ritual has at least two stages: a preparatory stage and the performance. The core of the ritual is that all present rise from their seats a little and then sit down again. This act is accompanied by a linguistic gesture said by all at once as they return to their seats. The linguistic noise made is [hɛ̃], depicting the noise associated with sitting down. This action is described in Ewe folk terms as either *así-ɖeɖé zikpui tó* [hand-RED-put chair edge] 'putting hands on the edge of chairs' or *zikpui-lé-lé* [chair-RED-catch] 'holding chairs'.

This leave-taking act is performed in the following manner: First, the spokesperson warns everyone present that the elder is going to pick up his chair. He then states that the elder has gotten up. On hearing this, everyone gets up a little and sits down again. This leave-taking ritual is not part of every encounter, but every "sitting" encounter has the preclosing and departure phase. Thus, for every such encounter there is a formal closure. In this respect, Ewe practice seems to be different from that of the Mampruli of northern Ghana, among whom, according to Naden (1986: 195), "at the end of business, interactants drift apart without any formal closure."

The Departure After the visitor has been granted permission to leave—and if necessary, after the closing ritual has been performed—the host proffers good wishes to the visitor, and the visitor responds. At this point, the visitor and host may shake hands and part. The host may see the visitor off or appoint someone to do this on his or her behalf. The choice of routine expressions at this stage depends on what the host-speaker perceives the visitor-addressee to be doing after the present encounter (see Ameka 1999 for a description of some parting expressions). For instance, is the interlocutor going to his or her home in the same village, to a different village, or to the farm or the market? Is it nighttime, and is the interlocutor going to bed? The encounter finally terminates when the host and the visitor part.

A Variety of Conventional Openers

It is usually asserted of African cultural linguistic groups that they have "a salutation for every conceivable occasion and situation" (Akindele 1990: 3). This comment was made with respect to the Yoruba, but Agblemagnon (1969) made a similar observation with respect to Ewe and compared it with French: "Each occasion in social life has a specific corresponding form of greeting. Instead of the impersonal and non-circumstantial 'bonjour' and 'bonsoir,' Ewe uses specialized formulas" (Agblemagnon 1969: 59, my translation).[2]

Although it is true that there is a special salutation for every event in many African communities, it is an exaggeration to consider all such expressions greetings. They are better seen as expressions used at the entry points of interactions. For instance, *agoo,* mentioned earlier, and its equivalents in other languages, such as *hodi* in Swahili, are openers rather than greetings, although some writers have characterized them as such. There are language-internal arguments for this view. The enactment of *agoo* is not reported in these languages as "X has greeted." In Ewe, for instance, it is not reported as *é-dó gbe* [3SG-put voice] 'He greeted'. Rather, it is delocutivized, and the expression is the content of the locution, as *é-dó agoo* [3SG-put *agoo*] 'He has said *agoo*'. Such an expression is not classified in Ewe together with expressions such as *ŋdí* 'morning' and *è-le agbea?* lit. 'Are you alive?' the enactment of which is reported with *é-dó gbe ná X* 'He greeted X'.

Furthermore, the semantics of *agoo* lacks some of the crucial components of greetings. The expression *agoo* has at least three uses in the West African littoral: to request permission to enter someone's premises, to request silence before a speech or an event,; and to ask for right-of-way. The common denominator of all these is attention-getting. The illocutionary semantics of the expression *agoo* can be paraphrased as follows:

I say: I want to do something.
I want you to know it.
I think I cannot do it if you don't want me to.
I say it because I want you to do something that would cause me to know I can do it.

This paraphrase does not contain some of the elements that I would say are criterial for a greeting; it has nothing to do with expressing good feelings to the addressee (see Wierzbicka 1987 for an explication of the English verb "greet").

Similarly, welcoming expressions such as the Ewe *woé de* lit. 'you have reached' and *woé zɔ* lit. 'you have walked' are not greetings, although they may occur as initial openers or as parts of greeting litanies, as in the long greeting sample quoted earlier (see 5b). Other salutations addressed to people at work, such as *ayikoo!* (Ameka 1994), or dining, such as *así le agba me loo* lit. 'hand in bowl', are interaction openers rather than greetings because it is after such expressions that proper greetings are exchanged. Thus there may be specialized salutations for "almost any conceivable situation," but these salutations do not constitute greetings. Well-being inquiries, however, constitute greetings, and I turn to these now.

Well-being Inquiries

"How-are-you" sequences and well-being inquiries are those turns during any greeting exchange in which the well-being of the interlocutors and their relatives are asked about. These questions may constitute the only opening or greeting turn. Formally, three types of interrogative structures are used in these sequences: propositional questions, signaled in Ewe by the question particle-clitic *=à;* "topic-only" questions, marked by the particle *ɖé,* which may be used to inquire about the well-being of people and places associated with the addressee but not of the well-being of the addressee him- or herself; and a manner content question introduced by *áléké́é* 'How is it?' as used in the earlier greeting sample. This last type seems to have gained greater currency among youths, because it feels like a translation of the colloquial English greeting as well as a popular greeting in Pidgin English, "How now?"

These questions may occur in two positions in the greeting exchange: at the beginning, functioning as conversation openers, or in the how-are-you sequence slot after the initial time-of-day greetings or welcoming routines. The propositional how-are-you questions such as *è-le agbe-a?* lit. 'Are you alive?' and *mìe-fɔ́-a?* lit. 'Have you (pl) risen?' tend to be used between equals and people who are familiar with each other. It is rude for a younger person to inquire about the well-being of an elder using these questions. This is a case in which the status of the interlocutors may determine the choice of the linguistic form used in the interaction.

These questions, unlike the English "How are you?" and "How do you do?" are genuine questions. Leech (1983: 132) quoted Arthur Guilterman to show that the English expressions are not true questions:

Don't tell your friends about your indigestion:
"How are you" is a greeting, not a question.

The English questions do not have to be answered faithfully; one is expected to answer them positively. Note that the response to "How do you do?" is its echo, "How do you do!" These are Pollyanna questions (Leech 1983: 147; and see Wierzbicka 2003 on the meaning of "How are you?" in English). The Ewe how-are-you questions have meanings, and because they can be faithfully answered either positively or negatively, they are real questions. For instance, if a parent greeted a child with the following question,

(8) *è-le* *nyuie-a?*
2SG-be-at: PRES well-Q
Are you well?

a felicitous response could be,

(9) *ao,* *ta* *le* *vé-ye-ḿ*
no head be.at: PRES pain-1SG-PROG
No, I have a headache.

Similarly, if the father of the addressee were sick, and the interlocutor asked about the father's well-being:

(10) *È-tɔ́* *dɔ́* *a?*
2SG-father spend.night.time Q
Is your father well? (lit. 'Did your father sleep/ spend the night (well)?')

a faithful response could be,

(11) *oo,* *é-fé* *lãme* *gblé*
no 3SG-POSS body spoil
No, he is unwell. (lit. 'His body is spoiled')

Contrast these responses with the situation in English, in which such negative responses are unexpected. Although it is possible to respond to "How are you?" in English with a negative answer, this tends to occur in contexts where the speaker indicates that she or he is aware that the negative response is not what is expected. For instance, although one can reply with something like "Lousy" or "I feel terrible," it is usually said in jocular manner to show that the norm is being violated.

One can conclude from all this that the Ewe questions are not only for courtesy but are genuine inquiries about the well-being of others. Their genuineness is also a reflection of the communality and of the inclusiveness themes that are enacted during social interactions. Language users can reflect on the genuineness of these questions. Van Jaarsveld (1988) reported on an experiment conducted in South Africa to test perceptions among Afrikaans-speaking students, on the one hand, and black African students, on the other, of responses to how-are-you questions. The students were asked what they would think if someone answered a how-are-you inquiry with "I have a headache and have no medicine." Among the 74 Afrikaans speakers, 37 thought the responder was looking for sympathy, and 13 believed he was being honest. The 59 black African students were split more sharply in the opposite direction: only 8 thought the response was a plea for sympathy, and 51 considered this an honest answer. For the great majority of the black Africans, then, the question and its answer were genuine and were to be viewed seriously. If this experiment were replicated, similar results would be obtained across various communities in Africa. Van Jaarsveld (1988: 100) quoted a Sesotho speaking informant's reaction to the purpose of these questions: "It gives people the opportunity to indicate their true feelings and circumstances, for example, illness, wanting help, etc." This represents the folk logic that underlies the faithful answers given to how-are-you questions in various African societies. The problems that can ensue when speakers of African languages transfer these understandings of well-being inquiries into English, for example, in intercultural contexts should be self-evident. Saville-Troike (2003: 36) commented: "Non-native speakers of English … complain that native speakers do not really care about the state of their health when they ask *how are you*? The non-natives are not recognising that this question is part of a greeting routine, which by nature has no meaning apart from its phatic function in communication." The claim that "How are you?" has no meaning apart from phatic function can be challenged, but what is at stake is whether the question should be answered faithfully or not.

Kecskes (2003: 112) distinguished between "situation-bound routines" and "situation-bound rituals." The former do not sound sincere, whereas the latter, which occur more often in tradition-oriented societies, are not considered insincere, "because these cultures seem to have agreed to accept the surrogate evidence for the true feeling." He further suggested that situation-bound routines relate directly to situations, participants, and actions, whereas situation-bound rituals relate the situation to other situations or agents. This distinction can be applied to the strategies for answering how-are-you questions. In English-speaking and other societies, the answers are routines that sound insincere, whereas in African societies they are rituals and are not considered insincere. Indeed, in Akan the situation of a positive answer to the question is related to another agent, God. The answer to *wo hõ te sen?* lit. 'Your body is how?'—*me hõ yɛ* 'I am fine'—is invariably prefaced by *Nyame adɔm* 'By God's grace'. Incidentally, such a formula has been adapted into English; sometimes only the preface is used as a response, adapted as "By his grace."

Topic-only greeting questions are asked about a place or a group of people with whom the addressee is associated. Typically, these questions are made up of a noun phrase that optionally ends in the particle *ɖé* in Ewe. An example is the following:

(12) *Mɔ́-dzí-tɔ́-wó* *(ɖé)?*
way-top-PERS-PL Q
How are the people on the road?

When such questions occur initially, they may substitute for either time-of-day greetings or welcome routines or attention getters. However, questions in which only the well-being of people is asked about, and no associated place is explicitly mentioned, cannot occur initially; they must occur after some other greeting expression. It is odd to start a greeting sequence with the question *ɖeví-á-wó (ɖé)?* 'How are the children?' Such a question can occur in the second turn in the greeting exchange, but not as an opener.

Responses to these questions are varied. The common responses are *wó-li* 'They exist' and *wó-dɔ́* lit. 'They have spent the night'. These questions perhaps reflect the questioner's seeking to know something about the topic, and it need not be the addressee's well-being. The well-being interpretation is imposed by the greeting context in which they are used.

I propose the following semantics for *X (ɖé)* greeting questions, where X is a noun phrase headed by a human or a locative nominal:

I am thinking about X.
I want you to know I feel something good toward X.
I don't know some things about X.

I think you might know some things about X (because you have been in the same place).
I say: I want to know something about X.
I say it because I want to cause you to say something that would cause me to know it.

When the question is about people, it is possible to elide the particle, *ɖé*. This happens especially when different groups of people are asked about during the greeting exchange. However, when the question is only about a place, *ɖé* ellipsis is not possible. Thus, in (5a), given earlier, when the questioner asks about the house—a place—the particle is used, whereas in (5b) all the questions are about people, and neither interactant uses the particle.

Using these well-being questions to ask about the addressee and other people and places associated with them is an enactment of an ideology of inclusiveness. Indeed, in many cases, inclusive plural pronouns or collective plural terms are used. Dzameshie (2002) related this to a cultural injunction that people should have care and concern for their fellow human beings (see also Egblewogbe 1990).

Sociocultural and Historical Dimensions

The sociocultural norm among the Ewe is that one should say something acknowledging another when the two come to be in the same place, whether they know each other or not. This explains why there are formulas for almost every conceivable situation, from having a meal to having a bath. In Ewe there is no restriction on who should initiate interactions determined by status in regard to age or office. All things being equal, a young person may greet an elder first or vice versa, and a chief may greet a commoner first or vice versa. In this respect the Ewe are different from other groups among whom the status of interlocutors determines who initiates greetings, such as the Gonja (Goody 1972). However, the "visitor" in general should initiate the interaction. This cultural norm can be spelled out in a cultural script as follows:

[B] Cultural script for interaction
[people think like this:]
if two people come to be in the same place
it is good if they say something of the kind one should say to the other at such a time
if they do this
they cause people to think/know that they are part of the same thing

One general constraint is that someone who is about to do something considered unclean or who is in an unclean condition, even if he or she is construed to have the visitor's role, should not open interactions. It is considered rude and insulting to the interlocutor. Some things considered unclean are going to the toilet or the rubbish dump or having a bath. People handling a corpse or carrying remains of a person should also not initiate interaction. This norm of interaction can be captured in the following cultural script:

[C] Cultural script for constraint on initiating interaction
[people think like this:]
if you come to be in the same place as someone else
if you are about to do something unclean
it is good if you do not say something first to the other person
people think it is very bad to do this

Apart from such contexts, the absence of the exchange of interactional formulas is viewed as a bad situation. The one who considers himself host may ask the other person whether the two of them "got up from the same bed." The reasoning is that if the two people had woken up in the same place, they would have greeted each other already, and so when they come to be in the same place later, they will not need to greet each other again. He might also ask, "Aren't you going to say anything to me?" (see Yahya-Ohtman 1995 on a similar question in Swahili). People who are not on speaking terms are investigated by the community's elders and leaders, and good relations between them are restored after arbitration.

Although these underlying cultural norms of interaction are resilient, the forms and modes of interaction have been affected by communities' contact with other groups. The Ewe, for example, have borrowed the English word "morning," adapted as *mɔ́ni,* and use it as a time-of-day greeting expression. They have also appropriated from English *kuɖími* 'good evening' and *gúdee* 'good day'. All these can be followed by an Ewe addressee phrase such as *ná wò* 'to you'. These English borrowings are used more in chance meetings. They invariably trigger a short form of the greeting. One is less likely to hear them in the context of planned encounters.

A related change is the emergence of a greeting exchange that could possibly be attributed to influence from other sources. In some southern Ewe communities, chance meeting greetings are enacted with the adjacency pair *me-dó gbe* [1SG-put voice] 'I greet' and *me-xɔ gbe*

[1SG-receive voice] 'I receive the greetings'. This could be a calque based on an Akan standard greeting, literally "I greet you." Considering that it has developed in communities close to the Togo border, where speakers might come into contact with French, it could also be a calque of the French *salut*. Whatever the source, the use of borrowed words and this new chance greeting are not looked upon favorably by the older generation.

Another observable change is in bodily gestures, especially those of females. Women show respect in greeting by lowering their bodies, as if about to genuflect and bow slightly. These days women seldom, if ever, lower their bodies in greetings. Both men and women still sometimes practice bowing slightly.

The use of salutation and identification address terms in opening routines has disappeared, especially in urban contexts, and not just among Ewe but also in other communities such as the Akan. The mode of inquiring about such identification terms has been replaced by questions asking for other forms of identification, such as "Who are you?" "Where are you coming from?" and Who is your father?" Some aspects of access rituals are stable, but others are changing in the West African communities.

Concluding Remarks

As people go about their daily activities in various communities of practice, they carry out several communicative rituals. In the foregoing I have looked at rituals for entry into and exit from interactions, especially among the Ewe of West Africa. In their performance, various ideologies are enacted, such as inclusiveness, hospitality, harmony, and communality. Furthermore, there are sociocultural constraints on communicative interaction, some of which I have tried to spell out in cultural scripts. The illocutionary meanings of some of the situation-bound utterances used in these interactions have been explored. For a holistic understanding of interactional ritual, we need to take into account the semantics of the formulas, the cultural constraints on their enactment, and the ideologies and values they embody.

In closing, I want to note some questions that the material discussed raises for our thinking about ritual communication. First, what is *ritual* about the linguistic forms and strategies described? As Richard Bauman asked in his commentary during the Wenner-Gren symposium, is there any reason other than the fact that Erving Goffman (e.g., 1967, 1971) referred to these as access rituals that we want to consider them rituals?

To the extent that they are enacted in culturally defined, predetermined situations, they possess an aspect of ritual. But this raises the question of the relationship between ritual and routine. Furthermore, access routines are ritualistic because of their interdiscursivity. In their enactment, speakers draw on standardized syntactic patterns and formulaic phrases, applying them in conventionalized frames for opening and closing interactions. Moreover, their patterning has metapragmatic function in the sense that they help "interactants inhabit culturally recognizable roles and perform culturally recognizable acts" (Perrino 2002: 229).

Notes

1. In the explication of Ewe utterances, I use the following abbreviations and conventions: COP, copula; DEF, definiteness marker; FOC, focus marker; HAB, habitual aspect marker; INTERJ, interjection; JUSS, jussive; LOG, logophoric pronoun; NEG, negation marker; NZER, nominalizer; PERS, personalizing suffix; PL, plural; POSS, possessive; POT, potential; PRES, present; PRO, pronominal; PROG, progressive; Q, question particle; QUOT, quotative; RED, reduplicative; SG, singular; SUBJV, subjunctive; VS, verb satellite; 1, first person; 2, second person; 3, third person. Tones are marked where relevant as follows: low tone by a grave accent, *à;* high tone by an acute accent, á*;* falling tone by a circumflex, *â;* and rising tone by a hacek, *ǎ*. Nasalization is indicated by a tilde ~ above or below the vowel, e.g. ã or a̰.

2. "A chaque circonstance de la vie sociale, correspond une forme déterminée de salutation. Au lieu du 'bonjour' et du 'bonsoir' impersonnels et non circonstanciels, l'Eve emploie des formules spécialisées."

six

Ritual and the Circulation of Experience

Negotiating Community in the Twentieth-Century Amazon

Suzanne Oakdale

In several Amazonian ritual traditions, biographical narratives merge with autobiographical narratives in ways that are difficult to disentangle according to classic definitions of autobiography and biography. In some cases the narrator assumes the identity of an ancestral figure. In others, the identity of the ancestral figure becomes subsumed and covered over by the identity of the narrator, even though the narrative itself is understood to be in some way biographical and to have been inherited from a member of a previous generation. In each of these types of performances the effect is a kind of "circulation" of experiences and perspectives between subjects from different time periods, distinct communities, or both.

In her discussion of Kalapalo biographies, Ellen Basso (1995) observed that accounts of subjective transformations were central to the way the history of the formation of new moral communities was told among the Kalapalo of Amazonian Brazil. In these accounts, warriors were described as coming to have common interests and perspectives with enemies as they began to view them as members of the same moral community. In her work on Kalapalo "self-cultivation," Basso looked at a variety of ways in which personal experiences were made to reach out to others through a process she called "translation." She suggested that this process might be central to the contemporary shaping of a "wide range of transnational negotiations" (Basso 2003: 85, 97).

In this chapter I look more closely at lowland Amazonian rituals that feature first-person narratives and in which there is understood to be a circulation of a point of view, a kind of translation of experience, between participants and various sorts of "others." To explore more fully how these events have the potential to bring about ideological shifts similar to the sort described in Kalapalo historical narratives, as well as some of their limitations, I focus on moments in which a group of Tupi-speaking Kayabi people have employed shamanic rituals with these features in the context of participating in new communities emerging within the twentieth-century colonization of the Brazilian Amazon.

The Kayabi, like the majority of lowland peoples, have undergone dramatic shifts in population, changes that involved forming new relations among themselves as well as with others. In order to explain how, in these contexts, rituals centering on first-person narrative accounts are understood to have the potential to encourage a circulation or generalization of a point of view, I draw on Greg Urban's (1989) work on the semiotic functioning of the pronoun "I" in narrative discourse, a discussion that itself built on and extended the work of others (Benveniste 1971 [1956]; Ricoeur 1974; Silverstein 1976; Singer 1984). Exactly how the "I" of Kayabi shamanic songs works is discussed here in the context of other Kayabi ritual songs as well as those of other lowland peoples.[1] Turning to particular historical moments, I look at the way shamanic rituals were employed in the formation of alliances made at times in the past century, discussing most fully an account of a shamanic ritual I recorded from one of the best-known twentieth-century Kayabi shamans, a man named Prepori. Prepori recounted how he orchestrated a shamanic ritual in the 1940s that worked to shape the way he and other Kayabi related to the Brazilian Indian Services, then called the Serviço de Proteção aos Índios (SPI). Although his account shows how standard first-person narratives featured in Kayabi shamanic ritual were employed to structure these relations, it also shows how he had to supplement them to bring about a generalization of experience among such diverse audience members as SPI officials and state-level politicians. Ironically, even as Kayabi shamanic ritual was used to structure new kinds of moral communities in the context of the Brazilian nation in both the 1990s and the 1940s, this type of ritual also functioned to display indigenous "culture," so that it simultaneously came to signal the unshared nature of some experiences and points of view.

Types of Discourse "I"

Following Urban (1989), in narrative discourse the "I" occurs predominantly in quotation marks. In some instances this takes the form of a "dequotative 'I,'" a term Urban (1989: 36) used to describe "the 'I' of quotation wherein the matrix clause has disappeared." This is an "I" that works "through a kind of theatrical substitution," pointing to "the speaker not with respect to the speaker's everyday identity or self, but rather with respect to an identity the speaker assumes through the text" (Urban 1989: 27). The imaginary self can function "as a blueprint for the everyday self," that is, as a type of ideal (Urban 1989: 49–50). Especially through fixed texts that are repeated over time, he argued, "the narrative 'I' becomes a genuinely cultural one" (Urban 1989: 49–50). The repetition of fixed texts that include this sort of first person is a demonstration of how the "same point of view, so to speak, can be taken up by different speakers/actors" (Urban 1989: 49–50). This process, therefore, is at the heart of the cultural construction of self (Urban 1989: 27). Moreover, the relationship between the everyday "I" and the "I" of narrative discourse "supplies the ground for sociability" (Urban 1989: 36). I suggest that versions of this "I" of narrative discourse (specifically, versions of the dequotative "I") may be important tools that can be marshaled when the need arises to bring people of different backgrounds to the point of sensing that they, too, can share a point of view, at least provisionally.

In Urban's model, the "I" in narrative discourse can have several relationships with the narrator's everyday self. Urban called the most extreme form of the dequotative "I" the "projective 'I.'" In this case the speaker speaks as though he or she has become merged with the presented character. This is the "I" of trance and possession, in which there is a total immersion within another (Urban 1989: 38). Slightly less extreme is what he called the "theatrical 'I.'" This is an "I" much like that found in theatrical traditions, "in which the individual speaks through the character he or she represents" (Urban 1989: 36). In this case there is role-playing, and the everyday self is hidden, but it is not as fully incorporated into another self as it is with the projective "I" of trance. Texts performed in the case of the theatrical "I" are understood to have been memorized, in contrast to texts in which the projective "I" is found, which audience members understand to be unfolding during the performance rather than to be repeated (Urban 1989: 42).

The sort of "I" that is most interesting to me here is not the fully projective "I" of trance and possession but the sort that is in-between the projective "I" and the theatrical "I." In this type, the narrator has not completely identified with the character he or she is presenting, but there is more subjective transformation and identification than exists in theatrical role-playing. My interest is in ritual texts showing simultaneous subjective engagement and identification with both the everyday self and the self of narrative. I do not look so much at how the "I" moves from an "everyday" to a "theatrical" and closer to a "projective" self and then back again, largely for lack of space (see Rumsey 2000). Rather, I focus on how, for long stretches in ritual songs, the "I" is simultaneously engaged with an everyday self and a radically other narrative self.

The Narrated "I" in Lowland Rituals

Although the relationship between the everyday "I" and the "I" of narrative discourse can be said to form a basis for sociability and the construction of self more universally (Rumsey 2000; Urban 1989), it takes on a specific shape in lowland Amazonian ritual traditions.[2] Likewise, although the assumption of another's narrative of personal experience as a speaker's own is found in a variety of contexts, such as between children and their caregivers (Miller et al. 1990) and among practical jokers (Bauman 1986), participants in many lowland rituals often take up the narratives of subjects who are, in comparison with these examples, extremely "other." The narrated "I" that is taken up in lowland rituals is often one that has been previously inhabited by deceased or mythic ancestors, as well as by enemies.[3] Urban described how, for example, during the narration of the creation myth among the Gê-speaking Xokleng of southern Brazil, narrators shifted from using the third person to using the first person, assuming the personae of the mythic characters themselves. He described how the "narrator frequently lapses into the first person pronoun even in presumably non-quoted portions of the narration" (Urban 1989: 39). This shift went along with subjective and acoustic changes: "The mesmerizing effect of the rhythm, coupled with the intense inward focusing and shutting out of the audience, produces a discourse 'I' that is, consequently, close to the projective 'I' of trance" (Urban 1989: 39). Through this use of first person, the narrator comes to assume the identity of an ancestor and subjectively to embody the continuity of culture (Urban 1989: 45).

Laura Graham (1995) found an even more complete identification with mythic ancestors in the ritual reenactment and narration of dreams among the Gê-speaking Xavante of central Brazil. In the ritual event she focused on, one elder recounted his dreams about interacting with and receiving songs from the mythical "first creators." As he described his dreams, he moved from describing being at a gathering with these figures to actually taking on their perspective. Using the first person, he recounted mythic episodes as if he were one of the protagonists. Shifting into rapid, breathy speech, he moved into Urban's fully "projective I," a state in which his everyday self was no longer present and in which he assumed the persona of a "first creator" (1995: 194), becoming an embodiment of cultural continuity.

In Kayabi ritual song genres, the everyday self also moves toward becoming merged with the personae of ancestors, although in a different way from that in the Xokleng and Xavante rituals discussed by Urban and Graham. This is particularly clear in a nonshamanic genre called *jawosi*. *Jawosi*, performed for a variety of reasons, are first-person songs about encounters with animals, trees, or objects that the audience understands as metaphorically referring to events in which the singer has interacted valiantly with subjects from other ethnic groups (Oakdale 2002, 2005). Details about the trees, animals, or objects, as well as what is known about the singer's background, provide clues to be interpreted by audience members about which ethnic group is being referenced. The majority of *jawosi* songs are also simultaneously understood to have been inherited from paternal relatives and to have referred to similar kinds of events in the lives of past generations of singers as well. When singers described for me how they understood these songs, it became clear that they simultaneously remembered how the songs related to the lives of their dead relatives (those people from whom they had learned the songs) and thought about how they related to their own lives. The lives of previous generations work as types of templates enabling singers to think about their own experiences in a similar form, despite radically changed historical circumstances (Oakdale 2002). The first-person pronoun is the pivot connecting the two.

Much as in the subjective states described for the Gê-speaking narrators, *jawosi* singers appear to turn inward as they sing. Although few singers are considered to be in dream or trance (as in the fully projective "I"), they do seem to have a "faraway" look. The ordinary or everyday "I" for these singers has not, however, been totally eclipsed by the personae of their ancestors. Audience members do not think about the songs primarily as relating to the lives of past singers. For example, audience members seldom even know the provenance of the songs, especially if they belong to a family other than the singer's. Instead, they think about the songs largely in terms of what they know about the life of the contemporary singer. Rather than embodying "cultural continuity," in the sense that past perspectives can be relived and embodied by present people, these songs point to the plasticity of very old, inherited forms, a plasticity that enables them to be meaningful in changed circumstances as the perspectives of ancestors are incorporated into the contemporary perspectives of the singers. Again, however, as in Gê narrative traditions, several selves overlap in these songs, selves that are normally separated by the passage of time.

The Panoan-speaking Yaminahua of Peru also have a song tradition in which inherited first-person songs are considered autobiographical (Déléage 2007). Similarly metaphorical, these songs are understood to relate to the singer's present life rather than to be moments in which the narrator disappears within the persona of another. But again, the "I" in these songs simultaneously refers to the present speaker and to a series of past narrators, presenting what Pierre Déléage called a "traditional I," a form that refers to the whole Yaminahua community, past and present (Déléage 2007: 92). Like *jawosi* songs, these demonstrate the way singers come to embody the somewhat generic ideals of adulthood. As singers move into this non-everyday "I" they undergo subjective transformations, and "powerful sentiments" move them to tears (Déléage 2007: 92).

Anne-Christine Taylor described spirit (*arutam*) quests among the Jivaroan-speaking, Ecuadorian Achuar in which she observed a similar assumption of a biographical template from a member of a previous generation, a template that became infused with the details of the life of the living subject.[4] The seeker of such auditory visions ideally comes to hear a spirit of a dead person who, when alive, was "an exemplary individual" (Taylor 1993: 666). This dead hero transmits to the living subject what Taylor called a "virtual biography," a "memory of a great biography shorn of all its particulars," or a "potential destiny" (Taylor 1993: 666, 667). As in the preceding examples, here again there is a kind of merging of biographies from subjects of noncontemporaneous generations in which the living does not so much disappear into the personae of past subjects as infuse these past personae with details from the present. It is as if the most basic outline of a theatrical script has been adapted for contemporary circumstances and audiences.

In addition to giving the sense that different subjects from distant time periods have come to share a single subjective position, the use of the first person in lowland ritual events can bring narrators into alignment with the "I" of subjects who belong to very different moral communities. Kayabi *jawosi* songs, for example, although understood to be inherited from paternal relatives, are also understood to be sung from the point of view of enemies (Oakdale 2005). The first Kayabi singer to have sung one of these songs is not considered to be the author. Rather, he overhears the song. Songs can be emitted directly from the bones or bodies of dead enemies as well as from virtually anything a singer has confronted while traveling away from Kayabi communities. Many of the songs that recount how a non-Kayabi dies at the hands of a Kayabi warrior are, moreover, sung from the viewpoint of the victim. The singer inhabits the perspective of this other, non-Kayabi person. Sometimes painted like the enemies they are impersonating, singers recount the emotions and thoughts of these individuals before they died. Although the story lines of these songs are just about the least "sociable" ones possible, they do allow singers to "temporarily regard themselves metaphorically as others," and hearers "to similarly participate in this imaginary system" (Urban 1989: 35).

As well as describing the enemy's subjective position as he or she is situated in (a losing) battle with a Kayabi warrior, many of these songs describe Kayabi warriors from the enemy's perspective. Most describe the Kayabi warrior as valiant or a person of renown. One even describes how the victim feels that the Kayabi warrior understands his own thoughts (Oakdale 2005: 126). *Jawosi* songs thus show not only how one role can be taken up by many subjects but also how one subject comes to see himself as an object by inhabiting the perspective of someone else who is very much an other. This narrative form therefore has the capacity to dramatize a type of socially produced self-consciousness in which the subject enters his own experience as an object "by taking the attitudes of others toward himself" (Mead 1956: 245).

Like *jawosi,* songs sung in shamanic cures for soul loss, called *maraka,* also dramatize the way different "enemy" subjects can come to share the same point of view (Oakdale 2005). *Maraka* rituals are three-night-long events in which a shaman sings in the first person about his dream travels in the spirit world as he goes to hunt for his current patient's lost soul. The songs are all sung from the perspective of the shaman as he travels in dream and seem to be much like personal reminiscences or dream narratives in Western traditions. They are, however, considered to be songs authored and sung first by spirits (*mama'e*), entities who can befriend shamans but who largely work for humans' demise. Spirits are jealous of Kayabi life and work to take human souls to their homes, ending their human victims' lives. While sleeping, the shaman overhears these entities' songs and repeats them for his human audience in *maraka* cures. Despite being accounts of the shaman's own travels, the songs are thus available to the shaman only secondhand. He is only the animator of the songs, not their author or principal. In this genre, the spirits first take on the "I" of the shaman, before he himself does.

In *maraka* songs, spirits see their world and themselves from the shaman's point of view, from his position as a visitor to their homes—the reverse of the Gê examples, in which living humans take on the perspectives of mythic characters and bring these characters into the human community. In *maraka,* beings that are akin to mythic ancestors in that they live in distant, normally invisible domains take on human perspectives and bring humans into their world. The spirits' assumption of the shaman's perspective through these first-person songs is also what allows him to experience their world. The shaman comes to understand his own dream experience once he quotes the spirits and takes up their point of view. Only once he hears their first-person *maraka* music and sings it is the shaman able to see their homes and villages. Interestingly, the patient who is a victim of soul loss understands where he or she has been in the spirit world only after listening to the shaman and, in a sense, merging himself or herself with the self of the shaman—who has of course taken the spirits' perspective, who in turn have previously taken the perspective of the shaman in his role as visitor to their homes. Audience members also say they feel as if they share the shaman's experiences as they listen to his songs, commenting that listening to the songs is like going visiting to the spirits' homes (Oakdale 2005).

The "I" of shamans' *maraka* songs comes close to being Urban's "projective I." Shamans are usually understood to be dreaming or sleeping as they sing. Their everyday personae are not only hidden, as in theatrical role-playing, but become partially merged with the spirit entities they are quoting: they become more like dream entities than like the people they are in everyday waking life. In many performances the spirits even come to reside in a shaman's hand or chest while he sings his cure. He is therefore listening to the music of these others as they sing and describe their faraway spirit homes—underwater, at the horizon, or deep in the forest or hills—from a position within his body. *Maraka* songs also describe how the shaman comes to take on the activities and postures of various spirits. They recount how shamans "imitate" the spirits, subtly describe how spirits look, sound, and behave, and then describe the shaman in similar terms (Oakdale 2005). Shamans report that they need to imitate spirits and follow their initiative on these dream voyages. They also point out, however, that they have to maintain some of their own volition while they are dreaming. They warn that if one were to follow the spirits too closely, it would lead to complete incorporation into the spirit world, a state from which no return is possible. In other words, they understand their own position as close to but just short of Urban's "projective I." A fully projective "I" would mean the permanent death of the everyday self.

In *maraka* there is also a choral refrain in which the "I" of the spirits and the shaman is taken on and quoted by yet another group. An all-male chorus repeats each line of the shamanic songs verbatim. These singers, too, report that they come close to having an experience that approaches Urban's "projective I." They say that they are overcome with emotion because of the beauty and brightness of the spirits' world they come to see through repeating the shaman's songs (Oakdale 2005).

In the case of Kayabi *maraka,* the distance between the characters animating the spirit world and the people in the human world of the on-the-ground performance is marked by the use of evidentials. *Maraka* songs employ at various points a tense and evidential marker, *ra'e,* which indicates that the events spoken about happened in the proximate past but that the speaker does not have firsthand, waking experience of the event. *Maraka* therefore bring the shaman and, to a lesser extent, the audience and chorus members close to a full merger with the perspective of spirits but then pull them back slightly short of it.

In the lowland traditions discussed here, these moments of openness to other perspectives are frequently times of musicality and song. In all the examples I have offered, song or speech that approaches musicality is part of the event. Song in the lowlands is also often understood to be a form that originates outside of or beyond humanity (Basso 1985: 70; Graham 1995: 114; Seeger 1987). If song, in these traditions, indicates quotation from other-than-human persons, then it has the potential to situate the singer within a radically distinct sort of perspective by its mere form. If the first person is used, the singer has the potential to become even further merged with or role-play a self very different from the everyday self. In traditions with this sort of ideology about music, however, song also functions as a kind of frame that tells the listener that this piece of communication was quoted, that it could not have been authored by a human narrator. In this respect, these sung forms are not entirely "dequotative," unless the human animator has so entirely become fused with the nonhuman author of the songs that he or she ceases to exist as a distinct entity. For Kayabi shamans this kind of fusion cannot be reversed, and there is therefore always some room, however infinitesimal, for the everyday "I" of the shaman as he assumes the "I" of the spirits.

Each of these lowland rituals, from a wide variety of peoples, presents images of extreme sorts of sociability by featuring the "discourse 'I.'" In many lowland rituals the discourse "I" allows living humans to come to engage at least partially in the perspectives of others who are unusually distant. They take on the "I" of mythic or long-deceased ancestors or of enemies. These kinds of rituals are therefore moments when the immediate community of people who share a way of life is open to subjectively engaging the perspective of very distant, extremely different, and sometimes dangerous sorts of others, at least temporarily. It stands to reason that these types of rituals, when seen more as historical events than as generic types of events (Kelly and Kaplan 1990), could be marshaled to play a key role in the negotiation of new kinds of relations in the dangerous and anxiety-producing situation of being incorporated into a national society.

Maraka Ritual and the Negotiation of New Social Relations

Maraka cures (as well as *jawosi* rituals) are in fact frequently put forward by Kayabi people as a viable means of negotiating new sorts of relations. In the Xingu Indigenous Park, for example, *maraka* rituals have been at the forefront of managing interethnic relations for a long time. The park is a multiethnic reservation encompassing a community of peoples, called the Upper Xinguans, who have resided in the area for hundreds of years, as well as others, some of whom, such as the Kayabi, were relocated to the park in the mid- to late twentieth century. As soon as the Kayabi came to the park, they gained a reputation among other groups, at least in the northern portion, as capable shamans. In general, Kayabi speak about *maraka* cures as one of the most appropriate vehicles for intergroup relations, especially among other Tupi-speakers. Although shamanic curing might be seen as a type of trade specialty, equivalent to the handicrafts produced by other groups in the park, cures can also be conceptualized as a way of making alliances and forming networks of relations, because they generate shared perspectives—the shaman and his spirit-authored, first-person narratives being the keys to the whole process. Rather than a skill to be traded, shamanic cures can be a way of expanding social relationships and sociability by generalizing a point of view.

In negotiating interethnic relations at the national level, this generalization of a point of view is often coupled with requests and expectations by non-indigenous Brazilians that shamans demonstrate "Kayabi culture" or the uniqueness of Kayabi perspectives and experiences. For example, in March 1992 the Brazilian National Indian Foundation (FUNAI) asked the Kayabi residents of the Xingu Park to send a drawing of a "Kayabi flag" and a tape of Kayabi music to represent "the Kayabi" at an event called the "Week of the Culture of Indigenous Brazilian Nations" (Semana da Cultura das Nações Indígenas Brasileiras). The request was addressed while I was at a park post. The director of the post, a Kayabi man, called the chiefs of the two most populous Kayabi villages to come discuss how to fulfill this demand. The three leaders, along with one of their wives and four other young men, decided that the music to send would be a tape-recording of a shaman's *maraka*. One of the men wrote down a few lines of a song and translated them into Portuguese. The flag that the group designed featured, in addition to other colors, red to stand for the red paint worn at "parties" such as *maraka* cures.

The Kayabi in the Xingu Park were relocated from territories far to the west of the park from the 1950s through the 1990s. Previously they lived in three areas that were somewhat isolated from each other along different rivers. Although the idea of a Kayabi nation or ethnicity (*étnia*) is common now (at least among Kayabi leaders communicating on the Internet), in 1992 this kind of unit was much less discussed. The families and clusters of families that came from different areas outside the park and lived in hamlets and villages spread throughout the park seldom seemed to present themselves in terms of this kind of shared community, at least in the contexts in which I was present. Although no one ever explicitly explained the choice to me in this way, it did seem as though *maraka* music was the most suitable type to send to the FUNAI event, because it had the potential to unite the most disparate positions into one shared "ethnic" perspective. It provided a powerful image of the way different perspectives could be unified through the shaman's sung narratives.

Of course in this case, few Kayabi people knew about either the request or the choice of music. The unification of perspectives was only hypothetical. It was a means of generating an imagined Kayabi nation only in the minds of the eight people who discussed the issue. Given that a portion of the *maraka* music was translated into Portuguese, this group might also have thought of the music as a means of generating a unification of perspectives across the indigenous groups and even the FUNAI officials participating in the distant urban event. Along with this possibility, however, was the fact that the music also represented the uniqueness of Kayabi culture vis-à-vis Brazilian national society and the other indigenous groups in Brazil. As the Kayabi flag was being drawn, one of the chiefs remarked, "All over Brazil, Indians are all drawing flags," marking this event, in his mind, as one infused with the cross-time simultaneity that Benedict Anderson (1983: 24) found so characteristic of contemporary nationalism. Through exercises like this one, generalized indigenous difference and a series of mutually exclusive indigenous cultures were being brought to mind at the same time that any sort of shared perspective was being produced.

Prepori's Account of a *Maraka* in Cuiabá

In 1993 I asked the elderly shaman Prepori to tell me about his life or, in more Kayabi phrasing, "where he had traveled." After eluding me for months, he finally consented to be recorded. Rather than the comprehensive life history I had been expecting, he narrated an account only of how he had developed his shamanic skills. In this respect it was similar to accounts shamans narrate before they sing in *maraka* cures, resume-like accounts explaining why the narrator has the authority to sing and cure. In importing this genre to shape the anthropological interview, Prepori was, in a sense, using *maraka* ritual to negotiate interethnic relations. In keeping with the *maraka*'s encouragement of a personal and subjective sense of a shift of perspectives, Prepori also addressed his story to my parents. After asking their names and directing me to translate it for them, Prepori said to my father, via the tape-recording, "Ray, are you hearing, Ray? I am going to make you see." Again ironically, as in the previous examples, as he translated his experience, enabling my father to "see," I was recording Kayabi "culture," those aspects that set Kayabi experience apart from that of me and my family. Rather than discuss the ritual aspects of the performance of Prepori's autobiographical narrative, I focus on a portion of his account that described one of his past *maraka* performances.

Prepori recounted, at one point, how he had used a *maraka* ritual to structure interethnic relations with government officials in the 1940s, a moment when Brazilian politicians were taking a nascent interest in indigenous cultures. He told about how, when he was still a young man and newly trained, he began to hold *maraka* rituals in front of whites. In the following excerpt, Prepori describes curing in the town of Cuiabá, capital of the interior state of Mato Grosso, in front of the governor of the state, a man who would in the 1950s personally finance the "pacification" teams sent out to contact some of the more isolated Kayabi remaining on choice land. He told his narrative in Kayabi, with the exception of the lines reproduced in italics, which he narrated in Portuguese.

> I went around singing maraka, singing maraka for the whites. Hoa. I went to the whites' big city, to Cuiabá. In that place, the whites made me sing again. Because you [whites] always pay people, they bought a *suitcase* for me. *The governor had [the guy we called "Mr.] Complication" buy it for me. He paid.*
>
> *There is another [spirit] that is called a* mama'e. *Those who are not a shaman cannot see them.*
>
> "Look, are you seeing the mama'e traveling around, flying?" I said to them. "For you all to see, it is circling here just like a hummingbird."
>
> "Where is it?" one white asked.
>
> It flew here, very close to my mouth. I grabbed it. First I was like this [with my mouth open]. Then I caught it [in my mouth]. Then I grabbed it from my mouth and put it in the white's hand. Then the white wrote it down for our father, for the general [i.e., Marshal Rondon, the founder of the Brazilian Indian Service (SPI)]. [He wrote:] *"Other Indians did not see how a Kayabi shaman did it, just the whites, the whites, just the governor."*
>
> *When I felt better again* [after the exhaustion of the performance], *we got up. The whole day I drank only Guaraná soda and coffee. Today I don't use coffee anymore. Coffee, Guaraná, until the next day. Ahhh, what a thing, the life of a shaman.*
>
> *"He just grabbed a piece of wood,"* said the governor [referring pejoratively to a cure by a different shaman]. He said, *"The only Kayabi, Tupi* [shaman] *is Prepori. I am going to ask that Marshal Rondon come see you, for you to work in front of your father* [i.e., leader]," the white said.
>
> *Then I brought in the dawn like this.* [Singing] *seven or eight hours, I did not stop. The whole day like this. At seven o'clock at night, we really started singing in earnest.*
>
> (Marakara'ãnga itekau. Tapy'yia upe marakara'ãnga tekau. Hoa, te wau kwepe tapy'yiawyra te pe, Cuiabá pe. A'eramũ je wimerimo tapy'yia jema'ema nũ. Aemepy tea je'ã peje pe ra'e. A'eramũ 'ngã *mala* mokũ prau jee. *Aí governador manda Enrolancia me comprar, né. Ele pagou.*
>
> *Tem outro se chama* mama'e. *Niguém que não é pajé não vê, não.*
>
> "Pesa te ekoa ema'ei r'ai ko mama'e rekoramũ te sa 'ngã," 'jau 'jau je pẽnupe. "Koa kau mynumyjawe."
>
> "Manamũ ajewei ekoi," 'jau tapy'yia.
>
> Koa akwapa au je te juruare. Ipyyka. Nara'ne jerekau. Koa je je ipyygi wei. A'eramũ je pyyka te juruare. Tapy'yia imua. A'erafutat tapy'yia ikwasia oreruwa upe, general upe: *"Outro índio não viu como pajé Kayabi vai,* tapy'yia, tapyyia *só, só governador."*

Quando eu fique bom, amanhecemos. Todo dia de manhã só Guaraná, café. Hoje não uso mais café não. Café, Guaraná até manhã, né? Aaaah [que] coisa, vida do pajé.

"Ele pega só pedaço de pau," 'jau *governador 'ĩ.* 'Jau, *"único, pajé Kayabi, Tupi é o Prepori. Então eu vou pedir para M. Rondon de vem ver você, para você trabalhar na frente de seu pai,"* 'jau tapy'yia *'ĩ.*

Aí eu amanheci assim. Sete ou oito horas, não parei. Dia tudo assim. Sete horas da noite começamos direto.)[5]

In this passage Prepori describes how, while singing in *maraka* style, he brought one of the *mama'e* spirits into the gathering. Because the white participant cannot understand the Kayabi of Prepori's dream songs, he cannot actually see the spirit, as other Kayabi in the audience presumably are able to do by merging or aligning their everyday selves with Prepori's extraordinary "narrated I." With respect to these Kayabi audience members, Prepori comments that the spirit is present for "all to see." The white, however, asks, "Where is it?" For this man, who cannot see because he cannot understand what he is hearing, Prepori thinks of a different, more tactile, way of bringing his perspective into alignment within his own. He captures a spirit in his mouth and places it in the man's hand. In this case, where not all audience members can fully understand or feel the force of the narrative "I," Prepori incorporates a novel way of merging the white person's perspective with his own. In Prepori's account, it is almost as if his *maraka* songs describing the world of the spirits have become a tactile "thing" that can be placed in someone's hand. Following the same route as his songs, the spirit that Prepori captures and places in the white man's hands comes first from the spirit world, then through his mouth, and then out to the nonshamans in the audience. In more mundane shamanic exorcisms, a shaman often heats his hand with his cigar and lets others touch it to feel the heat as an index of the presence of invisible objects that spirits have placed in human bodies. Although Prepori does not explain the nature of the spirit placed in the white's hand, I assume it was the presence of heat. Whatever its status, we are told that as a result of this maneuver, the white participant is fully convinced of the spirit world and consequently uses his own means of objectifying language—that is, writing—to pass the message on to the distant founder of the SPI, Marshal Rondon.

The time of Prepori's *maraka* in Cuiabá was a moment in which many Kayabi were becoming firmly enmeshed in the institution of the SPI in one way or another. The first Kayabi families had been officially "pacified" by the SPI by the late 1920s. By 1929, the majority of these Kayabi were settled and working at posts (Grünberg 2004: 57, 60). Establishing a system nearly tantamount to debt peonage, post officials organized Kayabi to work as rubber tappers and to purchase goods at post stores on credit to be paid off by their collection of rubber. As a result, SPI posts became significant sources of goods in the area. Although commercial rubber firms and religious missions were also important, they were less appealing because of their even more brutal working conditions and emphasis on religious instruction, respectively. Prepori described himself as moving between these institutions but as continually ending up tied to SPI as the best of a series of bad options.

The striking feature of Prepori's account of his *maraka* for politicians and SPI officials is the way he describes structuring their relationship by generalizing his shamanic point of view and including a white audience member in a novel way within his "discourse I," an "I" that originates with the spirits. Given that the SPI of the 1940s was following a policy of assimilating native peoples into the national society (Lima 1992), it is remarkable that Prepori's story describes a kind of negotiation of social relationships with these officials through a partial merger of their perceptions with his shamanic experiences. As he describes it, he brings this SPI official and perhaps even the distant Marshal Rondon to perceive his dreams of spirits.

Prepori's account, however, does not describe a generalization of this perspective to all those present or a general feeling of communitas during this *maraka* performance. He stresses the relationship between the Kayabi and the SPI and Brazilian government to the exclusion of other indigenous people present. As the white participant notes, "other Indians did not see how a Kayabi shaman did it, just the whites, the whites, just the governor." If SPI functioned like its current replacement institution, FUNAI, then indigenous communities likely jockeyed for its limited resources. Prepori's *maraka* is remembered as an attempt to bring about a kind of sociable sharing of perspectives only between white officials and the Kayabi. (Moreover, it is likely that the Kayabi involved were only Prepori and his following, not "the Kayabi" as an ethnic unit.) The governor is quoted, for example, as saying that Prepori is the only legitimate Kayabi or even Tupi-speaking shaman. The circulation of perspectives found in Prepori's *maraka* performance of the 1940s is, then—at least in Prepori's memory, as recalled in the context of the Xingu Park—one of the key means of negotiating this preferential alliance between his group and government officials. The most immediate, tangible result of the alliance is, in his account, that the governor buys him a suitcase.

Although the perspectives of the SPI officials, the governor, and the Kayabi present become partially aligned, there is also a simultaneous display of a distinct Kayabi "culture" in this performance. For the whites, it is an event worthy of being recorded because it is an example of cultural difference, and perhaps only of a generic sort. As Graham (2005: 637) pointed out with respect to contemporary Xavante ritual performances, these events may be "second-order indexicals" (Silverstein 1996a) signaling only "Native Amazonianness" or "indigeneity" for non-indigenous audiences. Therefore, while encouraging a circulation of experience and alignment of perspectives in the national context, Prepori's *maraka* also represents the exotic nature of Kayabi experience, something whites engage with only through a kind of generic objectification.

Conclusion

A wide variety of lowland Amazonian ritual traditions in which participants approach Urban's "projective I" are likely seen by the participants as having the potential to play a role in negotiating new types of transcultural and translinguistic communities, because they have the ready-made means of producing an alignment of perspectives. These rituals and their first-person narratives are not, however, automatically suited to encouraging sociability in such situations. Because of linguistic barriers, Prepori had to add commentary in Portuguese, as well as tactile sensations, to generalize or translate his perspective (which was ultimately the perspective of the spirits) to his audience of government officials in the 1940s. Similarly, for *maraka* songs to work to generate a sense of pan-Indian sentiment at the 1992 Week of the Culture of Indigenous Nations, the words had to be written down and translated. The important point is that these ritual narrative forms contain the suggestion and potential for aligning subjective perspectives. The details of the way this is worked out in specific situations are up to the genius of particular shamans. Over the course of his life, which ended in 2000, Prepori had been perhaps one of the most successful lowland shamans of his time to adapt ritual forms to new kinds of transcultural and translinguistic audiences, standing among others such as the Kalapalo shaman Posa (Basso 2003) and Davi Yanomami (Albert 2000).

Ironically, even as Kayabi shamanic ritual is adapted to promote a merging of perspectives among radically distinct types of people and to structure new types of communities in a national and international context, the same forms serve as emblems of cultural difference and the uniqueness of experience. Prepori, wearing an exotic shamanic costume, is in fact still featured on a postcard sold nationally to represent "the Kayabi" as "Indians of Brazil." As the image circulates throughout postal systems around the globe, this postcard version of Prepori's shamanic experience likely serves as a particularly generic marker of cultural difference for international audiences, rather than a means to a shared perspective.

Notes

The field research on which this chapter was based took place between 1991 and 1993 and was funded by an IIE Fulbright Grant for Doctoral Dissertation Research Abroad, a Predoctoral Grant (no. 5372) from the Wenner-Gren Foundation for Anthropological Research, and a Travel Grant from the Center for Latin American Studies at the University of Chicago. The historical research was funded in 2007 by a Field Research Grant from the Latin American and Iberian Institute and a Small Grant-in-Aid for Research at the University of New Mexico. In addition, the historical research that year was supported by a Snead-Wertheim Award for the study of history and anthropology at the University of New Mexico. The chapter benefited from comments by the participants in the 2007 Wenner-Gren symposium "Ritual Communication." I especially thank Michael Silverstein and the organizers of this event, Ellen Basso and Gunter Senft, for their insightful comments.

1. Following others (Silverstein 2001; Tambiah 1985; Toren 2001), I understand ritual moments not as radically different in kind from nonritual moments but as different only in degree. I use the term "ritual" to refer to events in which the greatest ritualization takes place. My examples of lowland rituals are not all ritualized to the same degree, but most tend toward the more extreme end of the continuum. The most ritualized events are those in which there is the greatest degree of patterning and ordering in sequences of words and action, formality, stereotypy, redundancy, and condensation (Tambiah 1985: 128). Because of these characteristics, such events create the sense of "stepping out of ordinary life into a temporary sphere of activity with a disposition all its own" (Tambiah 1985: 127).

2. This pattern is in keeping with Eduardo Viveiros de Castro's (1998) characterization of lowland cosmologies as "perspectivist."

3. The assumption of the "I" of distant ancestors is also found in Polynesian and Melanesian oratory (Merlan and Rumsey 1991; Rumsey 2000).

4. Because of the secrecy surrounding these quests, it is unclear to what extent the first-person pronoun is invoked.

5. This orthography is based on that used by the Summer Institute of Linguistics, a system also used by several Kayabi. I thank Aturi and Mairata for helping me write and translate this portion of Prepori's narrative.

seven

Communicative Resonance across Settings

Marriage Arrangement, Initiation, and Political Meetings in Kenya

Corinne A. Kratz

Efforts to generalize about the forms, functions, and uses of ritual communication (RC) cross-culturally might well founder when faced with the great formal variety and geographical diversity involved, not to mention differing notions of what counts as ritual (Basso and Senft 2006; Kratz 1982). Ritual language has been related to and contrasted with poetic, magical, and religious language, political oratory, and unmarked "everyday language" (a questionable category), although the formal-functional relations proposed are debated (Bloch 1974, 1975b, 1986; Brenneis and Myers 1984; Finnegan 1969; Irvine 1979; Keane 1997a: 48; Malinowski 1978 [1935]; Parkin 1984; Samarin 1976; Tambiah 1968, 1979). Yet language is just one of several communicative media combined in ritual, media that are scheduled and coordinated in ways that create frameworks for ritual goals such as social transformation. These frameworks are organized at multiple levels that might include the ritual as a whole, event sequences within the ritual, sign sequences within events, and the overall ritual system in a particular cultural-historical setting. To generalize about RC, then, it is more productive to consider formal-functional relations across the range of communicative media or in particular kinds of ritual events and to examine their pragmatic processes, patterns of coordination, and communicative resonances.[1]

In this chapter I explore such resonances among marriage arrangement, initiation, and political-legal meetings in Okiek communities in

Kenya in the mid-1980s.[2] The co-occurrence of iconic and indexical links that are relatively coordinated across several media and organizational features in a ritual event can produce a certain communicative resonance, which is most salient when there are multiple links and approximate parallels. These resonant indexical and iconic evocations may contribute to an event's pragmatic force, efficacy, and texture. This interarticulation is one process through which RC incorporates and condenses a range of situations, roles, and discourse styles from the broader communicative economy, weaving them together for the totalizing evocative effect commonly noted in ritual.[3] Okiek marriage arrangement provides an apt avenue for considering how participants work (and play) with the frameworks and conventions of ritual events, creating indexical and iconic connections with other communicative settings and forms (ritual and otherwise) through various structures, idioms, themes, and performative features.[4]

Consider, for example, the following excerpts from two ritual occasions. The first is from an encouraging address (*ceerseet*) to an Okiek girl during initiation, and the second, from wedding advice to a bride (*twekci laakweet; ntanap; yaamiis*). They differ in specific content yet share several discursive and poetic-rhetorical features (shown in boldface): rhetorical questions invoke gathered adults as embodied norm, sharp interrogative phatic prompts demand response (Kratz 1994: 192), and negative commands correct imagined misconceptions.

[Initiation address]
You think all these people—you think they didn't get initiated-i? Do you think all these died-i?
They didn't die.
So it becomes you that says, um—"I'll go and die."
Even— and you— And death-*i*—Even if disease takes you-*e,* it's still death.
You hear?
No matter what, it's still death. If disease takes you, it's still death.
So-a, you hear?
It's still death. There's no saying, "I didn't die because disease is what took me." You think you'll rise from the dead? *Don't say,* "I think I'll rise from the dead because disease took me."
You hear?
So you finish initiation, my child.

[Wedding advice]
All these [women] sitting here [who stayed with their husbands]—do you think they didn't have family?
Hee?
So are you the one now that will change our customs? Isn't there anyone you listen to? Are you deaf to all?
Hee?
We elders come, and we think we're coming to bless and give away a child—and **don't think** it's enemies you're going to [live with]. It's your country, like this.

As I discuss later, the resonance created through such common discursive and performative features harks back to initiation for the bride addressed and to multiple initiations and weddings for gathered adults—connections also likely to enhance the event's rhetorical persuasion. A different phase of marriage arrangement shows parallels to oratory in Okiek men's political-legal meetings (*kirwaaket*), and communicative patterns specific to marriage meetings characterize other extracts.

Until the mid-1950s, Kipchornwonek and Kaplelach Okiek based their economy on hunting game and collecting honey in highland forests in Kenya's Narok District. After significant socioeconomic transformations, most Okiek today are farmers and herders (Kratz 1990, 2007). Until the 1990s, most Okiek marriages were arranged through discussions between and within patrilineal families.[5] Okiek represent marriage arrangement (*kaiito*) as a collective enterprise completed through four (or more) meetings between the couple's families. Marriage extends and completes initiation into adulthood for young people, and marriage arrangement forges joint lineage action through discussion.

I cannot consider the full process here, or even an entire marriage meeting, which lasts for hours. Instead I sketch how event and participation structures, discursive themes, and pragmatic patterns and processes in marriage arrangement events relate to other occasions, highlighting moments when connections are most salient. For links to initiation, I concentrate on one final event of marriage arrangement, involving both bride and groom. Earlier meetings for formal interlineage discussions are the focus in tracing connections to political-legal meetings. On all these occasions—initiation, marriage arrangement, political-legal meetings—participants produce particular social relations, identities, and collectivities through discourse. This is not a seamless process but one often shot through with uncertainties, ambiguities, ambivalences, contradictions, and tensions (Kratz 1994; Peletz 2001). Social risks and conflicts of interest are often part of marriage arrangement. Okiek manage these complications through particular discursive themes and structures, simultaneously constituting and examining key social relations (Kratz 2000, 2005a, 2005b). In exploring the nature and workings of RC, it is important to consider how people manage and transform social relations and how the pragmatics of RC are oriented to these processes.

Initiation, marriage arrangement, and political meetings are all moments when Okiek practice overlaps and interacts with that of their neighbors, Maasai and Kipsigis, incorporating a regional perspective. Over time, Okiek adapt these practices as they engage with wide-reaching socioeconomic transformations and, increasingly, with state bureaucracies and policies (Kratz 2007). At the same time, other political meetings related to national and district campaigns and to local development projects have become more common in the area. Patterns of participation and communication associated with those meetings resonate in Okiek settings, too.

Rather than looking at an interarticulation of genres (Bauman 2004: 162, 2005; Briggs and Bauman 1992), then, I explore the interarticulation of events as part of the way RC is constituted and structured. To be sure, people create associations between events by using particular communicative genres and intertextual ties. Blessings, for example, help frame initiation ceremonies, marriage meetings, and political-legal meetings, although they differ across contexts (Kratz 1988, 1989). Type-token relations (e.g., between a general genre type such as a blessing and specific instances of it) and structures of similarity and contrast between tokens are important aspects of interdiscursive relations (Agha 2005a; Irvine 2005; Silverstein 2005). But resonances and relations between events take other forms, too, and occur in other media. For instance, structural iconicity in ritual acts and materials and in the sequence of ritual events ties together Okiek life-cycle ceremonies, indexing other ceremonies, even as these structural relations set up semiotic progressions and ceremonial differences across the life course. In a similar vein, Silverstein (1993: 48) noted that configurations of co-occurring indexical signs (which "may also or otherwise be quite distinctly functioning *qua* signs") are characteristic of metapragmatic indexicality.

Initiation and Marriage: Encouraging and Advising

An Okiek wedding (*-iilta murereet*) in the 1980s began at the bride's family home.[6] Early that morning, nearby relatives and friends gathered.

Also present were the groom, his parents and "best man," a child for the wedding procession, and some senior relatives who had participated in final discussions the night before. As female relatives anointed and dressed the bride in ritual attire, family and friends assembled in the outer room, talking quietly and drinking liquor if available. Children chattered and cried, people came and went. In this casual domestic scene, a senior man would begin to advise the groom and bride about how to treat each other and their new affines, instruct them in behavior appropriate to newly married status, and warn them of difficulties and responsibilities ahead. Other men and women offered counsel in turn, sometimes finishing outside as the wedding procession formed. After blessings, the procession began its slow journey to the groom's home, where the wedding rituals were completed.

This event was the bride's first official participation in a months-long (formerly years-long) process. In most cases, families met to arrange the marriage while she was secluded during initiation into adulthood.[7] If the wedding took place soon after seclusion, this might be her first encounter with residentially distant fathers and brothers since initiation began. At her wedding, the bride's position was analogous to one experienced during her first initiation ceremony. Performance patterns in that ceremony focused dramatic and rhetorical effects on her. She did not speak in any ritual event. When her fathers and brothers encouraged her with speeches, she could respond only through action, by braving initiation trials (Kratz 1994). At her wedding, the young woman again became part of a process that gave her no opportunity to speak. Again her relatives gathered to talk to her, advising the new couple. This time she was told to agree to the husband selected. Yet unlike recalcitrance during initiation, her refusal would not shame the family, for marriage was not a test of bravery, and she was now an adult. The advice was also public persuasion urging her to support the family's decision.

In most cases the groom had not participated in formal marriage talks either, but his parents did get his agreement before proceeding. He had also visited his future affines, perhaps bringing small gifts. If young, the groom had been initiated several years earlier, without encouraging speeches. Yet his situation required respectful behavior in new affinal relations, and this might recall elders' exhortations and advice during initiation for him, too. The uncertainties of marriage arrangement at this point center on the couple: will they stay together well and respect their affines? This threshold event concentrates the ambivalences of bride and groom. Seen simultaneously from the perspectives of a young single man or woman and a newly married man or woman, the changes and adjustments of marriage hold various attractions, burdens, and dilemmas (Kratz 2000). Bride and groom may not yet recognize all these implications, but mature adults relate telling experiences in their advice, exhorting them to behave properly. These retrospective narratives combine indirect advice, prospective suggestions, and warnings about situations the couple might encounter.

The persuasive aspect of wedding advice points to the uncertainties, ambivalences, and tensions inherent in Okiek marriage arrangement. The hortatory persuasion creates key parallels with *ceerseet* speeches to female initiates, using similar rhetorics invoking personal ties and responsibilities.[8] In a fuller analysis of *ceerseet* I noted, "The basic structure of encouraging speeches consists of a short opening vocative section followed by the longest, most variable section where encouragement is produced through persuasive argument and implied obligations. A short transitional section, usually with a metastatement about the speech or the situation, leads to the closing ... [in which] verbal encouragement is underlined with an encouraging gift" (Kratz 1994: 180). The examples in transcript 1 illustrate interdiscursive resonances between wedding advice and *ceerseet* speeches, as well as differences in themes, performances, and pragmatic patterns. Both speeches were delivered by a man I call by the initials AN, the first in June 1983 to encourage his sister Nini and her co-initiates, and the second three months later, at Nini's wedding.

In the interim the girls completed initiation and emerged from seclusion as marriageable young women. In the 1980s this made them prime targets for "theft" (a form of elopement) until they married, so the families tried to finish arrangements quickly (Kratz 2000: 144–145). The day after initiation ended, Nini and a co-initiate were indeed stolen. AN and his brothers tracked the group and brought them home a week later. The other initiate was married the next day, and Nini's wedding followed soon after, in both cases to the men to whom their families had promised them. As she was anointed and dressed, four senior men of her family began advising her husband. AN gave the first address to Nini herself, delivering it outside as the procession formed.

AN's advice invokes recent events both directly and indirectly. He first refers to Nini as "this bad person who won't listen" *(napiyaakitni)*, claiming his turn as "the one that got tired going about looking for them." With a vocative directing his advice to her, he begins. Reprised later in the advice, AN's preface echoes almost exactly the introduction and theme developed in his encouragement address three months before. Then, however, he was exhausted from going about finding things for initiation, at the girls' request.[9]

Transcript 1. AN's Encouraging Speech and Wedding Advice

Encouraging Speech	
AN: *aakocu/*	AN: You children/
anee ne kiang'etaate aceeng'aati kurpeetng'waang'-i/ ko tako anee ni/	I'm the one that went [running] about, getting tired looking for your things-i/ So this is still me/
kaopaarei kiamei-i?/ ma tako anee ni?// ayu ne kiopaarei in-//ne kiopwaan oleincinaan, "oi ceeng'— ceeng'aatenweec tukuuk"?// maawe aceengaat? toomasic-i? ayu ne kopwa kosyepaaten kityo paaiisyaanik en iyu?/ moosue paani—ma okweek inko kuurei-i?// ii?	Did you think I died-i?/ Isn't this still me?// When was it that you all said um-// that you all came and told me, "oi look for— go and look for things for us"?// Didn't I go and look? Haven't I gotten them yet-i? When is it that elders have simply come to sit here [in this house]?/ Don't you see now—isn't it you all that called them-i?// ii?
ko mainte kiy inko amwauwaak anee paani/ aleincaak anee paani/	So there's nothing that I tell you now myself/ I say to you now myself/
koang'et/ akopa okweek// ameta kaasiit—wakati yangu// kaasiisyekyuuk tukul/ akopa okweek// okasei-i?	I was exhausted/ because of you all// I leave my work—my time// All of my works/ because of you all// Do you hear-i?
ko koacokan/ akot taacokani paani/ aalte tuukyuuk/ akopa okweek/ ko ta atese taai-is kora// hm?//	So I was tired/ I'm still tired even now/ I sell my cows/ because of you all/ So [but] I'm still continuing// hm?//
ko se en anee paani inko amwauwaak-i//	So this what I tell you now myself-i//
aceer— atiny'e anee teeta akeenke/ aaltai kaaroon-i/ en laakokcaan tukul ko somok// atesunaak en tuuk cu kaace ko aaltai// si ing'aap in—/ okenter in—/ taeek inko kaokuuraati// oipaati opa ocut eropiyiasyekcaan kariisyek	I encour— I have one cow myself/ I'll sell it tomorrow-i/ for all those three children// I'll add it to the other cows I sold for you all// So that if um—/ you cheat um—/ the guests you invited// [then] you take it and go get into a [public transport] car with that money,

opeene eemeet inko opa opeene// ko aarteet ne aaltewaak kaaroon/ supeenta// koip ake tukul ishirini ishirini ishirini en okweek// ateswaak tuuk cu kaace aaltai/	and go to whatever country you end up going to// So it's a sheep that I'll sell for you tomorrow/ a female// Each of you will take twenty [shillings], twenty [shillings], twenty [shillings]// I add it for you to those cows that I sold/
Wedding Advice	
AN: *o piam atwekci kanto napiyaakitni// amu anee ne koang'et ace— aceeng'aati//*	AN: Oh first let me talk to this bad person who won't listen to what we say// because I'm the one that was tired from go— going about looking for them//
K: *s'itwekci//*	K: You talk to her//
AN: *Nini//*	AN: Nini//
ale ui-ais-i// amu caang' orkijanai en Oretyado// tena orkijanai nee? en iyaan//	I say go-ais-i// because there are many young men at Oretyado// How many are the young men? there//
R: *maiyuiitu cu pa Oretyado//*	R: Don't become like these ones of Oretyado//
K: *mankiriamaaken tukul// oo-oo/ opeci weeriit//*	K: Let's not all talk at once// oo-oo/ Let the young man [talk]//
AN: *o mutyo// kaikas-i? kale caang' Oretyado orkijanani// ikase-i// ui amu caang' ko iilkee/ ko intekee soksiseek/ ko intekee kariik-i// s'iwe— s'iwe isuen en iyaan in—/ iwe imeta ciici akikooniin// tuun any'on akase tuun kooroon/ akile in— "ny'on/ ny'on isue laakweetng'waang' amu ceepta otuupce"// ko maimeny'e kaau// ile "kaawe aineet"// iwe imeny'e ainaanaan// ui— ui cup-a paaiintani/ inkeroo-a/ ui cup paaiintaani anan icup intasatatnaan-e// ii? icup intasatatnaan anan icup paaiintooni// manan icup*	AN: Quiet// Have you heard-i? I say there are many young men at Oretyado// You hear-i// Go because there are many who anoint themselves/ and put on socks/ and put on beads-i// So you go— so you go and see them there in—/ you go and leave this person that we have given you to// And then I come and hear tomorrow morning/ that in— "Come/ come see your (pl.) child because she's your sister"// And you don't live at home// You say "I'm going to the river"// and you go and live at that river [i.e. go elsewhere, stay a long time]// Go— go curse this old man/ Where is he?/ Go curse this old man or curse that old woman-e// ii? You curse that old woman or you curse this old

in— sintanookuuk en iyaan// pakiteng'ing'uung'//	man// Or you curse your HuBrWi's there// your pakiteng' (HuFa)//
KS: *kikuurene pakiteng'// kikuurene paaiintoni//*	KS: He's called pakiteng'// This man is called that//
AN: caang' orkijana en iyaan// inken ile ma iyaan maapuunu kila aweenti Narok-i? oi iyaan apuunu aweenti Mau-i? ano ne maiany'on apunaati?// ma keetoonikcu maaruaati? maaru ng'aap ipiitoniin, maiarue amu inte Parkesui// ui-a s'any'on akas tuun kele-i/ kale "kaawe kaat aap— kaawe kaat aap ng'aa?// kaawe kaat aap ng'aa?// kaawe kaat aap ng'aa?"// aini amut asipu— aini amut asipaatiin-i// maasipu ot awe asuruun en Oretyado-i? cuun tapaanu? koisue Kimany'e kosipuun? inta Kimany'e kosipuun-iwe/ tos kikekucuuriten itiikcaan// kekiisiin// ole bahati amu anee ne kiny'o/ ma ciit ake// ui-a amu ayepe iit akas in— kiy inko— ng'aleekuuk tukul// s'isue kiy inko any'on aiten// hmm//	AN: There are many young men there// Don't you know that's where I usually pass all the time when I go to Narok-i? and that's where I pass when I'm going to Mau-i? Where is it that I usually come and pass?// Isn't it those houses that I usually go about and sleep in? Don't I usually sleep across there, I usually sleep there because Parkesui is there// Go-a so that I will come and hear that-i/ she said "I'm going to the house of— I'm going to the house of so-and-so// I'm going to the house of so-and-so// I'm going to the house of so-and-so"// And when I followed you recently— and recently when I went about following you-i// didn't I follow you until I found you with Oretyado-i? those far ones up there? Did you see Kimany'e following you? And if it had been Kimany'e that followed you-wei/ those ears would have been cut off// You would have had your throat cut// You say it's lucky because I'm the one that came/ and not someone else// Go-a because I will keep my ears open and hear um— what— all about you [all your words]// And then you'll see what I'll come and do [if you don't stay well]// hmm/

Advice to a bride often tells her to follow her family's decision, to follow her husband, but AN's refrain phrase here tells his sister to go, paralleling the idiom for initiation featured in *ceerseet.* He enumerates misbehavior she might adopt in her husband's home: go see all the fine young men and abandon the one we gave you, go curse your affines, go wander from house to house. He develops each example, describing the young men's adornment and the range of people she might curse and quoting her imagined excuses as she wanders. He intersperses a contrasting image of himself, coming: summoned by affines because of her misdeeds, coming during normal travels and hearing about her. His final comment reminds Nini that she was lucky it was he who found her; her other brother would have beaten her. Thus underlining his concern for her and her obligation to him, he warns that he will be listening for news of her behavior. He closes with a simple emphatic "hmmm."

Fuller analysis of poetic-pragmatic patterns in advice that day is beyond this chapter. But comparison shows that like encouraging speeches, AN's wedding advice creates rhetorical and pragmatic appeals through parallel syntactic structures and echo phrases that develop key themes, through imagined quoted speech and scenarios, and through phatic prompts punctuating the address to engage the bride (some as rhetorical questions). Notably absent is the display of strong but manfully contained emotion characteristic of *ceerseet,* which is shown by sighs, clucks, swearing, and lexical intensifiers (Kratz 1994: 193). Themes developed in the two events also vary with the different emotional tenors. The wedding advice echoes the genre from the earlier event, creating resonance through an interdiscursivity across types (Silverstein 2005: 9) based on similar sets of poetic-rhetorical features and patterns.[10] But relative to *ceerseet,* both the wedding event and its individual performances are less focused and less dramatic. To better understand the resonance between the two requires going beyond texts and language to other communicative media and aspects of the events.

Wedding advice is part of a multifocal event. Procession preparations take place concurrent with the advice-giving, unlike during *ceerseet,* when seated initiates face gathered adults. Similarly, the advice is addressed to both bride and groom, developing two perspectives and appeals. The gathering is also smaller, and time is limited, because the procession must start while the sun rises. As a result, the advice has fewer of the turns and repetitions through which a palpable consensus builds over the course of initiation. Both events address uncertainties, but their time frames and consequences differ. While wedding advice highlights good and bad examples, it urges broad patterns of behavior differentiated by gender, to start immediately but to continue into the future as a new way of life. If bride or groom ignores the counsel, he or she might be chastised in other meetings, the bride may be beaten or return to her family, and eventually the marriage may end. By contrast, the *ceerseet* appeals for immediate, pinpointed action: intense bravery the following dawn. If an initiate fails, she shames herself and the entire family.

Ceerseet speeches emphasize social relations between initiates and the speaker, underlining obligations that initiates fulfill through bravery. The series of speeches and thematic repetitions constitutes a collective appeal from gathered adults, but that appeal is based on personal relations and specific interactions recounted, as well as on general norms and expectations. Wedding advice draws on personal relations and incidents, too (e.g., AN's involvement when the bride eloped), but it invokes the whole lineage and jural relations and responsibilities (he followed her on behalf of the family). AN's advice, for instance, uses plural forms to tell Nini that she has been given to her husband and to issue the imagined summons about her misbehavior ("come see your (pl.) child"). He speaks both as an individual and as part of the lineage. His relation to Nini is one of lineage responsibility: he follows when she elopes, he listens to hear how she acts, and the family will protect her if her husband acts badly (as emphasized in advice to him). Wedding advice also highlights other relations, introducing new affines with kin terms and pointing out those present. One of Nini's fathers told the couple: "Remember that this old woman gets hungry. If you see she is sick … take over water for her. And go for firewood. You make *ugali* for your husband. And you cut the *ugali*-i, cut the *ugali,* and remember who? This old man. Go-a, friend, and take care of your wife's father. This is your wife's father."

During wedding advice, the distinction between lineages that dominated marriage meetings realigns to differentiate mature advisors and the couple. The authority of age is applied to re-create gendered differences of agency, power, and authority within the new household. The collective force of lineage actors remains important in finalizing and witnessing arrangements; it also becomes a potent rhetorical source in advising the couple. Others interject amplifying comments, as in AN's advice; when this becomes an alternation between speakers, advice can seem virtually co-narrated. Personal relations with bride and groom are invoked to induce them to heed the wedding advice. At the same time, a more inclusive collectivity comes into play. Members of both lineages merge into an adult collective that also becomes the avatar of "tradition" (Kratz 1993), arrayed in contrast to two junior individuals.[11] United by shared interests in concluding the property, resource, and personnel transfers of the marriage, the two sets of relatives join forces to encourage a lasting union between their children.

Other examples of wedding advice develop common themes, some using more narrative scenarios and humor. Less focused and dramatic than *ceerseet,* wedding advice reaffirms a wider range of relations and constitutes both the lineage collectives that are prominent during marriage meetings and a broader adult union relative to the couple. Yet both wedding advice and *ceerseet* address uncertainty about young people's behavior, invoking personal relations and obligations to exhort them to agree. For the bride especially, the event harks back to her recent initiation. For adults advising the couple, it might also recall other initiations, weddings, and the joys and sorrows of parenthood. But resonance between the occasions can potentially heighten emotion and affect for all involved as the new marriage begins and family relations realign.

The resonance between wedding advice and *ceerseet* builds through several forms of iconic and indexical interconnections that combine type-based and token-based interdiscursivity: the events' spatial organization, the general division between mature adult speakers and youths as addressees, the overlap between speakers who encourage and advise and at least one addressee (initiate or bride), some modes of appeal (drawing on personal relations, family commitments), the overall aim of persuasive exhortation through either encouragement or advice, and perhaps even specific language and phrases (as with AN's declared fatigue). These echoes and interarticulations between the events and the speeches help produce pragmatic effects in wedding advice, lending greater impetus to a more diffuse situation. They also mark and link the events as related modes of RC, aimed at persuading young people to follow paths laid out for them.

Making Collective Decisions in Two Contexts

Before the wedding, the two families arranged the marriage through meetings in which participants talked about, debated, and produced social relations, family histories, and—eventually—agreement about the union.[12] Managing such delicate discussions requires considerable social and political skill, and the process provides a rich focus for exploring the social dynamics, evocative rhetorics, and moral imaginations through which Okiek people constitute lineages, affinal connections, and other social relations. As Fabian argued (1994: 270), "because there are images illuminating intricate connections, and key words capable of unlocking semantic spaces, there may also be communicative events that suddenly open up insights into a complicated praxis." Okiek marriage meetings are just such events.

The resonances of marriage meetings are less densely concentrated than those of wedding advice and reach in several directions. Visits follow ritual procedures: for example, ideally there are four visits, the wife seekers arrive in procession carrying liquor marked with ritual plants, and women begin visits by sharing a small calabash of honey wine after libations. Ritual numbers, clothing, plants, and places of libation create iconic parallels and indexical links relating the occasion to other Okiek ceremonies with similar procedures and objects (Kratz 1987, 1994: 155–162).

During the discussions that occupy most of the meetings, however, the strongest discursive resonances reach toward political-legal meetings (*kirwaaket*), during which men settle disputes and discuss community concerns. Indeed, Okiek invoke such meetings as a source of procedures and ideals during marriage deliberations. At marriage talks in June 1983, for example, one father suggested, "Let's do what is done in a meeting and say-i/ say tosi-i 'Which one is liked?/ Do you follow Naresho's mouth? Do you follow another?'"[13] The ideology underlying these ideals was presented in October 1984 as a speaker sought to raise a new issue as a men's meeting finished:

S: Listen, o men/ And a meeting usually-i/ I say and a meeting usually-i/ isn't all dirt usually swept away-i [i.e., words finished]? Say yes indeed/

AO: That's how it is.

S: Yes/ And usually when we circumcise aren't you told, "Get up because you've become a man"/ "You leave what?/ all those boyhood words/ and take up those of manhood because you're a man."/ And a meeting, also a men's meeting like this very one/ that usually, usually—/ that [is when] we usually finish what? All words/ So since you've wanted-i/ to leave/ and you have finished all the [words] of the meeting-i/ and we bless, do you think we bless-o where one is still left?/ Isn't it tomorrow's [word] that we wait for-i?/ I also have a small thing/ o men/ Today when we are all met together/ and there is no good [word] usually in—/ if it's not a word that has been said/ where men are/ Because it's men who usually judge and counsel others/ Because there is no one that circumcises himself/ So that men—that word I want to throw out quickly/ there is a word that I heard/ that is talked about and disliked in our family/ Is it lies and gossip-i?/ or true?/ [Debating and deciding like] that is what's good because this is where all people [i.e., men] are [gathered]/ One that is said-e/ one that is said,/ that's the one that is good usually so-i/ so we can get to calm/

> everyone/ So when each is going-i/ to sleep-i/ we know that we finished such and such/ So if [someone] repeats his own [version and does the same thing again]/ elders tell him that we finished that one [already]./ And one that isn't said/ can it be finished?

Okiek regard men as capable of speaking well, reasoning clearly, and resolving disputes—"finishing words" in meetings. Problems should be discussed openly and resolved; men's meetings create a record and witnesses who remember history and other case precedents. During men's meetings and marriage meetings alike, Okiek describe speakers as "straightening out" (*-ciipta*) deliberations and "leading" or "following" paths (lines of argumentation). They use additional metaphors familiar from work on language in politics, disputes, and oratory (Bloch 1975b; Brenneis 1988; Brenneis and Myers 1984; Briggs 1996a; Comaroff and Roberts 1981; Hirsch 1998; Parkin 1984). Men's meetings are the prime occasions on which such discourse is manifest and realized in clear outcomes. In marriage meetings, the very circumstances make this ideal difficult to achieve. Features of event structure confound the desired discursive resonance with men's meetings.

Two significant differences relate to the participant mix and drinking, but other contrasts are worth noting. A complainant convenes a *kirwaaket* by calling together men from the area. Twenty to forty people gather in mid-morning, usually on a centrally located hilltop with shade trees.[14] Four to six men report from different communities in a formal, collective version of the news exchanges of individual greetings. After two elders bless the meeting, its genesis is described and discussion begins. Men sit or lounge on the hillside while individuals address the gathering. Each speaker stands in front, pacing as he talks, punctuating points by hitting the ground with his walking stick, sometimes enumerating points to structure an argument. Men squat near the front to get a turn or simply rise and go forward.

If the meeting concerns a dispute (e.g., about theft or land), the disputing individuals or lineage groups absent themselves after both sides are presented. The remaining men discuss and decide the case, then call the disputants back for the judgment. After final discussion, others may raise small questions or make announcements before additional blessings close the meeting. Many men then go to drink beer in nearby houses.

In contrast, marriage talks begin in the evening at the bride's parents' home. The first visit may be unannounced, but wife seekers make known subsequent visits so that the girl's senior male relatives will be present.

Elders from the groom's family, including his father and his mother or other senior kinswomen, bring liquor to the girl's home to enable the discussion. Most participants are men. All the girl's fathers and adult brothers can participate; her sisters' husbands and matrilateral relatives might also be consulted. Mature men (*paaiik*) from both families are regarded as essential, because of social and jural concerns that extend men's roles in political-legal meetings.[15] But unlike during those meetings, women are not excluded. The mother's assent is particularly critical, but other senior female relatives also speak.[16] All told, marriage meetings include ten to twenty people.

Formal talks begin with a metaphoric exchange between senior men that establishes the visit's goal. In the following exchange between the bride's father (N) and the groom's father (M), the food mentioned is liquor, and the young woman is the cow:

N: *Ei, aini ainy'on pakule. Aini ainy'on amtit, amu inkeri amtit-i... Mwai nee amtitni-iwe?*
Ei, and indeed, co-initiate. And indeed food, because here is food... What does this food say, friend?

M: *Ee. Wei, apare amtit—ko amtit, ko koceeng'e—koceeng'e teeta.*
Ee. Friend, I think it's food—it's food to look for—to look for a cow.

N: *Yu ana teeta?*
What's the cow like?

M: *Ko teeta inko esipa.*
It's a hairless cow.

Blessings inevitably follow this statement of intent, recognizing that good fortune brings the two families together. The men then establish whether the cow is already branded or reserved—that is, whether this is their first meeting—and recap any prior discussions.

Discussions continue for several hours in a process that discursively constitutes lineages as collective decision-making agents and in which people act simultaneously as individuals and as lineages. Each participant brings to the process different personal, social, and political perspectives, although these dynamics and conundrums of agency cannot be considered here (Kratz 2005a, 2005b). Partway through the discussions, the two sides separate and confer among themselves. Wife seekers should respond (*-wal*) respectfully to questions or challenges, which might raise disputed misbehavior by lineage members. Whatever happens, they should act like respectful affines in marriage meetings, offering iconic assurance about future behavior.

Like men's meetings, marriage talks are occasions of formal, collective decision-making. At times, men speak as they do during meetings—for example, defining an argument's structure by enumerating its elements and using extended turns with rhetorical questions that introduce pauses to emphasize points and engage listeners. In the following example, the speaker, AN, enumerates points to define options and structure his turn, incorporates one rhetorical question, and offers metacommentary about how discussion should proceed. Arrangements were failing because the bride refused to accept the groom; AN asks whether accounting of property for repayment should begin:

AN: *Aputi/ Kas amwauun ng'aleek-i/ ng'aleekcu ko tek kityo* [numerical hand sign]*// Ile aieeng'// Ng'aleekcu ko aieeng'//*
Affine/ Listen and I'll tell you words-i/ These words are just this many [numerical hand sign]// Say two// These words are two//

KT: *Mekonte toi ng'aleek inko kimwai-e//*
There are no longer any words to say toi [because she refused]//

AN: *Se paani akot in— amwauun-i// Inko kiyaakse-i/ yaakse// Inko kikany'e let-i//* [switch to Maa] *taany'u//* [switch back to Okiek] *Ng'aap-ayn ng'eetaat ne kimwai// Pakaac— manken anee cu kepa keuny'aati// Amu ma eceek inko yay nee?// inko yetiin kiy// Laakweet iny'eenkee inkonam ko— kopirtiitiit// Ko makinken inko ta tuun kimuuku-e// an ko ma// kake-i// Ako— akoweitokee//*
So now even in— I tell you-i// If it's asking for repayment-i/ ask for repayment// If it's waiting for a later one-i// [switch to Maa] wait// [switch back to Okiek] It's [words] of a man that we say [i.e., clear and true]// Leave— I don't know these ones that we go about hiding// Because we're not the ones that did what?// that refused you the thing// It's the child herself that started to— that became stubborn// And we don't know if we will be able [to convince her] later-e// or not// but-i// She— she went on her own//

Turn-taking during marriage talks might be explicitly directed by a senior man in the wife givers' family but is sometimes more a free-for-all. Focus often dissolves as side conversations grow and other concerns interrupt (cf. Myers 1986: 438). Metapragmatic direction returns attention to matters at hand. In the excerpt reproduced as transcript 2, people propose procedures for a lineage conference so that all will be heard. They comment on the kind of discussion desired and caution about the effects of drinking on the deliberations.

Transcript 2. Excerpt from a Lineage Conference during Marriage Discussions

N: *onameen-i/ keero onameen paaintaanaan kony'one-i/ kopun iyu/ koitey kiy/ akale Araapkiplet cu-o/ ma pa— Kap Changoroi iny'ee akeeng'ke inko kitiny'e-o/ ko Kap Changoroi ko inte [Ms: ko pukootyeetny'iin] ko pukootyeetny'iin ko muci kopir ng'aleekcu/*	N: Start with-i/ look start with that man who just came-i/ and pass this way/ and do this [that is, go around the room]/ I say these are Araapkiplet-o/ Isn't it— one Kap Changoroi person that we have here-o/ And the Kap Changoroi person who is here [Ms: He's her sister's husband] is her sister's husband and can talk about these words/
Ms: *komuci koyeteen/*	Ms: He can refuse [to give the bride to] them/
N: *komuci koyeteen komuci kokooita/ bas/*	N: He can refuse them and he can give her away/ Bas/
Ms: *cakten-a//*	Ms: Be quiet-a//
KW: *takikooci piik kotar lookooiyuekcwaak-i/ kiwal ak eceek/ ko akekas kiy inko kipoorci/*	KW: We will let people [i.e., men] finish their words-i/ [and then] we [women] will also respond/ when we have heard what has been done/
N: *opakaac ng'aleekcu/ amu tos kopwaani ng'aleekcu amu ra toi ne kitany'amali// pakaac amu pare kiperpereec*	N: Leave these words/ because these words will still come because today is the day that we really talk hard to them toi// Leave it because they think we are foolish//
Kt: *okas/ se lookooiyat kewale// omutyo amu mankekuikuiyen keiku Tukenik/ amu iceek maikokuikuiyen ak ceepyoosook//*	Kt: Listen/ This word that we respond [to them]// Quiet because we don't all talk at once and become like Tuken/ because they are the ones that usually all talk at once, along with women//
KS: *onkepire toi ra kura//*	KS: Let's take a vote today toi//
Kt: *makiwalcin-a toi ng'eelyeepiik aap ng'etaatik amu kit akemwai ko akemwai/ ipare kariam kaai tukul-i/ makas akeeng'ke?/ se-a keng'alaane/ ng'etaatikcuuk, kopakaa kopakok// ko kaikai*	Kt: We don't change the tongues of men toi because if we've said something it's been said/ Do you think everyone in this house has drunk-i/ and didn't hear one [word that was said]? Now-a when we are talking/ my men, women and men//

kekas-a lokooiyaat inko kimwai// amu ka tang'alaan ng'etaatik aieeng' kong'alaan somok/	it is better to listen-a to the word that is said// because if two or three men talk/
N: *kong'et-ais/ . . .*	N: It is finished-ais/ . . .
Kt: *ole akeeeeng'ke/ osue inko rotik ne okan osipi piikcuuk/ kekan kiam/ kipakaac ng'aleek// ko se inko ng'aleek ne akemwai/ inkesue kisip kaany'uun/ amu manamaakiis aieeng'u/ esiarit ak epulootit/ amu inko ko kele patpatpatpatpatpatpat/ ooc arriyia/ kole ake patpatpatpatpatpat/ ooc arriyia//*	Kt: Say ooooone [word]/ You see if it is liquor that you will first follow, my people/ and then we will eat first/ and leave words// And if it is words that we are saying/ let's see and follow [them] my household/ because two [things] cannot be [done] at the same time// [you can't hold both] a stick and a cow's stomach [reference to a proverb]/ Because if it's said patpatpatpatpatpatpat/ you are experts/ and another says patpatpatpatpatpat/ you're experts//
N: *oi moopar kiy liye/*	N: Oi don't [all talk at once] liye/

This description of marriage meetings sketches the foundation for interarticulations between marriage meetings and men's meetings, but transcript 2 also returns to what Okiek regard as two factors that can confound marriage discussions: the inclusion of women and the drinking that goes on during marriage talks. Each rests on a contradiction, and each serves as an excuse when marriage talks go awry. No discussion takes place unless liquor is brought, yet the alcohol that enables the meeting can bedevil discussion. Admonitions to avoid drunkenness, pay attention, take turns speaking, and retain focus are refrains throughout marriage meetings, especially as the evening wears on. Directions managing liquor distribution are a second refrain, sometimes interrupting the discussion. When meetings get out of hand, participants lament, "A word doesn't finish when beer has been drunk" (see transcript 3). The contrast with men's meetings is striking and is commented on explicitly.

Women's participation in consequential decisions contradicts Okiek notions of personhood. Moreover, with patrilineages defined as key actors in marriage arrangement, women's participation becomes doubly contradictory (cf. Jackson and Karp 1990: 20–21; Karp 1987). Their role in bearing and raising children, however, gives them the right to take

Transcript 3. Excerpt Complaining about Liquor

KS: *se keny'o pookitiik-ai tosi-i/ mos kekasaanu/*	KS: If drunkenness comes first-i/ then we no longer listen/
KW: *came-s ocei lookooiyaat ko ta amwaiun-i/ kekan— ko makiny'oe mayueek/*	KW: It's usually wanted that [when] I'm still telling you a word-i/ we first— liquor is not what is done first/
Ko: *ko makiny'oe mayueek/*	Ko: We don't do liquor first/
KW: *kikan kenaaaaam/ [KS: ot kong'et] ot kong'et/ ko kole kong'et-i/*	KW: First we taaaaaake [that word]/ [KS: until it finishes] until it finishes/ and when it has finished-i/
Ms: *ko akeamis paanaan/*	Ms: Then we eat/
Ko: *koakeamis/*	Ko: Then we eat/
KW: *kinam mayueek/ kiyaan ne maikitay/ pookeriny'uun/ ii? [Ms: kabisa] aini isue kiny'oe mayueek/ . . .*	KW: [But instead] we start with liquor/ that is what is usually done/ my DaHu/ ii? [Ms: Absolutely] And if you see we start with liquor/ . . .
Ms: *ko mos kisicin lookooiyaat ake tukul/*	Ms: Then we will no longer get any word [right]/
Ko/Ms: *makasaanu/*	Ko/Ms: It isn't listened to/
KW: *ikase? . . . oo kile/ mapeku lookooiyaat ne akeye mayueek/*	KW: You hear? . . . Yes, it's said/ a word doesn't finish when beer has been drunk/

part. Their husbands' lineages are perpetuated through women's reproductive capacity, so women are critical to re-creating the collectivities even though they are not themselves members. This paradox emerges during marriage meetings, where women have a say in lineage decisions. A girl's mothers, brothers' wives, and adult sisters can all attend and speak, although the event's structure frames their contributions in ways that minimize their influence and effect. Women speak only after men have begun to shape consensus.[17] Further, they speak after exchanges that might resemble men's extended, eloquent orations at legal-political meetings, a style most women have little opportunity to master. Transcript 4 shows complaints about women's participation when marriage discussions lost focus late one night.[18]

Transcript 4. Excerpt Complaining about Women

AN: *ipare singoi tuun inko kaaiyueek inko kile kipeenti, koik ceepyoosook ne intoen/ ne intoen/ ot koker kile inko kimwai?/*	AN: Do you think it's good for us to supposedly be doing marriage talks, and it becomes women who are leading/ who are leading [the words]/ until they close [i.e., stop] what we are talking about?
KwI: *otuuc ng'aleekcu/ opakaac tuun kaarooon-i/ ontanapkee ak in— kaany'iteenik ak iceek/*	KwI: Leave these words for later/ Leave them and tomorrow morning-i/ you advise each other with in— the affines too/
KwK: *oo/ koik tuun/ kintanapaatkee/ mainte inko yesai koik/*	KwK: Yes/ let it be tomorrow/ we will talk to each other/ There is nothing that refuses to become [what it will become]/
Kt?: *oo/ inkopar kiyaan/ inkoik lookoiyueek ng'aap tuun/*	Kt?: Yes/ let it be like that/ Let them become tomorrow's words/
[Many talk at once]	[Many talk at once]
AN: *ale os kecakte-i/ keng'alaan kopek ng'aleek aap ng'etaatik/ makiam amtit aap ciit-- hapana/ makiame amtit aap ciito kiam kityo murkuut// makimace keng'alaane koik ceepyoosook ce intoe lookooi/*	AN: I say when we get quiet-i/ we will talk until these words of men are finished/ We don't [just] eat someone's food— no/ We don't eat someone's food and just gulp it down [without saying the words]/ We don't want it to be that when we are talking, it becomes women who are leading the words/
KC: *amu nee asi ko akontoe ceepyoosook ko mookas/*	KC: Why is it that women were leading them and you didn't hear/
KW: *kale Kwaampaat Iyaya/ iny'ooru, ma maiong'ooceec ira/ ma maiong'ooceec-o kooko?*	KW: I say Kwaampaat Iyaya/ will you get it, don't you [men] usually accuse us [falsely] ira/ don't you usually blame things on us, grandson?
KwI: *ai ya-aa*	KwI: Oh no/

Okiek produce interarticulations between marriage talks and men's meetings in several ways, then, including iconicities in men's speech style and in event structure when both divide for deliberation. Such parallels create indexical links between the occasions. Metacommentary also identifies men's meetings as a model for formal decision-making that should be matched in marriage talks. But in practice these iconicities are fleeting and fragile. Marriage meetings are full of interruptions; focus periodically dissolves. Some occasions may be failed icons of men's meetings, with drunken fights erupting.[19] Okiek often attribute these shortcomings to the presence of liquor and women, identifying features of the event that systematically thwart the resonance desired. Various communicative media and event features can work at cross-purposes in creating resonance between marriage meetings and men's meetings, even as others align to connect to other ritual occasions.

Nonetheless, the discursive connections underline an enduring pragmatic resonance between the two events, just as persuasive exhortation was common to wedding advice and *ceerseet*. In both kinds of meetings, discussions constitute collective jural decisions that become part of an ongoing record, like the "legal chaining effect" Mertz (1996) described in legal opinions (see also Briggs 1996a: 26). Whether they concern lineage decisions about marriage or men's collective decisions about disputes or other issues, the meetings reconfigure social relations and reorient future action. In marriage meetings, this happens within a larger ritual frame established through acts that begin the visit, creating resonances that reach in several directions and situate the event within several domains of action.

Baraza: Emergent Resonance?

Men's meetings addressed many kinds of disputes in the 1980s, including matters related to the land demarcation that has led to far-reaching political economic shifts. At other meetings men discussed community work, roads, schools, and government policies—activities associated with one another as "development" (*maendeleo*). If the assistant chief was involved, the usual format of men's deliberative meetings also included announcements and exhortations about development, incorporating features of government meetings and rallies held throughout Kenya. However, they did not include the elaborate hierarchical structure and formulaic exchanges of political slogans of government rallies. Although some Okiek had attended rallies in nearby towns, the first *harambee* (self-help) fund-raising rally in my Kipchornwonek Okiek research area took place in October 1983. In my Kaplelach research area, the first "development meeting" of this sort was held in August 1993. Government councilors, district officers, chiefs, and local KANU (national political party) officials were invited for their first visit to the area.

Such government rallies and meetings contrast strikingly with locally convened men's meetings in terms of organization, participation conventions, language, and social relations. Before closing, I consider contrasts between the two to introduce these newer occasions through which additional resonances may be sedimenting into various contexts of Okiek life. In the early 1980s, government meetings had little consistent resonance in Okiek marriage arrangement, although one man jokingly called out the *harambee* slogan as people left a marriage meeting in 1983, and issues related to school-going daughters were becoming significant. Socioeconomic and demographic transformations in Okiek life accelerated as land demarcation and land sales proceeded from the 1980s into the 2000s, along with greater incorporation of the Okiek into national bureaucracies and policies. The appearance of government rallies, already common elsewhere in Kenya, was a sign of this.

At the time, most Okiek referred to the government meetings with the term for a men's meeting, *kirwaaket.* In July 1993 a young Okiot man helping to organize the August rally instead called it *baraza,* the common Kiswahili name.[20] By now Okiek might use both terms to distinguish the kinds of meetings. Haugerud and Njogu (1991: 1–2) characterized a *baraza* as "a staged political event where the weak meet the strong ... that links the state with particular localities ... [in] an arena of national culture-making." In the following summary, I supplement their thorough description of *baraza* (based on Embu District meetings) with examples from the two inaugural meetings in my research areas (Haugerud 1995: 60–107; Haugerud and Njogu 1991).

A "relatively authoritarian institution with the trappings of a participatory one" (Haugerud and Njogu 1991: 4), the *baraza* is a colonial and postcolonial institution originating in gatherings at which colonial officers learned about their districts, heard complaints, and made announcements. Today *baraza* are a regular part of national and district political campaigns and governance, often reported in national media. The setting differentiates participants: VIPs sit on chairs at the front under a sunshade, facing several hundred people seated on the ground, with a performance space between them. A master of ceremonies directs the planned program. The Okiek area meetings began with Christian prayer followed by a "traditional" blessing in Maasai or Kipsigis. Next, a series of performances welcomed guests with songs and spoken pieces in Kiswahili and Kalenjin by school choirs and women's groups. Invited VIPs might dance briefly with the women and "spray" singers with cash to favor a performance.

The master of ceremonies establishes jocular interaction with the assembly, engaging it with exchanges of political slogans and syncopated clapping sequences such as the following:

Okay, let's shake our fingers [i.e., do a KANU party sign].
And if I say "Haraaaambee!" you all say "Jogoo."
If I say "Where is our respected president?" you say "Jogoo."
If I say "Members of Parliament," you say "Jogoo."
"Councilor," "Jogoo."
"Our cows," "Jogoo."
"Our forest," "Jogoo."
Do you hear? If I say like that I want to hear it loudly.
[Having instructed them, he begins the exchange.]
Haraaaambee! (Jogoo)
Where is our honored president? (Jogoo)
Where is the vice president? (Jogoo)
Where is Minister Ntimama? (Jogoo)
Where is MP ole Tuya? (Jogoo)
Where is Councilor Koriata? (Jogoo)... [Six more exchanges follow.]

As speeches begin, the master of ceremonies introduces the reason for gathering and the area's development needs. VIPs then "greet the people" with brief addresses, beginning with local notables such as the school headmaster and the chief and moving up in rank. The guest of honor—perhaps a councilor or member of parliament—gives the last, longest address. Speakers use Kiswahili, code-switching to Maasai or Kalenjin and beginning or ending by exchanging political slogans with the audience.[21] This occupies the next hour or so at fund-raising meetings. At the end, VIP guests receive gifts such as sheep, goats, gallons of honey, hyrax fur capes, and other traditional crafts. They are fed well with meat, rice, potatoes, soda, and beer in a private setting at the event's start, end, or both.

The pragmatic sense of these extended performances was summarized in two comments at the 1993 meeting. Before the high-level VIPs arrived, the assistant chief advised that

> it is not food that is bringing people here today, but your troubles. There is no road here. There is a school, but no road. When people come, feed them, tell them your problems, and when they go say thanks. It is like when a guest comes to your home, you say thanks that they have come. Third, you can have just two men get up and tell them what your troubles are. Since it is the road you want to be done, ask for that. Then also ask them to arrange a harambee for you, ask them to get an opportunity for that. You have to ask the government for these things. Even if I'm a chief, I have no road and I have no school. I have to ask for it from the government.[22]

As people left the meeting, I was standing near the guest of honor. He commented in English to another guest, "We will do something for them. We have to do something for them." Both comments portray citizens as supplicants, although speeches also use metaphors of kinship and marriage to construe and construct relations and obligations between politicians and local people. The rally is an elaborate request for assistance, articulated in idioms of family, hospitality, and development. As elsewhere in Kenya, the dynamics are embroiled in political patronage and clientelism (Brinkerhoff and Goldsmith 2002; van de Walle 2002).

Baraza create an intricate display of hierarchy among political leaders and citizens through spatial organization, dress, speech, food, and gifts. Haugerud (1995: 9) observed that "communication tends to be unidirectional," but the meeting has a broad dialogic structure. The performative welcome by women and children and the community's request are answered with the guest of honor's final speech. Building to this, lower officials greet the people with staged dialogues and "a collusively 'hyped' display of support" (Haugerud 1995: 28–29). Unlike Okiek meetings in which men make jural and political decisions, "the baraza is not an arena for national policy debate and decision-making, but rather the forum in which such decisions are announced and justified.... Such gatherings offer platforms for political persuasion, for fundraising, for describing government programs and policies, and for instruction" (Haugerud 1995: 8–9).

Contrasts with Okiek men's meetings are many: among others, size, setting, participant structure, language, turn-taking, discourse structures, and inclusion of song and food. Indeed, the assistant chief's advice that just two men present a central request counseled against the very interaction and reiteration that define men's meetings. *Baraza* are "a secular ritual whose practice helps to reproduce the relations of domination that sustain the national political economy" (Haugerud

1995: 36). They are a ritual of contact and exposure rather than an arena of debate and deliberation (although Okiek men's meetings also have behind-the-scenes politicking).

Baraza allow rural communities to petition for government resources, seeking to establish relations with invited officials through gifts and display. They do not establish ongoing daily relations, but they provide grounds for future reminders and appeals. The politics of patronage personalizes bureaucracy. At the same time, *baraza* bring together people from a broad area as embodiment of the *wananchi* (Kiswahili: citizens, common people) in relation to the state. All are expected to contribute to gifts presented, schoolchildren and women must form performance groups, and participants in planning meetings develop the program and assign responsibilities. *Baraza* emphasized this collective identity for Okiek in my research area, which has become increasingly multiethnic in the past twenty years because of land sales and new settlement.[23] People learn nationalist rhetorics and idioms as they become caught up with requests for roads, schools, and other signs of development. The ritual communication of government *baraza* reproduces the national system of hierarchy and power as it extends into Kenya's rural settings. In this case *baraza* also promoted a sense of community based on common needs and development endeavors rather than on ethnicity and long-term interaction.

I cannot say how *baraza* might resonate with marriage arrangement or other Okiek ritual occasions today, in 2009. In the 1980s and 1990s *baraza* were uncommon in this Okiek area, and marriage arrangement was becoming transformed in any case. There seemed to be no significant resonance at that time between *baraza* and the wedding advice or *ceerseet* events already discussed. Some men's meetings included discussion of government policies affecting Okiek, but their format and communicative conventions did not resemble those of *baraza*. Elsewhere, however, resonances were developing.

In April 1984, the assistant chief's daughter married a youth with ambitions for work in development and government. Both men, particularly the assistant chief, attended *baraza* in various locations and had opportunities to hobnob with government officers and politicians in the district. The assistant chief's sister, a teacher, lived in town and was also engaged in development work. The wedding was an opportunity to show the family's affiliations and aspirations to modernity and political power, with innovations that might become common practice.[24]

The wedding had many distinctive features, including clothing brought from Nairobi, the capital, among which was a rented white lace wedding dress for the bride. The bride's relatives traveled in hired vehicles to her husband's home to celebrate; many commented on this departure from customary practice. The couple were advised as usual, and at length, before leaving, but on reaching the husband's homestead they did not enter his parent's house to be fed honey as usual. Instead, they sat under a sunshade constructed outside, with rows of chairs. The final event of the wedding consisted of speeches by men and women alike, each contributing to the new household. As in *ceerseet,* gifts were received ceremonially, recorded by the bride's aunt, and followed by excerpts of recorded music. The aunt announced the grand total, broke it down by location, and then called for one of the syncopated clapping patterns from government rallies.

The wedding presentations had been organized as a cross between *ceerseet* and a *harambee* fund-raiser, forging new kinds of resonance across contexts. This wedding may ultimately (retrospectively) be seen as a vanguard event of neotraditional Okiek practice, although it was not clear by the mid-1990s whether its innovations would become standard Okiek practice or remain an emerging family tradition, or whether other resonances with *baraza* might develop. Resonance is an ongoing production. Possible parallels and evocations through which it is created change over time as ritual events, idioms, and styles change and as new connections develop (Kratz 1993). New "meanings and values, new practices, new relationships and kinds of relationship are continually being created" (Williams 1977: 123,133), holding new possibilities through which communicative resonance might link events, contexts, and social practices.

Evocative Associations and Pragmatic Processes in Ritual Communication

RC is defined within broader communicative economies, with systematic contrasts and connections among communicative forms, media, and contexts. Such contrasts and connections provide resources for producing meaning, identities, social relations, and modes of power and authority. They also contribute to ritual's experiential textures and effects. The oft-remarked multivocality of ritual symbols condenses associations from multiple contexts and domains of meaning and action, but ritual performance is permeated by other interconnections as well. Communicative resonance is one process through which evocative interconnections are condensed in RC, indexing and relating other events and occasions to ritual events. Such resonance does more than recall and evoke kinds of events, however. For individuals, such structural parallels are also clothed in personal experience and memory, evoking, in the Okiek case, particular weddings, initiations, and personal relations. The resonance, then, creates potential emotional heightening even as it may reinforce pragmatic effects. Here I have explored communicative resonance across settings with Okiek examples, considering the way systematic contrasts and connections are produced in ritual events through multiple indexical and iconic relations between their spatiotemporal organization, participant structure, and discursive and pragmatic patterns and processes and those of other settings. Communicative resonance offers a productive way to consider how RC is structured, how people draw on RC to produce social relations and effects, and how RC and events transform over time.

The extent of communicative resonance in ritual events varies within and across cultural-historical settings, as do events with which resonances are established. This variability fuels the difficulty of formulating unchanging, generalized definitions of RC. Distinctions between RC and political, poetic, religious, magical, or everyday communication might be a matter of aspects, tendencies, frequencies, and continua, perhaps changing over the course of an event rather than being marked by clear diacritical forms. The multimedia nature of RC matters, too, for event structures may create parallels while discursive patterns create distinctions (or vice versa, as with Okiek marriage meetings and men's meetings). Communicative resonance identifies moments of relative coordination among a number of features, forms, and media that create links between events.

Okiek wedding advice, *ceerseet,* marriage discussions, political-legal meetings, and *baraza* illustrate the blurriness of the category "ritual communication" and underline the range of contexts potentially involved in communicative resonance.[25] They also show how interdiscursive relations in different media might reinforce one another to enhance resonance between events in some cases, whereas in others the connections conflict with other, contrasting event features, complicating or confounding resonances. State-oriented *baraza* were minimally invoked in Okiek marriage arrangement in the mid-1980s, yet they point to transforming identities and social relations and to new types and occasions of RC that may foster communicative resonance. Together these cases present a continuum of interconnection and contradiction among media, forms, and structures in different events, outlining the dynamics of communicative resonance.

In addition to identifying formal and performative resources and structural dimensions that contribute to communicative resonance, it is important to consider their involvement with pragmatic and metapragmatic processes in linked events. How might resonance evoking other occasions contribute to the social action and effects of RC? In the Okiek material, the parallels of encouragement and advice might have their strongest rhetorical effects on the bride—just initiated and being married—but they are relevant for others, too. Resonance between marriage discussions and men's meetings seems to invoke the latter's gravitas to further endorse lineage authority in marriage and—in Okiek metapragmatic commentaries—as procedural authority and model. More intriguing to consider is how formal-functional relations among semiotic resources relate to pragmatic patterns in linked events—for example, how RC constitutes collective persuasion or collective decisions from individual turns and contributions in different events, pragmatic tasks relevant to a number of occasions and cultural-historical settings. At the same time, in ceremonies such as Okiek initiation, ritual events are simultaneously part of the pragmatic trajectory and communicative orchestration of the ceremony as a whole.[26]

As collective decisions or persuasions are forged, RC also constitutes social relations and hierarchies, identities and collectivities, based on and producing notions of personhood, agency, causality, and society. Tensions and contradictions are integral to these processes, although the issues most prominent vary. For instance, *ceerseet* shows fundamental contradictions between Okiek ideas about gender and the willpower required for initiation (Kratz 1994: 195). In marriage talks, lineages are re-created as collective decision-making entities from cross-cutting individual relations and interests, simultaneously negotiating in the face of uncertainty about the young couple's future actions (Kratz 2000, 2005a). Fundamental contradictions related to gender are involved here as well. To what extent does communicative resonance invoke other settings characterized by similar contradictions and tensions, with their echoes and associations joining these dynamics?

Notes

Joanna Davidson and Michael Peletz provided helpful feedback on earlier drafts of this chapter. Discussions at the "Ritual Communication" symposium in Sintra were also much appreciated.

1. Defining and understanding RC requires several kinds of work, including detailed analyses of how modes of communication are used and combined in particular events; analyses that trace historical transformations in ritual occasions; and analyses that cut across events, occasions, and contexts. This work would identify the diverse communicative resources associated with ritual occasions and their varied uses and settings, situating RC in communicative economies of several scales and providing clues to discursive, pragmatic, and cultural resonances and social relations evoked within ritual.

2. My previous work examined ritual efficacy (the way Okiek constitute RC as social action) by analyzing the orchestration, coordination, and pragmatics of communicative media in initiation and the structural, semiotic, and pragmatic relations and progressions among Okiek life-cycle ceremonies (Kratz 1994); formal-functional relations among genres in ritual and conversational settings (1988a, 1988b, 1989); historical changes in ceremonial form and their representation (1993); and comparative ceremonial structures and styles among Okiek and their neighbors (1981: 363–67, 1988a, 1988b: 726–747). My current project on Okiek marriage arrangement follows initiates' continuing social maturation to consider how notions of personhood and identity develop over the life course in changing historical circumstances. I also consider the "micropolitical contestations" of marriage discussions that shape and link core social institutions (Ferguson 1999: 192; cf. Gluckman 1958; Kapferer 1983).

3. Other contributors to this volume use the notion of resonance to develop related analyses. Du Bois focuses more narrowly on how affinities are activated across utterances, noting that resonance across utterances can be divergent or convergent. Haviland's use of "resonance" is quite consonant with mine. He also underlines communicative multimodality and the social embeddedness of communicative interaction. Whereas I focus on resonance among particular, well-defined Okiek events, Haviland extends analysis to snippets of interaction in various daily settings. Silverstein (2005) also considered interdiscursivity across events.

4. A recent issue of *Linguistic Anthropology* concerned with "semiosis across encounters" extended related Bakhtinian perspectives (Agha 2005a; Bauman 2005). Despite recognition that such cross-context resonance is multimodal, however, much work on such interdiscursivity falls back on textual analysis alone, leaving aside other communicative media. These rich analyses of language use are potent resources for analyzing RC but are ultimately insufficient if other media combined with language in ritual are left out.

5. Land sales transformed the area's demography in the 1990s and, in tandem with increased educational participation and other changes, led to transformations in marriage arrangement and marriage patterns. Christian

churches also came to the area at this time, although mission stations and churches had long been in the region.

6. The next two sections draw from Kratz 2000.

7. Seclusion once continued for six to eight months but now is condensed into the month-long school holidays.

8. Okiek recognize similarities but describe wedding advice with verbs other than *-ceer* (encourage). The events differ in other ways: *ceerseet* are held at night during a dramatic series of ritual events, whereas wedding advice is given early in the morning, with a smaller group, as other preparations take place. Gifts are a distinctive feature of *ceerseet* for Okiek.

9. The close resemblance of AN's themes and wording in the two speeches suggests that he saw the two occasions as parallel in certain ways.

10. With the same speaker, there is strong token-based indexicality in this case, too.

11. Keenan (1974: 109) discussed a similar rhetorical joining in Madagascar weddings.

12. Okiek marriage arrangement has changed substantially over the last fifty to sixty years. Before cows were standard bridewealth, it was honey and hives. Today a "cow" might be a maize-grinding machine or a huge cooking pot. Indeed, a recent e-mail from a Kipchornwonek Okiot woman reported, "Marriage is no longer done through engagement, it's either by eloping, civil or religious" (S. Tanki, January 20, 2007). When I began working with Okiek in the mid-1970s, childhood engagement was still fairly common, and a future son-in-law visited for years before marriage. In the 1980s, the process described here was more or less universal among Kaplelach Okiek. The 1990s brought diverse social and economic transformations and associated shifts in marriage arrangement (Kratz 2007). These transformations ramify across many contexts and institutions, in varied, uneven ways. Major life transitions such as marriage provide critical moments when these transformations are recognized, debated, and lived as people negotiate divergent interests, changing situations, and unknown futures. These transformations and shifts are considered in my book *Looking for the Hairless Cow: Arranging Okiek Marriage.*

13. I omit Okiek text in this and the following example because of space limitations.

14. Meeting size varies by topic and jurisdiction; some multiethnic meetings are conducted in the Maasai language.

15. Men from the husband's family represent a guarantee of care for a married daughter, a warranty based on their influence and senior, supervisory relations with her husband. They form a joint judiciary with senior men of the bride's family if the marriage has difficulties. As elders describe it, the young woman's family gives her to her husband's family. If the marriage founders,

these men are witnesses to property transfers—a judiciary and guarantee, then, for the husband's family. "If the child [girl] then goes and runs away, they know what was said and they can repay things." They also resolve marital disputes when the wife returns home after mistreatment.

16. Women's participation is both essential and anomalous, a tension that emerges from the conjunction of gendered definitions of personhood and the dynamics of individual and collective personhood (Kratz 2000). Karp (1987) described a similar "paradox of agency" in Iteso marriage ceremonies. Brenneis (1984, 1996) showed how gender exclusion in meetings reinforced social hierarchies in Fiji. Kratz (1988, 1994, 2000) considered gendered differences in Okiek exposure to and ability in speech styles such as blessing and oratory.

17. In transcript 2, a senior woman (KW) notes this expectation.

18. Other complaints might focus on different features of marriage arrangement, such as accusing a girl's father of contravening lineage rights by "giving her away by himself."

19. Connections between ritual events might be realized more fully or portrayed as closer or more distant at different times, just as Briggs and Bauman describe strategies "used in minimizing and maximizing intertextual gaps" (1992: 155). Briggs also notes that relating events through narrative produces gaps and links, either or both of which might be emphasized by narrators and audiences (1996a: 24).

20. He tried to conduct the planning meeting in Kiswahili, indexing national and development domains of values, but the linguistic repertoire of the multiethnic gathering required switching to Maasai and Kipsigis. Okiek were assumed to understand both languages and to accommodate the narrower linguistic repertoires of immigrants into what was formerly an Okiek area. On Okiek multilingualism and accommodation, see Kratz 1981, 1986.

21. In the meetings Haugerud and Njogu described, speakers code-switched to Kiembu. As they noted, code-switching might signal different status claims to the assembled crowd and among the hierarchy of elites.

22. He spoke in Kiswahili; this is a running translation from my field notes.

23. Local *baraza* also provide ways for enterprising persons to become local liaisons with government bureaucracies and power by taking organizational roles and adopting the dress and language of those positions.

24. The assistant chief's family was certainly developing a distinctive, elite style of celebration relative to other Okiek. In December 1982 the assistant chief's brother married the daughter of a prominent local Maasai chief. The reception at his sister's house had an organization and gifts similar to those of the wedding event described for the assistant chief's daughter. The groom received his PhD several years after, later working for a development organization in Tanzania.

25. The dimensions of formalization that Irvine (1979) described are relevant to RC in many cases. She identified four aspects prominent in notions of formality: code structuring, code consistency, the invoking of positional identities, and situational focus. Are these combined in different ways, to different ends, in ritual events? Are there other relevant dimensions to include? How can this be extended to other media in RC?

26. Metapragmatic modes of framing events as ritual offer a productive topic for comparative analysis, as well as a kind of resonance across a range of occasions. For Okiek, blessings are invariably part of the explicit marking of ritual occasions. Blessings occur in each event discussed here, with occasion-specific themes and scheduling.

eight

Ritualized Performances as Total Social Facts

The House of Multiple Spirits in Tokelau

Ingjerd Hoëm

Ritualized performances present us with mirrors through which we can gain insights into the workings of society. Following this line of thinking, ritualized performances may also work as such mirrors, admittedly to varying degrees, for the people who produce and are engaged in ritualized behavior (see, e.g., Kapferer 1986 and Handelman 1998 for different expositions of these ideas). These ideas, though not novel, are still highly productive in the social sciences. Here I apply this perspective to address the issue of how people's conceptions and categorizations of the events of which ritual communication (RC) is an integral part contribute to shaping the experience and transformative potential of an event, within and beyond the event itself. I look at theatrical performances in Tokelau, a so-called non-self-governing territory of New Zealand. Tokelau comprises three atolls, Atafu, Nukunonu, and Fakaofo, lying five hundred kilometers north of Samoa in the South Pacific. Approximately fifteen hundred people live in the atoll societies. Another six thousand to seven thousand live in Tokelau communities outside of Tokelau—in New Zealand, Samoa, Australia, and the United States.

In what follows, I analyze a Tokelau theatrical performance as a total social fact in the Maussian sense (Mauss 1954 [1925]). In particular, I make use of three aspects of Mauss's perspective on gift exchanges. The first is the reciprocality of the relationship between the giver and the receiver of gifts, which creates what has been called an economy of *mana* (see Henare 2008). The second point follows from the premise of social reciprocity: a total social fact has ramifications in other spheres of society (religious, legal, economic, and political), beyond the immediacy of an exchange situation (Sykes 2005). Finally, local conceptions must be added to this perspective on gift exchanges as total social facts and as contests of social prestations in Mauss's terms. In order to incorporate local conceptions, I maintain a focus throughout the chapter on the way the frames of interpretation associated with a particular kind of event may shape the reception and hence the effects of the ritual communication represented in the event.

A Tokelau *fiafia,* or public festive gathering, is characterized by an exchange of gifts, both material and immaterial, ranging from food, mats, and money to speeches, prayers, dances, and various kinds of theatrical performances such as skits (*faleaitu*) and clowning. The exchanges take place between two or more groups or "sides" (*vaega* or *itu, faitu*), and their form is highly ritualized and competitive.

In pre-Christian times, the (Tokelauan, Samoan, etc.) genre of *faleaitu* 'house of spirits' was associated with the protection of spirits, *aitu* (for some examples of this and other aspects of spirit lore, see Hereniko 1995; Mageo 1984, 1996; Sinavaiana 1992). Today, although practices associated with Christian institutions are dominant, the 'house of spirits' retains this aspect of something out of the ordinary. People in Tokelau explain that what is said and done in the context of a public celebration, or *fiafia* (lit. 'to make happy, merriment, joy'), of which the *faleaitu* is an important ingredient, is judged differently from behavior outside such a context. What happens in the meeting house on such occasions is 'clean' (*mama*) almost by definition, and it is not to be taken seriously in the way that corresponding behavior would be outside this context (see Hoëm 2004).

The theatrical performance I present draws on multiple genres, practices, and discourses, ranging from the authoritative and potentially legitimating genre of *kupu mai anamua* 'words from the past' to descriptions of street children in urban New Zealand playing "spacies," or gambling machines. In this regard, aspects of the performance simultaneously resonate strongly with ancient ritual practices in Tokelau and carry textual resonances with other productions that with increasing frequency make indigenous culture an object of scrutiny across the Pacific.

Ritual practices in Tokelau, as can be gleaned from oral tradition, historical descriptions, and contemporary practices, are oriented toward increasing and achieving fecundity—of both humans and the natural environment—and toward making social organization work as a well-orchestrated and harmonious whole. This sought-after state is called *maopopopo,* which means "well-coordinated, of one mind, a group with a common purpose." This social body should be guided by *alofa,* which can be glossed as 'loving compassion', and should follow the principles of generalized reciprocity, *inati,* which ensures that all members receive equal portions of any communally distributed resource such as fish. Finally, patterns of interaction of respect and avoidance, *va,* between young and old, male and female, brothers and sisters, is still practiced in Tokelau today.

The "religious sphere proper" is the Christian church, represented by both Catholic and Protestant denominations. The church presides over the life-cycle rituals of baptism, first communion, marriage, and funerals, and people in general spend large portions of their lives in church-related activities. The ancestral past, as preserved in genealogies, songs, sayings, and other genres precious to Tokelauans, is an important part of life today, and knowledge thereof serves to regulate rights and obligations. Thus it gives shape and meaning to social relationships. This kind of knowledge is important and valuable because it represents the key to positions of power and respect. Except in its most general expressions, it is not openly shared or evenly distributed. Male elders, *toeaina,* are the expert custodians of this kind of knowledge, and occasionally an old woman, *lomatua,* may become recognized as knowledgeable as well.

Life in the atoll villages is communal in that the private sphere, in the Habermasian sense of the presence of a culturally recognized barrier between public and personal matters (see, e.g., Sennett 1977), cannot be said to exist. The Village Council, or *taupulega,* and the Women's Committee, or *komiti tumama,* each have a say in matters involving the internal running of the extended families (*kaiga*), such as household members' standards of hygiene and dress, their moral behavior, and their general conduct. They can even decide a *kaiga*'s future in the sense of ordering a household to leave Tokelau altogether. This punishment is severe, and to be cast out in this manner is a matter of great distress and shame.

The Shifting Sites of Ritual

The material I discuss involves a phenomenon that has been described as the "shifting of sites of ritual." The shift is associated with processes of modernization and was noted early on by Erving Goffman (1959, 1974). It commonly involves a change from the collective as subject and object of worship (Durkheim 1915) to the "cultivation of the self" (see also Bauman 1995). Another aspect of this social process is an increased ritualization of culture, such that the "naturalization" of practices (the establishing of a quality of "taken-for grantedness" of human life-worlds) becomes increasingly difficult to sustain, and therefore tradition and authenticity become contested entities (see Keesing 1992; also Briggs 1996b). It is possible to observe aspects of such processes in Tokelau society and in the Tokelau communities in New Zealand proper. Yet the ways in which these tendencies are conceptualized and accommodated differ, interestingly, in the two social environments. It therefore becomes increasingly important to understand how conflict and dissent are expressed and controlled, as well as how leadership is exercised and legitimacy achieved, in the face of increasing tension between competing visions of ways of life. The study of RC provides a particular intake to such processes of conflict management.

The Performative Self

In Tokelau, as in many other parts of the Pacific, conceptions of personhood equal a socially oriented self. An extroverted or communally oriented disposition is encouraged from early infancy. Robert Levy (1973) has described, on the basis of his ethnopsychological work in Tahiti, the pan-Polynesian occupation with *mata* 'face', in a way that seems to be a projection of Goffman's theory of the performative self (Goffman 1959). Polynesian forms of sociality, however, differ from the performative self described by Goffman in the extent of their collective orientation. That every situation is social, and that every social situation must be understood in terms of its social composition, produces an orientation that I have described elsewhere as *tulaga* 'sense of place' (Hoëm 2004).

This orientation can also be expressed in a collective readiness to perform and to take on the perspective of an other (a visitor, an other group or "side") and mirror it back to this other, most frequently through mimetic caricature. Another and more serious formal aspect of the representation of otherness is the greeting rituals that are integral parts of the opening sequences of any formal gathering. The ritual establishment of status in terms of inclusion and exclusion is achieved by the recitation of a *fakalupega* (Samoan *fa'alupega*), which is part of the opening section of the play described later.

Such characterizations and the differences in status and power accruing to them are typically relational, and most important, their value may be inverted in "nonserious" ritualized performances. This is part of the reason humorous and entertaining events are of such great social importance to Tokelauans: they contribute to the definition of social groups in terms of status relative to one another.

Ritual Communication and Theatrical Performances

The study of the way ritualized forms of language and other aspects of script or procedure combine to produce a particular kind of speech event and a particular vision of the world relates the study of human communication to issues of power (see in particular Bloch 1986). Social anthropology has added to the study of institutionalized production and inculcation of ideology the perspective in which ritual events may be seen simultaneously as the products of multiple life trajectories and as having institutional histories (Barth 1993; Herzfeld 1985). The challenge for this kind of approach still lies in analytically holding together the various perspectives and the situatedness of the respective producers, participants, and resulting event. In the subsequent presentation, I combine a linguistic and textual analysis with an exploration of the relationship between the intentions of the producers and enactors of a ritualized performance and recipients' use of various frames of interpretation in their reception of it.

The group Tokelau Te Ata, which produced the performance, chose a particular form of action theater called "theater for community development" (originally associated with the work of Paolo Freire, as developed by Augusto Boal and Jerzy Grotowski, among others; see, e.g., Schechner 1985). The structure of the performance is prototypical in that after a play has been presented, the audience is asked to comment upon its central issues. Audience members are also encouraged to suggest a different ending for the story they have just seen. By choosing this form, Te Ata wanted to address issues it considered important but found to be excluded from the dominant moral discourse in Tokelau society. Te Ata members also wanted to raise common awareness of significant events in Tokelau's history. They expect social change to take place by means of such action theater. In this case, the intended (or hoped for) social change would be for the excluded topics to enter Tokelau public discourse, and even for changes in some practices related to sexual abuse and intergenerational relationships to follow from this. Finally, they hoped to bring about a heightened sense of pride and the strengthening of a common, national sense of Tokelau ethnic identity.

The Theater Performance: A Challenge to Dominant Communicative Practices

The Tokelau theater performance that I analyze was an instance in which a relatively uncommon form, action theater, was presented in a communal setting.[1] The setting itself was influenced by the novelty of the production: it was communal, but people were gathered for the sole purpose of participating in the performance as a semiactive audience. This was in itself a great contrast to most other settings in which *faleaitu* and other kinds of performances (most commonly, dance and speeches) take place. The rule is that everyone present is likely to have to take part as a performer at one time or another during such events. The general form is for one *faitu,* or "side" (group or team) to "put on an item," as it is called in New Zealand (NZ) English. This "item" can be, for example, the popular *fatele* dancing, which is done by a group of men and women standing in gender-separated rows, one behind another and facing the other side, which sits at the other end of the village meeting house. When the dance is over, the conductor, or team leader, for the evening ends with the words *O fanatu e!* lit. 'Oh, going over there!'—in other words, "Over to you!" With this, the other side, which until now has been the spectator, becomes the performer by its acceptance of the challenge. Its members in turn present their dance for the others, who sit down in the role of recipients. In this manner, a competitive exchange of prestations typically takes place during these events.

The language and content of the dramas draw upon common speech genres, from *kupu mai anamua* 'words from ancient times', which include *muagagana* 'common sayings from old', or proverbs, to contemporary street slang in NZ English. Also included are the formal Tokelau language registers of *lauga* 'speeches', *pehe* 'songs', and *fakanau* 'spells'; the less formal language of the still highly ritualized style of *faleaitu* 'skits' and *faluma* 'clowning'; and everyday talk of varieties such as *alofaga* 'greetings', *faitala* 'gossip', and *tala pepelo* 'joking talk'.

The dramatic performance I describe was repeated in different social environments: in the Tokelau communities in New Zealand, in the Tokelau community in Samoa, and in the three atoll communities of Tokelau itself. It was received differently in the homeland and in the overseas communities. From the description of the social dynamics associated with this RC event, I hope to throw light on the way a set sequence of RC can be efficacious in qualitatively different ways. I examine the way the frames of interpretation that contribute to defining an event as being of a particular kind may bring about such variation.

Tokelau Te Ata sprang from a small network of relatives and friends who, in the early 1990s, lived outside Wellington, the New Zealand capital, in the Petone, Lower Hutt, and Upper Hutt Valley area. These people came together regularly and in different capacities as they attended the many functions—fund-raising events, sports gatherings, church services, and meetings (*fono*)—that connected Tokelau community members who lived overseas. Moreover, they formed a band, called Tagi, and met frequently for singing practice and occasionally for public performances.

Tagi means "lament" and is a standard part of Tokelau folk tales, or *kakai,* in which it most commonly occurs in the form of a short song performed by the storyteller on behalf of one of the characters in the story, who fervently desires something and turns the desire into a plea or petition in the form of a song (see, e.g., Vonen 1992). *Tagi* thus signifies a strongly felt wish and desire for something and a lament that the desire is not (at least yet) fulfilled.[2] The group members chose the name in order to show their attachment to Tokelau, their desire for good things for the Tokelau people, and their mourning of the distance between the present state of the Tokelau communities overseas and in the atolls and a happy, thriving society that successfully combined the ways and cultural inheritance from its past with the challenges of modern life. Members ranged from young to middle-aged, and some of them were moving into positions of community leadership at the time.

The band members all attended the so-called Easter Tournament, an annual pan-Tokelauan gathering at which contingents from Tokelau and the overseas communities met for religious services, sports tournaments, dancing, sharing of food, speeches, skits, clowning, and so forth. They had had their fill of such events, however, and thought it was time for something new. They conducted formal interviews with people who attended the tournament and asked for their opinion of the gathering: why they attended (most people from overseas said they attended in order to keep in touch with Tokelau things), whether they were satisfied with what such gatherings had to offer, and, if this was answered in the negative, what they would like to see instead. Quite a few respondents expressed dissatisfaction with the strong emphasis on Tokelau tradition—on preserving the correct Tokelau way, *faka Tokelau,* with all that implied: a dominant moral discourse with concomitant codes of behavior and an accompanying canon of performative genres. The canonical status of any performance—that is, its acceptance as proper according to Tokelau tradition—is ensured by the presence of elders (*toeaina* and *lomatua*) at rehearsals. The elders' acceptance of an "item," usually song and dance (skits and clowning are carried out mainly by elders and therefore are by definition legitimate), gives it legitimacy in the eyes of the community.

The results of the interviews encouraged the members of Tagi, who saw that others in the Tokelau community, outside their immediate circle, shared their desire to broaden the repertoire of expression. One of the group's members, and the prime mover behind this initiative, had some previous experience with the performance scene in Wellington. In particular, he knew the film and theater director Paul Maunder, who is known for, among other things, the controversy surrounding his production of the movie version of Albert Wendt's book *Sons for the Return Home* (Conrich and Tincknell 2006). Maunder expressed interest in helping facilitate a Tokelau theater production, and notes were distributed in the community saying that anyone who wanted to participate in the creation of a play about Tokelau's history was welcome to do so.

Elsewhere I have written in detail about the production of the play (Hoëm 1998, 2004). It suffices to say here that the invitation to participate resulted in a dedicated crew of eleven actors and associated members for the first play produced. This drama was called *Tagi,* too, and it dealt with significant events in Tokelau's turbulent past. The play followed Tokelau's history from mythological ancestry through a period of inter-atoll warfare and the decimation of the population by the Peruvian slave trade to the coming of the missionaries, ending with present-day life in the overseas communities. Some of these events were traumatic, and some of the knowledge associated with them is conventionally esoteric.

Texts and Ritual Communication

To illustrate the way the linguistic conventions of the play did and did not conform to established communicative practices in the communities, I reproduce four short sections of the text: the introduction, which is in two parts, a formal greeting, or *fakalupega,* and a recitation of genealogies (*gafa*); a *faleaitu,* or skit; a scene from "ordinary family life in New Zealand," including sexual abuse; and the end and resolution, a song about proper role behavior.[3] Following are the texts as they were originally presented, mainly in Tokelauan but with some lines in NZ English, accompanied by my translations. Insertions in parentheses are mine; insertions in brackets are stage directions. The use of Tokelauan posed a challenge for some of the younger actors, who were not fluent speakers.

	Ceremonial greeting
1a. *Fakalupega*	
Mamalu o te tatou kaiga: na matua,	The dignity of our "extended family": the mothers,
na tamana, na uo, ma te fanau a Tokelau.	the fathers, the friends, and the children of Tokelau.
Matou vaega nei, ka taumafai ki matou	Our group here will attempt to bring you
ke faka taunuku atu	
te matou fakafiafiaga, pe he tala foki,	our entertainment, and a story, too,
agai ki to tatou atunuku, ko Tokelau.	focused on our homeland, Tokelau.
Ko te matou tala foki, tulou,	Our story, with all respect,
ka fanatu lava i loto	is going to be in the Tokelau language.
i te gagana faka i loto i fale.	
Tulou te Faleiva.	Respects (to) the 'Nine-houses' (Fakaofo).
Tulou te Falefa.	Respects (to) the 'Four-houses' (Nukunonu).
Tulou te Falefitu.	Respects (to) the 'Seven-houses' (Atafu).

1b. *Gafa* (Genealogy)
Mai te ulugamatua ko Tonuia ma Lagimaina na tutupu ake ai na fale e fitu.
From the ancestral couple, Tonuia and Lagimaina, grew the houses that are seven (that is, Atafu).
Mai na lulu iena, e i ei, ko Vaovela, ko Laufali, ko Fekei, ko Pio, ko Levao, Laua, Malokie.
Mai te lulu a Vaovela nofo mai, Tonuia ma Lagimaina te ulugamatua, ko Vaovela, ko Hakalia, ko Moti, ko Tuilave, ko Teuila, ko Ioana, ko Heto.
From there came the offspring Vaovela, Laufali, Fekei, Pio, Levao, Laua, Malokie. From the offspring of Vaovela dwelling here, Tonuia, Lagimaina—the ancestral couple, (came) Vaovela, Hakalia, Moti, Tuilave, Teuila, Ioana, Heto. [Heto walks forward.]
E i ei te tuafafine o Tuilave, ko Muia. Ko Muia, ko Katalina, ko Valelia, ko Eheta.
There is the sister of Tuilave, Muia. Muia, Katalina, Valelia, Eheta. [Eheta walks forward.]

I te fanauga, toe liliu ifo kia Tuilave ... fanaifo ko Teuila, ko Ioana, e i ei te tamafafine ma te taina o Ioana ko Kaloline, ko Pule.
In (recounting) the process of bringing forth children, (we) once more turn down to Tuilave ... going down—Teuila, Ioana, there is the *tamafafine* (the offspring of sister's children) and the sister of Ioana. Kaloline, Pule. [Pule walks forward.]
Mai te lulu a Laufali, te ulugamatua ko Tonuia ma Lagimaina, ko Laufali, Malifa, ko Malae, ko Pou, Malia, ko Akata.
From the offspring of Laufali, the ancestral couple Tonuia and Lagimaina, Laufali, Malifa, Malae, Pou, Malia, Akata. [Akata walks forward.]
Mai te lulu a Fekei, te ulugamatua, Tonuia ma Lagimaina, ko Fekei, ko Lepeka, ko Tioni, nofo ia Tioni kia Fipe, te fanauga ko Hiohe, ko Huliana, ko Hulu. Ko Hiohe fanaifo ko Tahi, ko Teofilo, ko Nila.
From the offspring of Fekei—the ancestral couple, Tonuia and Lagimaina—Fekei, Lepeka, Tioni. Tioni living together with Fipe, the offspring Hiohe, Huliana, Sulu. Hiohe descended, Tahi, Teofilo, Nila. [Nila walks forward.]
Tuafafine o Hiohe, ko Huliana. Huliana, ko Pahi, ko Akapito.
Sister of Hiohe is Huliana. Huliana, Pahi, Akapito. [Akapito walks forward.]
Te tuafafine o Pahi, matua ko Huliana, ko Ana, ko Tioni.
Pahi's sister, mother Huliana, Ana, Tioni. [Tioni walks forward.]
Mai te toka tolu Hiohe, Huliana ko Hulu te taina o Huliana. Mai a Hulu, ko Taunehe, ko Hulu.
From the three Hiohe, Huliana (and) Hulu, Huliana's sister. From Hulu, Taunehe, Hulu. [Hulu walks forward.]
Mai te lulu a Pio, te ulugamatua ko Tonuia ma Lagimaina, ko Pio ko Fafie, Teaile, Te Hakalo, ko Taupe, Tekata, ko Loha, ko Luifala, Ateli, ko Huhana.
From the offspring of Pio—the ancestral couple Tonuia and Lagimaina—Pio, Fafie, Teaile, Hakalo, Taupe, Tekata, Loha, Luifala, Ateli, Huhana. [Huhana walks forward.]
Mai te lulu a Levao, ko Levao, ko Iakopo, Naomi, Ehekielu, ko Akenehe, ko au ko Falani.
From the offspring of Levao, Levao, Iakopo, Naomi, Ehekielu, Akenehe, me—Falani. [Stands up.]

2. *Faleaitu* (Skit)
Falani: *E fai mai tautou hiva ko manatua na aho koi aoga ai au.*
Keep on with your dancing (while) I recall the days I went to school.
Tioni: Ha ha.
Akapito: Oh.

Falani: *Io, Kima ma Hitolo ma Iaheto i te Hagato Iohefo i Masterton. He ko manatua ai te tala o matou.*
Yes, Kima and Hitolo and Iaheto (went to) the St. Joseph['s College] in Masterton. I don't remember the story about us.
Huhana: *Tauhaga fia?*
What year was this?
Falani: *Tauhaga fia? Ko te 1964, io ko te 1964 tena. E fai te aoga oi hau ai te felela oi ve mai Falani you ... swim? Oh yes, me good swim. I come from Tokelau. Hau ka te tatou vagea ko Heto, hau koe ki ei. Ko Heto ko Iaheto, ko Hitolo, ko au ko Hitolo. Hau koe ki ei. Tefea te tino e fai e ia te... Hau koe. Io ko au, io.*
Which year? In 1964, yes, it was in 1964. I was in school, and the brother superior came and asked me, Falani, you ... swim? "Oh, yes, me good swim. I come from Tokelau." (He said) "Come here and be our group, Heto, you come here. Heto, Iaheto, Hitolo, I am Hitolo. You come here. Where is the person who can be... Come you."
"Yes, me, yes."
Falani: *Ko te kau matamata e nonofo mai i luga i ko ni. Omai omai koutou. Manatua la ko teia te kautafa o te swimming pool, ko te ia te tino o te swimming pool.*
Io io, are you ready? Io.
[Falani, demonstrating what it was like:] The audience is sitting down there. Come here, come here, you. Remember that that is the side of the swimming pool, he is the person of the swimming pool.
"Yes, yes, are you ready? Yes."
Falani: *Kae tau te lima o Hitolo ki te itu o te swimming pool, veake ko ia kua malo. Na puna ake lava, kikila atu ki na tino matamata toe (puna ki lalo fano i te katoa).*
Hitolo's hand reached the side of the swimming pool (i.e., he had cut across it at the short end). It was like he had won. (He) surfaced, looking at the people who were watching.

3. *Holi kaiga* (Incest Scene)
In this scene, the character representing the first Tokelauan child born in New Zealand, a young female character called Hei, grows up and experiences difficulties because of cultural differences. The scene begins in a family home as the father returns from work. After dinner, an uncle shows up. The father and uncle drink beer, and then the father goes to bed. The uncle approaches Hei and throws his arms around her. The other actors now throw a blanket over Hei and the uncle, and one of the actors indicates by hand movements that the scene is "blacked out."

Although little is shown, it is clear that the uncle molests his young niece. Subsequently she gets into trouble. She meets street kids and plays "spacies" with them. Eventually she is taken into care by the welfare system, and her uncomprehending family is devastated.

4. *Pehe*	Song
Fatupaepae o te kaiga	Female head (lit. 'cornerstone') of the family
Fatupaepae o te kaiga	
E felau fakahoa te katiga	Sharing out, distributing the meal (the starchy food that goes with fish to constitute a full meal)
E felau fakahoa te utuga	Sharing out, distributing the fish shares
Tamatane o te uta fenua	'Senior male' of (commander of the work done in) the outer islets, where the coconut plantations are
Tamatane o vaka o utua	'Senior male' of the fishing boats going out from the village islet
Taofi ke mau	May these positions and actions stand firm
Ia kupu a tupuna e.	by (the power of) the words of the ancestors.
[Spoken by all] *"Ke ola ia Tokelau."*	"So that Tokelau may live!"

The *fakalupega* 'ceremonial greeting' (1a) is a conventional way of opening a formal gathering; it communicates proper respect (*fakaaloalo*) to all groups present. To name each group at the beginning of an event is important because it helps set the agenda by placing everyone in the correct relationship or position (*tulaga*) to the others present. In the present context, it also communicates that the play is for all of Tokelau, not just for one of the atoll communities. By implication, the play is not intended for a multicultural audience, either. The greeting frames the performance as a whole, but in an unusual and slightly ambiguous way: the presentation is characterized as both entertainment (*fakafiafiaga*) and a serious story (*tala*).

Section 1b presents the *gafa* 'genealogy' of the actors who participate in the play. To present a genealogy in public, except in the vaguest metaphorical terms, is highly unconventional. Genealogies are regarded as family property, and knowledge of them is jealously guarded. This kind of knowledge is vitally important in village life because it legitimates rights to land and positions. Usually, genealogical notes are kept as family treasures, and it is common that one person in each extended family is the custodian of such knowledge.

Furthermore, the way the genealogies are presented in this text, in order to demonstrate the position of an "ego," the individual actor, within a network of kin, falls outside the conventional usage of genealogies. In ordinary practice, genealogical links would be traced in support of claims to land, for example, through a particular genealogical position with concomitant rights and obligations. The mention of the individual actors by their first names in this text indicates that the individual aspects of their social personae are central to the following performance. Furthermore, the order in which the actors are introduced—the youngest first and the more senior members toward the end—is a reversal of common etiquette.

Text 2, the skit, or *faleaitu,* exhibits the structure common to the genre. A skit usually involves at least two people, who may take turns setting the scene, or one assumes the role of directing the skit. The director of the skit is asked or announces his or her intention to *fai mea malie* 'make something pleasant or sweet'. Then the director announces the topic or story of the skit, such as slave raiders or the biblical story of Noah. Alternatively, as in this case, it might be a story that the persons chosen for the skit have experienced themselves. The skit excerpted in text 2 illustrates the state of being "FOB," or "fresh off the boat," a derogatory New Zealand term for new arrivals from "the islands" who are ignorant of New Zealand ways. In spite of being Tokelauans and therefore good swimmers familiar with the sea, the actors are unfamiliar with swimming-pool etiquette at a Catholic boarding school and therefore make fools of themselves. In this part of the play, it follows that reference to the actors by their personal names is conventional.

In action theater, the director usually selects people from the audience to take part in a skit, positions them onstage, and tells them what to do. This procedure is copied here, but the participants are chosen from among the actors, which indicates that in fact we are witnessing a kind of meta-*faleaitu,* a play within a play. This kind of embedding of genres is common in Tokelau discourse, but the presentation of a play within a play in this manner was likely a first in the history of Tokelau performances. The content of the skit, however, is conventional.

Text 3 is my description of a scene depicting Tokelauan family life in New Zealand, including drinking and sexual abuse. To present such a scene in any form is definitely not part of the conventional repertoire of Tokelau performance or expressive culture, and the topic, sexual abuse and problems with public welfare, clearly lies outside the range of subjects deemed fitting for public mention and inclusion in performances. In this scene, the performers are represented as role players proper (mother, uncle, etc.), and not as projecting their personal selves or experiences.

Text 4 is the final song of the play, representing a resolution of the conflicting issues it has presented. It depicts the ideal man and woman according to Tokelau oral tradition. It ties their gender roles, such as female head of the extended family—the *fatupaepae* 'cornerstone'—to their respective places in the extended families and their roles in subsistence activities. It also presents the proper relationships of authority, leadership, and respect and stresses the value of sharing. Finally, it states that these practices, roles, and relationships are critical for the continuation of life in Tokelau and for Tokelauans. The song is part of the standard repertoire, and to use a song in this way, as a collective confirmation of a common purpose, is also typical.

The Reception of the Play

Another production by Te Ata, the result of which came to be called *Mafine*, "Woman," followed the production of the play *Tagi*. *Mafine* was about the role of women in the extended family and in Tokelau society; it stressed the conflict between individual hopes, aspirations, and desires and the larger collective's authority over individuals. In what follows, I concentrate on the reception of the first play, *Tagi*, but add a few comments pertaining to *Mafine* when describing the theater group's tour to Tokelau. For simplicity, I describe the overall reception in New Zealand and the reception in Tokelau and compare the two.

In the New Zealand Tokelauan community, the audience response to *Tagi* was overwhelming. People laughed , cried, and joined in singing the songs. The general reaction was that people were happy to "see the history of Tokelau come alive." To my knowledge, no one commented openly on the issue of sexual abuse, either in group discussions or in other media such as Tokelau radio programs. However, members of the theater group were approached in private by people who wanted to share their experiences with such problems and, they hoped, to get some advice. Critical comments were all centered on the legitimacy of the theater project in terms of tradition. Many people questioned Te Ata's right to represent Tokelau's history at all. The theater group had consulted with elders (*toeaina*) on various issues, but they had not allied themselves with one or more elders who could have been present at rehearsals and performances to lend credence to the project in terms of being done *faka Tokelau* 'the Tokelau way'. This did not happen for obvious reasons: one of the main motivating forces behind the project was precisely the wish to step beyond the accepted ways of behaving and communicating associated with the Tokelau way.

The part of the play that received the most public comment was 1b, the genealogical presentation of the actors' links to each other. Some people commented that the genealogies were incorrect, and others used the genealogical affiliations depicted in the play as a reason to dismiss the group's claim to a voice at all. This response came from the atoll Nukunonu, from which most of the actors were commonly considered to have come. The point is that the genealogies the group chose also show a link to Atafu, one of the other two Tokelau atolls. To stress a link to Atafu when they could easily have shown equally strong or stronger ties to Nukunonu seemed like a betrayal to the Nukunonu traditionalists. That the group chose this portrayal deliberately, in order to show that "we are all related, beyond atoll-affiliation, and hence should live together as one family or nation," was not understood or appreciated by all. Those who saw atoll affiliation as the most important point of identification rejected this stand.

Some of those who reacted strongly against this performance subsequently took up the challenge and, in typical Tokelau fashion—as in an exchange between "sides" at a *fiafia*—formed their own theater group and produced another play about Tokelau's history. Elders were present during the production of this play, and it contained no controversial parts. It consisted of a string of skitlike tableaux, and it ensured audience hilarity through scenes such as that of a man urinating over the side of a canoe in which a party of people is traveling to Tokelau in order to settle there. This "side," or mirror, theater group immediately placed itself in a position of competition vis-à-vis Te Ata. Its director, a little older than the leaders of Te Ata, was a community leader known and respected for his vast knowledge of Tokelau culture. The two groups competed fiercely for a while over who should represent New Zealand Tokelau at the Pacific Islands Cultural Festival, which was to be held in the Cook Islands. Finally, Te Ata decided to withdraw from the competition and, in an act of one-upmanship, applied to various bodies for funding to allow the group to go on tour to the Tokelau atolls.

Te Ata's breaking of communicative taboos in the play *Tagi,* in relation to the issue of sexual abuse, had some repercussions after the performances. One man in the "mirror" group, with a history of being an abuser, was said to have feared public exposure and loss of face and, in a fit of insanity, killed a member of his family before attempting to commit suicide. This was a personal tragedy and cannot be linked to the fact that the issue of sexual abuse had been made a part of public discourse. Some people did make such a connection at the time, however, and the members of the theater group felt badly about this turn of events.

The "tour to the homeland" took place around Christmas, a time of year when Tokelau experiences a great influx of people and a flurry of activities. Whereas the performances in New Zealand had only to be announced for large numbers of people to turn up, in Tokelau residents were busy with other things. Regardless, the theater group was received as a traditional *malaga,* a visiting party or touring group, and was provided with accommodation and gifts of food and speeches. It is expected of such a *malaga* that it reciprocate with speeches and entertainment of its own. Te Ata was given the meetinghouse, *falepa* or *falefono,* as a place to present its performances, and notice of them was spread by word of mouth throughout the villages. The reception during the performances was more subdued than that in New Zealand, but the round of comments and questions became livelier in Tokelau.

The comments were divided. Some people—community leaders and teachers—supported the need to address issues such as sexual abuse and the role of women. Others, mainly young people, defended "the Tokelau way" against what they perceived as an attack by Te Ata. Comments offered after the performances resembled those in New Zealand in their focus on what some people perceived to be misrepresentations of aspects of Tokelau culture. In the case of the play *Mafine,* which Te Ata also performed during the tour, some people stated that it was wrong, because they held that traditional, arranged marriages no longer occurred in Tokelau.

The issue of Te Ata's legitimacy in raising these issues, however, did not surface this time. Instead, on two occasions—on different atolls—a day or two after the performance, the group was invited to be the audience at a new play created by the village. That a "side" or mirror group emerged resembles what happened in New Zealand, but in this case the new production was explicitly produced for Te Ata, in an "O fanatu e!" (over to you) spirit, and not for a third-party audience (the Pacific Islands Culture Festival), as was the case in New Zealand. The new performance included only humorous parts. It, too, was about Tokelau's history, but it maintained the prototypical *faleaitu* style consistently. For example, it used gender-role inversion by having the last Tokelau *aliki,* or chief, played by a woman, to great audience hilarity. To my knowledge, there were no subsequent discussions or social repercussions in Tokelau, apart from some speculation about the individual actors and the possible resemblance of their real lives to the roles they had played.

The challenge presented by the group Te Ata had been properly received and contained by the reframing of the challenge to Tokelau norms of communication as a "side" event that properly called for an answer. The answer was then produced true to *faleaitu* and merry-making (*fiafiaga*) as it should be—and thus harmonious relationships and communicative norms were reestablished. The safeguarding of the *faleaitu* space was active in Tokelau in a way that it was not in New Zealand. Moreover, this safeguarding worked toward neutralizing the seriousness of the Ta Ata play's message, something that did not happen in New Zealand, where, if anything, the performance was taken so seriously that it remained problematic long after the event.

Events and Effects

I refer to the performance events I have described as "house of multiple spirits" and not simply "house of spirits," as *faleaitu* would normally be translated, because I want to stress that the theater group Te Ata drew on sources other than the traditional repertoire of Tokelau theatrical performances for inspiration. Thus it integrated into its production a broader range of "gods" or "spirits" and therefore more potentially conflicting forces than would otherwise have been the case. One strand of these forces was the social action or activist ethos that informs action theater. By expressing this ethos, the performers risked violating the traditional Tokelau conception of the *faleaitu* by breaking the cycle of playful reciprocity in performative exchanges. The only person who can be said to have knowingly entertained a desire to violate this conception, however, was the director, Paul Maunder, who frequently admonished the actors "not to become stuck in the clown"—that is, to go beyond the *faleaitu* tradition. A conflict of views on this point became apparent during the tour to Tokelau (Hoëm 2004).

The interpretive frame associated with the event in the New Zealand performance space defined it more or less as a theater performance as it is known in the modern, European tradition. (That tradition, of course, has also had its proponents of theater as a cathartic and transformative ritual.) When one looks at the event as a total social fact—beginning with the dynamics of audience reception, particularly the subsequent group formation and power struggle and the accompanying discourse about the definition of Tokelau tradition—the characteristic ritual exchange becomes apparent, although in an uncharacteristically serious and protracted form.

The performative event in Tokelau, as represented by the performers' interpretative frame, resembled that in New Zealand as just described. But because the local reception and process of group formation was more immediate, a different and local frame of interpretation and event structure was reinstated. This observation is supported by the fact that even though the local theatrical performances were instigated on the initiative of Te Ata members, who held workshops to teach the methods of action theater, the local producers rejected this form and instead produced *faleaitu* according to their own standards of Tokelau morals, aesthetics, and traditions. The dominant local conception of the performance space in Tokelau thus produced a ritualized answer, designed to rebut the challenge to its foundations presented by Te Ata, in a manner that, according to local standards of performative exchanges, was *malie*—sweet, harmonious, and appropriate.

When one compares the two sites of ritualized performances, a difference emerges in the way conflict was handled. In New Zealand, the serious frame of the theatrical performance produced an open conflict between the competing groups, whereas in Tokelau, the conflict was contained by the playfulness of the give-and-take exchange characteristic of the *faleaitu* space. This difference points us toward the recognition that the site for ritual activity is itself imbued with agentive power, more so than particular instances of ritual communication. However, this magic holds only as long as the actors who engage in the activity conceptualize it to be so. It is likely that in a situation of challenges to the legitimacy of leadership structures, the sites of ritual activity in particular will become contested. This is only to be expected, because ritual performances allow people a unique space in which to experience, maintain, and challenge what upholds the meaningfulness of their life-worlds. The "house of spirits" in contemporary Tokelau society can be an instrument of social control, but the genre can also represent an opportunity to reflect upon the sometimes harsh and difficult but occasionally hilarious aspects of life. The perspective of seeing ritual activity as a total social fact allow us to understand why this might be so.

Notes

1. Theater, mainly in the form of dramatic presentations of biblical stories, has occasionally existed earlier in a Tokelau context (Judith Huntsman, personal communication).

2. Mourning songs proper, that is, funeral dirges, also exist. They are called *haumate,* and one of the group members (Akapito Pasikale) is the composer of the first *haumate* to be produced in a modern context. It mourns the passing of most of the able-bodied men of Tokelau in the Peruvian slave raids of the 1860s.

3. The full text and translation of the play can be found in Hoëm 1995 (Tokelauan and English) and Hoëm 2004 (English).

nine

Unjuk Rasa ("Expression of Feeling") in Sumba

Bloody Thursday in Its Cultural and Historical Context

Joel C. Kuipers

Although there are many reasons to doubt the analytical validity of "ritual" as a universal category of ethnographic description (Beatty 2004), it has not prevented social scientists from widely applying the concept to emerging cosmopolitan forms of protest (Casquete 2006; Hobsbawm 1959; Jasper 1997; Juris 2005; Kershaw 1997; Polletta 2004; Szerszynski 2002). According to Szerszynski, ritual is common in settings of social protest because it helps link particular grievances to wider meanings and values; audiences are more likely to be sympathetic if they feel that the issues at stake transcend the particulars of the "here and now." Furthermore, because of the repetitive, stereotypic, and formalized features of ritual, the ritualistic actions of protest often evoke a sense of collective tradition, which may be useful as a rhetorical contrast with a state of affairs in the present. Like the other writers just cited, Szerszynski did not consider how the use of the word "ritual" to characterize such diverse forms of semiotic practice might obscure the profoundly different meanings associated with the term.

Even less has been written about the formal verbal chants that accompany such protest "rituals." McPhail, in a book about collective behavior in social movements (1991), attempted to bring some rigor to the study of protest chants by considering them as part of what he called "the elementary forms of collective behavior-in-common." Among these elementary forms he included "collective verbalization" (e.g., chants, prayers), "collective vocalization" (e.g., booing, hissing), and "collective gesticulation" (e.g., raised fist and "digitus obscenus," or raised middle finger). He went on to characterize protest chants in terms of the number of participants ("two or more"), their bodily orientation ("facing in a common direction"), the content of the chant ("common content"), and its rhythm ("common tempo").

Unfortunately, such characterizations of protest chants in terms of their "elementary forms" do little to help us understand this widespread phenomenon in its historical and cultural context. As Irvine warned more than twenty-five years ago, formal communication is not a single "thing" with fixed attributes. She observed that dimensions such as heightened code structuring, situational focus, and invocation of positional identities—all of which may appear in formal communicative events such as ritual chanting—vary considerably cross-culturally, historically, and even contextually (Irvine 1979).

In this chapter I examine a case in which the definition of what counted as ritual communication was undergoing rapid change. In the fall of 1998, five months after the downfall of the thirty-two-year Suharto dictatorship, students gathered in front of the district headquarters in the town of Waikabubak in West Sumba, Indonesia, to protest alleged cronyism by the district's regent. They were angry that one of regent's relatives, a member of the Weyewa ethnolinguistic group, had passed a civil service exam when records showed that he had never taken it. They chanted and sang songs for several days outside the office as the protest grew in force and intensity. At one point they chanted the regent's Weyewa 'hard name' (*ngara katto*), whereupon the regent's supporters reportedly took grave offense. In response, his relatives organized a counterdemonstration designed to "protect" him from personal insult. It was not interpreted in the cosmopolitan framework of contemporary protest ritual, however, but in the regional and local framework of territorial rivalry. Attempts were made to use customary forms of ritual communication to defuse the crisis, but it continued to escalate and resulted in the worst bloodshed in Sumba's recorded history.

Although it has been nearly ten years since the incident, known as Bloody Thursday, took place on November 5, 1998, it has reorganized politics and cultural life in the region in important ways. No one knows exactly how many deaths occurred on this one day; the official death toll is twenty-four, but all observers agree that the real number is considerably higher (Mitchell 1999; Vel 2000). Beginning with protests against the regent's alleged cronyism, a chain of events was unleashed that resulted, within days, in the migration of thousands of people seeking refuge in rural areas and a profound challenge to a decades-long trend toward urbanization and centralization of power and bureaucratic authority. The events were marked at key points by the use of forms of ritualized communication that variously challenged and reproduced the authority of spiritual and political power and its attendant models of ethnicity as a kind of performance. One commentator, Vel, believes these events were a cynical manipulation on the part of the leadership to control the decline of their authority. Perhaps. What such political interpretations do not explain is the logic behind the selection and use of symbolism, how and why the manipulation was effective at mobilizing large numbers of people, and how it was able to generate such passion.

After discussing the economic, cultural, and political background to this event, I examine in more detail some of the ceremonial features of communicative practice at the heart of the incident and the way these are related to changing ideas about the very structure and function of ritual communication on the island. The communicative features I consider in greater detail are *unjuk rasa* 'expression of feeling', *ngara katto* 'hard names', and *panewe tenda* 'ritual speech'.

Background

Sumba is a hot, dry island situated roughly at the midpoint between Bali and Timor in eastern Indonesia. For centuries it remained isolated from the waves of Indic, Muslim, and European influence that swept across the archipelago. Partly because of its location, its relatively inhospitable landscape, and its fiercely independent indigenous cultures, the island maintained its own thriving local system of ritual communication and exchange linked to ancestor worship and asymmetrical marriage alliance.

Linguistically, the island is divided into at least eight mutually unintelligible languages, with the greatest concentration of linguistic and dialect diversity in the southwest. Although the languages are clearly related and share many common features of grammar and vocabulary, these linguistic group distinctions are the basis for differentiating ethnolinguistic domains that were traditionally independent religiously, politically, and economically. The two ethnolinguistic groups I discuss in this chapter, the Weyewa and the Loli people, were recognized and politically enfranchised by the Dutch in the early 1900s (Kuipers 1998).

In the early twentieth century, however, as the Dutch extended and consolidated their bureaucratic and military control over the outer islands in order to restrict the practice of slavery and warfare, local leaders, or *rajas,* were increasingly recruited into the practice of "indirect rule" (Kahin 1949). Under this practice, the local leaders were the "regents," and the Dutch were the "administrators," providing military backup. Even after independence from the Dutch, the regents (such as Regent Rudolf Malo, the object of the 1998 protest) were recruited from locally prominent families.

These regents, or local *rajas,* were described by themselves and the Dutch as *kabani mbani* 'angry men' (fig. 9.1). In one incident in the early twentieth century, one of the first administrators on the island, Couvreur, described an uprising (*opstanden*) in the Laboya ethnolinguistic domain. "The village head, known as an *ata mbani*—an angry

Figure 9.1. A Sumbanese "angry man." Photograph by the author.

man, a willing fighter and terrorist among his circles, procured weapons and came after us in battle" (Couvreur 1914: 29). Not only are these men considered of high rank, but they are also highly verbal. The missionary Wielenga devoted an entire book to portraying the downfall of such a man, Oemboe Dongga: "He was a man of strength and brute force … he had a booming voice that could command. The sound of his voice, the sparkling of his eyes, and the gesture with which his right hand would reach for his long knife, was more than enough to make one take him seriously" (Wielenga 1928: 7).

Verbal fluency was essential to creating an impression of competence, ferocity, and ability to protect, if not from slave raiders then from malign spirits. Wielenga described his encounter with Oemboe Pati, the Weyewa *raja* in 1909:

> Then Oemboe Pati stood up and laid open the floodgates of his eloquence. He has no equal in all of Sumba. With unbelievable speed his words came out of his mouth, tumbling and splashing, one following the sound of the other. His countenance was taut and his carriage erect. Now and then making a single broad gesture with his right hand, he stood there talking, getting all excited, so that one thinks: with lashing words he flogs his enemies. In fact, it was a "word of welcome." To the ear of the uncomprehending, he spoke friendly words like a rabble-rousing braggart. Oemboe Pati cultivates his renown and makes an impression ... as one who is "powerful [*geweldigen*]." (Wielenga 1912: 330)

One of the reasons verbal prowess was so important to these leaders had to do with the central role of speech in Sumbanese life. In traditional Sumbanese ideology, all of life's sustaining natural and cultural rhythms and cycles are gifts from the ancestors, gifts that engender obligations and responsibilities. The seasonal and orderly cycles of planting and harvesting, of birth, marriage, and death, are all gifts from the ancestors. The knowledge contained in these gifts takes the form of the *panewe tenda* 'words' of the ancestors, by which the wisdom of the elders is transmitted from generation to generation. These "words" consist of a distinctive poetic style of ritual speech, formed from couplets in which the first line parallels the second in rhythm and meaning. Speakers draw from a more or less fixed stock of about three thousand such couplets and assemble them spontaneously on ceremonial occasions to create orations that must be fluent and eloquent and that often last all night (fig. 9.2). Traditionally, a key requirement of leadership was a mastery of ancestral wisdom, embodied in the ability to fluently use ritual speech (Kuipers 1990, 1998).

On this sparsely populated island, until well into the twentieth century Sumbanese tended to live in fortified hilltop ancestral villages (fig. 9.3), dominated by a charismatic "angry man" who was seen as a source of bounty and protector of the village. As the bureaucratic administration of the Dutch and later the Indonesian national government imposed a peace on these villages that made the need for such fortifications less immediate, villagers began spreading out farther and farther into the open countryside in search of fertile fields for their rice, corn, and root crops, as well as grazing land for cows, water buffalo, and horses. Nonetheless, they maintained loose ties with their "source" villages, returning periodically on ceremonial occasions.

By the 1980s the population of Sumba was growing quickly, roads reached into most corners of the island, and increasing numbers of

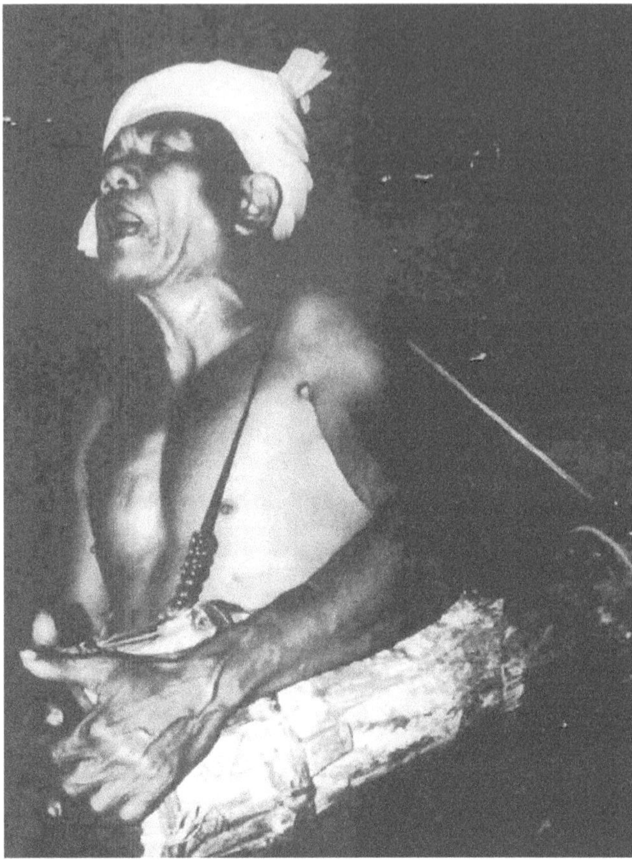

Figure 9.2. A Sumbanese ritual speaker. Photograph by the author.

Figure 9.3. A traditional Sumbanese village. Photograph by the author.

children were attending school and learning the Indonesian national language. Long sustained by a subsistence economy, the Sumbanese began to depend increasingly on cash crops for income and on imports for their lifestyle. At the same time, they felt increasing pressure to invest more in children's education and less in ceremonial enterprises such as ritual displays of oratory and animal sacrifice. They experienced state-sponsored political pressure to abandon the "primitive" and "feudal" ways of the ancestors and adopt Christian and modern ways.

By the early 1990s the majority of West Sumbanese had converted to Christianity and abandoned many of their traditional ceremonial practices. Charismatic traditional leaders, who had relied on their status as angry men and fluent speakers of ritual speech, found themselves increasingly marginalized in favor of Indonesian-speaking, school-educated bureaucrats (Kuipers 1998). The population of the polyglot regency capital, Waikabubak, was growing rapidly, because Waikabubak was a place for employment for the swelling ranks of high school and college educated Sumbanese. Although most businesses were owned by Chinese, most government employees were native Sumbanese, whose ethnic affiliations were becoming increasingly blurred because of mixed marriages or long residence outside the ethnic homeland. Ties to traditional customs became increasingly attenuated.

"Total Crisis"

As Vel reported, beginning in 1997 much of Indonesia entered into a state of "total crisis" (*kristal*). This emergency had at least three components: a climate crisis, a financial crisis, and a political crisis.

Although rainfall is never abundant on Sumba, the most bountiful rains tend to fall in the autumn months of November and December. Because of El Niño and other factors, the monsoon season in 1997 was disrupted, and much of the island experienced a drought. It was more serious in the east than in the western part of the island, where many rice fields are fed by underground rivers. Nonetheless, the economy of the entire island was affected. Then, instead of receiving an extended dry season in which to prepare for harvesting in the late summer, the island suddenly found itself drenched by rain in July and August 1998, which created flooding that destroyed many crops.

Although the World Bank sent food and financial relief to keep the farmers from destitution, the distribution was "delayed" and was inadequate. Rumors flew regarding the reasons for this and whether it was linked to corruption on the part of officials who were dealing with their own personal financial crises (Vel 2000). Resentment grew.

In addition, in 1997 the "Asian flu" financial crisis that hit Thailand, the Philippines, and Malaysia also began to hit Indonesia, and the currency was drastically devalued. As a result, commodities on which citizens had come to depend were suddenly much more expensive. The swollen ranks of government employees found that their salaries did not go as far as they once did; cattle exporters found their livelihoods seriously threatened by the expense of cattle feed and a shortage of buyers. Government commissions for new buildings and roads dwindled, and investment in other new projects dried up.

Linked in some ways to the first two crises was a political one. Faced with mounting opposition from ordinary citizens who found their savings suddenly disappeared, the government confronted widespread protests beginning in the fall of 1997 after investigations revealed corruption to have been important cause of the bank collapses. After years of relative prosperity and growth, the closing of banks because of bad loans, embezzlement, and cronyism was devastating. The mobilization of protest was unprecedented for Indonesia. Since the fall of Sukarno some thirty years previously, the Suharto regime had clamped down on all forms of dissent, continually reminding the people of the mass murders and chaos that followed the attempted communist coup of September 30, 1965, as a way of intimidating the population into cowed acceptance of repression. In this context, the sudden flowering of a culture of protest and dissent was shocking and new.

To understand how shocking these demonstrations were, it is instructive to examine accounts of protests from earlier times. Booth (1968) argued that in Indonesia of the 1960s, protests were often organized from above; were not directly against a leader but were appeals to the leadership, leaving formal legitimacy recognized; were rarely launched without the support of people even more powerful than the aggrieved group; and were largely "stage-managed." According to Ali (2001), the protests of 1997 and 1998 were different: they were a form of "democratization from below" in which ordinary citizens took to the streets to demand reforms of political leaders. He showed that by the fall of 1998, hundreds of protests and demonstrations were taking place each month in every province of Indonesia.

A generation of literate, Indonesian-speaking citizens had grown up in the years since the Suharto takeover in 1966, a generation that had known nothing but government repression and the stifling of dissent. The emergence of a culture of protest was an object of intense fascination all over the country. Newspaper readership soared. Commenting on the flowering of the culture of protest in Indonesia, Seth Mydans of the *New York Times* wrote: "With their jeans, sandals, long hair, and guitars, this is a student movement to take its place alongside the French and the American movements in 1968. Their continuing campus demonstrations kept alive the timid opposition to Mr. Suharto after he had been anointed to a seventh 5-year term in March of 1998 ... the students' ebullient and fearless occupation of the Parliament Building was the most visible part of the endgame that forced Mr. Suharto to step down" (Mydans 1998).

The student movement quickly developed its own new lexicon, which swept across the country. Among the key words were *reformasi,* for "reform of the government," and KKN, standing for "corruption, collusion, and nepotism."

Figure 9.4. Students occupying the Parliament building in Jakarta, May 1998. From http://id.wikipedia.org/wiki/Daftar_organ_gerakan_mahasiswa_1998.

Unjuk Rasa (Expression of Feeling) in October 1998

The implicit egalitarianism and solidarity of the students in the May 10 takeover of the Parliament building (fig. 9.4) was part of the interpretive context for the students who confronted the regent in West Sumba. On the morning of October 29, 1998, five months after President Suharto fell from power in Indonesia, more than two hundred demonstrators gathered in front of the regency office in Waikabubak, West Sumba, in Nusa Tenggara Timur, eastern Indonesia. Carrying a banner inscribed with phrases such as "Long live *reformasi* [reform]!" and "Regent Malo must step down," the demonstrators prayed, sang songs, and vowed not to retreat until their demands were met. By noon they were met by security officers, who ushered fifteen representatives to meet with the regent, Rudolf Malo, to explain their grievances and deliver their demands.

By 1:00 PM they met with Regent Malo. They asked why his nephew Nedi Kaka was listed as having passed the civil service exam when records showed that he had never even taken it. Demonstrators said the widespread practice of using surrogates (*joki*) to take tests under the names of other people was unfair, and the whole test should be nullified. The competition for government jobs was particularly intense that year because the currency devaluation and political instability in Jakarta had left the economy reeling, and unemployment was high. Furthermore, with the fall of Suharto and his GOLKAR party cronies, people began to complain openly about corruption and nepotism. When Regent Malo, himself strongly in the GOLKAR camp, denied wrongdoing and called the Nedi Kaka case an "administrative error" at the provincial level, the protesters were not satisfied (Kuipers n.d.).

Protests grew in size and intensity over the next seven days. The increasingly vocal throng created colorful banners and caricatures of the regent and his second in command. They sang vivid and provocative songs in their language, one closely related to and mutually intelligible with Weyewa, the regent's native language. The protesters' critique soon expanded to include the lavish renovations in the regent's residence. They demanded that the regent resign and his second in command be brought to jail (Kuipers n.d.).

The protesters were confronting the idea of a neocolonial hierarchy that allowed people like Regent Malo to acquire their positions in the first place and the crony system that allowed him to reproduce it through fake test results. That the event was construed as a challenge to hierarchy and not as being about competing ethnic groups is clear in the following exchange, which was reported to have taken place at midday on October 31, 1998, in the courtyard of the regent's office:

Regent: What are you doing here?
Demonstrators: We told you yesterday about the things you had covered up.
Regent: What have I covered up? Hey, you in the red shirt, come forward! [He indicates a protestor who is kneeling in a red shirt.]
Demonstrators: No! [They forbid him from coming to the podium.]
Regent: Oh, unfortunately, you have no manners!
Demonstrators: Is it we who have no manners or is it the regent? [Demonstrators: "The regent!"]

At some point during this exchange—probably at the point of the regent's metasemiotic reframing of the chanting demonstrators' behavior as a lack of proper "manners"—the protesters began to chant a culturally stigmatized nickname for the regent, his *ngara katto* 'hard name', Mette. At this point he withdrew from the scene and asked local security to step in.

The newly emergent culture of protest is visible even in the grainy photographs of the demonstration that I was able to obtain (fig. 9.5) (Reed 2005; Spanjaard 2000). Carrying banners (*spanduk*) bearing the phrase "We need a government that is clean and responsible and [that will] fight KKN [corruption, collusion, and nepotism]," the demonstrators saw themselves as participating in a formalized, stereotypical, and Indonesian-language genre of activity known as *unjuk rasa,* literally 'expression of feeling' but more commonly glossed in English as "demonstration." Although the regent described the demonstrators' expressions as personally insulting, the protesters drew on symbolism and forms of practice that linked their behavior to contexts far from Waikabubak.

Initially, supporters of the regent interpreted these shocking "expressions of feeling" as foreign behavior, akin to an external assault.

Figure 9.5. Protesters in West Sumba "demonstrate feelings" (*unjuk rasa*) against the regent in 1998. Reproduced by permission from *Pos Kupang,* 1 November 1998.

Although news of such demonstrations in favor of *reformasi* had made it to Sumba, never had one been enacted with such authenticity on Sumbanese soil. The alien practices of *tana dawa* 'the land of the Javanese' had penetrated to the courtyard of the regency. According to a security guard I spoke to, it felt like an "invasion."

What the regent's supporters quickly focused on, however, was the use of his "hard name" (*ngara katto*). In symbolic terms, use of such a stigmatized locution in a public setting is a violation of the relations of inside and outside. Only one's close kin and other intimates may use such a name, and even they only in contexts of relative intimacy. Violation of these norms is perceived as a threat and is a cause for anger, loss of face, and even spiritual imbalance.

As one can see from table 9.1, all Weyewa men and women have "soft" and "hard" names. Just as "Robert" is linked with the name "Bob" in English, so the regent's name, Malo, was linked with the name "Mette." Just as the use of "Bob" presumes a certain intimacy with its bearer, so does the name "Mette," although to a much greater degree and with much more serious implications for its improper use.

Although the use of these traditional Sumbanese names is declining in favor of "Christian" names such as "Rudolf," the Sumbanese names still exist, and most people are familiar with them and their "hard" counterparts, even if they seldom use them. In traditional contexts,

Table 9.1 Men's and Women's "Hard Names" (*ngara ndakke*) and "Soft Names" (*ngara katto*)

Men's Names		*Women's Names*	
Soft	*Hard*	*Soft*	*Hard*
Malo	Mette	Peda	Roki
Zairo	Zokke	Ninda	Rede
Lende	Rua/Ngedo	Leda	Ponne
Mbulu	Mbennaka	Dada	Tiala
Ngongo	Ngilla	Koni	Mbiri
Mbili	Kurri	Zoli	Lawe
Dairo	Lade	Wada	Lew
Mbora	Tyalo	Lali	Pindula
Mete	Rangga	Winni	Tannge
Lelu	Atu	Louru	Ladde
Dowa	Kelo	Mbuta	Ngapu
Mali	Keba		

children are considered soft and vulnerable, and so one must provide them with a "soft name" (*ngara ndakke*) that is spiritually 'compatible' (*modda*) with the child's character. Using a "coarse" or "hard" name to refer to a child is viewed as akin to physically assaulting something that is soft and helpless. People who feel kinship obligations toward the well-being of another are said to take offense if the hard name of one of their kin is used in an inappropriate way. To invoke a hard name in a public setting such as the 1998 demonstration can be interpreted in traditional terms as a challenge to one's feelings of kinship and ethnic loyalty.

Escalation

What was initially a challenge to the bureaucratic hierarchy and the regent's authority was then reinterpreted as a challenge to his person. When the regent's supporters in his home village heard of this challenge, they organized their own "expression of feeling" in support of their "family member." They rented several trucks, and reportedly five hundred men arrived and camped out in the regency headquarters to ensure that such insults "would not occur again." There were reports that the Weyewa men threatened to burn the entire town of Waikabubak.

By all accounts, the regent was appalled. Although gratified on one level that his "family members" had come out with such a show of support, he feared (rightly) that they had set in motion something that would be hard to control. He urged them to return to the Weyewa highlands as soon as possible. He said, "I am not the property of one ethnic group; I belong to the entire regency." As a way of emphasizing the transcendence of the regency over any single ethnolinguistic group, he attempted another metasemiotic reframing by referring to the regency with its couplet name, drawn from the lexicon of ritual speech: *manda eweta, pada elu* 'broad fields, beautiful meadows'.

What the Weyewa men who supported the regent did not count on was that a substantial gathering of men and women from the Loli ethnic group was not far away. In a coincidence reminiscent of Hawaiian history (Sahlins 1981), these men had gathered for a celebration of the new year festival of *poddu*. After several days of ritual restrictions and restraint, men and women wearing festive gear had gathered in a traditional ancestral village not far from the regency office and were preparing for a feast to release their prohibitions and welcome the new year through sacrifices of water buffalo and pigs (Rothe 2004). Although many of the participants had converted to Christianity, gathering on this one occasion for a "pagan" ceremony was an important opportunity to renew their identities as members of the Loli ethnolinguistic group and to see relatives. Having a large and threatening group of Weyewa men suddenly arrive on their doorstep to "protect" the regent was a galvanizing event that they perceived as an aggressive act.

According to Vel (2000), local leaders of the ancestral religion, whose authority had been dwindling for the past several decades, saw an important opportunity to recruit support. In the final stages of the *poddu* ceremony, a priest performed a divination requesting a blessing on a war against the Weyewa men. Three times the diviner consulted the augury, and three times it came out affirmative. Reports also circulated in the city of Waikabubak that Weyewa women were unsafe and should beware.

Although the Weyewa men got in the trucks and traveled the sixteen kilometers back to the Weyewa highlands, reports of violence and threats against Weyewa in the city put the citizenry on edge. On Wednesday, November 4, 1998, when rumors flew that a young man named Yohannes Motto had been murdered by a masked man in a Weyewa market (it turned out later that he had been beaten but survived), the houses of Rudolf Malo's relatives in Waikabubak were stoned. Beginning in the early evening on Wednesday, drums and gongs were beaten in many parts of the Weyewa highlands, mustering people to help protect their relatives. On that evening, a large party of Weyewa men, reportedly three thousand of them, gathered to march back to Waikabubak, the regency headquarters and the homeland of the Loli people. They marched through the night and arrived at the outskirts of town in the early morning. According to most accounts, although they wore ceremonial garb, they were unarmed and marched in the open on the highway, not stealthily in the woods. When they approached the town, however, they were met by Loli men who were gathered in the traditional ancestral village, Tarung, on the edge of town. As the latter poured out of the village, fighting erupted, only a few yards from police headquarters. The fighting continued uninterrupted until midday, when a torrential downpour finally dispersed the war parties.

When the rains ended, dozens of corpses lay in the fields and inside homes where the wounded had sought refuge. Angry mobs began to set fire to houses in the area, and by nightfall, hundreds of homes had been burned to the ground. Over the next several days, stores and offices remained closed. A mass exodus of Weyewa-speaking people began, leaving Waikabubak for the Weyewa highlands. Teachers, government officials, doctors, and small entrepreneurs no longer felt safe in this polyglot town that owed its existence to the idea of a state-enforced tolerance of ethnic diversity. Why the police did not intervene remains something of a mystery.

Ritual Speech and Reconciliation

One week after the bloodshed, the regent, police, traditional leaders, ministers and priests, and relatives of the victims all participated in a meeting at the subdistrict office in eastern Weyewa. Feelings of grief and tension remained intense. Following a question-and-answer period between the regent and the victim's families, the regent began sobbing so intensely that the meeting was disrupted and the microphone was handed over to the chief of police. Many questioned why the Lolinese head of the local parliament, T. L. Ora, did not attend. Regent Malo said it was because of illness, but few accepted that explanation. No direct meeting between Loli and Weyewa leaders had yet occurred.

Two weeks after the bloodshed, many stores and offices remained closed, and things had not yet returned to normal. Teachers had not been paid because the treasurer had fled the violence and had not yet returned. Rumors even circulated that the headquarters of the regency was going to be moved to the coastal town of Weetabula, in order to avoid conflict between the Weyewa and Loli peoples.

There were calls for the regent to step down. One commentator interviewed in the newspaper felt that the regent's behavior was cowardly and did not live up to the Sumbanese tradition of the bold and angry man in positions of leadership. Instead of himself being the protector, he ran and sought protection with the chief of police. "It's pretty strange that the regent himself actually fled during the fighting. Whatever the reason, the regent must take responsibility and he must step down."

The regent refused to resign. After his less than courageous conduct during Bloody Thursday, however, and his public weeping during the reconciliation meeting, he was effectively sidelined. Instead, leaders from the two subdistricts in which the fighting took place organized a reconciliation event themselves. It was held close to where the fighting had occurred, and a special hut was constructed in which the clan leaders held a ceremonial event in which they exchanged a water buffalo, pig, sword, and spear. Although most of the discourse was conducted in the Indonesian national language, traditional leaders from both Weyewa and Loli delivered orations in ritual speech. Those present felt that even though Loli and Weyewa were different dialects of the Sumbanese language family, ritual speech discourse provided a common idiom for expressing their reconciliation.

Discussion

In the context of the social and political upheavals of 1998, the students' selection of *unjuk rasa* 'expression of feeling' as part of what Charles Tilly (1979) called a "repertoire of collective action" would seem a reasonable strategy. Unlike the more traditional modes of dissent, which tended to be more like appeals for pity and mercy and involved the singing of "laments" (Kuipers 1998), *unjuk rasa* did not employ a familistic, kinship idiom of personalistic moral obligation as a way of legitimating its causes; the dominant themes were legal and bureaucratic and the formal interests of the injured parties. No reference was made to traditional obligations or reciprocities. This strategy made sense because of the notable success that Indonesian students had experienced in bringing down Suharto some five months earlier.

As a form of "collective verbalization," however, *unjuk rasa* was also an unfamiliar and thus potentially confusing genre in the repertoire of action. It is true that over the preceding decade, increasing numbers of Sumbanese students had been off the island and participated in such demonstrations on Java and elsewhere, but the majority of the population in Sumba had seldom, if ever, seen such a demonstration firsthand before. Although perhaps most of the adult population had seen or heard in the news about such events occurring in Java and were broadly familiar with the role of this form of collective action in bringing about the end of Suharto's rule, few had experienced it for themselves.

As a mode of formal communication circulating outside the island, *unjuk rasa* was part of a fairly well established Indonesian genre involving the use of written banners, marching, chanting and singing in unison, and gathering in public places (fig. 9.6). In Indonesia, elaborate forms of dress and even face and body painting are common. The performance of *unjuk rasa* creates a situational focus defined in terms of civil society, which is populated by "citizens" who share interests, rights, and a sense of equality.

In Sumba, however, where verbal performance has a long and venerable association with religious and political authority, chanting in unison is rare. In ritual speech contexts, when such chanting occurs, it is done only to confirm and ratify the speaker's discourse, never to challenge it (Kuipers 1990). The demonstrators' chanting represented a semiotic collectivization of oppositional voices that was not only unfamiliar but also threatening to observers.

The use of a hard name in most settings is usually little more than cause for irritation on the part of the namesake. When a hard name is

Figure 9.6. The Indonesian culture of protest on display at a 2006 anti-George W. Bush rally. From http://news.bmezine.com/2006/11/30/peace-out-jakarta/.

used in a public setting, and furthermore chanted in a context designed to suggest collective action, the logic of the naming system suggests that a protective response on the part of the audience is warranted—that is, protecting a "soft" family member against the "hard" words of an oppositional group.

The counterdemonstration of Regent Malo's kin, designed to do just that, was quickly recoded, however, in more traditional terms as a threatening act of territorial violation. This interpretation was particularly salient among the Lolinese ritual celebrants already gathered for the *poddu* festival. Once the territorial idiom had been invoked, efforts were made to recode the event once more by using the transcendent terms of ritual speech couplets—the regent referred to himself as the "property" of the entire region of West Sumba. It did little good. The drums of war were already beating, literally, and a tragic confrontation ensued.

One of the stunning ironies of the Indonesian-language phrase *unjuk rasa* 'expression of feeling' is that although it implies an externalization of an interior, individual condition or emotional state, in most cases in Indonesia it was in fact an event incited from above, by a leader or patron. Many protests were staged by members of the Suharto administration itself. In Suharto's Indonesia, little distinction was made between the private interests of those protesting and the interests of the demonstration's leadership. When students protested the regent's cronyism, therefore, a reasonable question among the regent's supporters was, "Who organized this?" Many looked at the Sumbanese political landscape and identified T. L. Ora, a Lolinese parliamentary leader who often disagreed with the regent, as someone who could potentially benefit from the protests. Even though many of the original protestors were from different ethnic groups—including Weyewa—the "feelings" being expressed were identified as those of the local parliamentary leader. This association reinforced the ethnic and traditional framework for the interpretation of the protest chant.

For the students, the stereotyped, repetitive chanting defined the protesters (at least to themselves) as part of a youthful group sharing progressive, democratic values, and it offered a critique of the cronyism and corruption of the Suharto regime. The audience they sought to communicate with and draw legitimacy from was not only local but also national. When they chanted the regent's hard name, they were not speaking in the voice of supplicants or wronged kinfolk but rather occupied an emerging cosmopolitan category of positional identities associated with 'university students' (*mahasiswa*).

For the regent's supporters, the collective verbal action of the protesters was interpreted in terms that had made sense throughout much of the thirty-two-year rule of Suharto: so-called expressions of feeling were usually little more than ventriloquations of the agenda of some powerful person. To them, the idea that someone such as the Lolinese parliamentary leader T. L. Ora would challenge Rudolf Malo in such a personal way in a public setting called for a response. Mostly unarmed, but in a belligerent and menacing posture, the supporters converged on the town of Waikabubak.

To the Lolinese celebrants gathered in the traditional hilltop village of Tarung, the sound and sight of a three-thousand-person throng of Weyewa marchers approaching in a confrontational manner on the main highway appeared not to be a mere counterdemonstration of feelings for the purpose of exchanging ideas. Even though the regent himself had tried hard to prevent the procession, the Weyewa crowd had organized itself hierarchically, as a group of subordinates defending the honor of their (unwilling) superior, the (not so) "angry man," Rudolf Malo.

Conclusion

No single framework, no unitary definition of ritual, no consensus point of view explains the Sumbanese tragedy of Bloody Thursday. Only by shifting back and forth between the frames of the student protesters, the Weyewa supporters of the regent, the Lolinese ritual celebrants, and the mourners in the aftermath—and their unfolding, reflexive, metasemiotic monitoring of each others' frames—can we begin to get a sense of the horrific logic of the "structure of the conjuncture" (Sahlins 1981) that brought about so many deaths. Just as the demonstrators tactically sought a sort of protection for their rude and challenging behavior by adopting the ritualized cadences of the cosmopolitan *unjuk rasa* genre of chanting, so the Weyewa supporters of the regent strategically interpreted what was essentially a gratuitous insult in more local terms as a form of ritualized communication expressing the collective will of a hierarchically organized force. That all these interpretive acts took place on an island beset by climatic, financial, and political crises, and still mourning the lost authority of the 'words of the ancestors' (*panewe tenda*), made this valorization of the very idea of ritual communication all the more compelling, if ultimately disastrous.

ten

Civility and Deception in Two Kalapalo Ritual Forms

Ellen B. Basso

The notion of a greater Amazonian "discursive area" was first proposed to describe a shared set of discourse forms and processes used by groups of people of distinct genetic linguistic affiliations (Beier, Michael, and Sherzer 2002). Although focused on language, the idea is of special interest for understanding how large-scale polities in precolonial Amazonia and Mesoamerica were formed, a matter currently being discussed by Americanist ethnographers and archaeologists.[1]

An important example of a discursive area with large-scale leadership structures is the southern region of the Terra Indigena do Xingu, Mato Grosso, Brazil (hereafter referred to as the "Alto Xingu"). It is a multilingual region in which live speakers of at least four mutually unintelligible languages. Hereditary leadership and large-scale ceremonial gatherings focused upon leaders' life-cycle events (ear-piercing, marriage, death), as well as an elaborate affinal civility register that apparently exists in all the local languages, provide a rare opportunity for examining the historical problem and seeing something of what Inomata (2006) called, in the context of the Classic Maya, "political theaters."

In the Alto Xingu, unlike in the multilingual northwest Amazon region, marriage with someone outside one's own language group is not required, and most people marry within their own group. Furthermore, language ideology identifies communities with their dominant languages and requires use of those languages during the intergroup ceremonial gatherings focused on hereditary leadership.[2] Yet despite this monolingual ideology, Alto Xingu people share a strikingly homogeneous set of values regarding personal behavior, life-status practices, kinship and marriage, mythological narratives, and material culture, together with a long-standing pattern of intersettlement trade specialization. Most likely, bilingual individuals have played an important role in the transmission of such features. Ceremonial monolingualism and the identification of local communities with particular languages may be a relatively recent development, an element within an invented tradition that was stimulated both by the loss of many ritual authorities during a period of eighteenth-century slave raiding and by outsiders' attempts to classify and distinguish local groups as "tribes." The latter have been portrayed as entering the region one by one, eventually coming to participate in what became a shared set of values and practices, the consequence of "intertribal acculturation" (Heckenberger 2005: 38). I prefer to think of these processes following my understanding of Kalapalo historical narratives, which focus not upon "tribal" units but upon specific interpersonal relationships and the nature and consequences of individual decisions to act with strangers in specific ways (Basso 1985).

The presence of shared forms of ritual communication is a striking characteristic of the Alto Xingu discursive area and is of special interest in regard to both the multilingual situation and the history of macropolitical formations. What is known of the details of these forms comes only from the Southern Carib language–speaking communities called Kuikuro (Franchetto 1983, 2000) and Kalapalo (Basso 1973, 1985, 2007), but there is evidence from ethnographic reports (Agostinho da Silva 1974; Galvão 1953; Gregor 1976, 2001; Ireland 2001; Monod-Becquelin 1975; Murphy and Quain 1955; Seki 1999) that similar styles are used by speakers of the three other local languages of the southern part of the region: Tupi, Arawak, and the nearly extinct "isolate," Trumai. It seems that the practices of ritual communication involved in leadership rituals and affinal civility each transcend language differences. Here, I examine the relations between these two forms of ritual communication as they are used by Kalapalo speakers and suggest a model for the way they have become related.

Affinal Civility

Humbling and related avoidance practices are central parts of affinal and leaders' civility, elements in a distinctly Kalapalo "theatrical I" (Urban 1989), which they call *ifutisunda*. In both familial and transcommunity ritual settings, aspects of the speaker's personal self are suppressed while multiple self-positionings and shared stances (Du Bois 2007) arise between people who otherwise do not or cannot communicate directly through language. The "theatrical I" is heard within and around the large communal family domestic household, where it is used as often between husband and wife, parents and their children, as between in-laws. Such relatives first begin to experience one another's deference, modesty, and overall politeness through distinctive clusters of speech and bodily action that accompany the giving and receiving of specially prepared food and finely hewn firewood, the presentation and use of important tools for body techniques (e.g., hair-cutting equipment and blood-letting tools), and the visual rearrangement of living spaces within the house in connection with puberty seclusion and new marriages (a young husband joins his bride's parents' household). As is always the case with enregistered speech, the interpersonal force of Kalapalo affinal civility depends on how (and whether) people manage the resources of this style. Successful users of the civility register cumulatively contribute to a continual doing or making of their familial relationships. Features of this multimodal and combinatorial style are summarized in table 10.1 (see Basso 2007 for more detail). The combination of these features—not their exclusive use with affines—makes the register stand out as a special kind of talk. In the examples that follow, relevant features are highlighted in boldface. See the note on abbreviations at the end of the chapter for a key to my word-by-word glosses.

Grammatical Features

A speaker's use of any one of three deontic demonstrative postpositions is important in the civility register insofar as these assert the necessity for a relative's personal decisions and choices but allow for omission of the harsher imperative form. *Aketsaŋe* and *aketsigey* (table 10.1) reference the speaker's own decision that another person act (and are used with a second-person addressee to soften an otherwise imperative function); *fetsaŋe* references the need or decision of the speaker to do something (see examples [1] and [6]).

Four of the twenty-four epistemic markers (EM) in Kalapalo appear frequently in the civility register.[3] Two EM specifically help speakers validate affinal projects. These are *-taka,* agreement with an interlocutor's description of experience or knowledge, and *-nifa,* with which the speaker asserts the necessity of an agreement. Kalapalo also use two other forms with contraspective semantics. With these, the speaker references something that is observed or stated but that the mind of the speaker wishes were otherwise; the speaker seemingly knows (or pretends to know) that there is little if any possibility of that happening.

Table 10.1 Features of Affinal Civility

Grammatical	*Semantic*	*Discursive*	*Interactive*
Deontic demonstrative postpositions: *aketsaŋe/aketsigey* (what is decided; in this manner); *fetsaŋe/fetsigey* (what is wanted)	Teknonyms: e.g., *ulimositsïpïgï* ('mother of our children who are no more'); *ulimowï* ('our children's father')	Avoidance: names; speech between parents-in-law and children-in-law in most circumstances	Domestic gestures: presenting food, firewood, valuable objects; cutting the new bride's hair; building her seclusion chamber; etc.
Epistemic particles: *taka, nifa; mukwe; kiŋi* (see text for explanations)	Metaphoric devaluations or inversions	Triadic communication	Self-presentation: younger person does not spit or pass wind in presence of elders; person is clean and well decorated when presenting gifts; gifts are carefully prepared and presented; etc.
	Kin terms for spouses and other in-laws; usual avoidance of "category" reference terms for in-laws	Validation/ verification expressions	Avoidance: no eye contact; no touching or use of personal items (hammocks, items of clothing, etc.)

The "positive contrafactual" clitic *mukʷe* 'wish in vain' has a "humbling" effect in the context of a requested activity, particularly when one makes an important request to a relative or to hereditary leaders. In contrast, the "negative contrafactual" *kiŋi* 'if only it were not so' is used in response to someone's bad news. In affinal civility, it occurs in response to someone's modest devaluation.

In example (1), a speaker uses the deontic postpositions *aketsaŋe* and *fetsaŋe* as well as the epistemic clitics *mukʷe* and *kiŋi*. A young unmarried man named Cuckoo tells his mother that he wants to try for his "dear uncle's daughter" (*awadyu endisï*) "even though it probably won't work out":

(1)

eŋu	***fe-tsa-ŋe***	***talo-ki***	***muk=ake-tsa-ŋe***
reason	DES-EX-I	no reason	EM=DEO-EX-I
awa-dyu		*i-ndisï-na*	*u-te-fo-ta*
uncle-END		3-daughter-DAT	1-go away-HYP-CI

Because I've decided for no particular reason to go try for dear Uncle's daughter, though it probably won't work out.

A speaker's use of the *-apa* taxis clitic links mention of projects of the interlocutor to the speaker's "conformity" to the interlocutor's wishes.[4] This can be complimented by the "agreement" EM *-nifa* and *-taka* used elsewhere in a conversation. In example (2), Cuckoo's mother supports his intention to try for his uncle's daughter, hoping that his wish will not be in vain, as he has modestly stated. Like her son, she uses *-te-*, the verb for "go away," to emphasize exactly what she is agreeing to. In (1), Cuckoo used *mukʷe;* his mother replies in (2) with *kiŋi:*

(2)

Eh he	***kiŋi***.	*Te-ke-**apa=ke-tsa-ŋe.***
Agreement	EM,	go.away-I-CONF= DEO-EX-I

May it not be so. I think you should go if that's what you've decided to do.

Semantic Features

"Affinal" semantic features appear at both the lexical and phrasal levels. They include kinship terms, teknonyms, and the practice of metaphorization as a way of devaluing or humbling one's gifts or wishes. Metaphors are also used to substitute for names that must be avoided.

Teknonyms and kinship terms used for affines are required forms that highlight many of the meanings involving validation and ratification of family projects. The Kalapalo use a vocabulary that expands the boundaries of the speaker's close family by referring to the wife as the husband's *iñandsu* 'sister' and the daughter's husband as her *efisu* 'younger brother'. Sisters-in-law become "sisters", and brothers-in-law, "brothers." After marriage, spouses refer to a parent-in-law as "our parent." In direct address, the father-in-law is "uncle" (*awa*), and the mother-in-law is "aunt" (*etsi*) (see Basso 1973, 1985). In indirect reference, especially when a person is speaking to his or her own parent, endearment terms are often heard, as in (1). Teknonyms are more restricted in usage and are never used in direct address.

Indirection on the topic of spousal intimacies often involves the use of metaphors. These metaphoric expressions allude to the partners' lying down together in a hammock and sleeping close to each other, as well as to their being able to eat together face to face and speak directly to each other (in contrast with the avoidance relatives). Descriptive nominals substitute for words for "husband" (*iño*) and "wife" (*ifitsu*) when they are uttered by an older relative to a younger person, as in example (3).

Devaluation, seen in grammatical features of civility, is also an important frame for metaphorization, in which the speaker modestly describes the inferior quality of someone or something to which he is connected. In (3), after a young woman has agreed to marry her suitor, his father-in-law offers him some of her refreshing cold manioc porridge, using an odd but striking metaphor. He is alluding to a woman's practice of gracefully blending the soup ingredients in water with her bare hand:

(3)

u-ntsi,	*ah*	***iñandsu***	***et-iña-ti-tsïgï***
2-young relative,	EXP	Z	3DT-hand-wash-Vt-COMP

ŋa-mba-ke
drink-Vt-I

My young relative, I assure you the sister has just finished washing her hands in this stuff, so drink it.

Example (4) comes from a conversation in which such humbling speech occurs in tandem with the "hoping against all evidence" epistemic marker *mukʷe*. An important young man has been given a wife, and because he will become a leader, they go to live in his settlement after he is with her family for a while. As they leave, her father tells him to mark her as released from puberty seclusion by cutting her bangs, which have been allowed to grow over her face. The woman's father uses the imperative mood when instructing his son-in-law to perform this rite. But the contrafactual *mukʷe* particle makes the request sound more like a wistful, improbable suggestion. As I show later, this usage is reminiscent of leaders' public oratory, during which repeated lines expressing ceremonial expectations include the *-mukʷe* clitic.

(4)
Iŋ-ke- ***muk^{w}e -tsï****-fa* *a=ña-gï-pa,*
look/think-I-EM-R-NT 2-path-POSS-D
When you're on your own path, I hope you'll know what to do with this,
i-ñandsu i-nïke-nï-miŋo *e-feke, e-feke.*
3-sister 3-forehead-Vt-POT 2-ERG, 2-ERG
you'll make the sister's bangs, you yourself.

Example (5) subsumes elements of all three lexical aspects in yet another fashion as a young husband asks his new father-in-law for permission to visit his family, together with his wives. The request is made somewhat indirectly. The young man avoids any direct reference to the marriage relationship as such. He calls his wives not "my wives" (*ufitsau*) but rather "sisters of mine I've found," a humbling remark. He speaks of "taking his sisters away," not mentioning that he intends to stay for some time with his own family. The father-in-law replies in a similarly elliptical fashion, using the kinship designation "your sisters" but acknowledging the marital relationship through the figure of "those who fan your fire." As in my other examples, kinship terms are used to reinforce the sense of family commensality that will persist, even away from the older person's domestic sphere. Yet nothing about where the young man and his wives will go is directly mentioned. Note that in the second line of (5), the narrator, speaking to his audience, does not hesitate to use the category term for "parent-in-law" (*-fotisofo*), which would never be used in affinal civility. His role is that of a distanced, didactic observer of the story's action, as is seen in the final line, his explanation to his listeners of the father's response.

(5)
Son-in-law: *"**Awa**,"* *Ø-nïg=i-feke.*
Uncle, say to-PERF-3-ERG
"Uncle," he addressed him.

Father-in-law: *"Ai,"* *Ø-nïgï-mbedya,* *i-fotisofo* *ki-lï.*
EXP, say to-PERF-PXA, 3-parent-in-law utter-PI
"What," the other answered when he said that to him, the father-in-law spoke.

Son-in-law:	*Eŋï-ta=**ke-ts=igey***	***i-ñandsu***	***fogi-dyu***
	do-CI=DEO-EX=DEM	3-sister	find-PI
	u-feke,	***iñandsu**-fa.*	
	1-ERG	3-sister-NT	
	I speak because I've decided to do something with these sisters I've found, these sisters I've found.		
Father-in-law:	***Eh he,***	*Ø-nïg=i-feke.*	
	Agreement,	say.to-PERF-3–ERG	
	"Yes, you should," he answered.		
	E-te-ke-fa,	*e-te-ke-**apa***	
	2-go.away-I-NT	2–go.away-I-CONF	
	Ø-nïg=i-feke.		
	say.to-PERF=3-ERG		
	"Go, then, go, if that's what you want to do," he said.		
	Iñadyo-mo-tsï-nifa	***e-ito-gu***	***ugi-ñi***
	Sisters-COLL-M-EM	2-fire-POSS	fan-N
	ige-ke,	*Ø-nïg=i-feke.*	
	3-take away-I	say.to-PERF=3-ERG	
	"I agree about that, you should take that pair of sisters, those who fan your fire," he answered.		

Discursive Features

Among affinal rituals organizing speech-centered interaction, of particular importance are avoidance practices. These provide the strongest psychological contrast between the civility style and other speech styles. Normally affines do not engage in activities within an intimate shared space. They avoid eye contact, refrain from walking in front of one another, and take care not to touch one another. A younger person will stand or sit or work behind an elder, in order to avoid the elder's direct glance. Looking at photographs of people at work, one sees that those who are still busily engaged during "breaks," their bodies oriented in a direction away from the main figures, are new sons- or daughters-in-law of the leaders who have organized the work. Houses are large enough to allow people to work somewhat apart from each other. At night, the newly in-married residents return to sleep in their hammocks after everyone else. "Restraint in the face of mistakes" might also be added to table 10.1. Consider the unfortunate youth living with the family of his future wife. Entering the dark interior of the house from the brilliant midday sun, he realized that he had walked (whistling, no less) directly past his father-in-law, who was sitting inside the doorway. Deeply embarrassed, this young man sat down near my hammock, clapped his hand over his mouth, and whispered, "I just walked in front of Uncle!" Faced with his son-in-law's blunder, the father-in-law simply pretended to ignore what had happened.

Probably the most striking feature of the affinal civility register is name avoidance, which involves the refusal to utter the names of parents-in-law, child's spouse, and spouse's opposite-sex sibling or words that evoke those names. Most child names are words for common objects and natural species, so people are always confronting situations in which forgotten names are suddenly remembered, to the embarrassment of the responsible parties. As a consequence of these avoidance practices, much affinal communication follows a "triadic" formula (Ameka 2004), with an intermediary acting to transmit a message between two avoidance relatives. In example (6), a husband asks his wife to tell her father, whom he refers to as "our parent," to collect firewood:

(6)

Husband:	***Uk^w-oto***	***fe-tsa-ŋe***	*i-ña*	*i-fa-ke*
	Dual-parent	DEO-EX-I	3-BEN	3-teach-I
	uk^w-oto-iña.			
	dual-parent-BEN.			
	Uk^w-oto	*i-ka-ŋu-ndomi.*		
	Dual-parent	wood-go.get-Vt-PURP		
	I want you to tell our parent, to let our parent know. Our parent needs to get firewood.			
Wife:	***Eh he ,***	***Ø-nïgi.***		
	Agreement,	say.to-PERF		
	"All right," she said to him.			
	Apa	*Ø-nïgi-feke,*	*e-i-ka-ŋu-ŋge-tu*	
	Father	say.to-PERF=ERG,	2-wood-go.get-Vt–I-DIS	
	fe-tsa-ŋe,	*e-i-ka-ŋu-ŋge*		
	DEO-EX-I,	2-wood-go.get-Vt-I		
	"Father," she said to him. "We want you to go get firewood somewhere, go get firewood."			
Wife's father:	*Eh he*	*Ø-nïgi.*		
	Agreement	say.to-PERF		
	"I'll do that," he answered.			

Ratification and validation are the particular means of developing discursive alignment through agreement responses. Appearing in almost all previous examples are two of these: the agreement response *eh-he* ("all right," "that's so," "I'll do that") and the "regret" response *eh he kiŋi* ("if only it were not so," "unfortunately that's so"). The latter is used affinally in response to a devalued or negative comment about the speaker's self, as in (2). Such responses appear after a relative describes some plans, requests, opinions, or even expository lessons, which are themselves made "civil" by the epistemic particle *-muk^{w}e,* one or more postpositions, and the conformative *-apa* clitic. Over time, ratification or validation of the interlocutor's speech by a listener-relative develops a shared stance, not only concerning the specific topics of the discourse but also helping to merge two speakers, sometimes very different from each other, into people committed to the shared marriage project.

Finally, affinal civility involves speakers' asserting the necessity of alignment. This is accomplished in part through use of the morpheme *wãke,* which has both epistemic and evidential features, referencing "distant past evidence that no longer exists but which is attested to by a speaker's own 'witnessing.'" Example (7) is an elaborate utterance in which a young man, speaking to his father-in-law, asserts his (legitimate) reasons for separating from his wife. He had hoped things would work out, but she has rejected him (hence the "positive to negative predication" EM *pile*):

(7)

*Taloki-la-ku-**wãke***	*w-e-nïgï*	*figey*
No reason-NEG-intensive-EM	1-come to-PERF	DEM

wãke	***muk^{w}e***	***wãke***	***e-ti-dyi-pïgï***
EM	EM	EM	2-emerge-Vi-PERF

***agiŋo**-feke*	*u-tifu-ne-nïgï*	*it-u-ŋu-pile…*
like-ERG	1-reject-Vt-PERF	3DT-pain-Vi-EM

Although it was for no reason at all before, perhaps in vain before, the person who was like your offspring painfully rejected me though I had hoped otherwise, she painfully rejected me though I had hoped otherwise.

W-e-nïgï	*ti-ku-ŋu*	***wake***	*e-iŋi-lu-iña*
1–come-PERF	REFL-pain-Vi	EM	2–see-PI-BEN

Ø-nïgï-f=i-feke	*t-idyogu-feke*
say to-PERF-EV-3–ERG	REFL-uncle-ERG

"It's painful for me to come to see you, to see you," he said that to his uncle.

Summary

Kalapalo affinal civility is an elaborate combinatorial style of "private" ritual communication used within the household. Grammatical, lexical, and semantic manipulations, together with bodily avoidance and other gestures, make this a highly marked discursive activity that is both a speech register and a genre of interpersonal ritual communication. Looking at the semantics of bodily gestures that go along with affinal locutions, one sees that they index the relationships of the parties involved. In Kalapalo society, persons within a marital relationship are by definition those who constitute a domestic, commensal household, sharing firewood, food, living space, and a special intimacy while being concerned with keeping a certain distance from one another.

***Anetu Itagiñu*: The Leader's Talk**

High noon, early September, on the central Brazilian *planalto.* It is the end of the dry season. The sun has baked the bare earth on the paths and in the plaza so hot that only those with the thickest calluses can walk outside. Most people are inside, resting from the early morning's work collecting and processing manioc. Fishermen, resting in the shade along the waterways, have yet to return to the settlement. Suddenly, from one of the houses close to the entrance road, a curious croaking sort of call begins: a signal from those inside the houses closest to the road that messengers have arrived to invite the Kalapalo to an *egitsu,* a ceremonial gathering focused upon hereditary leaders. What little talk there is stops, and the settlement falls silent, as two men, their faces and bodies darkened with charcoal and vegetable oil, walk quickly into the central area and kneel outside the *kuakutu,* the ceremonial house. No one comes to greet them; everyone remains inside. For half an hour the men remain motionless, until someone comes out of his house and guides them by their wrists into the *kuakutu,* where they will rest until a hereditary leader, returned from fishing, can properly greet them. An older woman who can speak to the Waura messengers in their Arawak language prepares a bucket of cold manioc porridge for their refreshment and carries it out to where the men are resting. After another hour or so, the oldest Kalapalo leader arrives home. He gives his fish over to the women of his household, bathes, and finally steps outside his house to acknowledge the messengers in the eloquent style that is called *anetu itagiñu* 'the hereditary leader's talk'. The root *-ta-,* a transitive speech-act verb with the sense of "tell to," in this context is associated with eloquence or oratory.

This is a genre distinctive to male *anetaũ,* Kalapalo hereditary officials (or "leaders" in this chapter) who are responsible for organizing and managing a variety of ceremonial events (Basso 1973, 1985). The leader's talk is used during public occasions that have a macropolitical focus, involving people from more than one community—the spear-throwing ceremony (*ifagaka*), the trade ceremony (*uluki*)—and those oriented around a leader's life-status rituals (*egitsu*)—a youth's ear-piercing, a pubescent girl's exit from several years of seclusion, followed by her marriage, and the memorial following a leader's recent death. All these are large-scale, collective events that occur each year in the Alto Xingu. They require lengthy preparations and culminate in participation by men and women from several or even all local settlements.

Ceremonials involve public orations performed by the older male leaders, who must use this genre at each step of the ceremonial process. Preparations for these events can sometimes take many weeks, if not months. Indeed, so closely connected with the status of hereditary leader are these orations that leaders, in the context of their work during ceremonial preparations, are often called *taiyope* 'associated with telling' and *tagioto* 'experts in telling'.

Anetaũ learn to use the leader's talk by practicing with older relatives, sometimes supplementing their knowledge with that of other important officials, to whom payment is given. At first practicing in private, hereditary officials are expected, as they mature, to know how to use *anetu itagiñu* well. Within a framework of relatively formulaic utterances, a good speaker is able to insert names of ancient leaders and places and to allude to contemporary regional concerns.

Kalapalo leaders were interested in discussing their use of this genre and allowed me to tape-record their particular versions. Their didactic discourses were framed as narratives that included step-by-step descriptions of activities and settings, interspersed with the leaders' quoting of their own speeches.

Egitsu ceremonials involve a lot of work, which the leaders spend much time planning and organizing. The leaders in each host settlement are assigned roles for each event. The *taiyope* take on the active organization and leadership of particular tasks such as cleaning the public entrance road, the central plaza, and the public path to the bathing area and gathering firewood, food, and fish for distribution. The *etiñï* 'askers' are younger men who travel, often long distances, to invite guest communities to participate in ritual events. Upon the guests' arrival, they are responsible for hosting them, greeting them in the distinctive leader's style, guiding them by their wrists to the seats prepared for them in the plaza, giving the visitors food prepared by their own household, escorting them to the campground or house where they will stay (usually on their own), tying up their hammocks, escorting them to the bathing place, and showing them around the community so that they may receive personal gifts from the residents.

The sponsor (*oto,* a word that also serves as "owner" and "expert") is the person whose relative is the focus of the event. His household is expected to provide food and payment in wealth to the other leaders. The sponsor also gives important gifts to the visiting leaders, who take their groups to the host's ceremony. The visiting leaders are expected to pay the messengers who have invited them, and in return they receive macaw feather ornaments from the sponsor.

As a ceremonial process, the *egitsu* begins with oratorical greetings and ends with eloquent departure speeches. Each step is marked by the leader's talk. Although the people being addressed directly are the speaker's fellow community leaders, the public and collectively oriented nature of the process suggests that at least tacit addressees are both the *otomo,* the collectivity of "ordinary" members of the community, and the *fagito,* visitors (whether they share a common language or not). One important function of the genre is thus to index the speakers' specific leadership roles, but a feature of special interest is the multivocal, dialogical nature of the genre.

Although nonleaders do not perform in this distinctive style and are not inclined to try to explain it to an outsider, it is clear that they can understand a good deal of what is said. Some ethnographers have described certain words in this style as "archaic," but many are best considered technical terms. Others are names from the past, the memory of which is supposed to be preserved by the leaders, who are themselves (in principle at least) descendants of ancient leaders. In fact, major epidemics and other catastrophes have broken the lines of descent in most cases, and my assistants observed that the current forms of *anetu itagiñu* were invented after the eighteenth-century slave raiding, during which all the *anetaũ* were taken away. Table 10.2 summarizes the important features of this genre.

The following examples are short excerpts from the *anetu itagiñu* recorded and discussed by two hereditary leaders who lived in Aifa settlement. Kambe, whom I first met in 1966, was one of two older Kalapalo leaders. His oldest son, Ageu, was the main leader in the same settlement after his father's death. Examples (A) through (E) represent the perspective of the community being invited to a ceremonial, which is in this context hosting the messengers. Example (F) is from the

Table 10.2 Features of Anetu Itagiñu

Grammatical	*Semantic*	*Discursive*	*Postural*	*Bodily*
Epistemic markers: contraspective *mukwe*; past assertive *wãke*; epistemic assertive expletive *ah* Evidentials: mythic "hearsay" and inherited, leader's knowledge; *-tï* personal experience *-tifa*: inherited historical knowledge *-kila/kita*.	Metaphoric and humbling references to marital relations, spouses, and in-laws	Chanting prosodic features: lowered overall pitch; monotonic melodic rhythm; rapid utterances; extended final vowels in opening and concluding segments	Use of special objects (bows, firearms, arrows, carried by speaking *anetau*); seats for visiting leaders; kneeling postures for messengers and visiting leaders	Leaders' jaguar ornamentation: pieces of hides, claw necklaces, body paint designs on wrestling champions who are also leaders
Affective and taxis clitics: gitse 'poorly, carelessly', *-gele*. 'as before in the past,' 'still'; *-ale*: uninterrupted	Kinship terms	Poetic chanting: repeated sentences; parallelisms	Donation of food and drink	Black paint (messengers)
Pronominal prefixes: 1st pers. sing., *-u*; 1+2, *ku-*; dual, *ukw-*	Technical vocabulary for *anetu* topics	Overlapping orations	Exchange of wealth between visiting and host leaders: shell belts, macaw feather headdresses	

perspective of the visitors after they have arrived at the settlement to which the messengers have invited them. This structural description obscures the fact that each "perspective" is a processual, or cultivated, intersubjectivity in which the speaker performs several voices.

Example (A) is the full text of Ageu's opening oration, in which this leader, standing outside his house while leaning on a hardwood bow, a symbol of office, calls to the other leaders to come out of their houses and ritually receive the newly arrived messengers. Visiting messengers are received by younger leaders who kneel before them, recite their acceptance speeches, and then remove the messengers' bark ankle wrappings. This lets the messengers know which individual leaders have accepted the invitation and will escort the rest of the community. This commitment requires that they give the messengers valuable shell belts. Which leaders will serve as the ceremonial escorts has been agreed upon prior to the messengers' arrival.

Many of the features shown in table 10.2 appear in this short opening oration (all relevant features in this and following examples are in boldface):

(A)

1 ***kïŋamuk^{w}e kïŋamuk^{w}e kïŋamuk^{w}e kïŋamuk^{w}e. kïŋamuk^{w}e kïŋamuk^{w}e***
Children children children children. Children children

2 ***Ah uk^{w}-oto-ko-iŋo-kugu muk^{w}e ali-tu-e, ali-ta-i,***
EXP dual-parent-PL-POT-INT EM cheer-Vi-I, cheer-CI-CL,
ali-ta-i, ali-ta-i, ali-ta-i, ali-ta-i, ali-ta-iii...
cheer-CIL-CL, cheer-CI-I, cheer-CI-CL, cheer-CI-CL, cheer-CI-CL...
Believe me, though they may not want to, both our relatives are coming, so cheer, cheer, cheer, cheer, cheer...

3 ***Ah kïtsï i-fati-gi-la-muk^{w}e a-ka-mba igey mu...***
EXP ugly 3-send-ADV-NEG-EM 3.-seated-Vi DEM EM...
Believe me, though they may not want to, sending no old and useless people (others will be) seated here...

4 ***Ah ukw-oto-ko-muk^{w}e-gele-al=igey. e-ŋoku u-limo***
EXP dual-parent-PL-EM-CONT-UT=DEM 2-messenger(s) 1-children
ata-nïgï-muk^{w}e igey, uk^{w}-atu-nda-ni-muk^{w}e igey.
EQ-PERF-EM DEM dual-invite-CI-ANT-EM DEM
Believe me, though they may not want to, our older relatives here again now as before. Though they may not want to, these messengers of yours, my children, are here, we are about to do the inviting here, though they may not want...

5 *Ah inde-ne-**muk^{w}e-ila*** ***uk^{w}-aŋa-mba-gitse uk^{w}-a-nïgï-ko***
EXP here-LOC-EM-NEG dual-be.seated-Vi-DEF dual-EQ-PERF-PL
at-ehe-muk^{w}e-ila agitse
EQ-PERS-EM-NEG DEV
Believe me, though they may not want to, here in this place, we two have been seated poorly, we two though we may not want to, continue to rest poorly.

6 ***Ah kïŋamuk^{w}e-ila-gitse ei-ŋoku-gu u-limo*** *ata-nïgï-lefa age*
EXP children-NEG-DEF 2-messenger-POSS 1-son EQ-PERF-MT more(?)
Believe me, and unfortunately there are no youngsters who are your messengers my children.

7 *Inde* ***muk^{w}e-lefa-gitse*** *ku-te-lu-ko* ***at-amo=kugu***
Here EM-MT-DEF 1+2-go away-PI-PL 2-relatives=completely
-gele-fa al=egey.
-CONT-NT UT=DEM
And with difficulty though we may not want to, we all leave this place, every one of your people, this time now as before.

8 ***Kïŋamuk^{w}e-la*** *agetsïkï* ***ei-ŋoku-gu u-limo*** *ata-nugu*
Children-NEG even more 2-messengers-POSS 1-children EQ-PERF
ku-te-lu al=egey
1+2-go away-PI UT=DEM
Not any youngsters now, more of your messengers are my children, (so) we all leave now as before in the past.

Several things are apparent from the free translation. First are Ageu's references to his own status as leader and the various positions he takes as such. These begin with his opening address to the "children," in which he calls the other (younger) leaders' attention to the visitors. Because in subsequent sections he will call out the other leaders to help assist with the greeting and acceptance of the invitation, "children" here references the speaker's primary leadership role as the oldest active *anetu.* (When several leaders share a task, as in the *uluki,* or trade ceremony, the speaker calls his fellow leaders "brothers"; see example [F].) In line 8, the speaker references this relationship of elder leader to younger leaders with regard to the messengers themselves, called *ulimo* 'my sons'.

Second is the devaluation of the work of the messengers and leaders themselves as "perhaps in vain" and "though they/we may not want to" (by the contraspective *-muk^{w}e*) and the self-humbling reception by the local leaders, whose efforts are described as "poorly" or "ineffectively" or "unfortunately" performed (by the affective particle *gitse*). Perhaps, they say, they are not (and cannot) be doing as well as the leaders of the past.

Third is the direct association of the intransitive experiencing of the two messengers through the speaker's use of the dual pronominal prefix *uk^{w}-* 'we two'. This last feature helps explain the two devaluation features as the speaker takes the "humbling" (*ifutisu*) perspective of the visiting messengers, young hereditary leaders serving their first important roles. This perspective is also indexed by the special posture of the messengers, who are seen at first kneeling, then seated with bowed heads.

Fourth, the leader also takes the position of his entire community, using the "inclusive we" prefix *ku-* when speaking of the trip they will take together to the hosts' ceremonial gathering. In this regard, the leader simultaneously distinguishes himself as a hereditary leader and includes himself in the collective group, whose participation is crucial to the success of the future ceremony.

Fifth, the expression *e(i)ŋokugu* 'your messengers' also appears to incorporate both the local leaders as a group and the entire community of potential travelers as relevant participants. The term for messenger (*eŋoku*) is one of the technical terms that is characteristic of this leader's talk; otherwise these visitors would be called *etiñe* 'askers'. The stance perspective (Du Bois 2007) of the messengers as reluctant participants appears in lines 2–4 ("even though they may not want to") and especially in line 5, where something more than the hosts' interpretation of their feelings is replaced by a sort of imagined reaction to the ritual incompetence of the speaker's own group ("we are seated poorly…"). This, too, is a form of stance-laden modesty.

Important as well are features that connect these ongoing ritual events to others that took place in the distant past. The speaker associates the arrival of youthful, vigorous messengers who have come to invite the people to travel to their settlement "this time, still" (*ale-egey*) with identical events in the past through use of the taxis particle *-gele* 'again', with the resultant sense of "they as before in the past." In both leaders' explanations of their speeches, Kambe and Ageu referred to the continuity of customary behavior, initiated by ancestral leaders in ancestral places. They do so using the traditional/customary hearsay knowledge/practice evidential clitic *ti/tu,* the evidential clitic *tifa,* referencing inherited customary knowledge (as is characteristic of leaders), and the inherited knowledge from prior generations (specific former experts) evidential *-kila.*

Example (B) is an excerpt from Ageu's response after members of his own group have accepted the messengers' invitation. This section of the ritual discourse is typified even more than the first by repetition and parallelism, through which Ageu develops a pronounced rhythmic chanting. As the local leaders kneel before the messengers in humble (*ifutisu*) acceptance of their invitation, Ageu speaks at length of the connection between these events, the participants, and the ancient past.

Lines 25 and 26 include the EM *wãke,* described in the section on affinal civility. The leader is able to bear witness about evidence from the past because it is inherited knowledge passed down from one leader to the next (Basso 1993; Franchetto n.d.). *Wãke* also appears later, in example (D), lines 110–119.

In multiple parallel couplets, names of ancient leaders and their activities are connected to the ritual event taking place in the here and now. Lines 29–30 mention Eusagu, *anetu ekugu,* the foundational leader of the settlement called Kalapalo. As in example (A), Ageu associates himself with these ancient leaders and their own young messengers (line 22). In line 21 Ageu speaks modestly of his expertise when alluding to his role as *itsugini* 'the greeter'. This is another technical term, a nominalization of the verb root *itsu-* 'call', that subsumes the acts of presenting special seats to the messengers, leading them by their wrists to be seated or to enter a house, presenting food, and of course the entire oratorical response to their presence.

In line 20, the messengers are said to "arrive quickly." In the ancient past these leaders were considered to be expert runners; I was told that the ceremonial wrestling I observed had replaced an original racing competition between members of different communities.[5] *Katundaluwa,* another technical term, refers to the messengers' appearance on the wide ceremonial entrance path (*taginda*).

(B)

20 *Uwitseke-gele* *a-ti-mbe-ga-ke* ***eŋoku***
quickly-CONT EXP-arrive-Vi-CI-I messengers
Now as before in the past, messengers arrive quickly.

21 *Ah* *itsu-gi-ni-ekugu* *oto-ila* *eti-mbe-ga-ke* ***eŋoku***
EXP greet-Vi-ANT INT expert-NEG arrive-Vi-CI-I messengers
Believe me, there is no expert who will greet them correctly, arrive messengers

22 *u-iñu-gu* *figu-mbugu* *katunda-luwa* *etimbe-ga-ke,* ***eŋoku***
1–shell collar-POSS grandchild-F entry.path-by.way.of arrive-Vi-CI-I messengers
The shell collars of those former grandchildren arrive on the entry road, messengers.

23 *Uwitse-ke-gele* *a-timbega-ke* ***eiŋoku***
move.quickly-I-CONT EXP-arrive-CI-I 2-messengers
Arrive quickly messengers, believe me.

24 *Ah* ***itsu-gi-ni*** *ekugu* *oto-ila* *eti-mbe-ga-ke* ***eŋoku***
EXP greet-Vi-N INT expert-NEG arrive-Vi-CI-I messengers
Believe me, there is no expert to greet them correctly, arrive your messengers.

25 *Eti-mbe-go-ki-dye- ti-ge-tu-fal=igey* *wãke.*
arrive-Vi-PL-ADV-SA-DES-RT-DIS-T-CONT=DEM EM
Again, inclined to arrive somewhere else like this now as in the past, I attest.

26 ***ei-ŋoku****-ge-tu-al=igey* *wãke*
2-messengers-RT-DIS-CONT=DEM EM
Messengers inclined like this somewhere else now as in the past, I attest.

27	*Ah*	*ŋele fisu-mbïgï*	***katunda-lefa***	*etimbe-ga-tiga-ke*	***eŋoku***
	EXP	they yB-F	walk.on.entry.path-MT	arrive-CI-HAB-I	messengers

Believe me, their younger brothers from the past accustom yourself to arrive on the entrance road, the messengers.

28	*U-wifu-gu*	*atu-wigu-mbïgï-**kila***	***eŋoku***
	1–ancestor-POSS	REFL-grandsons–F-EV	messengers

That's what I learned about my ancestor's grandson's from the past, your messengers.

29	***Eusagu**-fa tu-wigu-mbï-kila*	***eŋoku***
	(name)-NT REFL-grandson-F-EV	messenger

I learned about Eusagu's grandsons from the past, messengers.

30	***Eusagu** wigu-mbïgï*	***katunda-luwa***	*atimbe-ga-ke*	***eŋoku***
	(name) grandson-F	walk.on.entry.path-by.way.of	arrive-CI-I	messengers

Eusagu's grandsons from the past arrive on the entrance road, messengers.

Evidentiality: Inherited, Traditional/Customary, and Narrative Hearsay

Examples of evidential forms abound in leaders' didactic discourse. In example (B), lines 29–30, referring to the ancient leader by name, Ageu uses the rare evidential clitic (*-kila/kita*), which references concrete historical knowledge, that is, knowledge that has been passed down from a named person with firsthand experience. The personal experience evidential clitic *-tifa* references knowledge that has been inherited by the speaker through a chain of authorities, although these are not necessarily named as they are with the preceding morpheme. Example (C) is taken from Kambe's 1982 discussion of the leader's talk.

(C)

Uge ti-pïgï	*anet=ofo,*	*iñalu-ma*	*taloki-to-**tifa***	*i-tagi-ñu*
I make-PERF	leader=USU,	denial-EM	no reason-person-EV	3-speak to-N
iñalu.	*(EB: iñalu)*	*Anetu, Anetu, anetu-**tifa***		*i-tagi-ñu.*
denial.	(EB: denial)	Leader, Leader, leader-EV		3-speak to-N

I was taught to serve as a leader, none of the ordinary people in my experience speaks (i.e., eloquently), no. (EB: no). The leaders, the leaders are the ones who speak (eloquently).

Finally, in (D), Ageu uses the "simple narrative hearsay" evidential suffix, *-tï-/-ti,* which is restricted in use to narrators of mythic stories and leader's talk. This suffix references more than hearsay knowledge, because the value of *-t* comes from the speaker being himself indexed in other ways as an expert in what he is talking about—either what can be learned about the Beginning or, if the speaker is an experienced hereditary leader, the *anetu itagiñu.* In (D), Ageu impresses on his listeners the traditional nature of his knowledge about leaders from the distant past, using this suffix in the final clause of the sentence.

(D)

aŋ-olo	*figey*	*aŋi-folo,*	*aŋi-folo.*
EQ-DP	DEM	beginning-DPN,	beginning-DPN

This is the way of the ancients, the ancients.

Inde	*fegey*	*ati-ñe*	*a-tagi-mba-tofo-mbedya-lefa,*	*egey-fa,*	*ta-wa-**t=i**-feke.*
here	DEM	ask-N	3-tell-Vi-USU-PXA-MT,	DEM-T,	tell-F-**EV**=3-ERG

This is what the messengers here use for telling about what those other people did, and they even tell about what has been learned about them.

Tsufïgï, tsufïgï.
Over a long time, over a long time.

Ideology of Deception (Augene)

Kalapalo people have a great interest in *augene,* a (nominal) term that covers illusionary consciousness and deceptive action (Basso 1987). As I described in the section on affinal civility, familial politeness requires that speakers use a variety of metaphorical and other figures in which inversions and substitutions index respectful devaluation of the speaker's gifts and personal attributes in service to an affine. Moreover, hereditary leaders describe many instances of their ritual communication as *augunda* (the verbal form), with regard to the way they epistemically devalue the work and experiences of their ceremonial messengers and even their guests. Example (E) is taken from Kambe's quotation of his dialogue with the other leaders of Aifa once their visitors had arrived. Here he describes how he instructs them in the proper acts of welcome. But he modestly takes care to call them "brothers" and to note that he is the one who has agreed to take on this principal role, according to their wishes. In turn, they validate each of his remarks.

(E)

1 *Fisuandau fisuandau*
Brothers, brothers,

Uge ake-ts-egey	*faŋa-fi-tigi-ni*
me DEO-EX-DEM	seat-ADV-PERF-N

This is how I want to seat them.
[The guests then enter and sit on the seats set out for them in the plaza.]

2 *Fisuandau, fisuandau, ŋeŋoku* *uw-ata-nïgï-apa figey*
brothers, brothers, messengers 1–EX-PERF-CONF-DEM
My brothers, my brothers, as you asked me to, I have put the messengers
Ku-tsa-tofo-ko-na
1+2–EX-USU-PL-ALL
where we have what we use as our seats.

3 *ŋiŋ-ke-fofo* *ku-ŋeŋoku-gu* *ts-uGiñi-ke*
look.see-I-IT 1+2-messenger-POSS REFL-escort-I
The next thing you must think about is to escort these messengers of ours.
[Response by other chiefs]: *eh he, ohsi* (*Ø-nïgï-s=i-feke*)
agreement, HORT (say.to-PERF-CUST=3–ERG)
"All right, let's do it" (that's what they always say).

4 *uge-apa* ***u-augu-nda-ni***
me-CONF 1–deceive-CI-ANT
According to your wishes, soon I'll be the one to speak deceptively.
eh he.
agreement
"All right."

5 *ŋiŋ-ke-ap=ofo* *ukʷ-o-fofo umba-ke*
look.see-I-CONF-IT 1+2=USU drink-I
The very next thing we must think about is to give them something to drink.
[Leaders' response]: *eh he*
"All right."

In (F), excerpted from Ageu's speech of departure, the hosts address their departing visitors with statements of their continuity of experience with past ceremonial participants. The hosts take the stances of both their own communities and that of the guests; each has experienced both positions at one time or another. This excerpt is filled with instances of *augene*. There is a combination of witnessing (through *wãke*), modesty (through *-mukʷe*), and metaphoric inverting of that experience. Ageu speaks as if the guests have arrived very young and will return as mature men, but it is the stance of the guests that is being stated or, better, quoted.

(F)
110 *ah w-agi-su-tiki-mukʷe-fata=l=igey* *wãke*
EXP 1-lazy-PEJ-EM-SIM=UT=DEM EM
Believe me, no reason for my laziness perhaps in vain still this way as in the past.

111 *ah* *ege te-ta* *ti-giñu-feke-muk^{w}e-fata=l=igey* *wãke*
EXP DEM go.away-CI 1+3-sing-N-ERG-EM-SIM=UT=DEM EM
Believe me, you are going away singing to them perhaps in vain still this way as in the past, I attest.

112 *ah* *ŋeŋoku-gu-i-muk^{w}e-fata=l=igey* *wãke*
EXP messenger-POSS-CL-EM-SIM=UT=DEM EM
Believe me, messengers perhaps in vain at the same time still this way as in the past, I attest.

113 *ah-te-ta* *taiti-muk^{w}e–fata=l=igey* *wãke*
EXP-go.away-CL *=EQ-OP-EM-SIM-UT-DEM* *EM*
Believe me, at the same time may we go away, perhaps in vain still this way as in the past, I attest.

114 *ah* *sagiŋo-ila* *muk^{w}e-kugu-aka-mba* *igey* *wãke*
EXP same-NEG EM-INT-EM-XS DEM EM
Believe me, perhaps in vain not really the same you see, others this way in the past, I attest.

115 *ah* *ku-limo-feke* *muk^{w}e=(ekugu?) kw=aka-ŋa-mba* *igey* *wãke*
EXP 1+2-children-ERG EM=INT=seat-LOC-Vi DEM EM
Believe me, our children seated this way perhaps in vain vain as in the past, I attest.

116 *ah* *ku=te* *upïgï-ko-muk^{w}e-gele* *igey* *wãke*
EXP 1_2-go.away last-PL-EM-CONT DEM EM
Believe me, going away last this way, perhaps in vain now as before in the past, I attest.

117 *ah* *opi-tsomi-muk^{w}e-l=aka-ŋa-mba* *igey* *wãke*
EXP return-PURP-EM-like that=EM-LOC-XS DEM EM
Believe me, in order to return to be seated, perhaps in vain, I attest.

118 *ah* *fa-iŋo-tiki-muk^{w}e-gele* *igey* *wãke*
EXP mature.men-POT -EM-EM-CONT DEM EM
Believe me, as mature men, perhaps in vain this way, now as before in the past, I attest.

119 *ah* *u-te-lu-tiki* *to-ŋo-mu-i-gele* *igey* *wãke*
EXP 1–go.away-PL-EM DIS-LOC-EM-IRR-CONT DEM EM
Believe me, perhaps in vain there's no reason for me to go away somewhere this way now as before in the past, I attest.

Discussion

The question of how hostile or potentially hostile people are able to participate in collective ritual events such as those in the Alto Xingu can be answered only by careful examination of the ongoing interaction between participants, and especially of the affectively significant linguistic and perceptual means that are used. It is noteworthy that participants in the Alto Xingu leaders' rituals decorate themselves in a manner that suggests potential aggression. The messengers are decorated in the black paint of men about to engage in battle (see Basso 1985), the leaders themselves bear the marks of the most ferocious beast of all, the jaguar, and they carry weapons into the arena of ceremonial gatherings. Yet these attributes cannot be separated from other "peaceful" behaviors: the leaders humbly greet their visitors and offer them rest and refreshment. Later, wealth is exchanged among them. Leadership and leadership rituals thus become tokens of the (at least temporary, if not permanent, as is hoped for) relationships among their communities and between the individual members.

I agree with Surrallés (2003), who observed with regard to Amazonian welcoming ceremonies that attention needs to be paid to more than the "texts" of these events. Nonetheless, the linguistic details of such texts are indeed clues to the interpersonal events that concern us and cannot be regarded as performative consequences of an a priori affective foundation. From whence comes such a foundation? I suggest there are continually made links between the public, macropolitical ceremonial practices and the more private or micropolitical ritual practices described in this chapter. A focus on the interactions of the two, considered as an epistemically grounded "doing" or "making" of the interpersonal, relieves us from having to try to answer this chicken-and-egg question.

Affinal civility seems to enable the transposing the meanings of affinal activities such as gifting in one form or another to new situations. Kalapalo marriages should be seen as icons of that continual "making" of domesticity and its relational consequences outside the household, leading even to the success of more elaborate arrangements among people who do not share a single language. Thus the suppressed persona of the young husband, negotiating the perils of his wife's family's household, and that of his own father-in-law, who must show the newcomer an elaborated deference, jointly contribute developmentally to the complex dramaturgical "I" of the man who acts as the principal leader, someone who is at once himself, the local community of leaders, his own ancestors, and the visiting messengers.

As archaeologists have surmised, there are indeed some interesting connections between "kin" and "chiefly" polities. In the Alto Xingu, it is still possible to see these connections at work, in the continual working out of self-conscious identity construction on the part of hereditary leaders through kin-based discourse. Much more is involved, of course, than simple reference to "kinship ties." Affinal civility and the leader's talk share at least eight important indexical processes, instantiated by specific grammatical elements, lexical forms, and discursive and self-presentational techniques. Both registers involve some of the same epistemic and evidential markers, use of kinship terms, first-person inclusive "we," and dual pronouns, as well as practices identified as *augene* and *ifutisunda,* in the sense of humble, modest posturing through metaphorical inversions or devaluations.

A Kalapalo man's experiences of being first a young husband and later a father-in-law seem to provide the grounding for the ceremonial agency of hereditary leadership. This grounding—overall an aesthetic and affective grounding—is built upon evidential and epistemic features of the grammar, local language ideology, and pronominal features of self-presentation and referencing of personal and collective agency. Together, these elements are important in both the micro-political and macro-political ritual events. The multiple audiences for both, as well as the multiplicity of the speaking leader's positions, suggest they each enable but also transcend the interests of particular individuals, families, and even entire communities. It is in this context that references to continuity with ancient leaders and their practices, and the shift of emphasis to public acknowledgment of "settlements" or "communities" rather than specific interpersonal relations, become critical.

At first only partially and gradually revealed, the Kalapalo speaker's commitment to a certain "social truth"—a commitment to the perspectives of affinal or community others—is emergent. The repeated and repeatedly ritualized validation and verification of these others are expressions of commitment to a collective project. The acts contribute to the ongoing process both within a particular ritual communicative event and over time as both affines and leaders participate in one another's domestic and ceremonial goals. Evidentiality and epistemic marking in the context of narrative and didactic discourse about the past (mythic or inherited) appeals to "tradition" and "custom." The validation and verification forms (stereotyped utterances, expletives, and the use of certain epistemic markers, both grammatical and lexical) develop meaning-laden tropes for this "social truth."

Gestures and postures also index shared epistemic and affective stances. These at once instantiate personal agency and interpersonal alignment; the importance of bodily actions in both styles seems to have enabled them to be effectively shared across language boundaries. Where personal voices cannot be heard, either because they cannot be understood or because they have been suppressed in order to achieve at least temporary harmony, people may use the body to act out hidden predications. In such cases, the material body and its activities serve as safe and effective devices for communicating feelings of comfort, solidarity, patience, and respect, as well as a peaceful, humble demeanor (and at the same time, similarity or differences in identity, ethnic affiliation, and the like), especially if they contrast with the usual or expected behaviors of the participants. Not only do paralinguistic features have meaning in themselves, but in John Gumperz's words they also are "context-invoking meta-messages" or "contextualization cues."

Later, with repeated "form practice" (using these bodily acts in an increasingly predictable and eventually normative fashion), the same meanings are developed further through accompanying verbal locutions. As these locutions are experimented with, such semantics may come to be both paraphrased and metaphorized lexically in ways that conform to the language ideologies pertinent to these locutions. With the sharing of the semantics of acting out what cannot legitimately be spoken, meanings cumulatively pool as people continue to experiment in similar, continuously repeated contexts (marriage and other life-status events, shamanism, trade). A common normative discourse emerges, contributing to an invented history. With repeated use of these bodily acts in more predictable contexts, the same hidden meanings are developed further through accompanying verbal locutions, referencing ideological experiencing.

As Urban has written about Amazonian ceremonial dialogues and ritual wailing, a locution itself may in fact be a metacommunicative ideological statement as well as an index of relationship. Perhaps, as well, language ideologies developed from observations of the way people's ability to metaphorize, invert, and in other ways transform what was performed nonverbally may contribute to a sense that the "deceptive" functions of language predominate and serve positively as the means through which people create and manipulate what they already know and do. Within local networks of shared communicative codes, these stance-taking practices are enabled by grammaticalized and other forms of evidentiality and epistemology, varying use of pronominal prefixes, use of technical terms and devaluative metaphors, and the language of kinship classification. Thenceforth, their dialogical trajectory through social space.

Abbreviations in Interlinear Word-by-Word Glosses

ANT, anticipation mood; BEN, benefactive/dative; CI, continuous indicative; CL, proper inclusion copula; COLL, collective; CONC, concessive; CONF, conformative; COMP, completive; CONT, continuative taxis; D, deixis ("on flat surface"); DEF, deficient; DEM, demonstrative; DEO: deontic; DES, desiderative; DIR, directive; DIS, dislocative; DP, distant past; DPN, distant past nominalizer; DT, detransitive; E, emphasizer; EM, epistemic marker; END, endearment; ERG, ergative; EQ, equative copular verb; EV, evidential; EX, existential copular verb; EXP, expletive; F, former, of the past, deceased nominalizer; HAB, habitual; I, imperative; IR, irrealis; LOC, locative; M, modifier; MT, metonymic taxis; N, nominalizer; NEG, negation; NT: new topical reference; OP, optative; PC, personal customary; PERF, perfective aspect; PERS, persistent; PI, punctate aspect, indicative mood; PL, plural; POSS, possessive; POT, potential mood; PURP, purposive; PXA, shift reference "prior event, new participant"; REFL, reflexive; RT, repeated taxis; SA, same agent; SC, subject continuity; SIM, simultaneous taxis; TC, traditional customary; UT, uninterrupted taxis; USU, usuative nominalizer; Vi, intransitive verbalizer; Vt, transitive verbalizer; XS, subject discontinuity; Z, sister; 1, first person; 1+2, first person plural inclusive; 2, second person; 3, third person; =, vowel assimilation.

Notes

1. Archaeologists are concerned with the relationships between development of hereditary leadership, social inequality, and public ceremonial spaces, particularly what appear to have been structures designed for large-scale ceremonial gatherings (Clark 2004; Hill and Clark 2001; Inomata 2006; Schortman, Urban, and Ausec 2001). They are also concerned with the kin-based origins of these leadership structures, particularly intertextual relations between the discourses of leadership and kinship. With rare exceptions (Heckenberger 2006), however, these scholars fail to consider the practices recorded in the ethnographic literature.

2. As a consequence of marriage between people belonging to different language groups, as well as the flight of accused sorcerers who receive refuge among their relatives living in other communities, some residents speak more

than one local language. Seki (1999) commented on the "passive" multilingualism and bilingualism in the area, where in-married persons speak their own language to their spouse and children but not in public contexts. Franchetto (2001: 141) observed: "In-married persons strictly control their use of their own, and the local, languages: Outsider men do not actively participate in the local men's flute cult, sit apart from other men in the men's area in the plaza in an attitude of 'vergonha' [which means more than 'shame, embarrassment'; the Carib term is *ifutisu* and conveys the sense of humility and personal modesty]. Inside the family, the in-married person uses his or her language with the children (who become bilingual) while the local spouse speaks the local language. This may be understood by the in-married spouse but is 'carefully avoided.'"

3. I follow the definition of evidentiality as referring to *sources* of evidence and epistemology as concerning *evaluation* of evidence (Aikhenvald 2004; Basso 2008; De Haan 1999, 2001). I use the neutral terms "marker" and "morpheme" because there is some morphophonemic variability in the cliticization of these forms; in some contexts, at least some may be legitimately termed "particles."

4. Following Jakobson (1971: 135), I use the term "taxis" to refer to an important set of fifteen clitics that mark the phasal relations between two different narrated events.

5. The Brazilian linguist Bruna Franchetto was the first to collect, transcribe, and translate texts of the leader's talk. Her publications (esp. 1983, 2000, n.d.) include careful explanations of a number of Kuikuro examples. These are of special interest because Kuikuro and Kalapalo are closely related languages. Yet within a similar if not identical frame there are many differences, topically, lexically, and morphophonemically. For example, with regard to this particular example, the Kuikuro say that the messengers "run"; the Kalapalo say they "arrive quickly."

eleven

Private Ritual Encounters, Public Ritual Indexes

Michael Silverstein

Something happened to me yesterday /
Something I can't speak of right away /
Something happened to me /
Something oh so groovy /
Something happened to me yesterday!

—*The Rolling Stones*

My chapter concerns both ritual and communication, to be sure, but perhaps in a relationship one to the other that is different from that of other contributions to our discussion. My focus is on two examples of what we might term, initially, "private" and "solitary" rituals of individual humans in the two small-scale societies where I have worked. Each involves as well highly proprietary and circumspect indexical "communication" consequent upon such ritual experiences that, in a sense, always "retrospectively" shapes them as having been performatively effective ritual events, while in anticipation of the rituals, there is as well much "prospective" anticipatory shaping of a person's anxious ritual-readiness, as we may term it.

Among the Kiksht-speaking Chinookans of the Columbia River, the ritual in question comprises the securing of a "spirit power" by a pubescent or pre-adolescent young person that will endow the individual with a determinate life-cycle destiny; among the Worora and closely related Australian Aboriginal people, it is the way a man becomes "pregnant," i.e., fecund by-and-with a child, determining the child's "Great Name" and its social distribution as a denotationally deployable set of lexemes. These are, interestingly, rituals of the closest thing to "self-fashioning" we might find, among all the van Gennepian (1960) "rites of passage" so densely found in the social anthropological literature. An individual in each case has a conventionally structured, yet very out-of-observation encounter with cosmic alterity—with what we might even term "nature"—and comes away from the encounter culturally endowed for a new phase of life; indeed, in the second case, with the locally understood quickening power of life itself.

So whatever "communication" goes on in the central ritual moments here is between the non-human—one might even say "pre-human"—and human realms; both ritual moments, in fact, domesticate the forces of the non-human in-and-for some particular individual, who both prepares for and benefits from the consequences of the encounter. And the subsequent communication of what has, in fact, gone on in those central ritual moments must never occur through unrestrictedly circulatable narrative or equivalent denotational report. That a ritual encounter of such-and-such sort has happened is proprietary information, in general only indexically communicable in various restricted contexts, for example by one's demeanor, the qualities of one's body and social comportment that index prior, life-transforming experience, etc.

These cases seem to me to be interesting in several ways, both comparative and theoretical. Comparatively, they may add to the complexity of intersecting dimensions along which we would want to consider the general category of 'ritual communication': to what extent must the "communication" that presents itself in moments of ritual, for example, be centered on an interlocutory event, initiated in some sense by an intentional 'sender' (cf. Du Bois 1986; 1993), available as spectacle to an interested, ratifying 'audience' (cf. Bauman 1977; 1992)? Moreover, must the subsequent "communication" authorized and licensed by ritual be denotation-centered? And so forth, along several dimensions of contrast.

Theoretically, these cases bring up a central problem in the very analysis of ritual—or ritualized—semiosis, deriving from our cumulated understanding of these "performative"—i.e., indexically entailing or causally consequential—performances. Any adequate analysis of ritual eventhood must come to grips with the following universal property. Rituals as standardly illustrated in the anthropological literature are understood to be performative—transformative of the empirical world, even if in some very local way—*precisely as a function of their hypertrophied, reflexively calibrated metasemiosis* (see Silverstein 1981; 1993; 2004).[1] Layer upon layer of figuration in verbal, objectual-qualitative, actional and other modalities construct the bounded microcosm of ritual social-spacetime; what is dynamically figurated in this microcosmic event is understood to link it causally to consequences in the real world as a macrocosm. Such formal properties of rituals that, in effect, bound these events off from the everyday are directed to emphasizing—if not guaranteeing—their regimentation as autonomous entextualizations-in-context-of-belief that participants in the event experience as such, regardless of the degree to which effective Durkheimian "effervescence" results for each and every participant. It has generally been understood, moreover, that ritual efficaciousness depends on the calibrated *reflexivity* of the metasemiosis of which such an event is constituted, generally a result of the densely "poetic" structure (in Jakobson's [1960] sense) of ritual semiotic activities rendered into dynamic text ("entextualized") in one or more modalities (language; bodily arrangement and action; objects and their *qualia* and movement through the spacetime of the performance; music and other sonic signs; etc.).

But note that in the cases I bring up for consideration here, such private rituals seem to be densely metasemiotically characterizable only before- or after-the-fact, in this way producing their *worried expectation of being* or their *certainty of having been* "performative," in the sense of well-formed and therefore effective entextualizations of all their ritual conditions of possibility and co-organized sign manifestations that go into such an event. In both of these ritual encounters, there is a metasemiotic moment of self-transformation by self-recognition: "this is not 'ordinary nature' I am now confronting/ now confronting me; I feel it figurating my fate, my future."

Thus, there is an anxiety, in a sense, about such private rituals as I discuss here: will I have such an experience as I can describe in expectation, based on what others tell me? Have I in fact had this ritual experience on some prior occasion and am I therefore manifesting or able to manifest the fact? Has So-and-So had such a ritual experience? How do I read the indexicals he/she seems to be giving off as metasemiotically informative of the nature of the ritual event So-and-So seems, then, to have had? What is critically recognized both by the participant him/herself and certainly by any other(s) to whom the metasemiotic semiosis is manifest, is the explanatory value for subsequent behavior if one can interpret it as metasemiotic indexical signage of a private ritual encounter. Such retrodicted and therefore imputed performativity may well be part of the essential of such private life-transition ritual forms,[2] and we might see that the circulation of indexes licensed by such ritual occurrences both presumes upon these earlier events and, in an important way, retrospectively regiments and shapes them as having been previously effective ritual occasions in a particular person's life, that individual's recognition of which in the event is key. The ritual happening and its linked metasemiotic "reports" are interdiscursive without being intertextual (see Agha and Wortham 2005; Silverstein 2005: nn. 1, 7); the ritual happening is the interdiscursive target of which, then, the metasemiotic indexing becomes the necessary confirmatory regimentation.

We should also see these ethnographic instances in relation to what, in the West/First World, are some of the ideological "takes" on private, ritualized experience. To be sure, we in the Judaeo-Christian-Muslim traditions understand prayerfulness as one kind of ultimate private moment that leads us to ritual. Many people pray to a deity in moments away from normal sociality—think of orthodox Jewish men reciting prayers each morning in private while wearing their phylacteries, amulets that bind the metaphorical entrance-posts of the body (forehead-near-mind, upper arm-near-heart) like those placed on the doorposts of the observant Jewish residence. And many Jewish, Christian, Muslim and other worship services include segments during which each individual in the congregation—visible if not audible one to another—is called upon silently to engage in reciting prayers, whether formulaic or improvised. These acts of *aggregated, simultaneous (parallel) privacy-in-public* (cf. Hancher 1979) are distinct from segments where a congregation recites or sings aloud in unison (the paradigmatic ritual site and imagistic metaphor—unisonance—for a Benedict Anderson [1983, 1991] of the quasi-religiosity that underlies the culturalized phenomenology of nationalism). But what is important to understand here is that some institutional authority licenses private prayer, the experiencing of which in full as a semiotic event is available only to the participant engaging in prayer (though the performative effect of visible aggegration as such may give all participating mutual observers the "effervescent" feeling of collectivity notwithstanding, as a higher order by-product; note the service of the Eucharist in this respect in which the aggregate, serial incorporations of The Host by the congregants define the distributively realized corporate body of Christ).

Again, private, non–institutionally-licensed "ritual" behavior is, to a great extent, suspicious in modern Euro-American societies' rationalist ideologies: it is seen as "obsessive-compulsive behavior" and other "superstition"-indicating forms of dealing with uncertainty. Certainly, the little secret "ritual" acts we all perform under various circumstances—touching or carrying an amulet, whispering or muttering a sacred oath or disclaimer, organizing or arranging objects "just so," etc.—to guarantee the perlocutionary success of our interested undertakings, tend to become habitual. And as these become habitual, they are looked upon by others with at best an amused dismissal, and at worst they are looked upon as indexes of serious psychological dysfunction in an otherwise rationalized, secularized world of everyday life. We tend to be somewhat self-consciously embarrassed by having them called to attention, by virtue of which our anxiously and anti-ritualistically secular public persona seems to be called into question.[3]

Guardian "Spirit Power" Quest in the American Northwest

My first example is what is generally termed the "spirit power quest," once recognized as a widespread "complex" of indigenous North American spirituality and religious practice. Ruth Benedict did her very Boasian doctoral dissertation based on others' sources, "The concept of the guardian spirit in North America," published in 1923, on its distribution and variation over North American societies. My focus is on the practices among the easternmost groups of people speaking Kiksht, one of the Chinookan languages once spoken along the Columbia River from the Willamette River (south of present-day Portland, Oregon) to The Dalles. My own fieldwork, principally carried out from 1966 to 1976, is supplemented by material published starting a century ago by Edward Sapir and then his students, Leslie Spier and Walter Dyk, as well as from conversations with others working in this field more recently (David and Kathrine French, Dell Hymes, Robert Moore).[4]

Briefly summarized, the spiritual economy of the Northwest Coast societies revolved around the possibility that each individual might acquire special powers due to the encounter with a power-conferring avatar of the mythic characters connecting this world with the cosmogonic era in the very narratives of their doings told at night during the late autumn through early spring months. This stylized encounter would happen to a young person completely away from all other humans, in a private, ritual occasion of life-transforming offer of protection, sponsorship, and orientation toward a route of success in life. The avatar and the power conferred were termed *[i]-iułmaχ*, and it was a theme of continuing societal interest in any individual as to whether or not So-and-So "saw" and then, therefore "had" one or more such powers. As in so many different aspects of social life among Chinookans, quantity of power translated into the elaborately reticulated system of hierarchical rank; thus, having as many powers as one could attract was deemed important.

Acquiring and having many different such powers was an ideal state of affairs, endowing one with the confidence to ascend in society through the force of abilities of various kinds that gave one advantage over others and protected one from various forms of harm and malevolence. While some powers protected their possessors, others could be directed to intervene in the conditions of others, as in healing shamanism, and some, inherently malevolent, worked to the detriment of others, as in shamanic "shooting" of someone else's spirit, causing wasting disease through the presence of a foreign substance or object and ultimately death unless a stronger, countervailing power were secured through hiring a healing shaman to undo the damage to one's spirit.

Now Sapir had already encountered a kind of *-iułmaχ* anxiety vividly expressed by his half-breed colleague and interpreter, Peter McGuff (born ca. 1875), from whom Sapir took a dictation in summer, 1905, that he entitled "Winter Bathing" (Sapir 1909: 188–191). In this little dictation, which I have elaborately reanalyzed and discussed in Silverstein 1996b, Mr. McGuff talks about one among the several training regimes that Chinookan elders stipulated for pre-adolescent, even barely pubescent young people in order to prepare them for the acquisition of a spirit power. Since the spirit powers came to young people in the form of one of the animals or other characters of the cosmogonic era, when the topography, flora, and fauna were ordained as they should be for the coming of the current-era people (*Nadidanuit*);[5] consequently, paying attention to the cosmogonic myth-tellings and other sacred activities, such as spirit power dances, spiritually animated kinesis among the shamanically gifted, all of which took place during wintertime, was essential for young people. Not only Mr. McGuff, but my own consultants in the 1960s who were his consociates talked about falling asleep during the endlessly long evenings and nights of myth-telling, the "punishment" for which was to go for a solitary dip in the icy Columbia River or one of its tributaries in the pre-dawn chill. These were toughening routines, as my consultants recall them, designed to force the young person out into the world-at-large so as to gain confidence for the real spirit quest.

In spring- and summertime the world becomes empirically experienceable again, fit for human activities and inhabitances throughout its whole extent, rivers to lakes to forests to mountains, and everyone was active in pursuing the native economy of fishing, gathering, hunting and the preservation of foodstuffs. During this period in particular, young people would be sent out to isolated places in the middle of the night, given ritual tasks to accomplish (on the accomplishment of which the commissioning elder would check) such as the piling up of little stones, or the planting of a recognizable fabricated marker. The young person would be told to stay there all night, not returning until morning time. It was on these solitary vigils that one's *-iułmaχ* might come to one, telling the young person in a state of altered, van Gennepian removal-from-society that he or she would be protected by this power and be licensed to behave in ways that indexically revealed the power one had.

Here is the way one of my consultants describes it:

> Nobody goes out and get[s] the [*-iułmaχ*]—you know, like you would send the children. In the night we'd be someplace and tell 'em, "You go waaaaaay over there someplace, in [the middle of the] night." You don't want to get afraid the kid's gonna get et up by something; no, just let 'em go. They used to give you something, down by the [Columbia] River. They used to give you a little stick. You'd go up to that—I'll show you [= MS], where that bathing place [is] now, and th[ose] graves [on Washington State Highway 97 north of The Dalles Dam]. Well further down there's two holes there, o:hhhh big hole they go around in there. Five times and you put that stick on there. The next day this old person'll go up and look for that stick if [you] took it there. He'll find it there: "Yeah, he was here!" That was a marker. They used to tell me, "You take these hazel nuts, you go way up the hill there someplace, and you'll crack those nuts there and you'll eat it, and you'll leave the shells there." And this person'll go for sure. He'll go waaaaay up where he sent this kid. He'll find hazel nuts' peelings there: "Oh, well, he was here." See? They traced you to [determine] for sure [that] you was up there. That's for your own good, your own good: something'll come and talk to you; otherwise he'll put you to sleep. You'll go to sleep there. And this thing will be on to you that you're gonna be a powerful person."

Powers endowed one with strengths and abilities of various sorts. They also formed one's personality, constituting in effect a kind of ethno-psychodynamic explanatory framework for understanding people's characteristic ways of responding to the empirical circumstances of life. These characteristics are the realized, lived indexical consequences of having encountered specific spirit powers, and endow people differently. Thus, one consultant said of another, who was by that time blind, that even when she could see she used constantly to bat her eyelids just like a frog. This is clear evidence of a Frog Power ("Aq'wadat au ičaiułmaχ" 'Frog is indeed her power'), and the expectation therefore that she understands frogs when they "talk."[6] The mother's sister of a consultant "used to know that *skintxwa* [brown bear]; she used to wait on women—deliver babies," indeed, one of the conferred powers associated with this *–iułmaχ*.[7] Spier and Sapir (1930: 237) speak about the variety of manifestations of power, and their relative strengths, as follows:

> These guardian spirits … were by no means of the same potency. A shaman could not cure any one who had been bewitched unless his own spirit was more powerful than the spirit intrusive in the patient. Hopeless cases were those bewitched by the spirits of the grizzly, water-monster, mountain lizard, eagle, sturgeon, cougar, and turtle. Of these the grizzly and water-monster bewitchings were most fateful. Even the most powerful shamans would not attempt to cure these.
>
> Those who had sturgeon spirits were exceptionally brave; no matter what wounds they might have received they would not succumb, just as a sturgeon's vitality is great. It may be deeply cut without being killed. War chiefs almost always had for spirits, sturgeons, rocks, or trees. Some of them might be struck by arrows but they could not be wounded, and if they did penetrate, these men would not die. Only those who had weak spirits or none at all were killed.
>
> Certain spirits gave one the power to move stealthily, to hide readily, and be hard to shoot. Such were mountain lizards, snakes, small insects, and small birds. Only those with more powerful spirits could spy them out and shoot them.
>
> One who had a deer spirit became a good hunter of deer. He dreamed of where they were to be found. The deer talked to [told?] him. Such a man never ate deer meat, save when sick and about to die, he would ask for the flesh, eat a small piece and in a few days be well again.
>
> A man with a rattlesnake spirit would not be bitten by them. He could safely pick them up. He skinned them, dried the skin, and mixed it with his tobacco. Only such a man could smoke this. He could also send his snake (spirit) to bite someone.

We can see how carefully prepared for, indeed rehearsed was the solo ritual encounter with these forces of the extra-human world, the powers of which were realized within human society in these psychosomatic capabilities. People were attuned to the indexicals of spirit power, as they depended, in coming to satisfactory explanations of the course of human events of one or another sort, on reading such happenings in indexical terms.

Not having any powers at all was clearly a regrettable circumstance. As revealed to Sapir in 1905, Mr. McGuff, like my own consultants sixty and more years later, is clearly sad to realize he has none, and speculates on why that may be so.[8] (He thinks perhaps his ritual preparations were not sufficiently rigorous.) Yet even when one has encountered and been favored by a spirit power, one is enjoined from communicating about this most private, secret encounter. Doing so in denotational language, in particular, save when on one's deathbed, brings either withdrawal of the power or malevolence on the part of the power, causing one illness or even death. Here's one such unfortunate story from the cousin of the man (see note 7) who wanted his mother's *skintxwa* (Brown Bear) Power:

> Well I used to have pretty good [luck in attracting a *-iułmaχ*] like that. One time I was soooound asleep. My aunt used to know that [*skintxwa*] and she said—she told her son—ah, he told her, "Momma, I want you to leave what you had." And she told him, "No I give it to sister [= matrilateral parallel cousin]; he's gonna be—she's [gonna be] a woman. And she can tend to woman. She's a woman, but you're a man; you don't want to tend to a woman"—like a doctor does, you know. Well, she left that to me.
>
> And I was sleepin' one time and I woke up and I told the folks, "Well, the hazel nuts are ready, you folks ... that bush is all ready to pick now!" And this [hazel] bush wasn't, like that, *iktyana* ["whatchamacallit"], all over [in the countryside nearby]. And they told me, "Who told you?" They let me give it—that [*-iułmaχ*]—away. Quick I come [back and] said, "Oh, The [Brown] Bear!"
>
> If I never said I'da had it yet. But they made me kinda, you know, *dala'aχ* ['would-be; perhaps'] ... they tricked me so I had to say, "Oh, The Bear." I shouldn't have said, "The Bear," see? I should have kept this to my own self.

Here's another tale of loss of *-iułmaχ:*

> *-iułmaχ* that's a power. You get powerful, you know. Power, something; you know, you go and then you get a power, maybe a snake, or maybe a—ahh,... But you see how I didn't get nothing. I come to a place there and there was a whoooole bunch of—great big bunch of watersnakes. And I stood there and looked they were just like that [hands showing all curled together], a big bunch.

> So I tooked off and went home and I told—I went to a neighbor's—I said, "Ooohh you ought to see the snakes over there; come on, I'll show you!" And we went back there and there was noooo sight of snakes, nowhere. We looked around where I'd seen a bunch of snakes: they were gone!
>
> [MS: *Dala'aχ idmiGiwam* ('perhaps you're a [spell-casting] shaman') (laughs)]
>
> Yeah! Watersnake *dGiwam*. That's what it come—it showed to me but nobody else would [= was supposed to] see it but myself.

What is interesting about the whole *-iuɬmaχ* "complex" is its pervasive orientation of everyone to anxieties of encounter, secrecy, and control: a "complex," indeed, in our Western psychoanalytically informed sense! As we might try to discern if someone with whom we are dining just doesn't happen to like what has been served or is really and fundamentally a vegetarian of some degree, or—gasp!—a vegan, "spirit power" people read each other's likes and dislikes, abilities and attitudinal propensities in various empirical circumstances, etc., in such indexical terms. To be sure, then, attributions, i.e., ascriptions of the possession of spirit power(s) were a topic of discourse, a metapragmatic in the form of a kind of etiological explanation for how someone could manifest in certain ways. Why does So-and-So wear that particular species' hoof-rattle on her buckskin dress? Why does Such-and-Such not eat elk meat, though he gobbles up white-tail deer venison? How did Such-and-So manage to right his canoe and avoid drowning in the rapids of the Columbia, when no one else would be able to?

Two kinds of such ascriptions become more or less public facts in what we might call the degree-certain form of spirit power possession. Someone might earn a certain living by being a shamanic practitioner, both for good (diagnosis and healing) and for bad (causing illness and death). Here, what power or which powers someone controlled—at least in a record of doctoring feats in a hierarchy of strength—soon became matters of professional reputation. This is a whole area of experience that, all the while obeying the strictures on denotational revelation, narration, ostension, etc., is manifest to the community through particular power songs, associated paraphernalia and regalia, etc.—again, indexical emblems of the office of one's *-iuɬmaχ* (singular or plural). There are both serious stories about shamanic curing and hilarious parodies, as for example the trickster-transformer Coyote's Tartuffe-like antics pretending to be a curing shaman for purposes of getting close to young, virgin women and girls he constantly pursues.

The other venue for a somewhat public achievement of the status of power-holder was wintertime spirit power dancing. Particularly when someone seemed to be destined for shamanic status, that person's parents and close kindred would sponsor a coming-out dance, to which other, known powerful figures were invited in a kind of choreography of mutual recognition and mutual placement within the hierarchy of shamanic distinction. Ultimately with a logic not unlike that of the potlatch and this class of ceremonials—among Chinookans, particularly other life-cycle transitions where distribution of new names as well as of more obviously "thingy" property indexically diagrammed sponsors' assertions of status in an exquisite hierarchy of recognized and aspired-to rank—in winter shamanic dancing the powers of the cosmogonic universe were made flesh and were defined one in relation to another before the entire community of spectators.

At these extreme, quasi-professional and certainly public events, there was no question but that the players were laying claim to *-iułmaχ* possession, indeed manifesting how their spirit powers "possessed" them. For the majority of people, such powers were the dream and quest from an early age, though who had which power and why one thought so were matters of interpretation of indexical signs that thus served as the ratifying metasemiotic for the efficacy of the ritual acts in which spirit powers came to someone solitary and hopeful, yet probably somewhat both desirous and scared of the gift to be had at the very edge of empirical ordinariness.

Where Northern Kimberley (Australia) Babies Come From

My second example comes from my fieldwork among the people of Mowanjum Community during the mid-1970s, specifically focused on those for whom the first, or proprietary language was Worora.[9] The Worora have five distinct types of referring expressions used for indicating particular individual people, in addition to clearly analyzable definite descriptions (e.g., 'that bloke over there') and kinship expressions (e.g., 'your mother's brother'). These special expressions form each Worora individual's *naming set,* inasmuch as every individual is ultimately provided with all five types in some segment of the community, merely by virtue of being a social person, and inasmuch as the name-set elements show remarkable symmetries and asymmetries of characteristics that unify them as alternative true names in the way they are used. I shall label the five types of name-set element: [a] great name (translating Worora: *iŋumba Da:re:ya*), [b] *abia*-name (using the Worora baby-talk word for the symmetric "sibling"-like relation in the same or an alternating kinship generation in a patriline), [c] matronym (and pragmatic equivalents), [d] mother's decedent toponym, and [e] nickname(s).

The Worora term *–ŋumba,* which takes an inalienable possessive prefix (the form given in [a] just above is the unmarked third singular masculine possessed form with prefix *i*-), when used alone generally denotes a type [b] name-set element, as is shown in my data by answers to questions such as "What's his name?" So we might then take element [b] to be the prototypic name each individual person bears, the one that ties people together by a structure of egocentric kinship reckoning. By contrast, despite the importance—the ritual importance—I shall ascribe below to type [a], the great name, in the local metalinguistic term for type [a] the modifier *Da:re:ya* 'great' is the differentiating element of its lexemic shape, making it a fortiori a special type, not the general type. Element [b], the basic or prototype "personal name," is sometimes specified in conversation inquiring after identity with the modifier *abianaŋga* 'of his/her *abia*', in the default case understood to be fafa/fafasi. Interestingly, types [c] and [d], which turn out to be taboo forms of different degrees of potency—how one refers when one is enjoined from actually referring—do not even have Worora metalinguistic terms to describe them. At best, type [c], the matronym, was sometimes described in my presence with the descriptive phrase *garanaŋga:nja njiŋumba* or in local pidgin or creole English "mommy bilong 'em name," i.e., 'his/her mo's name [*sc., abia* name]'. Types [c] and [d] being, functionally, taboo- or avoidance-names, the avoidance seems to go so far as to leave the name-set elements themselves with no metapragmatic lexeme in Worora!

Now the most complex name-set element is clearly type [a], my focus here to highlight the private ritual that lies behind its bestowal and the restricted nature of its subsequent manifestation in use. The great name is really a whole set of lexical expressions that recall, allusively, and each in its own way, aspects of the event of self-announcement of the child-to-be encountered by his or her genitor. This curiously reflexive event of self-baptism is predicated with the verb form *bariy* -√(*y*)*i*/*u*-,[10] as in *bariy ge:ŋa* 'he *bariy*ed', with the child clearly the subject of the predication, not the future genitor, *before whom or toward whom* or in respect of whom it happens in a completely stylized way.

Interestingly, the whole event is described by informants in much the same terms as myth occurrences. Indeed, when a child *bariy*s, a conjuncture takes place of the mythic, or mythically ordained cosmos—what some call "The Dreamtime" for non-Aboriginal consumption—and the empirical world of flesh-and-blood (and semen and ova!). The essential characteristics are these. Usually while a man is out with his family or by himself on some hunting, fishing, and/or gathering outing, a strange occurrence involving a species or natural formation attracts his attention, as if to put him in a dream-like state. Indeed, some of my reports are of men falling asleep in a locale while resting from hunting or fishing, though they are quasi-awakened by the apparition. There is a lapse from the mundane, into some other realm in which the strange occurrence focuses a man, the eventual genitor, on the particular plant, animal, fish, weather-form, rock, etc., in which—or "with which," as the Worora say, using an instrumental phrase, note—the spirit of the child presents itself and refers to itself, sometimes only to say "This is me, daddy; I just did such-and-such!" The spirit of the child has indeed 'come up' (*bariy,* recall) in the paradigm case, because spirits (with their interactive potential in respect of humanity) are traditionally found, i.e., dwell, in deep, sacred, year-round pools of water, *wuŋgurr* 'sacred; sacrality' waters, at various sites throughout the clan territories, from which the direction of their emergence to interact with humans is always up. Children's spirits, too, thus dwell in these *wuŋgurr* sites, among other non-mundane types of actors such as mythic creatures resting there since The Dreamtime and reanimated by various human appeals through ritual practice.[11]

Now there is a real parallelism between these accounts of personal self-announcement and clan myths, in which the very same kinds of dramatic elements form the plots in The Dreamtime—the cosmogonic myth age—that result in consequences for the current state of things. The natural topographical formations and their place-names in Worora (and surrounding) territories almost always are explained as the commemorations of some mythic events engaged in at that spot by the *WandjuNas,* the earliest humanoid inhabitants described in myth-derived corroborrees and related sacra, as they interacted with the floral and faunal inhabitants, transforming them into the natural formations people encounter today. These myth-age characters traveled along what have become ritually salient geographical routes resulting in the topographical formations of stone, the pools of water (particularly the sacred *wuŋgurr* waters), etc., now named with placenames evocative of myth-age events. The myth-age inhabitants organized the social forms of society, the various social categories and prescriptive practices which, in the post-missionary period, are referred to, with missionary induced Mosaic allusion, by the term "The Law." Through these myth-age activities were created the various increase sites throughout the territory, sites at which clan propitiation of their animal and plant kinsmen (through totemic affiliation) takes place.

I am suggesting, then, that the event of self-announcement of the individual to his/her future genitor and the events of the myth age are similar in thematic content. I wish to suggest further that they result in a parallelism between two levels of an individual's relationship to the geographically experienced world. One such relationship follows from the individual pre-parturition event in historical time. The other follows from the recruitment of the individual to the totemic patriclan, the ahistorical or timeless relationship of every member of which in the encompassing world was determined by the events of the myth age.

Thus, as a member of a particular patriclan every person has rights in certain territories of his own clan, of the clan of his classificatory mothers' brothers, etc., including access to clan sacred *wuŋgurr* formations for rituals, deposit of sacra and bones, etc. At the same time, having *bariy*ed or come up at a certain location, this named spot, regardless of clan affiliation of the location—it is rarely within the territory of an individual's actual patriclan—becomes his/her personal *wuŋgurr* site. People claimed to feel a particular longing for the site, a particular indexical attachment.

Again, as a member of a particular patriclan, every person has agnatically derived kin-ties to certain patriclan-specific natural substances or species which the clan members are expected to propitiate and respect as "totem,"[12] a responsibility of descent stipulated by the myth age prototype of the species. But at the same time, having *bariy*ed or come up with a particular species, an individual has a special bond of identity with this species, not unlike that with their totemic clan kinsmen. One is not supposed to eat edible species with which one has *bariy*ed, but the sanction is not so strong as for the clan *gi:* species. One older woman remarked of the white bream species with which she *bariy*ed, "I am not supposed to eat that *wuŋgurru dja:ya* ('sacred fish'); still I am greedy for it." However, this same woman claimed that when she dreams of fishing, she goes off by herself and gets lots of (other) fish because of the special relationship.

Frequently, too, this special relationship to the circumstances of *bariy*ing explains some peculiarity or trait of an individual, whether physical or attitudinal or behavioral. One young man of about twenty-five in the mid-1970s *bariy*ed with a great big green crab (*ŋarruŋgunja*) at a place called Hall's Point in English, when his father was inside a cave with running water. Hence his hands are now like those of a crab, i.e., with characteristic palmar curling along with finger-curling and -spreading. Of course, the position of each patriclan and hence of its members in various systems of social relationship are also a consequence of their having had their essential properties ordained in the myth age.

There is, in short, a myth associated with each individual. It is first revealed to—or experientially involves—the genitor of each individual. In this event, the individual is constituted in ways and with consequences that seem isomorphic to the constitution of the larger, clan-level of social reality in which the individual will function. That is to say, the social order, itself a timeless structure of categories and rules ("the law") in native ideology, reproduces itself in the form of the to-be-born individual; the unique happening or sociohistorical event yields up a new individual spirit to the here-and-now order of actually existing consociates among the community. The "great name," like the various names at the clan level, is the commemoration of that individual myth, first and foremost associated with the ethnogeography of the known world. The myth of someone's *bariy*ing ties that individual to place, firstly, and as well to a particular instrumentality, circumstance, and manner.

The "great name" is, in a sense, a verbal allusion to that myth-like ritual happening—any or all of the following kinds of words: a toponym for the place-where-it-happened from among the ethnogeographical nomenclature; a flora- or fauna-type or even a species name, at several levels of taxonomized delicacy of division of the biotic world; a natural topographic formation-type, if relevant to the individual's mode of self-presentation; a descriptor of the manner of self-presentation or mode of apprehension by the genitor of the referent of the "great name." Any or all of these, used in discourse, alludes to the event and thus individuates the soul that *bariy*ed that way. One must then see in the various terms that constitute someone's "great name" alternate forms of what Kenneth Burke (1966: 369–372) would call "entitlements" of the individual's mythic origin, ways of calling it up by a radically telescoped and hence allusive indexical that functions as an historical metapragmatics and only thence as a denoting form.[13] No one of these forms *is* the name, it becomes clear from usage and commentary, and, taken together within a framework of understanding how *bariy*ing to one's future genitor takes place, all of these forms constitute the skeleton of a plot of such a mythic episode. They are then variant forms of allusion to the story of self-baptism or self-presentation, as first revealed to the genitor, and then repeated by him to the child's mother (genetrix) and other particular relatives who are taken into the circle of those who know the myth.

One aged *Yaudjiba* clan woman *bariy*ed with a crocodile (*goyo:ya* [n. masc.]), and hence her "name" is *goyo:yo:nja* 'crocodile [fem.]' adjusted for gender because of the referent. The event took place on a rough, treeless cliff in a spot called *wrrimbalo:ma*, part of a *wuŋgurr* site called *mara:rra* in the clan country of the *Larrinjuwa:ya* Clan, and hence her "name" is *wrrimbalo:ma* or, genderized appropriately, *wrrimbalo:nja*. This was, to be sure, a very surprising event for her father, since crocodiles are associated with tree-shaded waterholes (paradigmatic *wuŋgurr* sites, one should note), rather than with rough, treeless country. Whenever there is news to tell, the crocodile spirit pokes this woman with his nose, causing her to cry out from the blow. (I witnessed this while once at her campsite; visitors from afar arrived about a half-hour later!).[14]

Another, younger woman of the *Adbalandi* Clan appeared to her father seemingly within Ngarinjin territory, at a place called *bro:y ge:ŋa* inland from the old Kunmunya Mission site, at which in the myth age a kangaroo was involved in a particular incident along the Prince Regent River. A plains kangaroo (*wangali:na*) came casually hopping along to the woman's father, swaying from side to side (*buru:ba ge:ŋe:ri* 'he's swaying along'—just the way she walks nowadays, people in the know remarked—and hence her "great name" includes the form *buru:wala* (or Ngarinjinized, *búruwàla*), with characteristic feminine suffix *-wala* 'characterized by' on the stem of the verbal particle *buru:* 'sway'.

The stories of self-announcement are obviously inspirational for many of the people with whom I talked about this. As with myths, there seem to exist variant versions with different emphasis of detail on different recountings, providing relevance to a particular conversational situation as to etiology of some quirk or manner of the individual so named. People have a certain proprietary expansiveness in the feeling of a personal relationship to some species or formation or place, a natural outlet for ethnically specific and valued self-dramatization (which, in the contact situation in which Aboriginal peoples have long found themselves, is all the more to be appreciated). On such variant tellings, however, the narrator says in relation to the term for each detail, "that's X's/my name," or "and that's how X is/I am named (... named him/myself)"; i.e., all the principal canonical details are, under different circumstances, instantiations of the fact of one's "great name," the fact of one's spiritual or sociological self-baptism.

In the period of Christian missionization, people's "great names" are sometimes known to many through the mechanism of the missionaries' giving English-language "whitefella" first names or family surnames derived from them. But in general most people did not know others' personal *wuŋgurr* sites or other aspects of their "great names," let alone the individual myths they commemorate in full narrative form. There is, in fact, a positively formulated norm that the "great name" should be known and used in reference to an individual within a group that includes the genitor, to whom it was announced, the genetrix, whom the genitor has told the story only when she has become pregnant, and the "grandparental" (G^{+2}) individuals (and their classificatory equivalents) who eventually learn the circumstances of the baby's spiritual conception.

The event of self-presentation of a future child to his or her genitor is, in terms of stylization, baptismal force, etc., a private—indeed, dyadically structured and limited—ritual event. It gets its baptismal effect as its stylized narrative can be given an entitlement organized around the terms of where—what—how—in-what-manner, such metapragmatic descriptors of the ritual baptismal event becoming indexicals of the event as much as elements with proper-name like function in denoting the specific individual who *bariy*ed on that occasion. Now everyone knows what such an event consists of, even women who have never experienced becoming fertile with a child's spirit in this fashion; indeed, people are able to characterize what the type event consists of so that a young man who can become a father knows what to be prepared for, just as a young wife expects to learn the circumstances of spirit conception that quicken the fetus she will carry to term. So it is both in the particular, individual private rituals and in the general concept of this type of ritual that the framework of retrospective or prospective narration or lexical allusion to the circumstances of self-baptism regiment the form that the ritual takes, has taken, and will take, both in retrospect for every individual as a spirit-bearing social being who made his or her genitor fertile and *in potentia* for every male individual as a potential biological parent.

Concluding Question

As I said at the outset, both "ritual" events and events of "communication"—at least indexical communication, semiosis through indexical meanings of signs—are involved in such private, solitary and transformative life-cycle encounters that are locally understood to generate the essence of how people can be "read." The indexical semiosis in effect serves as the interdiscursive metasemiotic of the ritual event, in retrospect pointing to the authorizing legitimacy of the event believed to underlie the interpretability of such indexical signs as one's demeanor, and in a sense making clear to the knowledgeable what ritual seems to have occurred. Likewise, there is a vast and, in my fieldwork experience, anxious denotational metasemiosis in the form of orienting discourse about what such ritual events are, in general, all about, allowing people to have heightened sensitivity to the possibility of such private, solitary ritual encounters having happened or potentially happening.

One is primed and prepared to have a ritual encounter since culturally real and denotable entities and characteristics of vital importance to how individuals function in society emerge from such an event. Imagine, then, how acute the disappointment when either this kind of encounter does not take place, or seems to have taken place to no effect. One can be both power-less (in the Chinookan case) and child-less (in the Worora case),[15] unvalidated in both unfortunate circumstances as a citizen of a culture one exquisitely understands.

Might these rituals of life-transition be constituted minimally of *a chain of interdiscursive events that license and legitimate 'self'-realization and 'self'-fashioning in the act of recognition,* the private ritual encounter somewhere in the middle of the chain, without all of which—the anxiety-causing prospective metapragmatic priming as well as the anxiety-causing retrospective control over indexical proprietariness—one might not be able to tell the difference between the culturally "real" inside 'self' and 'other' and mere perceivable reality?

Notes

1. Given extreme limitations of space here, and wishing to move beyond what is already in the vast published literature, I take the generalization as a given, since it simply renders in appropriately semiotic concepts the cumulated disciplinary knowledge of anthropologists emphasizing now one, now another aspect of the universal mechanisms of ritual semiosis (not, note, its "explanation" in sociological or psychological, functional or historical terms). I ask readers unfamiliar with such matters to consult the references listed here, which develop each of the descriptive dimensions with extensive ethnographic examples.

2. For a certain segment of my co-participants, defined by age and media exposure, the logic is similar to the famous advertisement campaign by Clairol

hair coloring products, the tag-line for which across many media was, "Does she or doesn't she [color her hair]? Only her hairdresser knows for sure!" Here, crossing an age-grade or age-set threshold by virtue of having graying, therefore to-be-dyed hair that—ritually?—in the color-restoration iconically restores youth or at least youthful looks (the trope of *pars pro tota*) is a private act, prima facie knowledge of which is available only to an individual and to (in those days) her discreet hairdresser. Recall the longstanding controversy in the American press about whether or not the late Ronald Reagan had his hair dyed during his later political career culminating in the presidency in his seventh decade: the White House barber was even called upon by the administration to testify that Mr. Reagan's hair color was "natural." During the long drawn out Christmastime, 2006 obsequies for and remembrances of Gerald Ford as a humble, honest, and "genuine" Midwesterner , he of the purging of the White House of the noxious essences of the disgraced Richard Nixon administration (hubristic, dishonest, and false), once more the issue of Mr. Reagan's dyed hair emerged in the press—an indexical sign of the fact that Ford (and his post-presidential bosom buddy, Jimmy Carter)—headed the last of the what-you-see-is-what-you-get American presidential administrations. Note the way that the nostalgic exercise construes an era-boundary around the issue of "trust" about the self-narratives of the transformation/non-transformation of the presidential person.

3. In the *Science Times* section of the *New York Times,* Tuesday, January 23, 2007, pp. D1, D6, there is an article "Do you believe in magic?" by Benedict Carey, that discusses such private rituals, referring them, of course, in the current anti-sociological evolutionary psychological scientism of the times—as well as of the *Times*—to an evolutionary holdover in "the circuitry of the brain!"

4. See the pair of ethnographic summaries on Chinookan-speaking peoples, with all the references, in French and French 1998 and Silverstein 1990. Spier and Sapir 1930: 236–48 focuses specifically on spirit powers, and Silverstein 1996b explicates one of the preparatory rituals, so-called "winter bathing." In transcriptions, I employ Greek *χ* and *γ* for uvular, as opposed to velar, voiceless and voiced spirantized consonants.

5. Hence, during the wintertime sacred period, when the population resided in large villages of semi-subterranean houses, the cosmogonic myth cycles were regularly told, each telling concluding with the ritual formula "K'wabi*χ* a*γ*a Nadidanuit atgadiya..." 'Soon/close-by now the-People will come [*sc.,* from the mythic cosmogonic era] / come-up [*sc.,* to earth's surface]"; the deictic trope of proximad direction—horizontal movement 'hither' in the narrated cosmogonic world, vertical movement 'hither' to a sunny earth's surface in the wintertime world of narration—is quite telling.

6. A consultant who was this woman's matrilateral parallel cousin attributed the blindness to her very possession of this Frog spirit power, the frogs that communicate with her causing her to become, in effect, a blind seer of the future. Frog is an interesting mythic figure, it should be noted, as well as Toad; various human futurities seem to depend on their good graces.

7. Observe, then, the gender-specificity of some of the spirit powers. This particular woman's son asked his mother to help him train to receive *skintxwa* Power. "No; you're [a] man. You don't want to wait on [i.e., midwife] women. You leave that for your [female] cousin [to get]." Indeed, my consultant, the cousin, would have this Power but, but, but ...—as noted below.

8. Though ethnically identified as a Columbia River Native American, and educated at Chemawa, then the Oregon boarding school for the Anglophone deracination of such children, Mr. McGuff spoke Kiksht and Klickitat Sahaptin, and participated in local indigenous society, notwithstanding he was biologically only half "Indian," the other half African American. He served as Kiksht interpreter for Sapir in 1905, collaborating on recording and editing texts with Sapir during the next four years, and again as interpreter in Sahaptin (*Xwałχwaypam*) on Sapir's recommendation, for Melville Jacobs's first fieldwork in Klickitat in 1926.

9. The Worora-speaking (and related) patriclans traditionally inhabited the mountainous coastal and immediately interior country (plus the offshore Indian Ocean islands) from the eastern coast of King Sound to the Prince Regent River, in the region of Western Australia known as the Northern Kimberley. Inland were the Ngarinjin-speaking clans, and to the northeast, about as far as the present town of Wyndham, were the Wunambal-speaking clans, both of which groups constituted, with the Worora, a self-recognized cultural and social system of exchange. Today, representatives of all three traditional linguistic groups live in Mowanjum Community (though the site has shifted since my fieldwork), outside of their traditional territories, near the town of Derby at the southern end of King Sound. They have been gathered there in the first instance by missionaries after several intermediate moves since contact in 1915. It is only since the completed move to Mowanjum in 1961 that rapid social change has affected such indicators as learning Aboriginal languages, great increases in culturally-incongruous or even incomprehensible marriages and liaisons, submission to external modes of social control (local constabulary, state and federal "whitefella" law, etc.), and partial reorientation to a cash economy (for some, in the form of federal welfare checks). However, the naming system as reported here, and its underlying practices in ritual and belief, were just beginning to show signs of loss of vitality during my stay in ways and for reasons related to these other factors. Hence I feel that these data are far from memory ethnography, since very young consultants

then experienced these phenomena. In transcription, I employ capital letters for the retroflex series corresponding to alveolars

10. In Worora, almost every verb combines a (generally uninflected) particle that gives the specific lexical meaning with one or another of the auxiliary verbs that take all of the inflectional machinery of the predicating phrase, in particular all the cross-referencing inflectional pronominals that tell us who is doing what to whom, the tense/mode/aspect of the predicate, etc. In effect, since any given verbal lexeme occurs with only one or a small number from among the limited "auxiliary verbs"—like English *have* and *be* and its "SAE" congeners—these act like classifiers of the various verbal types, such as verbs of motion, verbs of continuing state, verbs of transitive action, verbs of sensation, etc. See Silverstein 1986. *Bariy* is a verb of translational motion occurring with the auxiliary -√(*y*)*i*/*u*-, the latter form translatable as 'go' when it occurs alone.

11. The stylized accounts I have of the relationship between this spiritual procreation –which, let us note, establishes a social relationship between the genitor and his child-to-be—and physical procreation all emphasize that the genitor periodically asks the genetrix if she is yet pregnant: "Have you found it [i.e., the child] yet?" "No." "All right; he keeps the name in his head." He reveals the name—i.e., the myth of spiritual procreation—only when it is certain that the genetrix is pregnant with a child. Observe that in the ethnobiology of the Worora, the genitor becomes fecund or fertile in an act of specific spiritual quickening, and that there is no specific relationship understood between any particular act of sexual intercourse and physical procreation, but rather continued intercourse after a man becomes fecund to transfer the child's essence to its genetrix's body, the signs of which are fetal growth. Note also that since in Worora language gender categories [masculine, feminine, (inanimate) things, places] for nouns denoting humans correlate with sex of denotatum, there sometimes have to be adjustments in gender category to the nouns for species, etc., to derive these components of the "great name." (An example is cited in the text below.)

12. The pseudo-transitive verb *gi: gu*-[ ]-√*dju*-, which takes as its nominal object the noun for the totemic plant, animal, mineral, etc., might be translated as "[ ] treats-as-totem; totemizes" whatever is stipulated by the nominal object.

13. "We'll always have Paris," says Rick Blaine (played by Humphrey Bogart) to Ilsa Lund (played by Ingrid Bergman) in *Casablanca*. He is not denoting the city, but the historical event they shared there, by which it is now "entitled" in each one's memory—as time goes by, that is.

14. This woman was also called by a nickname, *nje:ŋgalinja* 'her big toe [fem.]', used by her campmates and her generation mates, deriving from the prominently twisted large toes on her feet due to bunion-like deformities.

15. Or not a real child! For sometimes a woman may give birth to a *ra:y*, a demon outside the regime of normal sexual reproduction resulting from a man's spirit-fecundity. The *ra:y* masquerades as a properly developed term fetus, even resembling a malevolent deceased ancestor. The consequences of this are dire.

twelve

"While I Sing I Am Sitting in a Real Airplane"

Innovative Contents in Shuar and Achuar Ritual Communication

Maurizio Gnerre

Among the Shuar, approximately forty-five thousand northwestern Jivaroans of the Ecuadorian Amazon, most parts of a once-rich tradition of ceremonial and ritual events have been increasingly abandoned. The same process is taking place, at a slower rate, among the neighboring Achuar, approximately eight thousand northeastern Jivaroans of the Ecuadorian and Peruvian Amazon. The two peoples speak closely similar linguistic varieties and share a range of similar pragmatic-communicative forms, ritualized behaviors, ritualizations, rituals, and ceremonial events.[1] In this chapter I refer to two ritual genres still in use among both Shuar and Achuar.

In the past, both peoples were basically tropical forest hunters and horticulturalists, living in isolated longhouses. Everyday life was shaped and punctuated by many ritual genres, ranging from ritualizations not necessarily observable and perceivable to external observation to highly visible ones, culturally highlighted and linguistically named. Along this continuum, extending from the least to the most perceivable behaviors and events, were minor healing practices, magical (individual and private) formulas and songs, everyday visiting conversations, male and female initiations, shamanic curing performances, special verbal interactions, and full ritual cycles, such as the yearly celebration performed at the end of the "starvation season." The successful accomplishment of a feuding and (for the Shuar) a head-taking raid was celebrated with economically demanding, time-consuming, and highly elaborated ceremonies. Several of these rituals were constitutive, to different degrees, of Shuar and Achuar household specificity and of superordinate social cohesion.

In the twentieth century, Catholic and Protestant missionaries successfully converged on the Shuar and Achuar, at least in the endeavor of "domesticating" their social behavior and their bodies: the Shuar were "reduced" to "civilized" social and individual behaviors. As for the social dimension, they completely stopped feuding, quickly transitioned from polygamy to monogamy, abandoned their scattered longhouses and resettled in newly founded villages, and adopted cattle-raising and a new form of time allocation. Observable changes in the bodily dimension included the diffusion of Western-style clothing and the related reduction of body painting, male hair-cutting, and "well-behaved" body postures. Over the last five decades, not only missionaries but also state agents such as schoolteachers and low-level army officers were effective in these repressive, "civilizing" interventions. As a consequence of all these factors, very few forms of ritual communication (RC), or magical-communicative genres, out of the once wide range of them, are still in use among the Shuar, and a few more among the Ecuadorian Achuar.

Visiting conversations, for instance, in which voice use, body postures, gestures, and facial paintings and expressions were all semiotic components of the performance, inseparable from the spoken words, became obsolete as a consequence of new settlement patterns (Gnerre 1986). Currently, some forms of these conversations are part of a Shuar folklorized presentation of self, and some youngsters are able to perform them in a sort of distant and ironic representation of past Shuar ways of life.

Similarly, only a few Shuar elders still remember the main ritual cycles of the past, such as the highly complex *tsántsa* 'shrunken head' and the *uwí* 'peach palm' festivals.[2] The first was abandoned with the decline of head-taking raids. As for the second, performed in the past once a year, a famous Catholic missionary and researcher wrote thirty years ago that "if some elders dare to celebrate it, the 'modernised' youngsters make fun of them and boycott the celebration, jeering at them with jokes, so that the elders, under the pressure of witticisms and jests, have to conceal their beliefs not to expose them to a profanation" (Pellizzaro 1978a: 124). Certainly, sociopolitical transformations that had (and have) an enormous effect on Shuar-Achuar societies played a selective role in the persistence of and changes in some ritual genres.

In this chapter I focus on two ritual genres still frequently performed among the Shuar and Achuar. One is shamanic (public) singing, and the other is *ánent* singing, a "sung incantation, used ... to obtain some desirable result or win the favour of the addressee" (Descola 1997: 419). Shamanic chants and *ánent* are quite removed from each other as ritual genres, expressing different ways of acting and exerting individual powers. The first is performed by a trained shaman in front of an audience, whereas the second requires a private, often hidden, performance. The outputs of shamanic chants can be evaluated, but the *ánent,* performed far away from other humans, is out of reach of any possible evaluation of its achieved results. In both rituals, however, an audience of spirits and invisible entities is assumed to be present and addressed. Both rituals are parts of highly individualized knowledge and performances. The first is performed after the shaman has been "invited" (actually, hired) as a healer, and it takes place at night while he is under the effects of a powerful hallucinogen. He sings and acts in front of an often interacting and in any case participative audience, composed in most cases of a few persons, usually relatives of the patient being cured. At least one or two persons act more as participants than simply as audience.

The *ánent* genre, which is closer to a ritualized individual performance than to a ritual, is sung during the daytime or at twilight as a private and often hidden form of ritualized communication.[3] In most cases it is an individual exhortation or invocation to a powerful spirit; occasionally it is a metaphorical description of an emotional state or of an event and is performed in order to reach a faraway person or spirit. In some cases these songs can be performed at the borderline between having a fully magical purpose and being what we would identify as a "love song." This label is particularly evident when a woman or man sings it close to, but not facing, her or his partner.

The observable constructs of rituals and the verbal and nonverbal communicative forms that are often (but not always) co-extensive with them are filtered through thick layers of awareness, imagination, and social scrutiny. As Basso and Senft write in the introduction to this volume, RC, as performance, "is subject to evaluation by participants according to standards that are defined in part by language ideologies, local aesthetics, ... [and] relations of power among participants." "Evaluation" implies different levels of reciprocal control, scrutiny, and "intensity" that, together with the relations of power existing among participants, are sensitive to encompassing historical processes. These processes, reflected in and modifying specific kinds of RC, allow for the emergence of new sociocultural relations.

In Bauman's classic discussion of performance (1977), evaluation is based on the competence displayed by the performer.[4] The two ritual genres I discuss differ greatly in terms of audience-performer relations: shamans perform in front of an audience, exhibiting their magical powers, and thus are subject to evaluation, whereas *ánent* are sung in a strictly private and even "protected" way, and their performance seldom implies any exhibition of power. In shamans' performances, the audience always plays an important role. The relations between a shaman and his audience are conditioned by the power attributed to him, taking into account also his competition over power with other shamans. Often, for instance, ill persons are taken by their relatives to consult with two or more shamans, for each of whom it is extremely relevant to know who the person being treated is and whether she or he (or her or his relatives) have consulted with another shaman before.

Some Issues Addressed

According to Lévi-Strauss (1981 [1971]: 602–603), ritual singing "translates the urgent need," continuously renewed, for "reconstructing continuity starting from discontinuity." This is one possible perspective on the frame in which any RC takes place, but when we focus on ritual forms and their contents, we can claim that any ritual genre preserves culturally inherited components, often introducing into that frame newly built constructs. In other words, any form of "discontinuity" is grounded in a background of "continuity." Kuna (Panama) shamanic singing, for example, always reflects "implicitly, and in a cursory way, the mythological references on which it is ultimately founded" (Severi 1993: 15–16).

In this chapter I focus on "discontinuities," that is, changes and innovations, introduced in the contents of the two ritual genres, *ánent* and shamanic chanting. Most of these changes reside in references to external (global and national) technology, entities, institutions, and concepts.

In the examples I discuss, implicit reference to shared mythological knowledge is pervasive. This is particularly true in the case of Shuar shamanic singing. Mythological reference constitutes an often unsaid, semantically implicit background of "continuity," a background not only to Jivaroan ritual contents generally but also to the individual forms of each genre. For instance, a widely known *ánent* is the one sung by Núnkui, the female hero of Shuar mythology, which is sung by a narrator every time she (or even he) tells the main myth about

Núnkui. It is against this background of implicit continuity that images of "modern" and "external" objects and concepts are projected. It is primarily a background of formal continuity (in rhythmic, prosodic, and musical patterns and in voice use) that averts any risk of disruption of the implicit continuity.

It seems that the interstices providing communicative space for innovations in Shuar and Achuar ritual singing are created from re-adjustments between a persistent mythological reference, on which representation of self and of language is grounded, and current historical pressures. Although the two genres I discuss are quite different from each other, the feature shared by the examples I provide is their "modernizing" and "innovative" contents, which are constitutive of their rhetorical efficacy.

Unequal sociocultural relations, colonial or neocolonial domination, and new globalized perceptions are signaled somehow through rituals. Because this often happens before other communicative forms are affected, it seems that many forms of RC carry with them an anticipatory function. Under sociohistorical pressures, some rituals may disappear or be emptied of their value and meaning while others are provided with some type of continuity. Rituals can be kept in use only if their communicative components are provided with fresh, innovative contents and, often, new forms. Rejecting any unidirectional perspective of "external" pressures acting on local representations, ways of existence, and rituals, I adopt instead a dialectical interpretation in which changing local representations and performances somehow favor and enhance the effects of external pressures—even more so because of the Jivaroan way of sociability.

Descola (1986, 1996) interpreted Jivaroan "modes of relation" as dominated by a "predatory" attitude in which appropriation of external goods substituted for knowledge processes. "Predation" is also a way of appropriating externally originated concepts and the words used to express them; ultimately, it is a way of transforming knowledge into power. A sort of predatory absorption of the outside world interacts with sociopolitical transformations. Jivaroans' predatory attitude, their eagerness to absorb external goods and concepts, was perhaps the main factor triggering the large-scale reorganization of Shuar society that has taken place during the last fifty years. In 1965 the Shuar Federation was established, and two years later a radio station began broadcasting in Shuar for most of the day. In the late 1960s, a new political leadership of young men who had been boarding students in the Catholic missions became accustomed to producing long political radio talks. The new medium represented a communicative and linguistic challenge and opportunity at both the qualitative and quantitative levels. New strategies for a verbal-auditory rhetoric had to be devised, in the absence of a face-to-face visual component. The traditional Jivaroan one-to-one interaction was suddenly replaced by a communication of one to many (invisible) persons. Radio broadcasting helped change Shuar and, more recently, Achuar representations of "powerful" men (*kakáram*), increasing even further the importance of their speech and rhetorical abilities. On the quantitative level, new rhetorical features were the extremely long, wordy speeches, monologues in a mostly dialogical tradition.

When, from 1960 onward, literacy became increasingly widespread among the Shuar, a whole set of written texts was produced by young Shuar. Through the newly acquired tool of writing, they reelaborated part of their traditional narratives (mostly, but not exclusively, mythological ones) and even attempted to create a new literature in their own language (Gnerre 2000a, 2000b). Shuar teachers faced several metalinguistic challenges. In 1988 they produced a thick Spanish-Shuar dictionary (*Chicham nekatai*) in which they tried to find Shuar correspondences and glosses not only for common Spanish lexical items but even for the rarest and most obscure terms, such as *dantesco* 'Dantesque', *freudiano* 'Freudian', and *atómico* 'atomic'. Their implicit guiding aim was to show that their language was potentially able to convey all the "modern" and Western contents sedimented in the Spanish lexicon (Descola 2000). In the 1980s they also produced a textbook in Shuar and English, *Ii Jínti—Our Way,* to be used by Shuar students to learn English without the intermediary of Spanish. This book represented another effort to show how Shuar could face, in terms of sociolinguistic status and interlinguistic correspondences, a language perceived, at least by a few Shuar leaders and teachers, as more "powerful" than Spanish itself (Gnerre 1999a).

Corresponding to the Shuar's strong attitudes toward individuality, they fully expressed authoriality and personal style in their use of writing. In many shamanic chants and *ánent* we also find a search for uniqueness and individual characterization. Indeed, authoriality, authority, and personal style are pervasive, and each example of ritual performance should be discussed as a sample of such a creative attitude. In shamanic chants one finds different degrees of internal parallelism, as well as, at the same time, of overlap with other performances by the same shaman. Something similar can be stated for *ánent* singing. Although most of these songs are "inherited" by the performer—that is, learned from a relative of the same gender—innovations are introduced so that some degree of individual authorship is present in each case.

Jivaroan Language Ideology

The Shuar and Achuar ideology of language use and efficacy, framed, as it is, in a readiness to grasp and exhibit new abilities and concepts, parallels the attraction exerted on these peoples by external knowledge, techniques, and technological tools. Jivaroan peoples, although on the one hand highly jealous of their political system of extended families settled in isolated longhouses, have proved, on the other hand, to be very open to external material goods (Bustamante 1988; and see Wierhake 1985 for the Shuar) and conceptual novelties. In the past, to the extent that reconstruction is possible, intertwinings with other ethnic groups played constitutive roles in shaping Jivaroan cultures and languages.[5] An attitude open to external communication was revealed by the emergence, during the nineteenth century, of two pidginized language varieties, one based on Shuar and the other on Spanish, that were employed in relations with settlers and dealers from the Andean region (Gnerre 1984).

An example of this attitude of eagerness to absorb external knowledge and concepts comes from my own research. In 1971 I was doing fieldwork with my colleague Antonino Colajanni at the longhouse of a powerful Achuar man, the shaman Chumap'. He had heard through jungle "rumors" that white men had reached the moon sometime earlier (in 1969). One evening Chumap' asked me if this was true, and how it was possible. I told him that it was true, and that the men who had reached the moon had been sent in a special flying canoe-airplane, each person carrying with him three pots: one full of food, another of water, and a third of air, because on the moon there is no food, water, or air. Later the same night, during a curing session in his longhouse, Chumap' presented to his astonished audience the image of a white man traveling to the moon in his special canoe-airplane with three pots, to be able to survive where no food, water, or air was available.

From the second half of the nineteenth century, missionaries took advantage of the Jivaroan fascination not only for external goods but also for external "powers." They carried with them goods to be exchanged with locals who showed attitudes favorable to conversion (see Taylor 1981 for the Achuar concept of "God's wealth"). Jivaroan peoples incorporated not only material goods and their names but also external words referring to immaterial entities. They reinterpreted these words in order to codify them and provide new conceptual referents to the Jivaroan "invisible" world.[6]

Spoken (or sung) representations of relations with indigenous Quechua-speaking and mestizo Spanish-speaking peoples reflect one aspect of Shuar history, and in the case of mestizos, a relatively recent one. For centuries, Quechua-speaking peoples surrounded the northwestern Jivaroans. Indigenous and mestizo migrations from the Andean region of Ecuador to the upper Amazon began in the sixteenth century but from the late nineteenth century became a growing influx. At the same time—at least during the nineteenth century—a much less visible and invasive trend was taking place, in which Shuar dealers traveled to the Ecuadorian Andean markets in Ambato, Riobamba, Cuenca, and Loja. Many words from Spanish (let alone those from Quechua) referring to material goods and technological products were incorporated into the Shuar language. Most of these words were "gendered," in the sense that they were part of the male world, referring to "goods" such as weapons that allowed an increase of feuding. This shift triggered an endless chain of magical and physical acts of revenge. Between 1850 and 1960, feuding and revenge increased among the Shuar, and shamanic activity skyrocketed. The same things happened among the Achuar from 1960 onward (Steel 1999).

Communicative components of rituals are deeply rooted in socially shared ideologies of language and language use (Rappaport 1999; Robbins 2001a), as well as in representations of the communicating self. Historical changes always produce interstices among these dimensions, providing spaces for adjustments in RC. Some level of awareness plays a role in triggering changes in RC, in the encompassing frames of language ideology and representation of the communicating self. In some cases, these changes can ultimately lead to the disappearance of a certain ritual or the emergence of a new one.

A wide range of observable facts shows how Jivaroan language ideology is tightly connected to the representation of the communicating self. Each individual is the expression of a "nuclear" self-understanding, with a multifaced existential agency (*kakáram* 'strength', 'strong', 'powerful') different from that of anyone else (Gnerre 2007). Such a self-representation reflects on many ways of behaving, as well as on each individual use of language. For example, tentative, unofficial attempts by the Shuar Federation schooling system in the 1980s to standardize Shuar language clashed with individuals' rejections of standardized selected forms, which they perceived as restrictions on individual use of language.[7] Over the years, however, several of those linguistic choices became silently accepted. The widespread preference for Spanish as the main language in Shuar schools is likely grounded on avoiding linguistic forms of the native language that teachers and pupils dislike or even perceive as improper or flatly wrong. An "external" and already "made" written language like Spanish challenges no one's linguistic individuality.

Both of the ritual genres I discuss are deeply intertwined with this enduring Jivaroan ideology of language and representation of communicating self. In rhetorical performances by Shuar political leaders and in shamans' ostentation of magical power, unique or rare words are highly valued and implemented. With their endless morphological potentialities, the Shuar and Achuar languages permit the generation of an astonishing number of forms from each verb root. Consequently, persons willing to develop and use their rhetorical abilities can strengthen the efficacy of their discourse by producing forms rarely or never heard before.

A related dimension of Shuar language ideology is revealed by the constantly manifested need to provide spoken words with "emphasis." Speakers search for ways to enhance the enunciative power of words and to validate sentences in many circumstances, from everyday interactions to careful performances of mythological narratives. Some suffixes providing emphasis are used frequently; one of these is *-ka* 'itself, the same', which is used, for instance, after independent pronouns such as *wi* 'I' and *áme* 'you', producing *wíkya* 'I, myself' and *ámeka* 'you, yourself'.[8] The Shuar verse translated in the title of this chapter, "Kantámpranku awiúnkanam enkémturnai [while I sing I am sitting in a real airplane]," provides an example of the use of this suffix, which occurs after *awiún-* 'airplane' and before the locative suffix *-nam,* providing the meaning 'in the airplane itself'. Another suffix, *-api,* is frequently used in an evidential role, conveying the speaker's certainty about his or her assertion. During the twentieth century, some forms from the verbal root *t-/i/a/u* 'to say' assumed an evidential function and were increasingly employed, mostly in mythological narratives (Gnerre 1986), to close full sentences or even paragraphs. These forms, such as *tiniu ármya* 'they used to say' and *tau tímyayi* 'saying, it was said', evince the way an endless chain of similar performances and stress exists beyond the narrative being performed, and therefore the teller's commitment to the validity (more than the "truth") of the events being narrated.

Two Genres of Ritual Communication

Although in several South American traditions, some rituals imply the use of an esoteric language learned and practiced by "professionals"—as in the case of the previously mentioned Kuna (Panama) ritual genres described by Sherzer (1983) and Severi (1993)—this apparently does not occur in Jivaroan rituals. Shuar and Achuar ritual textuality, even if not "exoteric," is built on a layered metaphoric and rhetorical weaving. Although shamans receive special training and initiation, the textual complexity they produce seems comparable to that found in any "innovative" *ánent* sung by a person who has not been formally trained in that genre. However, as Taylor and Chau claimed (1983: 95–96), shamanic chanting, just like *ánent,* functions "as a meta-linguistic device used to differentiate otherwise similar types of linguistic expression. In other words [shamanic chants] serve to signal the 'otherness' of the language one is speaking in relation to 'normal' language, given the phonetical, lexical and grammatical similarity between the two forms of speech ... the Jivaro use song as a generalised equivalent for exotic language, that is to say, languages spoken by all other human and nonhuman (animal or supernatural) societies."

The "Penelope's web" of Jivaroan textuality is available to all adults, who, as self-proposing performers of an *ánent,* weave their text every time they sing, undo it, and weave it again on tatters of the previous canvas. The main aim of this never-ending web is to acquire and provide efficacy and performative strength even in the most intimate ritual genre, adjusting it all the time to the changing world, to face and metabolize the powerful pressures coming from the external, mestizo, "modern" world. The main strategy is to refer to the external world's symbolic goods and to name them. Incorporating some reference to external cultural worlds and powers plays a corroborating role in ritual speech and singing. To enhance the efficacy of both shamanic and *ánent* singing is to infuse into sung texts contents (referents) from the external world that, during the twentieth century, became identified with and symbolized by Western (mestizo) products and commodities. This vitalizing lymph lends enunciative and performative strength to the preexisting canvas. Agency, a central component in the performance of both ritual genres, is strongly evident in the exhibition of power (*kakáram*) present in the shaman's singing. It is also present in *ánent* performances, even if, as I have argued (Gnerre 2007), in much more graded forms, ranging from an openly and effectively exhibited agency to a shy and humble one.

Shamanic Chants

As Taylor and Chau (1983: 96) wrote, Jivaroan shamanic singing is a semiotic code in which "the relationship between song and alterity is specially clear...: shamans 'become drunk' (*namperíniawai*) in order to sing, and they sing because song as such is the language (in the sense of the ethnic or tribal language) spoken by their spirit helpers (*pasúk*) and the magic darts (*tséntsak*) they manipulate." Furthermore, the "language" used in those songs is conceptualized as a "foreign" language, even if it is not so in linguistic terms: it is just the ordinary language, implemented in the frame normally used, yet with a high density of metaphors and with many words from Spanish or Quechua as part of a rhetorical strategy meant to surprise or even astonish the audience. Taylor and Chau commented on the relationship of this "foreign" language to Quechua and Quechua-speaking powerful shamans: "The *tséntsak*'s song-language is ... explicitly referred to as a foreign language, most often the 'language of the Napo Quichua' or the 'language of the Cocama.' Quichua itself is considered the epitome of foreignness in terms of human speech, or, more accurately perhaps, a sort of precipitate of all possible foreign human languages;... Quichua thus plays a role strictly homologous to that of song, though restricted to human language, whereas song functions as an equivalent for *all* kinds of speech, human and not human; 'song' is therefore more inclusive" (1983: 96). In a sense, however, the shaman's singing is informative to an audience, which in many cases participates in his singing or at least encourages him (see Gnerre 2007).

With the increase of the number of shamans, triggered by some of the factors mentioned earlier, feuding and magical competition also increased. This was the context in which new, "modern" contents were introduced into shamanic singing. To boast some control over and acquisition of magical powers of external origin became a must for every shaman competing with others. A central part of the public exhibition of the shaman's power resides in the creative contents of his performances, necessarily different for each shaman and characterizing him and his magical performance like an individualizing seal or a special diacritic. It seems that traditionally, some degree of innovative content was achieved through boasting of magical powers received from Quechua-speaking shamans of the Napo River and in some cases even from Cocama shamans of the Peruvian Marañón. In more recent decades, a further strategy implemented to enhance the effectiveness of magical chants was that of exhibiting acquaintance or even familiarity with goods from the outside "modern" world.

Because shamans often claim that their singing is "dictated" or transmitted to them, as if broadcast over a radio by their friendly and collaborative *pasuk*, or protective spirits (see example [3] in what follows), the issue of the absence of intentionality could be raised (as in Du Bois 1993). In language use, predatory attitudes acquire a flavor of rhetorical manipulation that could border on a production of meanings without full control over them, or even without intention. Words, especially if they are wrapped in unfamiliar and even "exotic" sounds, are "goods" themselves, and their use, even if carrying with it a mysterious flavor, lends additional strength and power to ritual performances. Whenever possible, references to innovative items and only partially understood concepts are arrayed in such a way that cultural contact and social change become an intrinsic part of the discourse. In the majority of the examples I provide, the terms referring to external goods are accompanied by the word *apachi* 'mestizo, white person', making a clear statement of their valued external origin.

The texts transcribed here were recorded from the mid-1950s through the 1970s by Siro Pellizzaro, a Salesian missionary extremely knowledgeable about Shuar language and culture.[9] Therefore, the texts also represent a historical reference for decades when the Shuar were not yet in continuous contact with Ecuadorian national society, as they are today, and when the Achuar were still at an incipient stage of contact.

The order in which I present five selected segments of shamanic songs ranges, roughly, from a display of acquaintance with a "simple" yet rare and costly external good, a horse, to acquaintance with Western technological products—even an airplane. From each shamanic song I have selected a sequence of only a few verses. Because it is not my purpose to analyze in any detail the linguistic forms used, I stress only a few dimensions relevant to the theme discussed here. Although I offer no detailed linguistic analysis or gloss, I do mention a few key words showing textual continuity with the background mythological reference. Each segment is assigned a title representing its specificity in terms of interaction with the "modern" world. No free translations are provided, but rather some comments on the contents of each example.

(1) Horse. Sung by Ujúkam, a shaman who lived on the Kwánkus River, a tributary of the Santiago River in the southern Shuar area. Pellizzaro recorded several of his healing sessions in 1968, when Ujúkam was about fifty-five. In the segment transcribed here (Pellizzaro 1978b: 149), he represents himself as riding a horse (*kawái-*, derived from Spanish *caballo*) a possibility out of reach for most Shuar and a very uneasy practice in the tropical forest environment.

1 *kawáichinma ekémtunákutu*
on a little horse sitting (riding)
2 *chikiúruta winiákujáitianu*
trotting I am the one who comes
3 *umpúmpata winiájaitia*
blowing I come

Ujúkam's stress on the effectiveness and speed of his action against evil darts is symbolized by his riding a fast horse. *Umpúm-* (line 3) is a verb referring to the action of blowing, with many purposes. In this use it refers to the shaman's action of blowing his magical darts. The nominalized form *umpúmpata* refers to the shaman's special strength.

(2) Chamber pot. This is one of the oldest recordings made by Pellizzaro (in 1958) with the shaman Chumpi (also known as Martínez, at the time fifty-five) at Sáampis, in the area of Limón (central Shuar country).

1 *ekénsana imiánuchin imiánuchin*
sitting on my stool very very powerful
2 *tantán tantán, tantán tantán*
trotting, trotting
3 *apáchinia shikítmanta*
of the mestizo on their chamber pots
4 *jikiámtikran ipíkmanta*
trying to stimulate him opening its lid
5 *ayámsanku wi wi wi wi*
I come close I I I I

The "innovative" metaphor in this text is difficult to interpret. Chumpi seems to compare the traditional Shuar stool, a symbol of power of the big-man sitting inside his longhouse (*ekén-*), with the white people's chamber pot (*shikit-* lit. 'where to urinate or (defecate)', which is interpreted as a new kind of stool. An implicit mythological reference to Tsunki, the first shaman, can be traced, because he is always represented in Shuar narratives as sitting (*ekén-* in line 1) on his special and unique stool, an anaconda, in his underwater residence. In line 5, the verb *ayám-sa-* is a variant of the form *aniam-sa-* 'to come close (to somebody)'. The shaman is announcing that his spirit is coming close to him.

(3) Record player. This was sung in 1968 by Shakaim, a very old man, perhaps close to ninety, who lived at Tsuís, on the Santiago River close to the Peruvian border. Pellizzaro recorded several of Shakaim's healing sessions. Here I transcribe two segments of his outstanding songs, both referring to highly desired "modern" goods (Pellizzaro 1978b: 248–249):

1 *apáchinia Supairinia*
the mestizos' Supai
2 *achítkiajáitiaya*
I catch
3 *apáchinia witrúrian*
the mestizos' record player
4 *tsentsákruna kantamtíkrana*
my darts it makes to sing
5 *wisha achitmamtíkiana*
I also it makes to catch it

Here Shakaim invokes the "Quechua" spirit Supai (line 1) and then refers to a symbol of modernity, *witrúria,* from Spanish *vitrola* 'record player' (line 3), exhibited by wealthy mestizos (*apáchi*) at their parties—an object that fascinated the old shaman. In Shuar, *witrúria* assumed a more general meaning of speaking or singing box, and here it is used to refer to a radio, as shown by the use of the verb *achi-* 'to catch, to grasp' (lines 2 and 5). This verb provides a parallel between the "catching" of the Supai spirit and the "singing" darts (*tséntsak,* line 4) heard through the mestizos' singing box. It is through it that the shaman's darts "sing," as expressed through another Spanish-Quechua loan, *kanta-* (line 4).

(4) Outboard motor. In another chant (Pellizzaro 1978b: 204), Shakaim refers to another item that was relatively common among the mestizos settled on the Peruvian side of the Santiago River: the outboard motor, represented as painted in stripes of different colors.

1 *wawékana chichámenka*
of the witch doctors their (witchcraft) words
2 *asákma asákma mukúnniuítjai*
wiping out wiping out I use to suck
3 *apáchi mutúrparínia*
of the mestizos in their motor
4 *mutúrpariín arémpramu*
in their motor striped painted
5 *tímianái enkétra enketrawáitjai*
very powerful I use to put I use to put

The meaning is "I put the darts I suck in the mestizos' striped outboard motor." The outboard motor is obviously a powerful tool in a world of canoes and paddles, and its external painted appearance (*arémpramu,* line 4) is implicitly compared to a Shuar warrior's protective facial paintings (with red anatto stripes). In line 1, *wawék-* is a verb root meaning 'to bewitch', used here in a nominalized form, referring to bad witch doctors and their bad spirits.

(5) Airplane. This example of "modernizing" shamanic singing, which provided the title of my chapter, was part of a curing session held by Marián, a shaman who lived at Mayáik on the Santiago River. Pellizzaro recorded the session in 1968, when the shaman was about fifty.

1 *Panku kantaríniaka*
the main shamans their songs
2 *kantá kantámpranku*
singing while I sing
3 *awiúnkanam enkémturnai*
in a real airplane I am sitting
4 *enké enkémpranku*
sitting sitting myself
5 *tsentsákan máshiniam weamaruítkiuna*
within arrows all going myself

Marián refers to himself in a sort of a polyphonic perspective while singing the songs of *panku,* powerful shamans, inside an airplane (*awiún,* from Spanish *avión* 'airplane').[10] The airplane flies in the midst of many magical, invisible darts (*tséntsak*). Once again, the verb referring to shamanic singing is the Spanish-Quechua loan *kanta-* (line 2), also conveying an exotic meaning and giving the chant greater strength and efficacy. *Enké(m)-* is the same verb found in text (1) and a variant of the verb found in text (2), *ekén-* 'to sit'. Fast displacement seems to be a desired capacity for Jivaroan shamans, because three of five chants transcribed here are centered on that topic (with reference to a horse in [1] and to a motor-boat in [4]).

Magical Songs (ánent)

Ánent, magical songs, are sung by Jivaroans (for the Aguaruna, see Brown 1986) in many circumstances to address and possibly reach a spirit or a person—or, more likely, his or her *wakán,* or "soul." Taylor and Chau (1983: 93) wrote that "*ánent* are ... an essential aspect of the capacities of symbolic control exercised by men and women in their respective fields." These songs should be classified according to their function and use.

Ánent texts are jealously protected. Often they are sung in a low voice or with a closed mouth (in Shuar, *mekum-* 'to sing with the closed mouth'), or they are played (by men only) on their three-hole flute (*peem*) or on the Jew's harp (*tumánk*). The melodic line of the *ánent* has been analyzed by some ethnomusicologists (Belzner 1982; Salivas 2000). Even when addressed to a specific person, an *ánent* is rarely sung face-to-face to him or her; more likely, it is sung at a distance, allowing the addressee to listen to the chant. It is intended to be "sent" and sung when the performer is alone—which makes *ánent* difficult to collect. From among the huge number of *ánent* that Jivaroan people have memorized and constantly created and reshaped, only a very small proportion has been volunteered by the "owner" to researchers.

In the past, each woman and man had a repertoire of dozens of *ánent,* learned from a relative of the same gender who was willing to transmit his or her knowledge to a daughter or son, a niece or nephew. This still holds true for many, but not for all, Shuar and Achuar. In several cases these magical songs are said to have been received in a hallucinogen-induced vision. They were (and are) performed by males seeking their protector spirit (*arútam*) while hunting, participating in war expeditions, making weapons, and in many other circumstances. Women use to sing *ánent* on several occasions: while gardening and interacting with their cultivated plants and while taking care of their dogs. Other typical female circumstances for *ánent* performances are emotional and sentimental ones, in which cases the songs' themes range from conjugal love to self-compassion. One should ask whether this subgenre is itself a product of social changes and missionization.

Several circumstances and cultural frames for *ánent* performances have disappeared from the lives of the Shuar and other Jivaroans, especially for those sung as part of the feuding complex. Other cultural frames, however, have emerged. The five texts transcribed here are all female *ánent* of conjugal love, and as in the earlier examples of shamanic texts, they all invoke or refer to external goods or "innovative" representations of self. Three of the texts ([6]–[8], sung by one woman) were collected in the 1970s by Shuar students at the Bomboiza Institute from female relatives.

Text interpretation is always challenging, because Shuar and Achuar poetic language is complex in its morphological structure and in its pervasive metaphoric and metonymic semantics. In transcribing and translating my first three examples, I was assisted by Shuar collaborators. Because my focus is on contents and not on poetic style, I have provided transcriptions in edited versions from which several parallelisms have been eliminated.

(6) Red banknote. In several innovative *ánent,* reference to money (Shuar and Achuar *kuik/t*) plays a central role. This one, referring to Ecuadorian banknotes, was recorded at Pumpuéntsa in 1972. It was sung by Shíwiach, at the time about forty and one of the wives of Kawárim.

1 *Yatsutáchi yatsúta*
My little brother brother
2 *warí kuíki*
which money
3 *timiá surítkiáitiaj?*
so much do I hide from you?
4 *Papí kuitiáshi*
Paper banknotes perhaps
5 *Kapa kuítniasha*
red banknotes even
6 *wari ashímprukna*
quickly wasting
7 *aya sumáchukáitiaj*
not only to buy
8 *Warí kuítiakítia*
Which money is it
9 *imiá surímtinia?*
So much is to be hidden?

The reference is to red (*kapa*) paper (*papí,* from Spanish *papel*) money, at the time a large banknote worth one hundred sucres, then the Ecuadorian currency. The interesting and unusual aspect of this performance is that this is a male *ánent* sung by a woman. The "gender" of the text is revealed by the kinship address form *yatsú(ta)* 'brother' (male-to-male, used broadly also to mean "close friend"). The implicit reference is to a woman, perhaps a sister: "I do not hide from you even a large banknote (but I hide from you my sister)!" This *ánent* exemplifies an "occasional" polyphony, because Shíwiach, a woman, assumes somebody else's (a man's) *ánent.* This polyphony is completely different from that seen in shamanic chant (5), in which Marián fully assumes the chants of other shamans (*panku,* the most powerful ones) to express his identity with them.

(7) Table. This song, too, was recorded from Shíwiach, at the same time and place as the preceding one.

1 *Apáchi misaríntiajai* [repeated three times]
Of the mestizos I am a table

2 *Misa ajapámka chichám antúrmakáimi* [repeated twice]
The table if you throw away, words you will listen

Here the singer identifies herself with a table (*misa,* from Spanish *mesa*), a rare and unusual piece of furniture. She warns her husband not to throw it away—that is, not to abandon her—or he will have to listen to many bitter words from her. One might recall here the second shamanic chant, with its unusual reference to another object seen in a mestizo's house, the chamber pot.

(8) Daughter of the missionaries. Recorded from Shíwiach, at the same time and place.

1 *Patri nawantríntiajai* [repeated 3 times]
Of the missionaries I am the daughter
2 *Siniurítiajai siniuri nuáitiajai* [repeated twice]
I am a young lady a lady woman I am
3 *Nuwia atáksari, aya akupkamúitjai, apáwaru apáwaru*
When we were engaged, alone I was sent, my father (husband)
4 *Kajé kajéta awájtakmin puniár akújrátajme, puniár akujrátajme*
If you are mean to me, (with) a dagger I will stab you [repeated]

This is a unique *ánent* starting with the singer's self-introduction as "the daughter of the missionaries" and ending with a threat to stab her husband. The singer "exhibits" several Spanish words, to show her good education and deep involvement with the external world: *patri,* from the Spanish *padre* 'priest', *siniuritia,* from *señorita* 'young lady', and *siniuri,* from *señor,* lit. 'mister' but used here as a genderless term preceding *núa* 'woman', a Jivaroan word in assonance with *nuwia,* from *novia* 'fiancée'. The last word of the "external" set is also the most unusual: *puniar,* from Spanish *puñal* 'dagger'. Although all the texts selected for this chapter reflect aspects of cultural contact, this one represents some of the contradictory effects of missionization on forms of self-representation and discourse.

(9) Mestizo's hen. Recorded by Pellizzaro at Mayáikin in 1968 and sung by a woman whose name he was unable to recall in 1985, possibly the widow of a famous big-man who was killed a few years later.

1 *Apáchi atashchítjai* [repeated 3 times]
Of the mestizo I am the hen
2 *tuke tepértusata* [repeated 3 times]
always lie down on me

3 *netsép ajásuchi kasamprúmsamu atáshi*
my breast when grew I was a stolen hen
4 *Kajé kajéta awájtakmínkia, náintia kinkiájar weámunama*
If you are really mean to me, to blue hills I will go

The woman is exhorting her husband to treat her properly and to have frequent relations with her, just as when she was a spoiled girl, treated like one of the mestizos' hens. Otherwise she will abandon the house and run away to the blue (i.e., remote) hills.

In the past, hens (*atash'*, a word from Quechua) were valuable and desired goods, not only for Jivaroans but for most upper Amazon peoples. The reference to the blue hills is to the western pre-Andean region, which was intensively colonized by mestizos in the 1960s. In line 4 we find a formula that recurs in women's complaint *ánent: kajé kajéta awájtakmínkia* 'if you are really mean to me', already seen in example (8), line 4 (*kajé kajéta awájtakmin*), where the verb root *kajé-* characterizes a typical male behavioral posture in which a man acts rudely and often angrily.

(10) Airplane woman. Recorded by Pellizzaro at the same place and time; sung by Teesi, at the time forty-two.

1 *Awiúnk nua asana*
Airplane woman being
2 *ii ajámai wéakun*
seen done going (being seen while I go)
3 *tururурú winiájai*
making a big noise I come
4 *apawachíruwa*
my little father (my husband)

Teesi sends a cryptic message to her husband, saying that she has nothing to hide; she can be seen and heard as clearly as an airplane. From the local perspective, airplanes were—and still are—mysterious and challenging objects. They are often assumed to be symbolic referents, as we saw in Marián's shamanic chant (5) and see again in this *ánent*. In line 3, the reference to a noise (*tururúrú*) recalls the behavior expected from a friendly visitor, who is supposed to announce his arrival to the visitees.

Trends and Evolution

Massive social changes in the Ecuadorian and Peruvian Amazon have had consequences for two ritual genres, shamanic and *ánent* singing, both of which were highly sensitive to such changes, but for different reasons. Why have these two ritual genres persisted while most, if not all, others have faded away? The answer is that innovation and change have played a central role in their persistence. Indeed, it likely was the textual and performative fixity of other important rituals and ceremonial events, such as the annual peach palm festival, that hastened their obsolescence. The peach palm celebration, like several others, was publicly performed and publicly evaluated and controlled, whereas shamanic and *ánent* singing are both individual performances that allow individual manipulations. It seems, then, that a basic issue raised by my examples is that of the way in which individually performed rituals interact with historical changes (Kelly and Kaplan 1990).

Several researchers have been, and are, committed to settling the roles that rituals, and the communication associated with them, play in historical processes. In Tambiah's (1985) view, ritual potentially engages with the historical-political as well as the cosmological (or imaginative) dimension of social experience. Colonial pressures (more or less directly exerted), religious and state strengthening, modernity, and overall social change, as they engage with social representational dimensions, are often reflected and expressed through rituals, and more concretely through RC. Apparently, there are many more chances at an individual level for expressing these changes and adapting ritual performances to them.

To fully understand and contextualize the effects of social change on Jivaroan rituals, one should take into account the whole of their effects on Jivaroan language and communication. In such a broad context, it is likely that the changes in the contents of RC outlined here would be seen to have an anticipatory and "vanguard" status in changing communicative practices.

Historical changes continually produce interstices between socially shared ideologies of language, actual and individual language use, and representations of the gendered, enacting, communicating self. Rituals usually performed to achieve specific or even specialized purposes take advantage of these interstices. It is against this background that Shuar and Achuar shamanic and *ánent* singing have acquired more individualized and, consequently, reciprocally more competitive and rhetorically focused contents. Innovations in contents, however, play different roles in each of the two genres, building new, more competitive, or more focused images of the communicating self. The "innovative" trend found in the two genres reflects two quite different social, rhetorical, and argumentative motivations.

Shamanic ritual texts should be seen, at least in comparison with *ánent,* as macropolitical yet individual performances, adapting and filling interstitial spaces provided by the transition from the past small-scale dimensions of Jivaroan isolated settlements to modern villages. New settlement patterns, combined with new transportation facilities (roads, airstrips), led not only to an increase in the number of shamans active in each Shuar and Achuar area but also, predictably, to an increase in magical competition among them. Because shamans prefer to search for their power as far away as possible from the area where they will exert it, the increase in transportation facilities allowed many young males to travel to visit Quechua-speaking Amazonian peoples and even to the Andean region to acquire their magical "darts." Their "specialized" training became highly requested and costly, implying new and previously unthinkable economic possibilities, derived in many cases from successful cattle-raising. The competition over acquiring powers ran parallel to the shamans' willingness to exhibit them publicly, attracting external and even foreign researchers and "apprentices" (see, e.g., Rubenstein 2002). These new conditions triggered even greater competition among shamans, enhancing their verbal and conceptual creativity while exhibiting their acquaintance and familiarity with the outside world.

In a society like the Jivaroan one, with an attitude not just of openness to external influences but even a "predatory" one, shamans' arrays of "mysterious" lexical items, introducing references to external goods and concepts, are not surprising. Every shaman knows, however, that he must be sparing with his novelties in order to be able to exhibit them in his public performances—and all the more so since competition with other shamans, each equipped with magical powers and referential novelties, has increased.

Ánent magical songs, on the other hand, constitute micropolitical and fully individual performances. Combined economic, environmental, and social changes led to a shrinkage of the range of *ánent* types transmitted and kept in each person's use and to a decrease in individual repertoires. Drastic changes in settlement and economic patterns (villages, pastures, and cattle-raising) led to environmental depletion and the reduction of individual interaction with the spirits of the jungle and gardens, once addressed by men and by women, respectively. Changing sociocultural and cognitive conditions created new human-to-nature and human-to-human relations. A whole range of factors contributed to new male and female forms of self-representation. Among these I should mention at least the waning of the domestic gendered forms of socialization and training that were in use before schools were introduced; the obsolescence of male and female initiations and other once frequent ceremonies; the reduction of masculine hunting activities; and the adoption of a less individualized attitude toward male and female activities. Among all these significant changes, the decline in the transmission and practice of *ánent* performance holds a central place. Most *ánent,* once sung during many male and female activities, became part of the fading mental archive of remembrance. Only one of the once numerous types—*ánent* addressing themes of love and anger, jealousy and desire—grew in number and in creativity. This type is also the most available to researchers.

Innovative contents in different ritual genres are likely to emerge out of different motivations. In Shuar and Achuar shamanic singing, innovations are a response to growing "professional" competition, whereas in *ánent* singing they parallel a reduction of individual repertoires, providing new and rhetorically effective contents within the extant varieties.

Notes

I am grateful to the anonymous readers of an earlier draft of this chapter, who offered me insightful and helpful suggestions. For the interpretations and any imperfections, I am responsible.

1. In merely descriptive terms I use "ritualization" to refer to everyday, routine, minor actions and formulaic verbal utterances that take place while other longhouse activities are ongoing as usual. These are forms of human communicative performance present to different degrees of frequency and saliency in the cultural existence of any human group. With "rituals," on the other hand, I refer to fully observable communicative performances that take place in, and create, a special setting in which most other activities of residents are suspended. "Ceremonial events" require the participation of several residential groups, usually converging on one longhouse from several others, with the purpose of taking part and performing in them.

2. I write Shuar following the standard writing system adopted by the Shuar Federation and the Shuar school system. Most of the graphemes and the digraph should be read as in Spanish, with some minor differences: *e* is

pronounced as a high central-back unrounded vowel, *w* before *i* is pronounced close to [v], *j* is closer to [h] than to Spanish *jota, sh* is pronounced as [š], and *p, t,* and *k* become voiced when following a nasal. The velar nasal has phonemic status and is sometimes written as an underlined *n,* to distinguish it from alveolar *n.* All vowels can be nasalized and voiceless, but these features are usually not transcribed. For a basic phonological description, see Gnerre 1999b. I conducted fieldwork among the Shuar from 1970 to 1974, and among the Achuar between 1974 and 1978. After 1978, I went back to the upper Amazon approximately every two years, for two months each time.

3. *Ánent* is different from another sung genre, called *námpet,* which is publicly performed in a festive context. Both names are transparent, deriving from easily traceable verbal roots that are parts of a network of conceptual cross-references, which I do not discuss here, and key words, which I mention only in some of the comments on the texts I provide.

4. "Performance involves the assumption of responsibility to an audience for a display of communicative competence. This competence rests on the knowledge and ability to speak in socially appropriate ways. Performance involves on the part of the performer an assumption of accountability to an audience for the way in which communication is carried out, above and beyond its referential content. From the point of view of the audience, the act of expression on the part of the performer is thus marked as subject to evaluation for the way it is done, for the relative skill and effectiveness of the performer's display of competence. Additionally, it is marked as available for the enhancement of experience, through the present enjoyment of the intrinsic qualities of the act of expression itself. Performance thus calls forth special attention to and heightened awareness of the act of expression and gives license to the audience to regard the act of expression and the performer with special intensity" (Bauman 1977: 11).

5. There are several early examples of the Jivaroan attraction to external novelties. One dates to a late-eighteenth-century chronicle in which a Shuar man is described as fascinated while observing a white man writing. The Shuar tried to imitate the hand posture and movements of the writing man and to repeat aloud the Spanish words he was pronouncing.

6. In Shuar discourse and magical singing are found some key words from Quechua-speaking peoples. A central concept in the Shuar lexicon for the "hidden" world, *wakán,* often translated into Spanish as *alma* 'soul', can be traced to an Andean voice and concept, *waka* (Gnerre 2003). An old name for "God," recorded in early documents, was *kumpanama,* a word analyzable as 'in the place of [*-nama*] mestizo people [*kumpa-,* from the Spanish *compadre* 'godfather']', where *-(d)re* was analyzed by Shuar as a possessive suffix. Another word of the same set is *yus,* from the Spanish *Dios,* used in several *ánent* but

apparently not in shamanic singing. In my examples, some shamans identify their powers and protective spirits (*pasuk*) with the Quechua spirit *supai*. This name was recorded in the early Quechua-Spanish dictionaries (as *çupay*) with the meanings "devil, phantasm, shadow of a person" and "a vision, a sprite, an elf."

7. The Shuar Federation became a central reference for many other indigenous peoples of the Amazon and played an important role in Ecuador.

8. In the form *wi-kya,* derived from *wi-ka,* we find an example of the Shuar rule of palatalization: the insertion, or "echo," of [y] as a reflex of [i] in the previous syllable.

9. In the 1980s I frequently consulted with Pellizzaro at the mission where he resided, at Chiguaza, in the northern Shuar region. At that time he gave me many of his valuable transcripts and some copies of his tapes, suggesting that further linguistic and textual analysis should be carried out, as he was busy with other projects. He had published some of the texts, without any linguistic comment, in one volume of the *Mundo Shuar* series (Pellizzaro 1978b). In most cases Pellizzaro was unable to retrace the exact situation in which he had been allowed to tape-record a healing session. For a few cases, however, he was able to recall who the patient was and what his or her history was of previous consultations with other shamans.

10. In Shuar and Achuar, *panku* is derived from Quechua *banku* 'a shaman's teacher'. According to Harner (1972), the Quechua term derives from the Spanish *banco* 'bank', understood as a physical deposit of magical powers. According to Descola (1997), it refers to the big-man's stool.

thirteen

Interior Dialogues

The Co-Voicing of Ritual in Solitude

John W. Du Bois

Two of the outstanding qualities of ritual are its contribution to the impersonal construction of social authority (Du Bois 1986; Durkheim 1915) and its mediation of the individual's unfolding subjective experience (Briggs 1993; James 1902). Yet ritual's paradox remains: How do the social and the individual, the impersonal and the subjective, connect? Can we construct a vision of ritual to unify what has been sundered?

In our quest to come to terms with the nature and significance of ritual, we may come to notice, without at first attaching any great significance to it, that perfectly ordinary occasions arise in the course of everyday life in which ritual finds a voice—or rather, is given a voice by its practitioners. On such occasions the ritual practitioner turns out to be, often enough, an ordinary layperson like ourselves, and the voice we hear is characteristically tinged with the personal tones of its author. Taking the opportunity to observe the mundane rituals that surround us, we contemplate the subtle yet potentially unsettling character of what happens when the ritual text meets the voice of the individual who would enact it. The encounter of a seemingly timeless text with the uniquely personal voice of its present performer calls into question some of our most basic assumptions about the separation between the worlds of ritual and ordinary discourse. At stake, too, is something larger: the accompanying ontological assumptions regarding the nature of the social actions and entities, including ritual signs, that populate our life-world, and of the lived experience of the individual who works to find meaning by way of ritually mediated discourse.

The variety of ritual to be analyzed in this chapter is apparently sufficiently innocuous that it has remained largely unnoticed, undocumented, and untheorized, even as it represents a recurring reality in the daily lives of millions of believers worldwide. The genre mixes layers of scriptural citation leavened with pious commentary, presented in small portions suitable for daily reading. In the single instance examined here, we meet a solitary layman, entirely alone in a room, who is speaking aloud. No others are present to hear him perform, as he habitually does each morning, a ritual reading of a short religious text specified for that day. The following excerpt comes from the middle portion of the text:

(1) 94 *A child of the light confesses instantly and stands bared before God,*
95 *a child of darkness says oh I can explain that away.*

The reading unfolds routinely, largely in accordance with the expected pattern for the practice. But at least one feature sets this instance apart. The present speaker, unlike most, talks back. Departing from the script before him, he responds to the preceding lines, after a pause of 3.7 seconds' duration, in his own words:[1]

(2) 96 (3.7)
97 (TSK) (H) That is the difference.
98 (1.6)
99 The light,
100 and the dark.
101 (0.7)
102 (H) Confession,
103 (0.7)
104 and self-explanation,
105 (0.5)
106 Self-explanation is (0.2) ego.
107 (1.0)
108 (H) .. Id.
109 (0.4)

The dialectic between the text and the speaker's response to it is explored in detail in what follows, but a few preliminary comments are in order here. Although printed for mass circulation and destined to be part of a massively shared, synchronized performance realized by dispersed members of a common religious orientation, the text in its moment of distributed reading is locally enacted, embodied, situated, and, ultimately, appropriated and personalized. By responding in his own voice, the speaker introduces a new layer of dialogic imbrication to the already complex strata of embedded metadiscursivity (Silverstein 1993, 2005) entextualized in this ritual genre. Yet belying its apparent authority, the ritual text's vital dependence on processes of personal performance render it vulnerable to confrontation by alternative discourses, opening ritual up to the unfinalizability of polyphony and heteroglossia (Bakhtin 1981 [1934]; Voloshinov 1973). Crucially, the contingency of the dialogic response allows it to veer between the poles of affirmation and contestation.

One way to think of the tension between institutionalization and personalization of ritual is in terms of what Foucault characterized as "the mode of action that an individual exercises upon himself by means of the technologies of the self" (1988: 225). Technologies of the self can be understood as the structures that subtend practices of ethical self-formation, involving "forms of subjectivation" through which the individual constructs at once a "relation to oneself" and a relation to generalized moral codes of behavior (Foucault 1988: 225). The idea naturally lends itself to anthropological analyses of practices in which the individual deploys some cultural resource (such as a ritual text) to reshape aspects of her own subjectivity (cf. Hirschkind 2006; Mahmood 2001; Robbins 2004) in the construction of moral personhood (Shoaps 2004). (The ritual text to be analyzed in what follows seems to present a paradigm case.) Disenchantment with the totalizing tendencies of the Durkheimian perspective has long since motivated a turn from monolithic interpretations of society-level functions of ritual to more nuanced views of the heterogeneous meanings ascribed by individual participants to their own ritual practice, including subjective experience. Whether a shift in this direction reflects a change in the world or only in our preoccupations with it, there is value in probing the individual's personal participation in, and response to, ritual.

The traditional anthropological concern with ritual faces uncertainty today, in part because its object of study is no longer what it once was. Arguably, a worldwide trend is under way that threatens the living continuity of certain forms of ritual, especially large-scale public rituals linked to traditional religions under pressure. Such trends may be compared to the catastrophic loss of endangered languages worldwide, although the analogy, and the analysis, remains controversial (Hill 2002). At the same time, other ritual forms are on the rise, especially those associated with the global expansion of some varieties of Christianity and Islam (Hirschkind 2006; Keane 1997c, 2002; Mahmood 2001;

Robbins 2005). Whether the cultural consequences of globalization are blamed or simply noted, the effect on the observer class has at times been to motivate an escape to safer fields of inquiry. But this is hardly the time for anthropologists to give up on ritual. What is called for instead is a renewal of the terms of engagement. Subtle shifts in theoretical perspective can reform expectations regarding what we hope to receive from ritual in pursuit of the anthropological enterprise.

In pursuing a dialogic approach to ritual, the present line of research seeks to renew and extend anthropology's long-standing exploration of the centrality and power of ritual in social life while probing as well the more intimate dimensions of human subjectivity. In examining the individual's exploitation of received ritual forms for processes of self-formation in daily life, the need arises to address the contingent aspects of ritual's locally situated realization. To frame the problem, my analysis draws on an array of conceptual tools including participation (Goffman 1981b), voice (Agha 2005b; Keane 1999), indexicality (Ochs 1996; Silverstein 1976, 2003), and the technology of self (Foucault 1988; Mahmood 2001; Robbins 2004). These issues are situated within an overall dialogic perspective (Bakhtin 1981 [1934]; Voloshinov 1973), within which Bakhtin's ideas on "interior dialogicization" (Bakhtin 1973 [1929]; cf. Cohn 1978) and "internally persuasive discourse" (Bakhtin 1981 [1934]; cf. Rampton 2006) are especially relevant to the rhetorical efficacy of "voices from without ... which can speak in the language of a voice within" (Burke 1950; cf. Du Bois forthcoming). In addition, given that the act of reading is centrally at issue, the observations of literary theories of "interior monologue" (Bickerton 1967; Chafe 1994; Cohn 1978; Humphrey 1954), hermeneutics (Ricoeur 1976), and reader response criticism (Iser 1978) become relevant. The whole is organized under the general rubric of stance (Du Bois 2007), as developed further in what follows.

In the rest of this essay I present a dialogic approach to the analysis of ritual discourse in its personal dimensions, exploring the nexus between text, voice, and subjectivity as a matter of the structure of participation in ritual. Methodologically the work is grounded in observable aspects of ritual practice, analyzed in terms of stance (Du Bois 2007). The first section briefly delineates a contrast between the visible exterior and the subjective interior as they relate to ritual. In the next section I undertake an extended analysis of the event that provides the main focus of the chapter: a solitary performance of a ritual discourse in which a dialogic back-and-forth develops between reader and text. The penultimate section moves to a more generalized theoretical characterization of the role of voice in ritual, depicting what I call co-voicing as a form of participatory engagement with the ritual text, as framed within stance theory. Finally, the conclusion highlights some of the broader implications of the dialogic perspective for understanding ritual in social life.

Ritual: Exterior or Interior?

In any attempt to define ritual, one immediately encounters a question that has generated debate over the ages: Where does ritual reside? Is it external, such that it can be taken as sufficiently defined by its procedure? On such a view, ritual is constituted by a behavioral surface, a configuration of acts, signs, bodies, and objects accessible to the external gaze, amenable to imitative reproduction by its observers. By this token the realization of ritual is objective (Rappaport 1974, 1999), occurring appropriately under conditions of effective enactment regardless of the subjectivity of those who do the enacting. Or is ritual rather internal, a process that penetrates into the individual psyche (James 1902; cf. Briggs 1993; Lienhardt 1961; Rampton 2006)? Among the many variants of this position, one version holds that ritual demands a certain subjective involvement by the actor in the act, presupposing a configuration of intentionality to be located variously within the soul, psyche, or consciousness of the ritual participant (Bauman 1983; Hanks 2000; Keane 1997b, 2002; Shoaps 2002).

That there are deep and long-standing divisions concerning the proper answers to these questions, fueled in part by divergence of religious doctrine, is well known. The philosophical and sociological dimensions of the problem are no less daunting than the theological, evoking such fraught issues as objective and subjective dimensions of experience and of sociality. Although it is tempting to sidestep such issues entirely, if only to avoid raising problems we are unlikely to be able to resolve, the question of ritual's external and internal aspects—obvious and opaque, objective and subjective (Rappaport 1974; Turner 1975)—refuses to be entirely set aside. The ritual participants, who feel themselves to be doing something more than merely producing patterns of behavior to be analyzed, annotated, or reproduced, are not to be ignored. Ritual participants not only weave but inhabit and indeed embody the fabric of social life. Even as ritual life is conducted in public spaces, it reveals an interior as well as an exterior dimension, whether we speak of spiritually potent ritual located in religious practice (Abu-Lughod 1986; Bauman 1983; James 1902; Shoaps 2002) or interaction ritual found in daily encounters (Basso 2007; Goffman 1967). The realization of the ritual act must encompass not only the events of the visible exterior but also those that penetrate to the affective interior. In ritual, the subjective animates the objective as much as the objective mediates the subjective.

In taking account of the personal involvement of the individual in ritual, it is important to avoid falling into a merely psychologizing account (Rampton 2006). It proves useful to attend closely to specific details of the individual's dialogic practice, in order to appreciate how the situated actions indexically mediate relations between the ritual text and the subjectivity of its performer. Such an analytic methodology can yield more secure results, with far-reaching implications for the way the realization of ritual contributes to its own force and significance in social life. It is to this kind of close analysis of ritual practice that I turn in the next section.

Ritual in Solitude

The initiating complication that drives the present inquiry arises in an encounter with a specific form of ritual, briefly exemplified earlier. Although drawn entirely from a recording of one man talking, the discourse can hardly be described as a monologue. Paradoxically, it presents a challenge not only to reified notions of the ritual text but also to certain interactional approaches to discourse (a.k.a. talk in interaction) that sometimes insist on the need for two bodies to make an interaction (Schegloff 1999: 408).

The circumstances bear some clarification. The recording was made under my direction using a portable digital tape-recorder I had set up in advance to record for four hours continuously. The speaker, who lives alone, took the recorder home and turned it on in the morning when he awoke. He wore the recorder and microphone on his person as he moved freely about the house. Because no outsider was present, the resulting recording appears reasonably natural, in the sense that the speaker seems to behave more or less as he would have without the tape-recorder present.

In the common parlance, solitary speaking is sometimes referenced as "talking to oneself." Such a pat formulation is at best incomplete and at worst prey to unspoken prejudicial assumptions, but in any case it is too crude to capture the significance of what happens on occasions like the present one. More productively, the phenomenon of self-talk has recently been receiving serious, theoretically motivated attention from psychology (Baars 1997; Morin 1993) and other cognitive sciences (Fields 2002), updating an interest that can be traced back to the work of Vygotsky and others. Although most discussion of self-talk is framed almost exclusively in psychological terms, a notable exception appears in the brilliant sociological speculations of Goffman (1978), who acutely discerned a dimension of sociality in the unaccompanied individual's use of "response cries" to manage the presentation of self even when ostensibly "alone." The present work continues along these lines, addressing the social rather than the psychological dimensions of self-talk, but I depart from Goffman in attending closely to extended, transcribed samples of naturally occurring discourse.

Despite the solitary conditions of its production, the event at issue here unexpectedly reveals itself as dialogically constituted, in an almost literal sense. The recording begins with Daniel, as I will call him, waking and going about his morning activities. During the course of these events he often speaks aloud, providing a running sotto voce commentary on the activities he is engaged in. His comments often seem to derive from associations triggered in some way by his present circumstances. We may speculate that, living alone, the widower Daniel tends to speak aloud when others might only think the words to themselves.

Turning to the event itself, we observe a context that is in some respects familiar. It is morning. A man sits holding a book in the compact form of a daily devotional reader, *My Utmost for His Highest* by Oswald Chambers (1935), a best-seller among Christian religious tracts. Daniel's first task is to ascertain which page-long text he should read, from among the many in the book. Following the conventions of daily devotional practice, he makes the selection via a calendrical procedure (in effect a minor divination; Du Bois 1993, forthcoming). The book specifies a text for each day of the year, so the day's date becomes consequential for the unfolding ritual reading:

(3)	1		(1.8)
	2	DANIEL;	Today is March the,
	3		(0.8)
	4		(Hx) twenty- .. what -f:ourth:. (Hx)

Daniel somewhat hesitantly decides that the current date is March 24. But after a few moments of uncertainty (omitted here), he revises his estimate:

(4)	12	DANIEL;	(TSK) (H): Or twenty-third.
	13		I guess.
	14		.. Yeah.
	15		(0.3)

What Daniel accomplishes in this sequence may seem trivial, but it turns out to be important for grounding the ritual character of what happens next. What is established is not merely a fact about a date but the calendrical authority that motivates the selection of a particular text for the day's reading. Daniel then proceeds to the ritual reading proper:

(5)	16	DANIEL;	(TSK) (H) *Am I carnally minded.*
	17		(H) (TSK) (H)
	18		(0.6)
	19		*Whereas there is among you .. jealousy and strife,*
	20		*are ye not carnal.*
	21		(2.3)

Italics here indicate passages of reading, as opposed to speaking in one's own voice.[2] It bears pointing out that the status of this utterance as read speech is indexed not so much by the use of a special vocal quality per se as by its rhythmic regularity, moderation of intonational variability, and, especially, the absence of disfluencies and word-search pauses within the boundaries of a single sentence.

Daniel starts his reading with the title at the top of the printed page: "Am I Carnally Minded?" (line 16). He takes a breath, then another, then pauses (lines 17–18). Although we cannot know what is going on in any particular pause, certain observations and speculations are possible. Pauses and vocalisms such as in-breath are abundant in the vicinity of the read passages; more precisely, they seem to occur more often at discourse boundaries, especially between sentences. Although the presence of a scripted text, mapping out fully which words are to be spoken next, should obviate the need to pause for word searches, some sentences nevertheless trigger a following pause. These often seem to be those calling for some contemplation, if not a response. Thus, pause distribution may reflect moments of cognitive activity by the reader (Chafe 1994), an index of dialogic reader response (Iser 1978; Riffaterre 1990) to the "assimilation point" associated with the completion of a sentence.[3]

Be that as it may, Daniel goes on to read the opening biblical epigraph (lines 19–20). Chambers's source was evidently the English Revised Version of the Bible (1881): "For whereas there is among you jealousy and strife, are ye not carnal?" (1 Corinthians 3:3). In reading aloud, Daniel deploys a voice that cannot be considered exclusively his own, if only because he has yet to invest it fully with his own stance (Basso 2007; Du Bois 2007). Partly cued by details of the manner of speaking, the reading voice subtly restructures the participation frame for the utterance at hand. For Daniel the reading voice is a provisional one, creating a kind of temporary buffer for ritual propositions. This leaves open the question of whether we are to interpret the stance that would normally be implicit in an active voicing of the read proposition as present—whether it counts as the speaker's current committed stance or not.

Daniel goes on, reading now from words evidently originating not with the Bible but with the devotional pamphlet's author, Oswald Chambers:

(6)	22	DANIEL;	(TSK) (H) *No natural man knows anything about carnality.*
	23		(0.4)
	24		(H) (TSK) *The flesh lusting against the spirit,*
	25		*that came in at regeneration,*
	26		*the spirit lusting against the flesh,*
	27		*produces carnality.*
	28		(2.4)

After a substantial pause (line 28), Daniel continues with a passage from the apostle Paul, which elicits additional layers of voicing and revoicing. On the printed page, what appears in *My Utmost for His Highest* for the date March 23 is the following (Chambers 1935: 83):

(7) "Walk in the Spirit," says Paul, "and ye shall not fulfil the lusts of the flesh"; and carnality will disappear.

Although Chambers does not cite his source, the portion in quotation marks is from Paul's letter to the Galatians (Galatians 5:16, King James Version). In Daniel's reading this is realized as follows:

(8)	29	DANIEL;	(TSK) (H) (0.2) *Walk in the Spirit,*
	30		*says Paul.*
	31		(0.2)
	32		(H) #*and ye shall not fulfill the lusts of the flesh,*
	33		(0.2)
	34		(H) (TSK) (H) *and carnality will disappear.* (Hx)

Up to this point (excerpts [5]–[8], lines 16–34), the reading has proceeded uneventfully as a faithful reproduction of the printed text, augmented only by the bodily behaviors that commonly accompany human vocal production, such as breath and pause. What determines the course of events, its seems, is the script laid down by the devotional pamphlet. Cast in the role of a mere animator of the unhindered words of the text, Daniel seems ordained to transmit a mix of propositions formulated variously by Oswald Chambers, the apostle Paul, and the biblical author. But in the next increment of the discourse, cracks begin to appear in the seamless voicing, amid indications that Daniel will now deploy his own voice to engage dialogically with Paul's. (The previous excerpt is repeated here for context.)

(9)	29	DANIEL;	(TSK) (H) (0.2) *Walk in the Spirit,*
	30		*says Paul.*
	31		(0.2)
	32		(H) #*and ye shall not fulfill the lusts of the flesh,*
	33		(0.2)
	34		(H) (TSK) (H) *and carnality will disappear.* (Hx)
	35		(H) (TSK) Walk in the Spirit,
	36		yeah.
	37		(0.4)
	38		#(H) (TSK) #n_Kay.
	39		(0.5)
	40		(H) Okay.

A superficial analysis might hold that Daniel "repeats" (Norrick 1987; Tannen 1987) the same words twice, a few moments apart (in lines 29 and 35). But once the question of stance is considered for these two utterances, it becomes problematic to maintain that, when Daniel speaks the words "Walk in the Spirit" a second time in line 35, he is merely "repeating" the same stance action he has already achieved in line 29. And whereas the words may in some sense be the same—though surely not their precise prosody and pronunciation—the voice is another matter altogether. The difference becomes clear if we distinguish the specific vocal quality (phonation style, etc.) employed on a given occasion of speech production from the voice as a mark of identity. Identity as applied to voice is a complex and subtle matter, but we can provisionally define it as involving a recognizable index of a social being or socially constituted positionality capable of constancy across renewable occasions of participation in dialogic engagements. Voice in this sense, which we may characterize in stance terms as the voice-position, is not reducible to voice quality in the phonetic sense.

Although Daniel's vocal quality does not change systematically between his two acts of voicing, we may still recognize a shift in voice qua voice-position. To be sure, because multiple voices can be laminated together in one polyphonous utterance (Günthner 1999), sorting them out can be challenging, to the extent that it draws on cues across multiple orders of indexicality (Silverstein 2003), among other things.

It should not need to be said, but perhaps it does, that the fact that speakers sometimes manipulate multiple voices need have nothing to do with "hearing voices," another folk characterization of a pathology sometimes associated with self-talk. According to the scholarly literature on such issues, in the healthy version the multiple voices are managed as an internal matter under the control of a coherent self; in the unhealthy version they may seem to be controlled by an external source.

One easily overlooked cue to relations between stances (and the voices they imply) is sequence (Schegloff 2007). When Daniel's voicing of his "own" words follows his voicing of Paul's, the sequence reflects recognition of two voices apparently taking turns and, in the process, realizing distinctively positioned stances. (The language of turn and sequence is invoked here, even when no other conversationalist is physically present, on the basis of cues that typically accompany turn-taking [Schegloff 2007: 14; and see Du Bois forthcoming.]) The new contribution made by a second voicing is to shift to the self voice, the better to take a stance indexing commitment (Kockelman 2004). Once stance is taken into account, it becomes clear that the first voicing represents a stance lead, and the second, a stance follow (Du Bois 2007: 161–168).

That the present discourse is organized as an alternation of voices taking stances receives some support from what Daniel does next. He confronts the issue that has been at stake all along: whether he will be content with a mere animation of the ritual text (lines 29–34), enacting a provisional voicing of words that remain alienated from him as the stance of another, or will move to align with the prior stance. In line 36 he makes his initial move, departing from the script to interject a clear expression of his own stance alignment, using the convergent alignment marker "yeah" (Du Bois 2007). This "yeah" is introduced in postposed position, that is, at the end rather than the beginning of the response (Raymond 2000). In lines 38 and 40 this positioning is confirmed, if slightly softened, with the stance follow marker "okay" (expressed in two variant pronunciations). "Okay" here serves to mark consent to someone else's proposal. By substituting "okay" for "yeah," Daniel downgrades his participation, marking his move as stance follow to Paul's stance lead. He thus consolidates both his alignment with the stance of the ritual text and his recognition of its priority. The uncertain balance between alternative contingent outcomes—will he follow Paul's lead or not?—is resolved. He has made the move from entertaining a textually proposed proposition to making it count now as his own stance.

To represent the subtle interplay of virtual voices, it is useful to introduce a new coding convention. Supplementing the standard transcriptional practice of notating the identity of the speaker (qua animator) at the start of each new "turn," a further annotation is introduced to indicate what type of voice-position the speaker is inhabiting. Among the general voice types implicated in reading aloud, we may distinguish the *text voice,* in which the speaker primarily animates the words of the text, from the *self voice,* in which the speaker fills both animator and author roles (roughly speaking).[4] One first writes the standard speaker attribution label (here marking the animator role, in effect), then an equal sign (=), and then the annotation specifying the author role. Applied to the previous two passages, lines 29–34 would be analyzed as indexing a text voice (DANIEL=TEXT), whereas lines 35–41 reflect a self voice (DANIEL=SELF). Obviously, such labels serve only as rough guides to aspects of the dynamic flux of vocal polyphony and should be taken with a grain of salt.[5] Yet even partial attempts to annotate vocal positionalities can be useful in calling attention to aspects of the participation frame as it is dynamically constructed in discourse.

In the next installment of the text, the reader is confronted with a question. Refusing to treat the question as merely rhetorical, Daniel responds with an expressive interjection:

(10)	41	DANIEL=SELF;	.. (AHEM) (AHEM)
	42	DANIEL=TEXT;	(TSK) (H) *Are you contentious.*
	43		.. *easily troubled about trifles.*
	44	DANIEL=SELF;	Oh boy.

Responding with an affectively intensified interjection ("Oh boy"), Daniel seems to acknowledge that the term "contentious" fits him. "Oh boy" goes well beyond the option of a minimal stance alignment marker (e.g., "yeah") to participate empathically in an affectively loaded dialogic exchange between differentiated voices.

This is not to suggest that the exchange is symmetrical, which would be absurd: only one of the voices is capable of responding to the other in real time. As Ricoeur pointed out (1976: 75), in the "asymmetric relation" between text and reader, "only one of the partners speaks for the two." In contrast to the relative fixity of the text voice, the self voice has the luxury of contingent response, choosing the terms of its engagement. Still, when the text voice animates what is formally marked as a question (*Are you...?*) addressed to the reader (*you*) and bearing on emotions (*contentious, troubled*), an interactionally appropriate response is forthcoming: Daniel answers with an affective expression of the self voice.

The examples adduced so far have been relatively tame in presenting a more or less consensual convergence of alignment between text and self voices. But dialogic engagement is not all sweetness and light; the meeting of stances at the juncture of self voice and text voice need not be so harmonious. To allow for a dialogic response opens the text to a dialectic of contingent alternatives, exposing it to the very real possibility of divergence and even contestation between voices. We start to get a sense of what is at stake in the next portion of the reading. (The preceding lines are repeated here for context.)

(11)	42	DANIEL=TEXT;	(TSK) (H) *Are you contentious.*
	43		.. *easily troubled about trifles.*
	44	DANIEL=SELF;	Oh boy.
	45		(0.4)
	46	DANIEL=TEXT;	(H) (0.7) *Oh but no one who is #a Christian ever is.*
	47		(1.1)
	48	DANIEL=SELF;	What absolute nonsense.
	49		(4.4)
	50		The way Paul talks,
	51		there would have been no reason for Christ to have come in the first place,
	52		because everyone's supposed to be perfect already.
	53		(1.8)

Upon reading what he takes to be Paul's words, *Oh but no one who is a Christian ever is* (line 46), Daniel responds, after a pause, in his own voice. He evaluates Paul's stance with the harsh assessment, "What absolute nonsense" (line 48).[6] In voicing such a critical evaluation, Daniel gives the clearest evidence yet that he is involved in something more profound than merely animating the words of another. He faces a deeper question: To what extent will he sign on as (co-)author of the words? In stance terms, the choice is whether to make the stance his own through convergent alignment or to reject it through divergent alignment. If Daniel does not shy away from sharp divergence at times, his very independence lends meaning to his voicing of the ritual stance. As an apparently free agent—according to the ideology of the so-called liberal subject—he seems to wield his free will as he chooses to deploy his own voice and words, whether to reject, embrace, or otherwise define a nuanced alignment with the ritually offered stance.

In the next "turn," Daniel shifts back to reading in the textual voice:

(12)	54	DANIEL=TEXT;	(TSK) (H) *Paul says,*
	55		(0.3)
	56		*they are.*
	57		(2.5)
	58		(TSK) #(H) *He connects these things with carnality.*
	59		(3.1)

Daniel reproduces these words with no explicit evaluation. After a pause, he goes on to read three more sentences of Chambers's text, the last of which (lines 64–65) elicits a notable response:

(13)	60	DANIEL=TEXT;	(H) *Is there a truth in the Bible that instantly awakens petulance in you?*
	61		(0.4)
	62		(H) (TSK) (H) *That is a proof that you are yet carnal.*
	63		(0.8)
	64		(TSK) (H) *If sanctification is being worked out,*
	65		*there is no trace of that spirit left.*
	66		(1.7)
	67	DANIEL=SELF;	(H) (TSK) (H) No: #,
	68		#that,
	69		(0.3)
	70		That's (0.7) (%) crap.

Daniel shifts to his own voice in line 67, after a pause and in-breath (lines 66–67), which are typical correlates of the beginning of a new turn (Du Bois n.d.). The initial "no" in his own voice indexes the beginning of a divergent alignment, relative to the words of the ritual text he has just finished animating. He goes on to render his verdict on the prior proposition via the metapragmatic assessment "That's crap" (line 70). "Crap" is a pretty strong word to use in assessing a biblical exegesis, but that's just what Daniel does. Yet the word "that," though apparently innocuous in comparison with "crap," is no less devastating in its own way. It is used here to demarcate a portion of the prior discourse as an object, an utterance whose stance can be evaluated. (This may in fact be the typical, if underappreciated, function of "that": to point to something in the prior discourse, constituting it as an object cognitively accessible to participants [Ariel 1998; Hanks 1990, 2006; Webber 1991].) Faced with the proposition *If sanctification is being worked out, there is no trace of that spirit left,* Daniel moves to define it as his (reflexive) stance object, apparently even before he knows what to call it. He first utters "that," then pauses (lines 68–69), then again "that's" and another pause (line 70), before he goes on to deliver his blunt evaluation, "crap."

I turn now to the closing moments of this intertextual engagement. (Lines 94–109 were presented earlier, in excerpts (1) and (2); lines 71–93 and 110–116 are omitted in the interests of space.) As he reads the final sentences of the prescribed text for the day, Daniel stays mostly in text voice until the end:

(14)	117	DANIEL=TEXT;	(H) (TSK) (H) *What is the proof that carnality has gone?*
	118		(0.2)
	119		(H) # *Never decei:ve yourse:lf?*
	120		(1.0)_((MOVES_PAPER))
	121		*When carnality is gone it is the most real thing imaginable.*
	((7 LINES OMITTED))		
	129		(H) (TSK) (H) *You will never cease to be the most amazed person on Earth,*
	130		*at what God has done for you.*
	131		(0.6)
	132		*on the inside.*
	133		(1.0)
	134	DANIEL=SELF;	(TSK) (H)
	135		(1.9)
	136		Okay, (Hx)

Upon completing the prescribed reading (in line 132), Daniel pauses, takes a breath, pauses again, and finally responds with a simple "Okay" (line 136). As in the case discussed earlier, Daniel's "okay" here indexes a stance follow aligned with the ritual text's stance lead. It comes across as rather tepid, but Daniel doesn't leave things there; the "continuing" (or "comma") intonation of line 136 hints at more to come. And Daniel indeed goes on to recast his overall evaluation of the text he has just finished reading. Amid a sequence of pauses, clicks, throat-clearings, and other vocalisms, he elaborates a further dialogic response—now whispered, but in his own voice:

(15)	137		(1.6)
	138	DANIEL=SELF;	(TSK) (H)
	139		(2.3)
	140		<WHISPER> Yeah </WHISPER>.
	141		(0.7)
	142		(TSK)
	143		(1.3)
	144		#(H) (AHEM) (AHEM)
	145		Mhm,
	146		(0.2)
	147		(TSK)
	148		(1.9)

So this is the way the whirl with the text ends, not with a bang but a whimper. After this Daniel moves on to other activities and topics.

Yet close examination reveals some significance to be found amid the pauses and vocalisms, in the subtle sequencing of stance alignment markers. Compared with his initial "okay" (line 136), Daniel's subsequent "yeah" and "mhm" (lines 140 and 145) represent a nuanced shift in alignment, from acceptance of the stance of a differentiated other to a more direct personal appropriation of the text's ritual stance. As the final explicit response in his own voice, the sequence of alignment markers can be heard as a gradual upgrading of his commitment, indexing his deepening inhabitance of the position voiced—and now co-voiced—in his dialogic performance of the ritual text.

The Ritual Stance

What, if anything, can stance theory bring to the problem of ritual? I began this essay by acknowledging the gap between the entextualized, decentered, authoritative aspects of ritual form and the subjectivity and contingency that attend its local realization by particular participants.

Although the issue may seem moot for mass media products such as devotional publications, it is only masked by the apparent completeness, self-sufficiency, and autonomy of the text. To close the gap, it is important to consider how the users of ritual materials forge a relationship between themselves and their texts. Stance theory can help to model the structures and processes involved in the construction of a participation frame for intersubjective engagement with ritual forms.

Stance can be defined as a triplex act in which the speaker as subject (1) evaluates an object, (2) positions a subject (canonically the self), and (3) aligns with other subjects (Du Bois 2007). The triune stance model is fundamentally dialogic. It builds on the structure of engagement between speaking subjects who jointly construct, in the inter-individual territory of distributed cognition (Voloshinov 1973; Hutchins 1995), an intersubjective framing of their respective subjectivities. Through repeated processes of stance alignment, each co-participant's expressions of subjectivity come to be structured in relation to the others'. For ritual in solitude, with only one (living) speaker in the room, it may appear that the issue of intersubjective alignment is moot. Once we take the perspective of voices rather than individuals, however, the pervasive relevance of stance alignment comes into focus.

Consider, for example, the relationship between Daniel's voice and the represented voice of the apostle Paul, as discussed earlier.[7] (Portions of excerpt 9 are repeated here for convenience, condensed to highlight the parallels between the voices.)

(16)	29	DANIEL=TEXT;	(TSK) (H) (0.2) *Walk in the Spirit,*
	30		says Paul.
	((4 LINES OMITTED))		
	35	DANIEL=SELF;	(H) (TSK) Walk in the Spirit,
	36		yeah.

As noted earlier, Paul's stance is enacted as an imperative admonishment to *Walk in the Spirit* (line 29), to which Daniel responds in his self voice, first reproducing the words he has just spoken (line 35) and then introducing the postposed stance alignment marker "yeah" (line 36). Figure 13.1 represents the structural relations between the stances taken by Paul and Daniel as constructed in this "exchange." In the terms of the stance triangle, Paul's role as first stance subject is represented by a speaker label at the upper left node of the triangle. His stance utterance, the directive *Walk in the Spirit,* is represented along the vector beginning from this node and sloping downward to the right. Daniel is represented as the second stance subject, with his speaker label at the lower left node of the triangle and his stance utterance represented along the vector sloping upward to the right. What the two stance vectors point to, canonically, is the shared stance object. How to characterize a shared stance object in the present case is not so easy to pin down, but it can be provisionally defined as the principle of moral obligation, "what one ought to do."

Figure 13.1. Co-voicing the ritual stance.

For the present discussion, however, what matters most is the third stance vector, depicted in the vertical line connecting the two stance subject positions. This represents the dimension of alignment between Daniel's and Paul's stances. It is important to clarify that alignment is not, as I use the term, a simple binary opposition but a scale of continuously variable degrees. Certainly the polarity of alignment may be dichotomized as convergent versus divergent, which leads some analysts to divide the territory categorically into "alignment" versus "disalignment." But in a more nuanced approach, it becomes crucial to recognize alignment as a continuous variable, if only because it is actively negotiated as such by participants.

As a process, the implementation of alignment is not symmetrical: it may be initiated by one participant. This lends alignment a directionality, shown in figure 13.1 by an arrow directed from the second subject to the first (from Daniel to Paul). This analysis reflects the fact that it is Daniel's stance marker "yeah" that indexes convergent alignment between the two stance subjects. Even if the paired utterances in lines 29 and 35 are identical in words, propositional content, and perhaps illocutionary force, once we consider the matter of voicing, the difference could not be clearer: in this structuring of stance participation, one speaker leads, the other follows.

It may seem that in treating Daniel's voice as engaging directly with Paul's, I am committing an unpardonable oversimplification of the intertextuality and polyphony in play, neglecting a whole series of embeddings of Paul's words—first in the Bible, then in Chambers's pamphlet, and then in Daniel's reading voice. The "original" participation frame, after all, can be construed as a matter strictly between Paul and the Galatians. But the status of the Bible as scripture lends it a semiotic openness that transforms the scope and reach of its address. As a ritual text its participation frame is hyperactivated, as it were, inviting us to hear Paul's admonishment to the Galatians as extended universally, even to ourselves. Read in a ritual attitude of participatory openness, the text calls us as new readers to construct ourselves as addressed participants, filling roles once taken by its original audience. As Ricoeur wrote (1976: 93), "the letters of Paul are no less addressed to me than to the Romans, the Galatians, the Corinthians, and the Ephesians." This builds on the "omnitemporality" of the text, which "opens it to unknown readers." By such means, ritual links participatory permeability to constituted authority, inducing a unique capacity for mediation across participation frames. This may be necessary for ritual to function effectively as a center of semiosis (Silverstein, this volume).

What is remarkable in Daniel's discourse is not so much his habit of talking out loud when alone but his ritual attitude: from the outset he approaches the text at hand as a suitable partner for dialogic engagement. And yet his practice may not be so unusual after all, if we set aside the issue of self-talk. The dialogic connection depends first on separation: the criterion of interaction is that each partner must wield a distinguishable voice. Once differentiated, the dialogic partner has the potential (whether exercised or not) to make contingent contributions that will shape, at least in part, the emerging stance.

To approach a ritual text with a preparatory orientation to dialogic engagement is to adopt a ritual attitude of a certain kind, without which the outcome may be limited to mere vocal animation of prescribed words on a page. This at least is the recurring Protestant critique of ritual's formalistic tendency (Bauman 1983; Keane 1997b, 2002; Shoaps 2002). There doubtless exist forms of ritual practice designed to be carried out in a detached manner, as in some kinds of divination (Du Bois 1993). But in individualistic forms of religious practice such as the one considered here, this is clearly not the ethos.

Conclusion

If ritual has long been favored as a point of entry for anthropological probings into the salient structures of culture and society (Durkheim 1915), in recent years this privileged status has come into question. Ritual awaits a new role in a theoretical landscape transformed by a multiplicity of concerns including practice (Bourdieu 1991; Silverstein 1998), linguistic ideologies (Kroskrity 1998; Robbins 2001b; Silverstein 1985), the social imaginary (Gaonkar 2002; Taylor 2002), technologies of the self (Foucault 1988; Mahmood 2001; Robbins 2004), modernity and its "posting" (Rampton 2006), "afterology" (Sahlins, cited by Robbins 2005), and other contemporary preoccupations. It is difficult to say how much the disciplinary crisis of confidence in anthropology, of which diffidence about the theoretical import of ritual is only one indicator, is connected to the actual crisis of ritual in the world that anthropology proposes to represent. In the face of sociocultural disruption driven by accelerating processes of globalization, the fraught contradictions among jostling forms of tradition, modernity, and postmodernity give rise to a complex pastiche that seems to offer little to bewildered subject populations except a choice between self-referential skepticism and doctrinal fundamentalism. Yet amid this flux, ritual is not so much abandoned by its practitioners as it is transformed via new forms and practices, new projects and interpretations. Against this background, a neglected dimension of ritual stands a chance of becoming visible, even if it was present all along. Ritual's capacity to induce and embrace the contingent responses of new participants suggests that, even in its interior dimensions, ritual has always been already dialogic.

In previous work I have emphasized the way ritual's recurrent structural properties serve to systematically imbue it with social authority (Du Bois 1986, 1993), tying its functional efficacy within a community of discourse to the social construction of its own entextualization. Without taking anything away from the import of social authority, entextualization, or structural universals, I would here redress the tacit imbalance by foregrounding a role for the voices of ritual participants—among whom must be included not only ritual speakers but also hearers and readers. To theorize personal participation is to frame the issue of subjectivity so as to recast the active social construction of *inter*subjectivity as a locally situated project of participants. And the project remains social, indeed intersubjective, even for the individual in solitude. The polyphony of dialogic voicing introduces the potential for socially distributed agency into any utterance. Yet it is precisely ritual's formal constitution as an "objectively" entextualized *technology* of the self that opens up a usable channel for continuously modulated vocal participation in the ritual frame. In ritual, the text voice puts a stance on the table, and the self voice endorses it (or not). The alternation of voices yields a sequential organization not unlike what can be observed in turn-taking, a structural principle long recognized for its contributions to the manifestly social activity of multiparty, face-to-face interaction. The words of a solitary participant can be demarcated into the equivalent of "turns" by recognizing the distinctiveness not only of successive phases of verbal action but also of alternating voices whose positionality is differentially indexed by the stanced utterances they realize. As ritual subjects are drawn into the active construction of intersubjectivity, ritual in its actual enactment comes to resemble, more than might have been expected, the dialogic negotiation of stance alignment in interaction.

I began by posing a fundamental question for the understanding of ritual: How can the gulf be bridged between the impersonal authoritative form of ritual and its affect-laden subjective experience? The answer has to begin with the fact that ritual is not (only) something we do but something we experience in the doing. As active agents in the realization of ritual, we find our selves changed by the activity. Entering the participation frame of ritual co-voicing, we are transformed—as is the ritual itself, in the contingencies of its renewed manifestation. Through ritual we submit to a discipline beyond ourselves, a technology of the self, that has the power and apparently the purpose to induce change in our subjectivity, to penetrate into interior domains of affect, apprehension, and affinity. But this destabilized subjectivity is not left to float freely, untrammeled in an interior realm of imagination and solipsism. What goes on in the interior is dialogue, and dialogue always reaches ultimately to the exterior. There it finds itself constrained by the encounter with another subject, another voice wielding a stance of its own. Ritual is designed precisely to mediate the reflexive engagement between the implied voice of a prior text and the present voice of one who would reenact it. It is in this sense that ritual is constructed dialogically, through the collaborative achievement of co-voicing.

When the solitary individual faces the ritual text, the conditions for dialogic engagement are stripped to the bare minimum. What the case under analysis—in which the protagonist not only animates but also talks back to the ritual text—reveals is a penetration of the dialogic principle into the deepest levels of the realization of ritual. In this instance the process turns out to hinge on the dialogic configuration of personal involvement in ritual technologies of the self, which makes possible the production of particularized, situated meanings via culturally generalized materials.

Under conditions of solitude, sociality does not disappear. If anything, the solitary social actor challenges us to come to terms with the full scope of sociality, revealed now in its dialogic guise. Dialogic practice is seen to organize even such activities as self-talk and private ritual, which in turn help create an inherently dialogic organization of persons. Ritual text and ritual practice thus emerge as two distinct phases of a single semiotic life cycle that together implicate a third term: a dialogic self that both constructs and is constructed by the circulation of discourse between public and private domains, crossing the exterior-interior divide. Whether in solitude or in public, ritual stands as perhaps the paradigm case among technologies of the (dialogic) self. The critical contribution of ritual co-voicing is to construct a frame for individual participation that links contingent, subjective dimensions of personal meaning to the compelling authority of ritual form, with its ramified links to ideological structures in an intertextual maze of meaning extending to the horizons of the sociocultural field.

Notes

An earlier version of this chapter was presented at the Wenner-Gren symposium in Sintra, Portugal, that gave birth to this volume. I would like to thank the participants in that event for their many stimulating observations and insights on ritual, as well as feedback on this chapter, both of which substantially benefited the work. I particularly appreciate the generosity of Ellen Basso and Gunter Senft as organizers, editors, and creative contributors to the whole. Thanks are due to the Wenner-Gren Foundation for the remarkable support that made such a vibrant intellectual exchange possible and for its knack for location, location. I thank Wally Chafe for bringing to my attention the literary theories of Humphrey, Cohn, and Bickerton, as well for his insights on interior monologue. Thanks also to three anonymous reviewers, whose comments improved this work significantly. For her deep support and encouragement, I thank Mira Ariel. Finally, I wish to acknowledge my continuing debt to the man whose voice is heard in these pages, whose collaboration in a particularly intimate piece of research allowed me to witness the private practices of a creative soul—without whom there would be nothing to say.

1. The excerpts are transcribed following the system of conventions known as Discourse Transcription (Du Bois et al. 1993) as recently updated to "DT2" (Du Bois n.d.). For the sake of clarity, the excerpts are presented in a slightly simplified transcription. The transcription conventions employed are the following: {LINE}, each line of the transcription represents one intonation unit; DANIEL;, speaker attribution label; =TEXT, role or voice enacted by speaker; *italics,* reading voice (ad hoc local convention); (1.7), pause, with duration in seconds; .., very short pause (less than 0.18 second); colon (:), prosodic lengthening of previous sound; em dash (—), truncated intonation unit; (H), in-breath; (Hx), exhalation; (TSK), alveolar click; (%), glottalized vocalism; (AHEM), throat-clearing; @, laugh (one per pulse); #word, uncertain hearing of word; <WHISPER> words </WHISPER>, beginning and end of whispered voice quality.

2. I use italics here in preference to the standard convention of Discourse Transcription ("DT2" revised practice; Du Bois n.d.), which is to enclose the read words within angle brackets as follows: <READ> words </READ>. Given the prevalence of reading throughout this analysis, the use of italics as an ad hoc local convention seemed more user friendly.

3. For those steeped in the rhythms of conversational interaction and the interactional significance of the sequential location of pauses between speakers' alternating turns (Schegloff 1999: 408, 2007: 14), it is important to recall that in the solitary situation, the absence of real-time, co-present co-participants (though surely not of co-participants in the intertextual sense) provides a reprieve from competition for the floor. One key consequence is a modification of the conditions governing allotment of time for the current speaker's preferred activities, including, speculatively, cognitive processes such as silent speech or even silent ("interior") dialogue.

4. Goffman's influential partitioning of the speaker role into animator, author, and principal is suggestive but ultimately inadequate to account for the interplay of polyphonic voices, as when the implied voices of a ritual text meet the living voices of ritual participants. The hope to subsume Daniel's voicing under the rubric of a mere animation of Paul's (or Oswald Chambers's) words becomes still more difficult to sustain as the dialogic engagement unfolds. Yet promoting Daniel to author will not make the problem go away. What matters more, perhaps, is the tension between the animator and author roles, a tension that may be an integral component of the dialogic construction of social relations by processes of co-voicing. To the extent that they

help us articulate this tension, animator and author are provisionally useful categories, but they capture only a part of what is needed for a fully dialogic understanding of the participation framework within which ritual comes into being. The issue merits further examination in light of Irvine's (1996) critique of the Goffmanian participation model, Hanks's (1996) extension of the debate to embrace ritual, and so on.

5. Note also that vocalisms such as breathing and throat clearing are typically attributable to the self voice, regardless of how the line as a whole is labeled.

6. Although my primary concern here is with what Daniel makes of the text as he reads it aloud, one possible alternative reading of the original is worth mentioning. Close perusal of this passage suggests that Chambers intended the words *Oh but no one who is a Christian ever is* (line 46) as a representation, perhaps, of the imagined response of a prideful Christian, who boasts that the mere fact of being a Christian automatically protects one from error. The intrusion of the interjection *oh* into the written passage can be heard as evoking the language of direct quotation from an oral source (Heritage 2002), thus tending to support the view that this is a representation of the voice of an imagined reader, not of Paul. Chambers originally delivered his homilies as oral performances before audiences. His words were transcribed in real time by his wife, Biddy, a trained stenographer who later edited and published the texts posthumously. Whatever vocal cues might have been present in Chambers's original live performances to index the ventriloquated response of a misguided listener, they did not survive the transition to the printed page. Where Chambers scripted a heteroglossic positionality for the recalcitrant reader's "answering word" (Voloshinov 1973: 102), thereby introducing an additional layer of complexity into the participation frame, Daniel apparently misses the implicit cues signaling a shift in voicing and so attributes the words to Paul. This is the more understandable in that on this page of text, the use of quotation marks is otherwise reserved exclusively to signaling Biblical quotations.

7. For the sake of simplicity, I treat the complement clause following *Paul says* as Paul's utterance in his own voice. A more thorough treatment would take into consideration the many layers of complex metapragmatic embedding that are introduced by the present text's profoundly intertextual pedigree, implicating sources of the Bible, its transcriptions and translations, Oswald Chambers's lectures, Biddy Chambers's real-time transcriptions, her editing and posthumous publication of selections in the form of a devotional volume, and more. This is an interesting story, but not for this occasion.

References Cited

Abu-Lughod, Lila. 1986. *Veiled sentiments: Honor and poetry in a Bedouin society.* Berkeley: University of California Press.

Agblemagnon, F. N'sougan. 1969. *Sociologies des sociétes orales de l'afrique noire: Les Ewes de sud Togo.* The Hague: Mouton.

Agha, Asif. 1994. "Honorification." *Annual Review of Anthropology* 23: 277–302.

——. 2005a. "Semiosis across encounters." *Journal of Linguistic Anthropology* 15 (1): 1–5.

——. 2005b. "Voice, footing, enregisterment." *Journal of Linguistic Anthropology* 15 (1): 38–59.

—— and S. E. F. Wortham, eds. 2005. "Discourse across speech events: Intertextuality and interdiscursivity in social life." *Journal of Linguistic Anthropology* 15 (1): 1–150.

Agostinho da Silva, Pedro. 1974. *Mitos e outras narrativas Kamayura.* Bahia: Universidade Federal da Bahia, Coleção Ciência e Homem.

Aijmer, Karin. 1996. *Conversational routines in English: Convention and creativity.* London: Longman.

Aikhenvald, Alexandra. 2004. *Evidentiality.* Oxford: Oxford University Press.

Akindele, Femi. 1990. "A sociolinguistic analysis of Yoruba greetings." *African Languages and Cultures* 3: 1–14.

Albert, Bruce. 2000. "O ouro canibal e a queda do céu: Uma crítica xamânica da economia política da Natureza (Yanomami)." In *Pacificando o branco,* edited by Bruce Albert and Alcida Rita Ramos, 239–276. São Paulo: Editora UNESP.

Ali, Denny J. 2001. "Democratization from below: Protest events and regime change in Indonesia, 1997–1998." Ph.D. dissertation, Department of Political Science, Ohio State University.

Ameka, Felix K. 1987. "A comparative analysis of linguistic routines in two languages: English and Ewe." *Journal of Pragmatics* 11: 299–326.

——. 1992. "The meaning of phatic and conative interjections." *Journal of Pragmatics* 18: 245–271.

——. 1994. "Areal conversational routines and cross-cultural communication in a multilingual society." In *Intercultural communication: Proceedings of the 17th International LAUD Symposium, Diusburg 23–27 March 1992,* edited by H. Pürschel, 441–469. Bern: Peter Lang.

——. 1999. "'Partir c'est mourir un peu': Universal and culture specific features of leave-taking." *RASK International Journal of Language and Communication* 9 (10): 257–283.

——. 2004. "Grammar and cultural practices: The grammaticalisation of triadic communication in West African languages." *Journal of West African Languages* 30: 5–28.

——. 2006. "'When I die, don't cry': The ethnopragmatics of 'gratitude' expressions in West African languages." In *Ethnopragmatics: Understanding discourse in cultural context,* edited by Cliff Goddard, 231–266. Berlin: Mouton de Gruyter.

—— and Anneke Breedveld. 2004. "Areal cultural scripts for social interaction in West African communities." *Intercultural Pragmatics* 1: 167–187.

—— and James Essegbey. n.d. "Mido Evegbe." Manuscript.

Anderson, Benedict. 1983. *Imagined communities: Reflections on the origin and spread of nationalism.* London: Verso.

——. 1991. *Imagined communities: Reflections on the origin and spread of nationalism.* 2nd ed., London: Verso.

Arewa, E. Ojo, and Alan Dundes. 1964. "Proverbs and the ethnography of speaking folklore." *American Anthropologist* 66 (6), part 2: 70–85.

Ariel, Mira. 1998. "The linguistic status of the 'here and now.'" *Cognitive Linguistics* 9: 189–237.

Atran, Scott. 2002. *In gods we trust: The evolutionary landscape of religion.* New York: Oxford University Press.

Austin, John L. 1962. *How to do things with words.* Oxford: Clarendon Press.

Axelrod, Robert. 1984. *The evolution of cooperation.* New York: Basic Books.

Baars, Bernard J. 1997. *In the theater of consciousness: The workspace of the mind.* New York: Oxford University Press.

Bakhtin, Mikhail M. 1973 [1929]. *Problems of Dostoevsky's poetics.* Translated by C. Emerson. Minneapolis: University of Minnesota Press.

——. 1981 [1934]. *The dialogic imagination: Four essays.* Edited by Caryl Emerson and Michael Holquist. Austin: University of Texas Press.

——. 1986. *Speech genres and other late essays.* Austin: University of Texas Press.

Barnard, Timothy P., ed. 2004. *Contesting Malayness: Malay identity across boundaries.* Singapore: Singapore University Press.

Barth, Fredrik. 1993. *Balinese worlds.* Chicago: University of Chicago Press.

Basso, Ellen B. 1973. *The Kalapalo Indians of central Brazil.* New York: Holt, Rinehart and Winston.

——. 1985. *A musical view of the universe.* Philadelphia: University of Pennsylvania Press.

——. 1987. *In favor of deceit: A study of tricksters in an Amazonian society.* Tucson: University of Arizona Press.

——. 1993. "A Kalapalo testimonial." In *La remontée de l'Amazone: Anthropologie et histoire des sociétés amazoniennes,* edited by Phillipe Descola and Anne-Christine Taylor. *L'Homme* 33: 379–407.

——. 1995. *The last cannibals.* Austin: University of Texas Press.

——. 2003. "Translating 'self-cultivation.'" In *Translation and ethnography,* edited by Tullio Maranhão and Bernhard Streck, 85–101. Tuscon: University of Arizona Press.

——. 2007. "The Kalapalo affinal civility register." *Journal of Linguistic Anthropology* 17 (2): 161–183.

——. 2008. "Epistemic deixis in Kalapalo." *Pragmatics* 18: 215–252.

—— and Gunter Senft. 2006. "Ritual communication." Organizers' statement for Wenner-Gren conference held in Sintra, Portugal, March 16–23, 2007.

Bauman, Richard. 1977. *Verbal art as performance.* Prospect Heights, Ill.: Waveland Press.

——. 1983. *Let your words be few: Symbolism of speaking and silence among seventeenth-century Quakers.* Prospect Heights, Ill.: Waveland Press.

——. 1986. *Story performance and event.* Cambridge: Cambridge University Press.

——. 1992. "Performance." In *Folklore, cultural performances, and popular entertainments,* edited by Richard Bauman, 41–49. Oxford: Oxford University Press.

——. 2004. *A world of others' words: Cross-cultural perspectives on intertextuality.* Malden, Mass.: Blackwell.

——. 2005. "Commentary: Indirect indexicality, identity, performance. Dialogic observations." *Journal of Linguistic Anthropology* 15: 145–150.

—— and Charles Briggs. 1990. "Poetics and performance as critical perspectives on social life." *Annual Review of Anthropology* 19: 59–88.

Bauman, Zygmunt. 1995. *Life in fragments: Essays in postmodern morality.* Oxford: Blackwell.

Beatty, Andrew. 2004. "Ritual." In *The social science encyclopedia,* vol. 2, edited by J. Kuper, 888–891. London: Routledge.

Beier, Christine, Lev Michael, and Joel Sherzer. 2002. "Discourse forms and processes in indigenous lowland South America: An areal-typological perspective." *Annual Review of Anthropology* 31: 121–145.

Belzner, William. 1981. "Música, modernización y occidentalización entre los Shuar de Macuma." In *Amazonia ecuatoriana: La otra cara del progreso,* edited by Norman Whitten, 150–169. Quito: Abya-Yala.

Ben-Amos, Dan. 1969. "Analytical categories and ethnic genres." *Genre* 2: 275–301.

Benveniste, Emile. 1971 [1956]. *Problems in general linguistics.* Translated by Mary Elizabeth Meek. Miami: University of Miami Press.

Berger, Peter L., and Thomas Luckmann. 1966. *The social construction of reality: A treatise in the sociology of knowledge.* New York: Doubleday.

Bickerton, Derek. 1967. "Modes of interior monologue: A formal definition." *Modern Language Quarterly* 28: 229–239.

Bloch, Maurice. 1974. "Symbols, song, dance and features of articulation: Is religion an extreme form of traditional authority?" *European Journal of Sociology* 15: 55–81.

——. 1975a. "Introduction." In *Political language and oratory in traditional society,* edited by Maurice Bloch, 1–28. London: Academic Press.

—— ed. 1975b. *Political language and oratory in traditional society.* London: Academic Press.

——. 1986. *From blessing to violence: History and ideology in the circumcision ritual of the Merina of Madagascar.* Cambridge: Cambridge University Press.

Bloom, Paul. 2004. *Descartes' baby: How the science of child development explains what makes us human.* New York: Basic Books.

Booth, Anne. 1968. *Public protest in Indonesia.* Athens, Ohio: Ohio University Press.

Bourdieu, Pierre. 1977. *Outline of a theory of practice.* Cambridge: Cambridge University Press.

——. 1990. *The logic of practice.* Stanford, Calif.: Stanford University Press.

——. 1991. *Language and symbolic power.* Cambridge, Mass.: Harvard University Press.

Boyd, Robert, and Peter J. Richerson. 2005. *The origin and evolution of cultures.* New York: Oxford University Press.

——. 2006a. "Solving the puzzle of human cooperation." In *Evolution and culture,* edited by Stephen C. Levinson and Pierre Jaisson, 105–132. Cambridge, Mass.: MIT Press.

——. 2006b. "Culture and the evolution of the human social instincts." In *Roots of human sociality: Culture, cognition, and interaction,* edited by N. J. Enfield and Stephen C. Levinson, 453–477. Oxford: Berg.

Boyer, Pascal. 1994. *The naturalness of religious ideas: A cognitive theory of religion.* Berkeley: University of California Press.

——. 2002. *Religion explained: The human instincts that fashion gods, spirits, and ancestors.* London: Vintage.

Brenneis, Donald. 1984. "Straight talk and sweet talk: Political discourse in an occasionally egalitarian community." In *Dangerous words: Language and politics in the Pacific,* edited by Donald Brenneis and Fred Myers, 69–84. New York: New York University Press.

——. 1988. "Language and disputing." *Annual Review of Anthropology* 17: 221- 237.

——. 1996. "Telling troubles." In *Disorderly discourse: Narrative, conflict and inequality,* edited by Charles Briggs, 41–52. Oxford: Oxford University Press.

—— and Fred Myers, eds. 1984. *Dangerous words: Language and politics in the Pacific.* New York: New York University Press.

Bricker, Victoria R. 1974. "The ethnographic context of some traditional Mayan speech genres." In *Explorations in the ethnography of speaking,* edited by Richard Bauman and Joel Sherzer, 368–388. Cambridge: Cambridge University Press.

Briggs, Charles L. 1988. *Competence in performance. The creativity of tradition in Mexicano verbal art.* Philadelphia: University of Pennsylvania Press.

——. 1993. "Personal sentiments and polyphonic voices in Warao women's ritual wailing: Music and poetics in a critical and collective discourse." *American Anthropologist* 95: 929–957.

—— ed. 1996a. *Disorderly discourse: Narrative, conflict and inequality.* Oxford: Oxford University Press.

——. 1996b. "The politics of discursive authority in research on the 'invention of tradition.'" *Cultural Anthropology* 11: 435–469.

—— and Richard Bauman. 1992. "Genre, intertextuality, and social power." *Journal of Linguistic Anthropology* 2 (2): 131–172.

Brinkerhoff, Derick, and Arthur Goldsmith. 2002. *Clientelism, patrimonialism and democratic governance: An overview and framework for assessment and programming.* IQC no. AEP-I-00-00-00005-00, Task Order no. 4801-003-01. Cambridge, Mass.: Abt Associates.

Brody, Jill. 1991. "Indirection in the negotiation of self in everyday Tojolab'al women's conversation." *Journal of Linguistic Anthropology* 1: 78–96.

Brown, Michael. 1986. *Tsewa's gift: Magic and meaning in an Amazonian society.* Washington, D.C.: Smithsonian Institution Press.

Brown, Penelope. 1997. "Conversational structure and language acquisition: The role of repetition in Tzeltal adult and child speech." Paper presented at the annual meeting of the American Anthropological Association, Washington, D.C., Nov. 27.

—— and Stephen Levinson. 1978. "Universals in language usage: Politeness phenomena." In *Questions and politeness: Strategies in social interaction,* edited by Esther N. Goody, 256–289. Cambridge: Cambridge University Press.

Brown, R., and A. Gilman. 1960. "The pronouns of power and solidarity." In *Style in language,* edited by Thomas A. Sebeok, 253–276. Cambridge, Mass.: MIT Press.

Burgess, Anthony. 1962. *A clockwork orange.* London: William Heinemann.

Burke, Kenneth. 1950. *A rhetoric of motives.* New York: Prentice-Hall.

——. 1966. "What are the signs of what? (A theory of 'entitlement')." In Kenneth Burke, *Language as symbolic action: Essays on life, literature, and method,* 359–379. Berkeley: University of California Press. [Orig., *Anthropological Linguistics* 4 (6): 1–23 (1962); repr., *Anthropological Linguistics* 35 (1–4): 476–497 (1992).]

——. 1967. *Philosophy of literary form.* 2nd ed. Baton Rouge: University of Louisiana Press.

Bustamante, Teodoro. 1988. *La larga lucha del kakaram contra el Sucre.* Quito: Abya-Yala.

Byakutaaga, Shirley C. 1991. "Empaako: An agent of social harmony in Runyoro/Rutooro." *Afrikanistische Arbeitspapiere* 26: 127–140.

Cancian, Frank. 1965. *Economics and prestige in a Maya community: The religious cargo system in Zinacantan.* Stanford, Calif.: Stanford University Press.

——. 1992. *The decline of community in Zinacantán: Economy, public life, and social stratification, 1960–1987.* Stanford, Calif.: Stanford University Press.

Carsten, Janet, and Stephen Hugh-Jones. 1995. "Introduction: About the house. Lévi-Strauss and beyond." In *About the house: Lévi-Strauss and beyond,* edited by J. Carsten and S. Hugh-Jones, 1–46. Cambridge: Cambridge University Press.

Case, William. 2002. *Politics in Southeast Asia: Democracy more or less.* Richmond, U.K.: Curzon Press.

Casquete, Jesus. 2006. "Protest rituals and uncivil communities." *Totalitarian Movements and Political Religions* 7 (3): 283.

Caton, Steven C. 1986. "Salam tahiyah: Greetings from the highlands of Yemen." *American Ethnologist* 13: 290–308.

Čermák, František. 2004. "Text introducers of proverbs and other idioms." In *Phraseologismen als Gegenstand sprach- und kulturwissenschaftlicher Forschung,* edited by Csaba Földes and Jan Wirrer, 27–46. Hohengehren: Schneider Verlag.

Chafe, Wallace L. 1994. *Discourse, consciousness, and time: The flow and displacement of conscious experience in speaking and writing.* Chicago: University of Chicago Press.

Chambers, Oswald. 1935. *The golden book of Oswald Chambers: My utmost for His Highest; selections for the year.* New York: Dodd, Mead.

Charteris-Black, Jonathon. 1999. "The survival of English proverbs: A corpus-based account." *DeProverbio* 5 (2) www.deproverbio.com/DPjournal/DP,5,2,99/Black/survival.htm.

——. 2005. *Politicians and rhetoric: The persuasive power of metaphor.* Basingstoke, U.K.: Palgrave Macmillan.

Clark, John E. 2004. "Mesoamerica goes public: Early ceremonial centers, leaders, and communities." In *Mesoamerican archaeology: Theory and practice,* edited by Julia A. Hendon and Rosemary A. Joyce, 43–72. Oxford: Blackwell.

Cohn, Dorrit. 1978. *Transparent minds: Narrative modes for presenting consciousness in fiction.* Princeton, N.J.: Princeton University Press.

Comaroff, John, and Simon Roberts. 1981. *Rules and processes: The cultural logic of dispute in an African context.* Chicago: University of Chicago Press.

Conrich, Ian, and Estella Tincknell, eds. 2006. *New Zealand fictions: Literature and film.* New Zealand: Kakapo Books.

Couvreur, A. J. L. 1914. Memorie Van Overgave. Afdeeling Soemba [Memoires]. Unpublished archival material. Zug, Switzerland: Interdocumentation.

Cowie, A. P., ed. 1998. *Phraseology: Theory, analysis, and applications.* Oxford: Clarendon Press.

Damon, Frederick H. 1982. "Calendars and calendrical rites in the northern side of the Kula ring." *Oceania* 52: 221–239.

Danielson, Peter. 1998. *Modeling rationality, morality, and evolution.* New York: Oxford University Press.

De Haan, Ferdinand. 1999. "Evidentiality and epistemic modality: Setting boundaries." *Southwest Journal of Linguistics* 18: 83–102.

——. 2001. "Encoding speaker perspective: Evidentials." *Language Diversity and Linguistic Theories Symposium Proceedings: Linguistische Berichte, Sonderheft* 9: 201–216.

Déléage, Pierre. 2007. "A Yaminahua autobiographical song: Caqui caqui." *Tipití: Journal of the Society for the Anthropology of Lowland South America* 5: 79–95.

Descola, Philippe. 1986. *La nature domestique: Symbolisme et praxis dans l'écologie des Achuar.* Paris: Editions de la Maisons des Sciences de l'Homme.

——. 1996. "Constructing natures: Symbolic ecology and social practice." In *Nature and society: Anthropological perspectives,* edited by Phillipe Descola and Gisli Pálsson, 82–102. London: Routledge.

——. 1997. *The spears of the twilight: Life and death in the Amazon jungle.* London: Flamingo.

——. 2000. "Un dialogue entre lexiques." In *Les rituels du dialogue: Promenades ethnolinguistiques en terres Amérindiennes,* edited by Aurore Monod Becquelin and Philippe Erikson, 313–327. Nanterre: Société d'Ethnologie.

Devereaux, Leslie. 1995. "Experience, re-presentation, and film." In *Fields of vision: Essays in film studies, visual anthropology, and photography,* edited by Leslie Devereaux and Roger Hillman, 56–73. Berkeley: University of California Press.

Ding Choo Ming and Abdul Rahman Arba'eyah. 2002. "Daripada Kamus Peribahasa Melayu Digital ATMA kepada Perkamusan Bahasa Berkomputer." *Dewan Bahasa* (July): 48–59.

Dixon, R. M. W. 1971. "A method of semantic description." In *Semantics: An interdisciplinary reader in philosophy, linguistics and psychology,* edited by D. Steinberg and L. A. Jakobovits, 436–471. Cambridge: Cambridge University Press.

Du Bois, John W. 1986. "Self-evidence and ritual speech." In *Evidentiality: The linguistic coding of epistemology,* edited by Wallace L. Chafe and Johanna Nichols, 313–336. Norwood, N.J.: Ablex.

——. 1993. "Meaning without intention: Lessons from divination." In *Responsibility and evidence in oral discourse,* edited by Jane H. Hill and Judith T. Irvine, 48–71. Cambridge: Cambridge University Press.

——. 2007. "The stance triangle." In *Stancetaking in discourse: Subjectivity, evaluation, interaction,* edited by Robert Englebretson, 139–182. Amsterdam: John Benjamins.

——. forthcoming. "Co-opting intersubjectivity: Dialogic rhetoric of the self." In *The rhetorical emergence of culture,* edited by Christian Meyer and Felix Girke. Oxford: Berghahn.

——. n.d. "Representing discourse." Manuscript, Department of Linguistics, University of California, Santa Barbara. Excerpts available at www.linguistics.ucsb.edu/projects/transcription/representing.

—— Stephan Schuetze-Coburn, Susanna Cumming, and Danae Paolino. 1993. "Outline of discourse transcription." In *Talking data: Transcription and coding in discourse research,* edited by J. A. Edwards and M. D. Lampert, 45–89. Hillsdale, N.J.: Erlbaum.

Duranti, Alessandro. 1981. *The Samoan fono: A sociolinguistic study.* Canberra: Pacific Linguistics.

——. 1985. "Socio-cultural dimensions of discourse." In *Handbook of discourse analysis,* vol. 1: *Disciplines of discourse,* edited by Teun van Dijk, 193–230. New York: Academic Press.

——. 1997. "Universal and culture-specific properties of greetings." *Journal of Linguistic Anthropology* 7: 63–97.

Durkheim, Emil. 1915. *The elementary forms of the religious life.* Translated by J. W. Swain. London: Allen and Unwin.

——. 1982 [1895]. *The rules of sociological method.* London: Macmillan.

Dzameshie, Alex K. 2002. "The forms, functions and social value of greetings among the Ewes." In *New directions in Ghanaian linguistics,* edited by Felix K. Ameka and E. Kweku Osam, 381–408. Accra: Black Mask.

Egblewogbe, Eustace Y. 1990. "Social and psychological aspects of greeting among the Ewes of West Africa." *Research Review* (n.s.) 6: 8–18.

Eibl-Eibesfeldt, Irenäus. 1984. *Die Biologie des menschlichen Verhaltens: Grundriß der Humanethologie.* Munich: Piper.

——. 1989. *Human ethology: Foundations of human behavior.* New York: Aldine de Gruyter.

—— and Gunter Senft. 1987. *Studienbrief Rituelle Kommunikation.* FernUniversitat Gesamthochschule Hagen, Fachbereich Erziehungs- und Sozialwissenschaften, Soziologie, Kommunikation—Wissen Kultur.

Enfield, N. J. 2009. *The anatomy of meaning: Speech, gesture, and composite utterances.* Cambridge: Cambridge University Press.

—— and Gérard Diffloth. 2009. *Phonology and sketch grammar of Kri, a Vietic language of Laos.* Cahiers de Linguistique—Asie Orientale 38, no. 1.

Evans-Pritchard, E. E. 1940. *The Nuer: A description of the modes of livelihood and political institutions of a Nilotic people.* Oxford: Oxford University Press.

Fabian, Johannes. 1994. "Jamaa: A charismatic movement revisited." In *Religion in Africa: Experience and expression,* edited by Thomas Blakely, Walter van Beek, and Dennis Thomson, 257–274. London: James Currey.

Feld, Steven. 1982. *Sound and sentiment: Birds, weeping, poetics, and song in Kaluli expression.* Philadelphia: University of Pennsylvania Press.

Ferguson, James. 1999. *Expectations of modernity: Myths and meanings of urban life on the Zambian Copperbelt.* Berkeley: University of California Press.

Fields, Chris. 2002. "Why do we talk to ourselves?" *Journal of Experimental and Theoretical Artificial Intelligence* 14: 255–272.

Finnegan, Ruth. 1969. "How to do things with words: Performative utterances among the Limba of Sierra Leone." *Man* 4: 59–69.

Firth, Raymond. 1967. *Tikopia ritual and belief.* London: Allen and Unwin.

——. 1972. "Verbal and bodily rituals of greeting and parting." In *The interpretation of ritual: Essays in honour of A. I. Richards,* edited by J. S. La Fontaine, 1–38. London: Tavistock.

Földes, Csaba, and Jan Wirrer, eds. 2004. *Phraseologismen als Gegenstand sprach- und kulturwissenschaftlicher Forschung.* Hohengehren: Schneider Verlag.

Foley, William A. 1997. *Anthropological linguistics.* Oxford: Blackwell.

Fortes, Meyer. 1966. "Religious premisses and logical technique in divinatory ritual." *Philosophical Transactions of the Royal Society of London, Series B, Biological Sciences* 251 (772): 409–422.

Foucault, Michel. 1988. "Technologies of the self." In *Technologies of the self: A seminar with Michel Foucault,* edited by L. H. Martin, H. Gutman, and P. H. Hutton, 16–49. Amherst: University of Massachusetts Press.

Fox, James. 1974. "'Our ancestors spoke in pairs': Rotinese views of language, dialect, and code." In *Explorations in the ethnography of speaking,* edited by Richard Bauman and Joel Sherzer, 65–85. Cambridge: Cambridge University Press.

——. 1977. "Roman Jakobson and the comparative study of parallelism." In *Roman Jakobson: Echos of his scholarship,* edited by D. Armstrong and C. H. van Schooneveld, 59–90. Lisse: Peter de Ridder.

Frake, Charles O. 1975. "How to enter a Yakan house." In *Sociocultural dimensions of language use,* edited by M. Sanches and B. G. Blount, 25–40. New York: Academic Press.

Franchetto, Bruna. 1983. "A fala do chefe: Generos verbais entre os Kuikuru do Alto Xingu." *Candernos de Estudos Linguisticos* 4: 4–72. Campinas, Brazil.

——. 2000. "Rencontres rituelles dans le Haut-Xingu: La parole du chef." In *Les rituelles du dialogue,* edited by Aurore Monod Becquelin and Philippe Erikson, 481–510. Nanterre: Societe d'Ethnologie.

——. 2001. "Línguas e história no Alto Xingu." In *Os Povos do Alto Xingu: História e cultura,* edited by Bruna Franchetto and Michael Heckenberger, translated by Cesar Gordon Jr., 111–156. Rio de Janeiro: Editora Universidade Federal Rio de Janeiro.

——. n.d. "Les marques de la parole vraie en Kuikuro, langue Caribe du Haut Xingu (Bresil)." Manuscript (www.AILLA.texas.org).

French, D. H., and K. S. French. 1998. "Wasco, Wishram, and Cascades." In *Handbook of North American Indians,* vol. 12, *Plateau,* edited by Deward E. Walker Jr., 360–377. Washington, D.C.: Smithsonian Institution.

Galvão, Eduardo. 1953. *Cultura e sistema de parentesco das tribos do Alto-Xingu.* Boletim do Museu Naciuonal, n.s., vol. 14.

Gándara, Lelia. 2004. "'They that sow the wind…': Proverbs and sayings in argumentation." *Discourse and Society* 15: 345–359.

Gaonkar, Dilip Parameshwar. 2002. "Toward new imaginaries: An introduction." *Public Culture* 14: 1–19.

Garfinkel, Harold. 1967. *Studies in ethnomethodology.* Englewood Cliffs, N.J.: Prentice-Hall.

Geertz, Clifford. 1957. "Ritual and social change: A Javanese example." *American Anthropologist* 59: 32–54.

——. 1966. "Religion as a cultural system." In *Anthropological approaches to the study of religion,* edited by Michael Banton, 1–46. London: Tavistock.

——. 1973. "Deep play: Notes on the Balinese cockfight." In Clifford Geertz, *The interpretation of cultures,* 412–453. New York: Basic Books

Gergely, György, and Gergely Csibra. 2006. "Sylvia's recipe: The role of imitation and pedagogy in the transmission of cultural knowledge." In *Roots of human sociality: Culture, cognition, and interaction,* edited by N. J. Enfield and S. C. Levinson. Oxford: Berg.

Gibson, James J. 1979. *The ecological approach to visual perception.* Boston: Houghton Mifflin.

Gluckman, Max. 1954. *Rituals of rebellion in south-east Africa.* Manchester: Manchester University Press.

——. 1958. *Analysis of a social situation in modern Zululand.* Rhodes-Livingstone Institute, Paper 28.

——. 1963. "Rituals of rebellion in south-east Africa." In Max Gluckman, *Order and rebellion in tribal Africa: The Fraser lecture,* 110–136. Manchester: Manchester University Press.

Gnerre, Maurizio. 1984. "Shuar de contacto y español de contacto." In *Relaciones interétnicas y adaptación cultural entre Shuar y Achuar,* 211–226. Quito: Mundo Shuar.

——. 1986. "The decline of dialogue." In *Native South American discourse,* edited by Joel Sherzer and Greg Urban, 307–341. New York: Mouton de Gruyter.

——. 1999a. "*Ii jinti—Our way*: An English textbook from the Amazon." *Anglistica* 7: 59–78.

——. 1999b. *Profilo descrittivo e storico-comparativo di una lingua amazzonica: Lo Shuar (Jívaro).* Naples: Istituto Universitario Orientale.

——. 2000a. "Cazando sapos: El triste humorismo de un diálogo Shuar." In *Les rituels du dialogues: Promenades ethnolinguistiques en terres Amérindiennes,* edited by Aurore Monod Becquelin and Philippe Erikson, 285–311. Nanterre: Société d'Ethnologie.

——. 2000b. "From head-hunters to writers: A Shuar myth and an oration." In *Translating native Latin American verbal art,* edited by Kay Sammons and Joel Sherzer, 197–210. Washington, D.C.: Smithsonian Institution Press.

——. 2003. "La história semántica de la voz *huaca.*" In *Il sacro e il paesaggio nell'America indigena,* edited by Davide Domenici, Carolina Orsini, and Sofia Venturoli, 371–384. Bologna: CLUEB.

——. 2007. "'Io,' agentività e genere nelle modalità comunicative shuar (Amazzonia)." In *Agency e linguaggio: Etnoteorie della soggettività e della responsabilità nell'azione sociale,* edited by Aurora Donzelli and Alessandra Fasulo, 113–141. Rome: Meltemi editore.

Goddard, Cliff. 1998. *Semantic analysis.* Oxford: Oxford University Press.

——. 2000. "'Cultural scripts' and communicative style in Malay (Bahasa Melayu)." *Anthropological Linguistics* 42: 81–106.

——. 2002. "Ethnosyntax, ethnopragmatics, sign-functions, and culture." In *Ethnosyntax: Explorations in grammar and culture,* edited by N. J. Enfield, 52–73. Oxford: Oxford University Press.

——. 2004. "The ethnopragmatics and semantics of 'active metaphors.'" *Journal of Pragmatics* 36: 1211–1230.

—— ed. 2006. *Ethnopragmatics: Understanding discourse in cultural context.* Berlin: Mouton de Gruyter.

—— ed. 2008. *Cross-linguistic semantics.* Amsterdam: John Benjamins.

——. n.d. "'Follow the way of the rice plant': The semantics of proverbs in English and Malay (Bahasa Melayu)." Manuscript submitted for publication.

—— and Anna Wierzbicka, eds. 2002. *Meaning and universal grammar: Theory and empirical findings.* 2 vols. Amsterdam: John Benjamins.

—— and Anna Wierzbicka, eds. 2004. *Special Issue on Cultural Scripts.* Intercultural Pragmatics 1 (2).

Goffman, Erving. 1959. *The presentation of self in everyday life.* New York: Doubleday.

——. 1963. *Stigma: Notes on the management of spoiled identity.* New York: Simon and Schuster.
——. 1967. *Interaction ritual: Essays on face-to-face behavior.* New York: Doubleday.
——. 1971. *Relations in public: Microstudies of the public order.* Harmondsworth, U.K.: Penguin.
——. 1974. *Frame analysis: An essay on the organization of experience.* New York: Harper and Row.
——. 1976. "Replies and responses." *Language in Society* 5: 257–313.
——. 1978. "Response cries." *Language* 54: 787–815.
——. 1981a. *Forms of talk.* Philadelphia: University of Pennsylvania Press.
——. 1981b. "Footing." In Erving Goffman, *Forms of talk,* 124–159. Philadelphia: University of Pennsylvania Press.
——. 1983. "The interaction order." *American Sociological Review* 48: 1–17.
Goodwin, Charles. 1986. "Between and within: Alternative sequential treatments of continuers and assessments." *Human Studies* 9: 205–217.
—— and Marjorie Harness Goodwin. 1987. "Concurrent operations on talk: Notes on the interactive organization of assessments." *IPrA Papers in Pragmatics* 1: 1–52.
Goody, Esther N. 1972. "'Greeting,' 'begging' and the presentation of respect." In *The interpretation of ritual,* edited by J. S. La Fontaine, 39–72. London: Tavistock.
Gossen, Gary H. 1973. "Chamula Tzotzil proverbs: Neither fish nor fowl." In *Meaning in Mayan languages,* edited by Munro S. Edmonson, 207–233. The Hague: Mouton.
——. 1974a. *Chamulas in the world of the sun: Time and space in a Maya oral tradition.* Cambridge, Mass.: Harvard University Press.
——. 1974b. "To speak with a heated heart: Chamula canons of style and good performance." In *Explorations in the ethnography of speaking,* edited by Richard Bauman and Joel Sherzer, 389–413. Cambridge: Cambridge University Press.
——. 1985. "Tzotzil literature." In *Supplement to the Handbook of Middle American Indians,* vol. 3, edited by Victoria R. Bricker and Munro Edmonson, 65–106. Austin: University of Texas Press.
Graham, Laura. 1995. *Performing dreams: Discourses of immortality among the Xavante of Central Brazil.* Austin: University of Texas Press.
——. 2005. "Indigeneity and instrumentality." *American Ethnologist* 64: 622–641.

Gregor, Thomas. 1976. *Mehinaku: The drama of daily life in a Brazilian Indian village.* Chicago: University of Chicago Press.

——. 2001. "Casamento, aliança e paz intertribal." In *Os Povos do Alto Xingu: História e cultura,* edited by Bruna Franchetto and Michael Heckenberger, translated by Cesar Gordon Jr., 175–192. Rio de Janeiro: Editora Universidade Federal Rio de Janeiro.

Grünberg, Georg. 2004. *Os Kaiabi do Brasil central.* São Paulo: Instituto Socioambiental.

Gumperz, John J., and Dell Hymes, eds. 1972. *Directions in sociolinguistics: The ethnography of communication.* New York: Holt, Rinehart and Winston.

Günthner, Susanne. 1999. "Polyphony and the 'layering of voices' in reported dialogues: An analysis of the use of prosodic devices in everyday reported speech." *Journal of Pragmatics* 31: 685–708.

Hancher, Michael. 1979. "The classification of cooperative illocutionary acts." *Language in Society* 8 (1): 1–14.

Handelman, Don. 1988. *Models and mirrors: Towards an anthopology of public events.* Oxford: Oxford University Press.

Hanks, William F. 1990. *Referential practice: Language and lived space among the Maya.* Chicago: University of Chicago Press.

——. 1996. "Exorcism and the description of participant roles." In *Natural histories of discourse,* edited by Michael Silverstein and Greg Urban, 160–202. Chicago: University of Chicago Press.

——. 2000. Dialogic conversions and the field of missionary discourse in colonial Yucatan. In *Les rituels du dialogue: Promenades ethnolinguistiques en terres Amérindiennes,* edited by Aurore Monod Becquelin and Philippe Erikson, 235–254. Nanterre: Société d'Ethnologie.

——. 2005. "Pierre Bourdieu and the practices of language." *Annual Review of Anthropology* 43: 67–83.

——. 2006. "Joint commitment and common ground in a ritual event." In *Roots of human sociality: Culture, cognition and human interaction,* edited by N. J. Enfield and Stephen C. Levinson, 299–328. Oxford: Berg.

Harner, Michael. 1972. *The Jívaro: People of the sacred waterfalls.* Garden City, N.Y.: Anchor Books.

Hasan-Rokem, Galit. 1992. "Proverb." In *Folklore, cultural performances, and popular entertainments: A communications-centered handbook,* edited by Richard Bauman, 128–133. New York: Oxford University Press.

Haugerud, Angelique. 1995. *The culture of politics in modern Kenya.* Cambridge: Cambridge University Press.

—— and Kimani Njogu. 1991. "State voices in the countryside: Politics and the Kenyan baraza." *Working Papers in African Studies* 159. Boston University African Studies Center.

Hauser, Marc D. 2006. "Moral ingredients: How we evolved the capacity to do the right thing." In *Evolution and culture,* edited by Stephen C. Levinson and Pierre Jaisson, 119–145. Cambridge, Mass.: MIT Press.

Haviland, John B. 1967. "Vob: Traditional instrumental music in Zinacantan." Harvard Chiapas Project. Manuscript.

——. 1977a. "Gossip as competition in Zinacantan." *Journal of Communication* 27: 186–191.

——. 1977b. *Gossip, reputation, and knowledge in Zinacantan.* Chicago: University of Chicago Press.

——. 1988. "A father-mother talks back: The micro-creation of context in Tzotzil." Paper presented at the workshop "Contextualization of Language," Konstanz, Germany, October.

——. 1993. *Merolicos.* Paper presented at the annual meeting of the American Ethnological Society, Santa Fe, N.M., April 16.

——. 1994. "Lenguaje ritual sin ritual." *Estudios de Cultura Maya* 19: 427–442.

——. 1996. ""We want to borrow your mouth": Tzotzil marital squabbles." In *Disorderly discourse: Narrative, conflict, and inequality,* edited by Charles L. Briggs, 158–203. New York: Oxford UNiversity Press.

——. 1998. ""Mu'nuk jbankil to, mu'nuk kajvaltik; He is not my older brother, he is not Our Lord": Thirty years of gossip in a Chiapas village." *Etnofoor* 11: 57–82.

——. 2000. "Warding off witches: Voicing and dialogue in Zinacantec prayer." In *Les rituels du dialogue: Promenades ethnolinguistiques en terres amérindiennes,* edited by Aurore Monod-Becquelin and Philippe Erikson, 367–400. Nanterre: Société d'ethnologie.

——. 2005a. "'Whorish old man' and 'One (animal) gentleman': The intertextual construction of enemies and selves." *Journal of Linguistic Anthropology* 15: 81–94.

——. 2005b. "Selling with fear: Merolicos in Mexico." Paper presented at the conference "Language and Text Variation in Business and Economics," University of Florence, Feb. 3.

Heckenberger, Michael J. 2005. *The ecology of power: Culture, place, and personhood in the southern Amazon,* A.D. *1000–2000.* New York: Routledge.

Heeschen, Volker. 1987. "Rituelle Kommunikation in verschiedenen Kulturen." *Zeitschrift für Literaturwissenschaft und Linguistik* 17: 82–104.

Henare, Manuka. 2008. "On an economy of mana." Paper presented at a round-table discussion, European Society for Oceanists conference, Verona.

Hereniko, Vilsoni. 1995. *Woven gods: Female clowns and power in Rotuma.* Suva, Fiji: University of Hawaii Press/Center for Pacific Islands Studies.

Heritage, John. 2002. "*Oh*-prefaced responses to assessments: A method of modifying agreement/disagreement." In *The language of turn and sequence,* edited by C. E. Ford, B. A. Fox, and S. A. Thompson, 196–224. Oxford: Oxford University Press.

Herzfeld, Michael. 1985. *The poetics of manhood: Contest and identity in a Cretan mountain village.* Princeton, N.J.: Princeton University Press.

Heywood, John. 1972 [1546]. *The proverbs of John Heywood, being the "Proverbes" of that author printed 1546.* Edited by Julian Sharman. Folcroft, Pa.: Folcroft Library Editions.

Higbee, Kenneth L., and Richard Millard. 1983. "Visual imagery and familiarity ratings for 203 sayings." *American Journal of Psychology* 96: 211–222.

Hill, Jane H. 2002. "'Expert rhetorics' in advocacy for endangered languages: Who is listening, and what do they hear?" *Journal of Linguistic Anthropology* 12: 119–133.

——. 2005. "Intertextuality as source and evidence for indirect indexical meanings." *Journal of Linguistic Anthropology* 15: 113–125.

Hill, Jonathan D. 1993. *Keepers of the sacred chants.* Tucson: University of Arizona Press.

Hill, Warren D., and John E. Clark. 2001. "Sports, gambling, and government: America's first social compact?" *American Anthropologist* 103: 331–345.

Hirsch, Susan. 1998. *Pronouncing and persevering: Gender and the discourses of disputing in an African Islamic court.* Chicago: University of Chicago Press.

Hirschkind, Charles. 2006. *The ethical soundscape: Cassette sermons and Islamic counterpublics.* New York: Columbia University Press.

Hobsbawm, Eric J. 1959. *Primitive rebels: Studies in archaic forms of social movements in the nineteenth and twentieth centuries.* Manchester: Manchester University Press.

—— and Terence Ranger, eds. 1992. *The invention of tradition.* Cambridge: Cambridge University Press.

Hoëm, Ingjerd. 1995. "A sense of place: The politics of identity and representation." Ph.D. dissertation, University of Oslo.

——. 1998. "Clowns, dignity and desire: On performance, reflexivity and identity." In *Revising ritual: Performance, media, identity,* edited by Felicia Hughes-Freeland and Mary Crain, 21–43. London: Routledge.

——. 2004. *Theater and political process: Staging identities in Tokelau and New Zealand.* Oxford: Berghahn.

Howe, Leo. 2000. "Risk, ritual and performance." *Journal of the Royal Anthropological Institute* (n.s.) 6: 63–79.

Humphrey, Robert. 1954. *Stream of consciousness in the modern novel.* Berkeley: University of California Press.

Hutchins, Edwin. 1995. *Cognition in the wild.* Cambridge, Mass.: MIT Press.

Huxley, Sir Julian, ed. 1966a. *A discussion on ritualization of behavior in animals and man organized by Sir Julian Huxley.* Philosophical Transactions of the Royal Society of London, Series B, Biological Sciences 251, no. 772.

——. 1966b. "Introduction." In *A discussion on ritualization of behavior in animals and man organized by Sir Julian Huxley.* Philosophical Transactions of the Royal Society of London, Series B, Biological Sciences 251, no. 772, 249–271.

Hymes, Dell. 1968. "The ethnography of speaking." In *Readings in the sociology of language,* edited by Joshua A. Fishman, 99–138. The Hague: Mouton.

——. 1972. "Models of the interaction of language and social life." In *Directions in sociolinguistics,* edited by John J. Gumperz and Dell Hymes, 35–71. New York: Holt, Rinehart and Winston.

Inomata, Takeshi. 2006. "Plazas, performers, and spectators: Political theaters of the Classic Maya." *Current Anthropology* 47: 805–842.

Ireland, Emilienne M. 2001. "Noções Waurá de humanidade e identidade cultural." In *Os Povos do Alto Xingu: História e cultura,* edited by Bruna Franchetto and Michael Heckenberger, translated by Cesar Gordon Jr., 250–286. Rio de Janeiro: Editora Universidade Federal Rio de Janeiro.

Irvine, Judith T. 1974. "Strategies of status manipulation in the Wolof greeting." In *Explorations in the ethnography of speaking,* edited by Richard Baumann and Joel Sherzer, 167–191. Cambridge: Cambridge University Press.

——. 1979. "Formality and informality in communicative events." *American Anthropologist* 81 (4): 773–790.

——. 1996. "Shadow conversations: The indeterminacy of participant roles." In *Natural histories of discourse,* edited by Michael Silverstein and Greg Urban, 131–159. Chicago: University of Chicago Press.

——. 2005. "Knots and tears in the interdiscursive fabric." *Linguistic Anthropology* 15: 72–80.

Iser, Wolfgang. 1978. *The act of reading: A theory of aesthetic response.* London: Routledge.

Jackson, Michael, and Ivan Karp. 1990. "Introduction." In *Personhood and agency: The experience of self and other in African cultures,* edited by Michael Jackson and Ivan Karp. Uppsala: Uppsala University.

Jakobson, Roman. 1960. "Closing statement: Linguistics and poetics." In *Style in language,* edited by Thomas A. Sebeok, 350–377. Cambridge, Mass.: MIT Press.

——. 1971. "Shifters, verbal categories and the Russian verb." In Roman Jakobson, *Selected writings II,* 130–147. The Hague: Mouton.

James, William. 1902. *The varieties of religious experience: A study in human nature.* New York: Longman Green.

Jasper, James M. 1997. *The art of moral protest: Culture, biography, and creativity in social movements.* Chicago: University of Chicago Press.

Joyce, Richard. 2006. *The evolution of morality.* Cambridge, Mass.: MIT Press.

Juris, Jeffrey S. 2005. "Violence performed and imagined: Militant action, the black bloc and the mass media in Genoa." *Critique of Anthropology* 25 (4): 413–432.

Kahin, George M. 1949. "Indirect rule in East Indonesia." *Pacific Affairs* 22 (3): 227–238.

Kahn, Joel S. 2006. *Other Malays: Nationalism and cosmopolitanism in the modern Malay world.* Singapore: Singapore University Press/ Copenhagen: NIAS Press.

Kapferer, Bruce. 1983. *A celebration of demons.* Bloomington: Indiana University Press.

——. 1986. "Performance and the structuring of meaning and experience." In *The anthropology of experience,* edited by Victor Turner and Edward Bruner, 188–203. Urbana: University of Illinois Press.

Karp, Ivan. 1987. "Laughter at marriage: Subversion in performance." In *Transformations of African marriage,* edited by David Parkin and David Nyamwaya, 137–153. Manchester: Manchester University Press.

Keane, Webb. 1997a. "Religious language." *Annual Review of Anthropology* 26: 47–71.

——. 1997b. "From fetishism to sincerity: On agency, the speaking subject, and their historicity in the context of religious conversion." *Comparative Studies in Society and History* 39: 674–693.

——. 1997c. *Signs of recognition: Powers and hazards of representation in an Indonesian society.* Berkeley: University of California Press.

——. 1999. "Voice." *Journal of Linguistic Anthropology* 9: 271–273.

——. 2002. "Sincerity, 'modernity,' and the Protestants." *Cultural Anthropology* 17: 65–92.

Kecskes, Istvan. 2003. *Situation-bound utterances in L1 and L2*. Berlin: Mouton de Gruyter.
Keenan, Eleanor. 1974. "Norm makers, norm breakers: Uses of speech by men and women in a Malagasy community." In *Explorations in the ethnography of speaking*, edited by R. Bauman and J. Sherzer. Cambridge: Cambridge University Press.
Keesing, Roger. 1992. *Custom and confrontation: Kwaio struggle for cultural autonomy*. Chicago: University of Chicago Press.
Kelly, John D., and Martha Kaplan. 1990. "History, structure, and ritual." *Annual Review of Anthropology* 19: 119–150.
Kershaw, Baz. 1997. "Fighting in the streets: Dramaturgies of popular protest, 1968–1989." *New Theatre Quarterly* 13 (51): 255–276.
Kessler, Clive, Joel S. Kahn, and Francis Loh Wok Wah, eds. 1992. *Fragmented vision: Culture and politics in contemporary Malaysia*. Sydney: Allen and Unwin.
Key, Catherine A., and Leslie C. Aiello. 1999. "The evolution of social organization." In *The evolution of culture: An interdisciplinary view*, edited by Robin I. M. Dunbar, Chris Knight, and Camilla Power, 15–33. New Brunswick, N.J.: Rutgers University Press.
Knight, Chris D. 1999. "Sex and language as pretend play." In *The evolution of culture: An interdisciplinary view*, edited by Robin I. M. Dunbar, Chris D. Knight, and Camilla Power, 228–247. Edinburgh : Edinburgh University Press.
—— Robin I. M. Dunbar, and Camilla Power. 1999. "An evolutionary approach to human culture." In *The evolution of culture: An interdisciplinary view*, edited by Robin I. M. Dunbar, Chris Knight, and Camilla Power, 1–11. New Brunswick, N.J.: Rutgers University Press.
—— Camilla Power, and Ian Watts. 1995. "The human symbolic revolution: A Darwinian account." *Cambridge Archaeological Journal* 5: 75–114.
Kockelman, Paul. 2004. "Stance and subjectivity." *Journal of Linguistic Anthropology* 14 (2): 127–150.
——. 2006. "Residence in the world: Affordances, instruments, actions, roles, and identities." *Semiotica* 162: 19–71.
——. 2007. "Agency: The relation between meaning, power, and knowledge." *Current Anthropology* 48: 375–401.
Kratz, Corinne A. 1981. "Are the Okiek really Masai? or Kipsigis? or Kikuyu?" *Cahiers d'Études Africaines* 79 (XX, 3): 355–368.
——. 1982. "Language and communication in ritual contexts." Manuscript.

——. 1986. "Ethnic interaction, economic diversification and language use: A report on research with Kaplelach and Kipchornwonek Okiek." *Sprache und Geschichte in Afrika* 7: 189–226.

——. 1987. "Chords of tradition, lens of analogy: Iconic signs in Okiek ceremonies." *Journal of Ritual Studies* 1: 75–96.

——. 1988a. "The unending ceremony and a warm house: Representation of a patriarchal ideal and the silent complementarity in Okiek blessings." In *Property, power and ideology in hunting and gathering societies,* edited by James Woodburn, Tim Ingold, and David Riches, 215–248. Oxford: Berg.

——. 1988b. "Emotional power and significant movement: Womanly transformation in Okiek initiation." Ph.D. dissertation. University of Texas, Austin.

——. 1989. "Genres of power: A comparative analysis of Okiek blessings, curses and oaths." *Man* (n.s.) 24: 299–317.

——. 1990. "Sexual solidarity and the secrets of sight and sound: Shifting gender relations and their ceremonial constitution." *American Ethnologist* 17 (3): 31–51.

——. 1993. "We've always done it like this ... except for a few details: 'Tradition' and 'innovation' in Okiek ceremonies." *Comparative Studies in Society and History* 35: 30–65.

——. 1994. *Affecting peformance: Meaning, movement, and experience in Okiek women's initiation.* Washington, D.C.: Smithsonian Institution Press.

——. 2000. "Forging unions and negotiating ambivalence: Personhood and complex agency in Okiek marriage arrangement." In *African philosophy and cultural inquiry,* edited by Dismas Masolo and Ivan Karp, 136–171. Bloomington: Indiana University Press.

——. 2005a. "Kinship in action: Managing uncertainty in Okiek marriage arrangement." Paper presented at the conference "Imagining Kinship," University of Michigan, Ann Arbor, March 19–20.

——. 2005b. "Wild bees, hairless cows, and hidden enemies: Imagining relatedness and fate in Okiek marriage arrangement." Manuscript.

——. 2007. "Uncertainties and transformations in Okiek marriage arrangement." Paper presented at the conference "Place versus Path: Reconfiguring Nomads to Fit the State," University of Bergen, Norway, June 7–10.

——. n.d. "Looking for the hairless cow: Arranging Okiek marriage." Book manuscript in preparation.

Krebs, John R., and Richard Dawkins. 1984. "Animal signals: Mindreading and manipulation." In *Behavioural ecology: An evolutionary approach,* 2nd ed., edited by J. R. Krebs and N. B. Davies, 380–405. London: Blackwell.

Kropp Dakubu, Mary Esther. 1981. *One voice: The linguistic culture of an Accra lineage.* Leiden: African Studies Centre.

——. 1987. "Creating unity: The context of speaking prose and poetry in Ga." *Anthropos* 82: 507–527.

Kroskrity, Paul V. 1998. "Arizona Tewa kiva speech as a manifestation of a dominant language ideology." In *Language ideologies: Practice and theory,* edited by B. B. Schieffelin, K. A. Woolard, and P. V. Kroskrity, 103–122. Oxford: Oxford University Press.

Kuipers, Joel C. 1990. *Power in performance: The creation of textual authority in Weyewa ritual speech.* Philadelphia: University of Pennsylvania Press.

——. 1998. *Language, identity, and marginality in Indonesia: The changing nature of ritual speech on the island of Sumba.* Cambridge: Cambridge University Press.

——. n.d. "Personal names and changing modes of inscribing identity in Sumba, eastern Indonesia: 'Bloody Thursday' in linguistic and social context." In *Asian naming systems,* edited by C. MacDonald and Yangwen Zheng. Singapore: National University of Singapore Press. In press.

Langer, Susanne K. 1951. *Philosophy in a new key: A study in the symbolism of reason, rite, and art.* Cambridge, Mass.: Harvard University Press.

Laughlin, Robert M. 1975. *The great Tzotzil dictionary of San Lorenzo Zinacantan.* Washington, D.C.: Smithsonian Institution Press.

——. 1980. *Of shoes and ships and sealing wax: Sundries from Zinacantan.* Washington, D.C.: Smithsonian Institution Press.

Leach, Edmund R. 1966. "Ritualization in man." In *A discussion on ritualization of behavior in animals and man organized by Sir Julian Huxley.* Philosophical Transactions of the Royal Society of London, Series B, Biological Sciences 251, no. 772, 403–408.

Leech, Geoffrey N. 1983. *Principles of pragmatics.* London: Longman.

Levinson, Stephen C. 2006a. "Cognition at the heart of human interaction." *Discourse Studies* 8: 85–93.

——. 2006b. "On the human 'interaction engine.'" In *Roots of human sociality: Culture, cognition, and interaction,* edited by N. J. Enfield and S. C. Levinson, 39–69. Oxford: Berg.

Lévi-Strauss, Claude. 1963. *Structural anthropology.* Harmondsworth, U.K.: Penguin.

——. 1966. *The savage mind.* Chicago: University of Chicago Press.

——. 1981 [1971]. *The naked man.* Translated by John and Doreen Weightman. New York: Harper and Row.

——. 1987. *Anthropology and myth: Lectures 1951–1982.* Oxford: Blackwell.

Levy, Robert. 1973. *Tahitians: Mind and experience in the Society Islands.* Chicago: University of Chicago Press.

Liénard, Pierre, and Pascal Boyer. 2006. "Whence collective rituals? A cultural selection model of ritualized behavior." *American Anthropologist* 108: 814–827.

Lienhardt, Godfrey. 1961. *Divinity and experience: The religion of the Dinka.* Oxford: Clarendon Press.

Lim, Kim Hui. 2003. "Budi as the Malay mind: A philosophical study of Malay ways of reasoning and emotion in *peribahasa.*" PhD dissertation: University of Hamburg.

Lima, Antonio C. de Souza. 1992. "On indigenism and nationality in Brazil." In *Nation-states and Indians in Latin America,* edited by Greg Urban and Joel Sherzer, 236–258. Austin: University of Texas Press.

Mageo, Jeanette Marie. 1984. "'Ferocious is the centipede': A study of the significance of eating and speaking in Samoa." *Ethos* 17: 387–472.

——. 1996. "Spirit girls and marines: Possession and ethnopsychiatry as historical discourse in Samoa." *American Ethnologist* 23: 61–82.

Mahmood, Saba. 2001. "Rehearsed spontaneity and the conventionality of ritual: Disciplines of *ṣalat.*" *American Ethnologist* 28: 827–853.

Malinowski, Bronislaw. 1923. "The problem of meaning in primitive languages." In *The meaning of meaning: A study of the influence of language upon thought and of the science of symbolism,* by C. K. Ogden and I. A. Richards, 296–336. London: Kegan Paul, Trench, Trubner.

——. 1935. *Coral gardens and their magic.* 2 vols. London: Allen and Unwin.

——. 1968 [1929]. *The sexual life of savages in northwestern Melanesia.* London: Routledge and Kegan Paul.

——. 1974. *Magic, science and religion and other essays.* London: Souvenir Press.

——. 1978 [1922]. *Argonauts of the western Pacific.* London: Routledge and Kegan Paul.

——. 1978 [1935]. *Coral gardens and their magic,* vol. 2. New York: Dover.

Mauss, Marcel. 1954 [1925]. *Essai sur le don/The gift.* London: Cohen and West.

McPhail, Clark. 1991. *The myth of the madding crowd.* New York: Aldine de Gruyter.

Mead, George Herbert. 1956. *The social psychology of George Herbert Mead.* Chicago: University of Chicago Press.

Merlan, Francesca, and Alan Rumsey. 1991. *Ku Waru: Language and segmentary politics in the western Nebilyer Valley, Papua New Guinea*. Cambridge: Cambridge University Press.

Mertz, Elizabeth. 1996. "Consensus and dissent in U.S. legal opinions." In *Disorderly discourse: Narrative, conflict and inequality,* edited by Charles Briggs, 135–157. Oxford: Oxford University Press.

Mieder, Wolfgang. 2001. *International proverb scholarship: An annotated bibliography. Supplement 3 (1990–2000)*. New York: Peter Lang.

——. 2004. *Proverbs: A handbook*. Westport, Conn.: Greenwood Press.

——. 2005. *Proverbs are the best policy: Folk wisdom and American politics*. Logan: Utah State University Press.

Miller, Peggy, Randolph Potts, Heidi Fung, Lisa Hoogstra, and Judy Mintz. 1990. "Narrative practices and the social construction of self in childhood." *American Ethnologist* 17: 292–311.

Mitchell, David. 1999. "Tragedy in Sumba: Why neighbours hacked each other to death in a remote part of Indonesia." *Inside Indonesia* 58 (April–June), www.insideindonesia.org/content/view/694/29/.

Monod-Becquelin, Aurore. 1975. *Le pratique linguistique des Indiens Trumai (Haut Xingu, Mato Grosso, Brésil)*. 2 vols. Paris: SELAF.

Moore, Sally F., and Barbara G. Myerhoff, eds. 1977. *Secular ritual*. Amsterdam: Van Gorcum.

Morin, Alain. 1993. "Self-talk and self-awareness: On the nature of the relation." *Journal of Mind and Behavior* 14: 223–234.

Murphy, Robert, and Buell Quain. 1955. *The Trumai Indians of central Brazil*. Seattle: University of Washington Press.

Mydans, Seth. 1998. "Indonesia's students: An unrelenting force for change." *New York Times,* November 13, A3.

Myers, Fred. 1986. "Reflections on a meeting: Structure, language, and the polity in a small-scale society." *American Ethnologist* 13 (3): 430–447.

Naden, Tony. 1980. "How to greet in Bisa." *Journal of Pragmatics* 4: 137–145.

——. 1986. "Social context and Mampruli greetings." In *Pragmatics in non-Western perspective,* edited by George Huttar and Kenneth Gregerson, 161–199. Arlington, Tex.: University of Texas at Arlington.

Ndoleriire, Oswald K. 2000. "Cross-cultural communication in Africa." In *African voices,* edited by Vic Webb and Kembo-Sure, 268–285. Cape Town: Oxford University Press Southern Africa.

Norman, Donald A. 1991. "Cognitive artifacts." In *Designing interaction: Psychology at the human-computer interface,* edited by J. M. Carroll, 17–38. Cambridge: Cambridge University Press.

Norrick, Neal R. 1985. *How proverbs mean: Semantic studies in English proverbs*. Berlin: Mouton de Gruyter.

——. 1987. "Functions of repetition in conversation." *Text* 7: 245–264.

Nyaku, Frank K. 1985. *Hogbedede*. Accra: Language Centre, University of Ghana.

Oakdale, Suzanne. 2002. "Creating a continuity between self and other: First-person narration in an Amazonian context." *Ethos* 30: 158–175.

——. 2005. *I foresee my life: The ritual performance of autobiography in an Amazonian community*. Lincoln: University of Nebraska Press.

Obelkevich, James. 1994 [1987]. "Proverbs and social history." In *Wise words: Essays on the proverb*, edited by Wolfgang Mieder, 211–252. New York: Garland.

Obeng, Samuel Gyasi. 1996. "The proverb as a mitigating and politeness strategy in Akan discourse." *Anthropological Linguistics* 38: 523–549.

Ochs, Elinor. 1990. "Indexicality and socialisation." In *Cultural psychology*, edited by James W. Stigler, Richard A. Shweder, and Gilbert Herdt, 287–308. Cambridge: Cambridge University Press.

——. 1996. "Linguistic resources for socializing humanity." In *Rethinking linguistic relativity*, edited by John J. Gumperz and Stephen C. Levinson, 407–437. Cambridge: Cambridge University Press.

Owings, Donald H., and Eugene S. Morton. 1998. *Animal vocal communication: A new approach*. Cambridge: Cambridge University Press.

Parkin, David. 1984. "Political language." *Annual Review of Anthropology* 13: 345–365.

——. 2001. "Ritual." In *International Encyclopedia of the Social and Behavioral Sciences*, edited by N. J. Smelser and Paul B. Baltes, vol. 20, 13368–13371. Amsterdam: Elsevier.

Peeters, Bert, ed. 2006. *Semantic primes and universal grammar: Evidence from the Romance languages*. Oxford: Oxford University Press.

Peirce, Charles S. 1965 [1932]. "Speculative grammar." In *Collected papers of Charles Sanders Peirce*, vol. 2, *Elements of Logic*, edited by C. Hartshorne and P. Weiss, 127–269. Cambridge, Mass.: Harvard University Press.

Peletz, Michael. 2001. "Ambivalence in kinship since the 1940s." In *Relative values: Reconfiguring kinship studies*, edited by Sarah Franklin and Susan McKinnon, 413–443. Durham, N.C.: Duke University Press.

Pellizzaro, Siro. 1978a. "Uwí en la actualidad Shuar." In *La celebración de Uwí*, 121–137. Quito: Museos del Banco Central del Ecuador.

——. 1978b. *Uwishin*. Quito: Mundo Shuar.

Perrino, Sabina M. 2002. "Intimate hierarchies and Qur'anic saliva (Tëfli): Textuality in a Senegalese ethnomedical encounter." *Journal of Linguistic Anthropology* 12 (2): 225–259

Persson, Johnny. 1999. *Sagali and the Kula: A regional system analysis of the Massim.* Lund Monographs in Social Anthropology 7. Lund: Department of Sociology, Lund University.

Polletta, Francesca. 2004. "Can you celebrate dissent? Holidays and social protest." In *We are what we celebrate: Understanding holidays and rituals,* edited by J. E. Bloom, 151–177. New York: New York University Press.

Radcliffe-Brown, Alfred R. 1940. "On joking relationships." *Africa: Journal of the International African Institute* 12 (3): 195–210.

Rampton, Ben. 2006. *Language in late modernity: Interaction in an urban high school.* Cambridge: Cambridge University Press.

Rappaport, Roy A. 1974. "The obvious aspects of ritual." *Cambridge Anthropologist* 2: 2–60.

——. 1999. *Ritual and religion in the making of humanity.* Cambridge: Cambridge University Press.

Raymond, Geoffrey. 2000. "Questions in interaction." Ph.D. dissertation, Department of Sociology, University of California, Los Angeles.

Reed, Thomas V. 2005. *The art of protest: Culture and activism from the civil rights movement to the streets of Seattle.* Minneapolis: University of Minnesota Press.

Richerson, Peter J., and Robert Boyd. 2005. *Not by genes alone: How culture transformed human evolution.* Chicago: University of Chicago Press.

Ricoeur, Paul. 1974. "The question of the subject." In *The conflict of interpretations: Essays in hermeneutics,* edited by Don Ihde. Evanston, Ill.: Northwestern University Press.

——. 1976. *Interpretation theory: Discourse and the surplus of meaning.* Fort Worth: Texas Christian University Press.

Riffaterre, Michel. 1990. "Compulsory reader response: The intertextual drive." In *Intertextuality: Theories and practices,* edited by Michael Worton and Judith Still, 56–78. Manchester: Manchester University Press.

Robbins, Joel. 2001a. "Ritual communication and linguistic ideology: A reading and partial reformulation of Rappaport's theory of ritual." *Current Anthropology* 42: 591–614.

——. 2001b. "God is nothing but talk: Modernity, language, and prayer in a Papua New Guinea society." *American Anthropologist* 103: 901–912.

——. 2004. *Becoming sinners: Christianity and moral torment in a Papua New Guinea society.* Berkeley: University of California Press.

——. 2005. "Humiliation and transformation: Marshall Sahlins and the study of cultural change in Melanesia." In *The making of global and local modernities in Melanesia: Humiliation, transformation and the nature of cultural change,* edited by Joel Robbins and Holly Wardlow, 3–21. Burlington, Vt.: Ashgate.

Roseman, Marina. 1991. *Healing sounds from the Malaysian rainforest: Temiar music and medicine.* Berkeley: University of California Press.

Rothe, Elvira. 2004. "Wulla Poddu: Bitterer Monat, Monat der Tabus, Monat des Heiligen, Monat des Neuen Jahres in Loli in der Siedlung Tarung-Waitabar, Amtsbezirk der Stadt Waikabubak in Loli, Regierungsbezirk Westsumba, Provinz Nusa Tenggara Timur, Indonesien." PhD dissertation, Ludwig-Maximilians-Universität, Munich.

Rubenstein, Steven. 2002. *Alejandro Tsakimp: A Shuar healer in the margins of history.* Lincoln: University of Nebraska Press.

Rumsey, Alan. 2000. "Agency, personhood and the 'I' of discourse in the Pacific and beyond." *Journal of the Royal Anthropological Institute* (n.s.) 6: 101–115.

Sacks, Harvey. 1975. "Everyone has to lie." In *Sociocultural dimensions of language use,* edited by Mary Sanches and Ben G. Blount, 57–80. New York: Academic Press.

——. 1992. *Lectures on conversation.* London: Blackwell.

Sahlins, Marshall D. 1981. *Historical metaphors and mythical realities: Structure in the early history of the Sandwich Islands kingdom.* Ann Arbor: University of Michigan Press.

Salivas, Pierre. 2000. *Musiques jivaro: Une esthétique de l'hétérogène.* Paris: Université Vincennes-Saint Denis.

Samarin, William, ed. 1976. *Language in religious practice.* Rowley, Mass.: Newbury House.

Sapir, Edward. 1909. *Wishram texts.* Leiden: E. J. Brill.

Saville-Troike, Muriel. 2003. *The ethnography of communication: An introduction.* 3rd ed. Oxford: Blackwell.

Schechner, Richard. 1985. *Between theater and anthropology.* Philadelphia: University of Pennsylvania Press.

Schegloff, Emmanuel A. 1968. "Sequencing in conversational openings." *American Anthropologist* 70: 1075–1095.

——. 1999. "Discourse, pragmatics, conversation, analysis." *Discourse Studies* 1: 405–435.

——. 2007. *Sequence organization in interaction: A primer in conversation analysis*, vol. 1. Cambridge: Cambridge University Press.

—— and Harvey Sacks. 1973. "Opening up closings." *Semiotica* 8: 289–327.

Schortman, Edward M., Patricia A. Urban, and Marne Ausec. 2001. "Politics with style: Identity formation in prehispanic southeastern Mesoamerica." *American Anthropologist* 103: 312–330.

Schottman, Wendy. 1995. "The daily ritual of greeting among the Baatombu of Benin." *Anthropological Linguistics* 37: 487–523.

Searle, John R. 1969. *Speech acts: An essay in the philosophy of language*. Cambridge: Cambridge University Press.

——. 1995. *The construction of social reality*. New York: Free Press.

Seeger, Anthony. 1987. *Why Suyá sing*. Cambridge: Cambridge University Press.

Seki, Lucy. 1999. "The Upper Xingu as an incipient linguistic area." In *The Amazonian Languages,* edited by R. M. W. Dixon and Alexandra Y. Aikhenvald, 417–430. Cambridge: Cambridge University Press.

Senft, Barbara, and Gunter Senft. 1986. Ninikula: Fadenspiele auf den Trobriand-Inseln, Papua-Neuguinea. *Baessler-Archiv* NF 34: 93–235.

Senft, Gunter. 1985a. "How to tell—and understand—a 'dirty' joke in Kilivila." *Journal of Pragmatics* 9: 815–834.

——. 1985b. "Emic or etic or just another catch 22? A repartee to Hartmut Haberland." *Journal of Pragmatics* 9: 845.

——. 1985c. "Trauer auf Trobriand: Eine ethnologisch/linguistische Fallstudie." *Anthropos* 80: 471–492.

——. 1986. *Kilivila: The language of the Trobriand Islanders*. Berlin: Mouton de Gruyter.

——. 1987. "Rituelle Kommunikation auf den Trobriand Inseln." *Zeitschrift für Literaturwissenschaft und Linguistik* 17: 105–130.

——. 1991. "Mahnreden auf den Trobriand Inseln: Eine Fallstudie." In *Verbale Interaktion: Studien zur Empirie and Methodologie der Pragmatik,* edited by D. Flader, 27–49. Stuttgart: Metzler.

——. 1996a. "Phatic communion." In *Handbook of pragmatics: Supplement 1996,* edited by J. Verschueren, J.-O. Östman, and J. Blommaert, 1–10. Amsterdam: John Benjamins.

——. 1996b. "Past is present, present is past: Time and the harvest rituals on the Trobriand Islands." *Anthropos* 91: 381–389.

——. 1997. "Magical conversation on the Trobriand Islands." *Anthropos* 92: 369–391.

——. 1999. "Bronislaw Kasper Malinowski." In *Handbook of pragmatics: Supplement 1998,* edited by J. Verschueren, J.-O. Östman, and J. Blommaert, 1–20. Amsterdam: John Benjamins.

——. 2003. "Wosi milamala: Weisen von Liebe und Tod auf den Trobriand Inseln." In *Anabasis: Prace Ofiarowane Professor Krystynie Pisarkowej,* edited by I. Bobrowski, 289–295. Kraków: LEXIS.

——. 2006. Review article: "A biography in the strict sense of the term. Michael Young, *Malinowski: Odyssey of an anthropologist 1884–1920,* Volume 1." *Journal of Pragmatics* 38: 610–637.

Sennett, Richard. 1977. *The fall of public man.* New York: Knopf.

Severi, Carlo. 1993. *La memoria dell'uomo bianco.* Florence: La Nuova Italia.

Sherzer, Joel. 1983. *Kuna Ways of Speaking: An Ethnographic Perspective.* Austin: University of Texas Press.

——. 2002. *Speech play and verbal art.* Austin: University of Texas Press.

Shoaps, Robin Ann. 2002. "'Pray earnestly': The textual construction of personal involvement in Pentecostal prayer and song." *Journal of Linguistic Anthropology* 12: 34–71.

——. 2004. "Morality in grammar and discourse: Stance-taking and the negotiation of moral personhood in Sakapultek (Mayan) wedding counsels." Ph.D. dissertation, Department of Linguistics, University of California, Santa Barbara.

Silk, Joan B. 2002. "Practice random acts of aggression and senseless acts of intimidation: The logic of status contests in social groups." *Evolutionary Anthropology* 11: 221–225.

Silverstein, Michael. 1976. "Shifters, linguistic categories, and cultural description." In *Meaning in anthropology,* edited by Keith H. Basso and Henry A. Selby, 11–55. Albuquerque: University of New Mexico Press.

——. 1981. "Metaforces of power in traditional oratory." Lecture presented in the PERL Lecture Series, "The Rhetoric of Politics," University of Chicago, and at the Department of Anthropology, Yale University.

——. 1985. "Language and the culture of gender: At the intersection of structure, usage, and ideology." In *Semiotic mediation,* edited by Elizabeth Mertz and Richard Parmentier, 220–259. New York: Academic Press.

——. 1986. "Classifiers, verb classifiers, and verbal categories." *Proceedings of the Berkeley Linguistics Society* 12: 497–514.

——. 1990. "Chinookans of the Lower Columbia." In *Handbook of North American Indians,* vol. 17, *Northwest Coast,* edited by Wayne Suttles, 533–546. Washington, D.C.: Smithsonian Institution.

——. 1993. "Metapragmatic discourse and metapragmatic function." In *Reflexive language: Reported speech and metapragmatics,* edited by John A. Lucy, 33–58. Cambridge: Cambridge University Press.

——. 1996a. "Indexical order and the dialectics of sociolinguistic life." In *Proceedings of the third annual symposium about language and society*, edited by Risako Ide, Rebecca Parker, and Yukako Sunaoshi, 266–295. Texas Linguistic Forum 36. Austin: University of Texas, Department of Linguistics.

——. 1996b. "The secret life of texts." In *Natural histories of discourse*, edited by Michael Silverstein and Greg Urban, 81–105. Chicago: University of Chicago Press.

——. 1998. "The improvisational performance of culture in realtime discursive practice." In *Creativity in performance*, edited by R. Keith Sawyer, 265–312. Greenwich, Conn.: Ablex.

——. 2001. "Comments on 'Ritual communication and linguistic ideology,' by Joel Robbins." *Current Anthropology* 45: 606–608.

——. 2003. "Indexical order and the dialectics of sociolinguistic life." *Language and Communication* 23: 193–229.

——. 2004. "'Cultural' concepts and the language-culture nexus." *Current Anthropology* 45 (5): 621–652.

——. 2005. "Axes of -evals: Token vs. type interdiscursivity." *Journal of Linguistic Anthropology* 15 (1): 6–22.

Simon, Herbert A. 1990. "A mechanism for social selection and successful altruism." *Science* 250: 1665–1668.

Sinavaiana, Caroline. 1992. "Where the spirits laugh last: Comic theater in Samoa." In *Clowning as critical practice: Performance humor in the South Pacific*, edited by William E. Mitchell, 192–218. Pittsburgh: University of Pittsburgh Press.

Singer, Milton. 1984. *Man's glassy essence: Explorations in semiotic anthropology*. Bloomington: Indiana University Press.

Sobrevilla del Valle, Dení. 2000. "Desempeños discursivos de un personaje urbano: Los merolicos, una aplicación de la oralidad." Master's thesis, CIESAS, Mexico, D.F.

Spanjaard, Helena. 2000. *"Reformasi Indonesia!" Protest art, 1995–2000*. Delft, Netherlands: Museum Nusantara.

Spier, Leslie, and Edward Sapir. 1930. *Wishram ethnography*. Seattle: University of Washington Press.

Steel, Daniel. 1999. "Trade goods and Jívaro warfare: The Shuar, 1850–1957, and the Achuar, 1940–1978." *Ethnohistory* 46: 745–776.

Surrallés, Alexandre. 2003. "Face to face: Meaning, feeling and perception in Amazonian welcoming ceremonies." *Journal of the Royal Anthropological Institute* (n.s.) 9: 775–791.

Sweeney, Amin. 1987. *A full hearing: Orality and literacy in the Malay world*. Berkeley: University of California Press.

Swettenham, Frank. 1906. *British Malaya*. London: John Lane and Bodley Head.

Sykes, Karen. 2005. *Arguing with anthropology: An introduction to critical theories of the gift*. London: Routledge.

Szerszynski, Bronislaw. 2002. "Ecological rites." *Theory, Culture and Society* 19 (3): 51–70.

Tambiah, Stanley J. 1968. "The magical power of words." *Man* (n.s.) 3: 175–208.

——. 1979. "A performative approach to ritual." *Proceedings of the British Academy* 65: 113–166.

——. 1985. *Culture, thought, and social action: An anthropological perspective*. Cambridge, Mass.: Harvard University Press.

Tannen, Deborah. 1987. "Repetition in conversation: Towards a poetics of talk." *Language* 63: 574–605.

Taylor, Anne-Christine. 1981. "La riqueza de Dios: Los Achuar y las misiones." In *Amazonía ecuatoriana: La otra cara del progreso*, edited by Norman Whitten, 115–143. Quito: Mundo Shuar.

——. 1993. "Remembering to forget: Identity, mourning, and memory among the Jívaro." *Man* 28: 653–678.

—— and Ernesto Chau. 1983. "Jivaroan magical songs: Achuar *ánent* of connubial love." *Amerindia* 8: 87–127.

Taylor, Archer. 1962 [1931]. *The proverb, and an index to the proverb*. Hatboro, Pa.: Folklore Associates.

Taylor, Charles. 2002. "Modern social imaginaries." *Public Culture* 14: 91–124.

Tilly, Charles. 1979. "Repertoires of contention in America and Britain: 1775–1820." In *The dynamics of social movements*, edited by J. McCarthy, 126–155. Cambridge: Winthrop.

Toren, Christina. 2001. "Comments on 'Ritual communication and linguistic ideology,' by Joel Robbins." *Current Anthropology* 45: 608–609.

Turner, Victor. 1967. *The forest of symbols: Aspects of Ndembu ritual*. Ithaca, N.Y.: Cornell University Press.

——. 1969. *The ritual process*. Chicago: Aldine.

——. 1975. *Revelation and divination in Ndembu ritual*. Ithaca, N.Y.: Cornell University Press.

Urban, Greg. 1989. "The 'I' of Discourse." In *Semiotics, self, and society*, edited by Benjamin Lee and Greg Urban, 27–51. Berlin: Mouton de Gruyer.

——. 2002. "Metasignaling and language origins." *American Anthropologist* 104: 233–246.

van de Walle, Nicolas. 2002. "Africa's range of regimes." *Journal of Democracy* 13: 66–80.
van Gennep, Arnold. 1909. *Les rites de passage: Étude systématique de la porte et du seuil, de l'hospitalité, de l'adoption, de la grossesse et de l'accouchement, de la naissance, de l'enfance, de la puberté, de l'initiation, de l'ordination, du couronnement, des fiançailles, et du mariage, des funérailles, des saisons etc.* Paris: La Haye.
——. 1960 [1909]. *The rites of passage.* Translated by M. B. Vigedom and G. L. Caffee. Chicago: University of Chicago Press.
van Jaarsveld, Gerrit J. 1988. "Goeimorgen, good morning, kgosto, dumela, sawubona: Opening routines and misunderstandings." *South African Journal of Linguistics* 6: 93–108.
Vel, Jacqueline A. C. 2000. *Tribal battle in a remote island: How district leaders in Sumba (eastern Indonesia) combat the fading of their authority. Violence in Indonesia, its historical roots, contemporary manifestations.* Leiden: Leiden University.
Viveiros de Castro, Eduardo. 1998. "Cosmological deixis and Amerindian perspectivism." *Journal of the Royal Anthropological Institute* 4: 469–488.
Voloshinov, V. N. 1973. *Marxism and the philosophy of language.* Translated by Ladislav Matejka and I. R. Titunik. New York: Seminar Press.
Vonen, Arnfinn Muruvik. 1992. "A Tokelau folktale: The tale of Alo." In *Kupu mai te Tutolu/Tokelau oral literature,* edited by Ingjerd Hoëm, 89–168. Oslo: Institute for Comparative Research in Human Culture/ Scandinavian University Press.
Waterson, Roxana. 1990. *The living house: An anthropology of architecture in South-East Asia.* Singapore: Oxford University Press.
Watts, Ian. 1999. "The origin of symbolic culture." In *The evolution of culture: An interdisciplinary view,* edited by Robin I. M. Dunbar, Chris Knight, and Camilla Power, 113–146. New Brunswick, N.J.: Rutgers University Press.
Webber, Bonnie L. 1991. "Structure and ostension in the interpretation of discourse deixis." *Language and Cognitive Processes* 6: 107–135.
Weiner, Annette B. 1976. *Women of value, men of renown: New perspectives in Trobriand exchange.* Austin: University of Texas Press.
——. 1983. "From words to objects to magic: Hard words and the boundaries of social interaction." *Man* 18: 690–709.
Werlen, Iwar. 1984. *Ritual und Sprache, Zum Verhältnis von Sprechen und Handeln in Ritualen.* Tübingen: Gunter Narr.
Wheelock, Wade T. 1982. "The problem of ritual language: From information to situation." *Journal of the American Academy of Religion* 50: 49–71.

White, Geoffrey M. 1987. "Proverbs and cultural models: An American psychology of problem solving." In *Cultural models in language and thought,* edited by Dorothy Holland and Naomi Quinn, 151–172. Cambridge, Mass.: Cambridge University Press.

Whorf, Benjamin Lee. 1956. *Language, thought, and reality.* Cambridge, Mass.: MIT Press.

Wickler, Wolfgang. 1966. "Mimicry in tropical fishes." In *A discussion on ritualization of behavior in animals and man organized by Sir Julian Huxley.* Philosophical Transactions of the Royal Society of London, Series B, Biological Sciences 251 (772), 473–474.

Wielenga, Douwe Klaas. 1912. "Riesen op Soemba." *De Macedonier* 15: 328–334.

——. 1928. *Oemboe Dongga: Het kampoeng hoofd van Soemba.* Kampen: Kok.

Wierhake, Gudrun. 1985. *Cultura material shuar en la historia.* Quito: Mundo Shuar.

Wierzbicka, Anna. 1987. *English speech act verbs: A semantic dictionary.* Sydney: Academic Press.

——. 1996. *Semantics: Primes and universals.* Oxford: Oxford University Press.

——. 2003. *Cross-cultural pragmatics: The semantics of human interaction.* 2nd ed. Berlin: Mouton de Gruyter.

Williams, Raymond. 1977. *Marxism and literature.* Oxford: Oxford University Press.

Winick, Stephen D. 1998. "The proverb process: Intertextuality and proverbial innovation in popular culture." PhD dissertation, University of Pennsylvania.

Wittgenstein, Ludwig. 1953. *Philosophical investigations.* Oxford: Blackwell.

Yahya-Othman, Saida. 1995. "Aren't you going to greet me? Impoliteness in Swahili greetings." *Text* 15: 209–227.

Yankah, Kwesi. 1995. *Speaking for the chief: Okyeame and the politics of Akan royal oratory.* Bloomington: Indiana University Press.

Yngve, V. H. 1970. "On getting a word in edgewise." In *Papers from the sixth regional meeting, Chicago Linguistics Society,* edited by M. A. Campbell, 567–578. Chicago: University of Chicago Press.

Young, Michael. 2004. *Malinowski: Odyssey of an anthropologist 1884–1920.* New Haven, Conn.: Yale University Press.

Youssouf, Ibrahim Ag, Allen Grimshaw, and Charles Bird. 1976. "Greetings in the desert." *American Ethnologist* 3: 797–824.

Index

Note: Italicized page numbers indicate tables and illustrations